BATTERSEA PLACE

***

BATTERSEA

PLACE

LIBRARY

Battersea Place
by LifeCare Residences

FINE WINE
EDITIONS

THE FINEST WINES OF
CHAMPAGNE

A Guide to the Best Cuvées, Houses, and Growers

MICHAEL EDWARDS

Foreword by Hugh Johnson | Photography by Jon Wyand

First published in Great Britain 2009 by
Aurum Press Ltd
7 Greenland Street
London NW1 0ND
www.aurumpress.co.uk

A catalogue record for this book is available from the British Library.

ISBN 978 1 84513 486 0

10 9 8 7 6 5 4 3 2
2016 2015 2014 2013 2012

Typeset in Didot and Gotham
Printed in China

Fine Wine Editions
Publisher Sara Morley
General Editor Neil Beckett
Editor Stuart George
Subeditor David Tombesi-Walton
Editorial Assistant Vicky Jordan
Designer Kenneth Carroll
Layout Rod Teasdale
Map Editor Eugenio Signoroni
Maps Red Lion
Indexer Ann Marangos
Production Nikki Ingram

Contents

Foreword

by Hugh Johnson

Fine wines detach themselves from the rest not by their pretensions but by their conversation—the conversation, that is, that they provoke and stimulate, even, I sometimes think, by joining in themselves.

Is this too surreal a thought? Don't you exchange ideas with a bottle of truly original, authentic, coherent wine? You are just putting the decanter down for the second time. You have admired its colour, remarked on a note of new oak now in decline and a ripe blackcurrant smell growing by the minute, when a tang of iodine interrupts you, the voice of the sea as clear as if you had just parked your car on the beach and opened the door. Picture the Gironde, the wine is saying. You know the slope with its pale stones and its long grey view. I am Latour; how can you forget my siblings with their family taste of sweet iron? Keep me on your tongue and I will explain everything: my grapes, the sun I missed in August, and the baking September days up to harvest. Is my strength draining away? Then I am old, but all the more eloquent; you see my weak points now, but my character is clearer than ever.

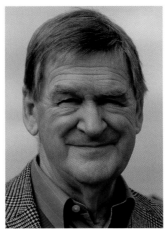

He who has ears to hear, let him hear. The vast majority of the world's wines are like French cartoons, *sans paroles*. Fine wines are thoroughbreds with form and mettle, even on their off days or when they are outrun. If a seemingly disproportionate number of words and, naturally, money are lavished on them, it is because they set the pace. What do you aspire to without a model? And far from being futile, aspiration has given us, and continues to give us, more thoroughbreds, more conversation, and more seductive voices to beguile us.

Just 20 or 30 years ago, the wine world was a plain with isolated peaks. It had crevasses, not to mention abysses, too, but we did our best to avoid them. The collision of continents thrust up new mountain ranges, while erosion turned barren new rock into fertile soil. Do I need to mention the clambering explorers, the pioneers who planted at high altitudes with aspirations that seemed presumptuous at the time? If they started by making wine with little to say, those who persevered found a new grammar and a new vocabulary, to add its voice to conversations that will soon, it seems, be worldwide.

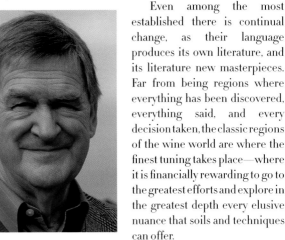

Even among the most established there is continual change, as their language produces its own literature, and its literature new masterpieces. Far from being regions where everything has been discovered, everything said, and every decision taken, the classic regions of the wine world are where the finest tuning takes place—where it is financially rewarding to go to the greatest efforts and explore in the greatest depth every elusive nuance that soils and techniques can offer.

Champagne is one such region. Its very privilege, the unique space it occupies as a symbol of luxury and success, obliges its practitioners to strain for continual improvement. Banality is a constant risk. The best producers know that they must surpass themselves to keep their image brilliant in a world of shortcuts and discounts.

The object of this book, and of this series as a whole, is to recognize the leaders, to investigate their methods and philosophies, to acknowledge the finest wines currently being made, and to eavesdrop on the conversations that will bring future pleasures.

Preface

by Michael Edwards

The image of Champagne is changing subtly as it comes to be recognized as a fine wine in its own right, rather than just a symbol of celebration and triumph. It was not always so. In 1993, when I was researching my first book, *The Champagne Companion*, I remember feeling like an extraterrestrial being, having asked if my planned itineraries of visits to Champagne producers could include as many small growers as great houses. The spin machine moved quickly into action, hinting darkly that growers could make good Champagne but only by accident: it was the magic sorcery of the blender, the *chef de cave*, in a big house that really counted.

We know better now. Great Champagne depends, like all fine wine, on great grapes from privileged vineyards, tended with care and love for the plants, the soils, and the environment. It is no accident that traditionally the best *chefs de cave* have been the children of Champagne growers—and the younger generation often has degrees in agronomy as well as oenology.

The big change in Champagne over the past 15 years has been the accelerating advance of the finest growers, whose Champagnes now feature strongly on the best wine lists of restaurants in Paris, London, New York, San Francisco, Tokyo, and Hong Kong. These artisan producers and the very small band of truly exceptional *grandes maisons* are the heroes of this book, because they share a love of their land and pride in their terroirs that are every bit as complex as those of Burgundy and Alsace—if less talked about, until now.

At the last count, there were reckoned to be 22,000 different Champagne labels from the 15,000 grape farmers, 400 négociants, and innumerable, ever-more-powerful cooperatives. This book takes a very selective approach to these sources, profiling 90 of my favorite producers— a personal crème de la crème—whose wines show the "restrained exuberance" (Jean-Claude Rouzaud's phrase) of the very best Champagne. Those noted under "Finest Wines" are, in keeping with the definition used for this series, those that I think are most worth writing about, be it for their absolute quality, for some other intrinsic interest, or for their value.

As fascinating as the influence of a precise terroir can be on the creation of great wine, it isn't everything. And as fashionable as the concept now is of single-vineyard Champagnes, I quite often found in my research that the more complex wines were often *assemblages* of three sites, in one or more villages, rather than being the products of only one. Even when the terroir of a vineyard was not that special, the Champagne could still be spectacular, thanks to respectful viticulture and brilliant winemaking.

Michael F. Edwards

To Louisa, well met in Verona

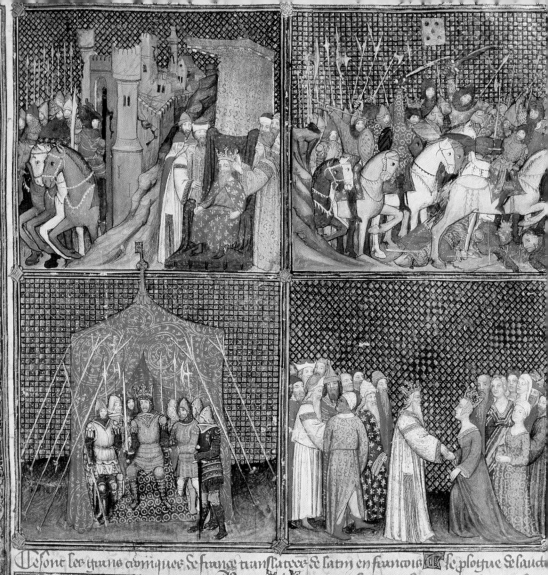

Ce sont les croniques de france translatees de latin en francois. Le prologue de lacteur

Cil qui
ceste
euvre
come
ce de
tous
ceulx
q ceste
histoi
re liront
Salut
en nr
seigneur
Pour
ce que pluseurs se doubtoient de la verité de

euvre a faire par le commandement de ce
home quil ne pot ne ne dut refuser. Mai
pour ce que sa lecture et la simplesce de so
engin ne souffisent mie a traittier dun
si haulte hystoire. Il prie au commencemen
a tous ceulx qui ce livre liront que se qui
y trouveront a blasmer quilz le sueffrent p
ciaument sans villenie et recompresiona
Car si come il a dit devant le deffault de le
ture et de loquence qui en lui sont et la si
plesce de son engin le doivent excuser par
raison. Si sachent tous quil traittera au p
briefment quil pourra car longue parolle
et confuse plaist petit a ceulx qui lescoutten
mais la briefve parolle et dite apertement

Holy Oil to Liquid Gold

Champagne has been the wine of celebration and consolation for centuries. At moments of supreme happiness and triumph, there is nothing quite like it; when times are hard, it raises morale as no other drink can. But for a full appreciation of why the wine of Champagne is so special and something more than the bringer of bubbling happiness, it is best to look at the region's culture in the broadest sense—through the land and the grapes, to the fluctuating fortunes of the province, and, of course, to the resilient and resourceful people who make the wine.

Chalking it up

The *falaises de Champagne*, those rocky outcrops of chalk found 90 miles (145km) northeast of Paris, provide an ideal environment for growing classic wine grapes in the great vineyards of the Montagne de Reims and the Côte des Blancs. The very pure chalk layered beneath these famous slopes is called belemnite, after the extinct sea creatures from whose remains it is formed. Like a sponge, belemnite soil stores excess water for dry periods but also has the ability to store heat in wetter ones, which is something of a boon in the veering extremes of current climate change. Long before the science of geology was established, the growers of Champagne preferred belemnite to micraster soil, formed from the fossil remains of sea urchins, which is less porous. Belemnite and micraster chalk deposits are the major geological resources of the Paris Basin that extends north to the Channel ports and resurfaces in the white cliffs of Dover and the chalky South Downs of Kent and Sussex, where good sparkling wine is also made.

Back in Champagne, there are deep veins of belemnite chalk in satellite districts such as Vitry-le-François, some 20 miles (32km) southeast of Châlons-sur-Marne, that provide an excellent base for Chardonnays of vigorous minerality. Chardonnays of quite a different character are cultivated on yet another type of crumbly chalk called Turonian. Especially on the great south-facing hill of Montgueux, just west of Troyes, the wines have a sumptuous, golden fruitiness, shaped by this softer Turonian chalk, as well as by the warmer temperatures regularly reached on this sunny hillside.

On the Montagne de Reims, Pinot Noir also thrives, on soils that are a mix of chalk and sandstone, the latter lending an elegance to the inherent richness of the great black grape, whereas in the Aube district of southern Champagne, Pinot Noir produces wines of bright, exuberant fruitiness on deeper Kimmeridgian soils of clay, limestone, and marl. But then the Aubois villages, vineyards, and, to some extent, the wines themselves are to many eyes, noses, and palates more like Burgundy than Champagne.

Wines of kings and monks

Vine-leaf imprints from a rock thought to be 60 million years old have been found in the Champagne region. But for the practical purposes of winemaking, grapes were probably first being cultivated in this northeastern province of France (at that time Roman Gaul) about 50 years after the birth of Christ. Yet everything stalled in AD 79, when Domitian, a protectionist Roman emperor, decreed that the vineyards of Gaul be uprooted. One of his successors, Probus, a gardener's son, lifted the ban 200 years later, and the hedonistic Romans soon came to love the wines from Champagne. They must have tasted like the nectar of the gods compared with the dyspeptic Roman wines of the time, which were touched up with bizarre seasonings ranging from seawater and pitch to myrtle berries and poppy seeds.

Later, in the dying Empire of the 5th century, a pagan Frankish warlord called Clovis defeated

Left: A manuscript showing the baptism of Clovis with holy oil—a legend of crucial significance for Champagne

the Romans and declared himself king of the land around Reims. His grip on power was soon threatened by a Germanic tribe of Goths from the east. Clovis's wife, a Christian, persuaded him to pray to God for deliverance. So Clovis vowed that if he defeated the Goths, he would convert to Christianity. Having then routed his new foes, Clovis and his victorious army were baptized on Christmas Day 496 by St Rémi, bishop of Reims. (The Romanesque basilica named in the saint's honour is one of the loveliest churches in town.)

Some 300 years later it was alleged by an archbishop of Reims that Clovis was anointed with holy oil brought down from heaven in an ampule by a dove and that this sacred liquid had survived. The role of the archbishops of Reims in the anointing and crowning of the French kings, from Hugh Capet, the first "king of the Franks", in 987 onwards, established their city rather than Paris as the spiritual capital of medieval France. Although Capet himself was crowned at Noyon, 37 of his successors came to Reims for their coronations, the last being the Bourbon Charles X, who was crowned in 1825. Reims's saintly status proved a boon for the vineyards. Successive monarchs made large donations to the Marne's monasteries, which became seminal institutions of winemaking until the French Revolution of 1789. Early religious orders saw nothing venal in the enjoyment of wine. Drawing on an 8th-century rule of the nuns at the Hôtel-Dieu in Reims, Nicholas Faith quotes one clause stipulating that "if any of the sisters says anything abusive to another or swears wickedly, she shall not drink wine that day".

It took another 900 years before the notion of a sparkling Champagne became a reality. Throughout the Middle Ages, drinkers preferred to make the distinction between the *vins de la*

rivière, from vineyards above the Marne, and the *vins de la Montagne*, from the higher slopes of the Montagne de Reims. The wines from the best vineyards were as highly rated in the times of the Capetian kings as they are today. In the early 13th century, that brilliant opportunist King Philip Augustus liked to refresh himself with the wine of Hautvillers while he plotted to drive John of England from his French dominions. Later, the Tudor king Henry VIII was partial to the wine of Aÿ, and in the late 1600s the Sun King, Louis XIV, drank little else but the wine of Bouzy. All were essentially still wines and supposed to be red in colour; they were actually more pink-tinged—what the French called *oeil de perdrix*, or partridge eye—and made mainly from progenitors of the Pinot Noir grape.

The first sparkling wines

Pierre Pérignon, a Benedictine monk and cellar master of the Abbey of Hautvillers (1668–1715) has been called the inventor of sparkling Champagne. It certainly makes a good story to imagine that a blind monk could have created such a glamorous drink associated with seduction and the demimonde. But actually it is a romantic myth, since Pérignon was not blind (he merely blind-tasted), and the wines of Champagne always had a natural tendency to sparkle gently. In the cold climate of the Marne, the grapes had to be picked in late autumn, and there was simply not enough time for the yeasts, present on the grape skins, to convert the sugar in the pressed grape juice into alcohol before winter put them to sleep. In the spring, the yeasts woke up, the fermentation started again and triggered the release of carbonic gas—hence the trace of sparkle in the wines. Some Champenois would have you believe that deliberately making their wine sparkle was one of the few genuine revolutions in winemaking. In truth, this "revolution" was really an evolutionary

Left: The Abbey of Hautvillers, home to Dom Pérignon
Over: Aÿ, whose wines were favoured by Henry VIII of England

development that took place over nearly 200 years. Tom Stevenson has adduced convincing evidence that "the English [...] invented Champagne, and did it six years before the French made their first sparkling Champagne, and over 70 years before the oldest Champagne house was established" (*Christie's World Encyclopedia of Champagne & Sparkling Wine*, pp. 8–11).

For Dom Pérignon, the wine was always more important than the bubbles. The fact that it sparkled was probably a nuisance that he tried to control rather than to encourage, and if he did deliberately, maybe even reluctantly, start to make sparkling Champagne, he probably did not do so until the mid-1690s. None of this, however, diminishes his place in history as the father of the modern Champagne industry. Pérignon's real achievements—truly dramatic for his time— were recorded by his immediate successor, Frère Pierre. They included inventing the "coquard" press; making a clear, still, white wine from black grapes; understanding that in Champagne's marginal climate, blending wines from different vineyards generally produced a more balanced drink than making an unblended wine from a single plot; adopting bottles made from *verre anglais* ("English glass"), which were able to withstand the pressure that built up inside them; and reintroducing cork as an effective closure with which to seal them.

From abomination to the height of fashion

Although there are plenty of glowing literary references to the silvery foam in sparkling Champagne in the early 18th century, the final victory of the bubbles was not won for at least another hundred years. The serious-minded Champenois seem at first to have hated the new fizzy wine, which was dismissed by the merchant Bertin du Rocheret in 1715 as an abominable drink, its effervescence belonging rightly to

Above: King Louis XV of France, who enacted important laws affecting Champagne's distribution and packaging

beer, chocolate, and whipped cream. "The Devil's Wine" was naturally irresistible to the decadent Regency court at Versailles.

The beginnings of the modern Champagne trade really date from 1728, when Louis XV removed the restrictions on transporting wine in bottles that had previously held back sales of sparkling wines. The next year, Ruinart opened for business as the first recorded Champagne-making house. In 1735, the king issued rules recording the size and capacity of the Champagne bottle, as well as decreeing that the cork must be securely tied down with string (the technique known as *ficelage*, which has been revived by a few modern producers). And in 1743, Claude Moët, a French citizen whose family were of Dutch origin, established what was to become the biggest firm of all: Moët & Chandon. As sales doubled in the half-century before the French Revolution, the future potential for sparkling wine was reflected in the price of land in the Côte des Blancs—up 800 per cent as landed families, such as the Robert de Robertsons from the Nord *département*, settled there and planted the new Chardonnay vines on the chalky hillsides. Then, as now, these wines sparkled more vigorously.

The Champagne houses did well out of Napoleon's military campaigns. Wherever the emperor was victorious—Austria, Prussia, Poland—a Champagne salesman quickly followed to offer his wine and set up a sales network for future business. In the debacle after Waterloo (1815), the Champenois typically turned even national defeat to their advantage. Famously, Jean-Rémi Moët, Claude's son, encouraged the occupying Russians to take the wine, in the sound belief that they would be back. And so it was. Russia soon became the biggest export market for Champagne, after England.

Technique, trust, and the tsar

In the 19th century, three technical innovations were further catalysts for the expansion of the Champagne trade. In 1818, Antoine Müller, Veuve ("widow") Clicquot's cellar master, solved the problem of removing the unwanted deposit that forms in Champagne as a result of the second fermentation. Antoine devised *pupitres*, which were inverted V-shaped desks with holes in them. The bottles were placed neck down in the holes so that they could be turned and tilted every day until the deposit settled safely on the cork, a process known as *remuage* (roughly translated into English as "riddling"). In the hands of a skilled worker, the deposit could then be expelled from the bottle with minimal loss of wine.

An even more significant invention, in 1836, was the *sucre-oenomètre* ("wine-sugar meter"), the

creation of Jean-Baptiste François, a pharmacist in Chalôns-sur-Marne. From this date, the Champagne-maker could more accurately add the right amount of sugar to the wine to make it sparkle, with less risk of the bottle exploding because of too much pressure. A little later, Louis Pasteur made his groundbreaking discovery of yeasts and their fundamental role in the fermentation process—something that had been a mystery to earlier winemakers.

Armed with these advances, the Champagne trade expanded dramatically between the 1840s and the turn of the 20th century, and many firms sprung up offering their wines at low prices. The public quickly became disillusioned, however, with these cut-price Champagnes, which could be sold under any name or label. As a result, there was a growing demand for brands in which drinkers might have confidence. Several of the best brand names were established by German immigrants—the Bollingers, the Krugs, the Heidsiecks, and the Mumms—who were finer linguists than the French merchants and better able to penetrate world markets. The Alsace-born Louis Roederer became a principal supplier of Champagne to Russia, and in the 1870s his house created the ultra-rich Cristal to satisfy the sweet tooth of the Romanoffs. It came in a clear, glass (occasionally crystal) bottle, with a flat bottom and no punt, so that the tsar's taster could quickly spot if there was anything suspicious about it. As a nod to these distinguished origins, the Cristal bottle is essentially the same today.

Style shift: from sweet to dry

Until the mid-19th century, all Champagne was pretty sweet, for reasons of commercial expediency. To meet increasing demand, the Champagne houses always added a high dose of sugared liqueur to the Champagnes, so that they would be drinkable within 12 months of the

harvest. But by the 1860s, a few firms had begun to label their wines "dry" in response to a new trend, fostered by the British, towards a drier and more mature type of Champagne. But truly brut (literally "raw", signifying very dry) Champagne as we now know it was not really made before 1874, when the remarkably tenacious Madame Pommery launched that legendary vintage in the teeth of opposition even from her own staff. The 1874 Pommery took Victorian London by storm. Such a dry version ushered in a revolution in Champagne, since thereafter it came to be seen as a wine not only for toasts or dessert but one that could be consumed at any time of the day or night.

Fin du siècle to famine and riot

The Belle Epoque was, in Don Kladstrup's words, "the Golden Age of Champagne". At home, actresses' admirers drank fizz from their ladies' slippers in *salons particulières*. Abroad, aspiring Champagne salesmen made daring coups—none more so than George Kessler, Moët's US agent. At the New York launch of Kaiser Wilhelm's yacht in 1903, Kessler had the chutzpah to switch a bottle of Moët White Star for a bottle of German Sekt. Wilhelm was incensed, while Moët was delighted with the attendant publicity.

Yet the glamour of the era was being replaced in France by social tensions, such as the rising anti-Semitism after the Dreyfus case, and a general sense of anxiety among ordinary Champenois about their livelihoods. Because of the improved French railways, cheaper grapes from the south had flooded into the Ile de France, undercutting those of Champagne's growers and causing a dramatic fall in their incomes. Relations between growers and the houses, who were often all too happy to buy cheaper grapes from elsewhere, became increasingly bitter. Drawing on Hervé Luxardo's *Le Peuple Français*,

Left: Léon Bakst's *The Luncheon* (1902) reflects Champagne's fashionable status at the beginning of the 20th century

Kladstrup quotes a grumbling Champenois grower thus: "They [the merchants] live in châteaux, we live with holes in the roof."

To make matters worse, the authorities' attempts to map out the limits of *Champagne viticole* were treated with suspicion by the growers. The vignerons of the Marne claimed that their soil alone was suitable for Champagne's classic grapes, while the Aubois growers in the south asserted that their vineyards, cultivated first by the Cistercians at Clairvaux, were part of the ancient province of Champagne, with Troyes as its historic capital.

The French government vacillated, tempers flared, and it all ended in tears on 12 April 1911, when the Marne growers ran amok in Aÿ, looting the cellars of merchants they suspected of trading in grapes of other regions, and emptying barrels of wine into the streets. Miraculously, there was little loss of life. Both sides drew back from the brink, and a compromise was reached. The classic heartland of the Marne would be known as Champagne; the Aube as Champagne Deuxième Zone. The Aube's second-division status was eventually repealed in 1927, when it became part of an enlarged *Champagne viticole*.

Hard times: war, prohibition, depression

During World War I, Reims was virtually destroyed by incessant bombardments from German artillery. The city was completely rebuilt in the 1920s, with elegant Art Deco architecture along wide boulevards. The widespread temperance movement that also followed the Armistice was, however, bad news for the Champenois. The United States went dry with the advent of Prohibition in 1920. Much of Canada and Scandinavia followed suit. Then came the Great Depression. Growers in Champagne suffered real hardship. The great Le Mesnil grower Alain Robert recalls that his father regarded a single orange on Christmas Day as a particular treat.

Above: "Uphill work conquers all things" (Virgil)—a plaque in Aÿ commemorating the resilient spirit of the Champenois

The market today

Recent years have been very good for Champagne. For the ten years since the eve of the Millennium, the region has never looked so prosperous. And with four bountiful crops since 2004 and the houses hungry for grapes at rising prices, the vignerons appear to be sitting pretty. Euphoria has ruled as demand for Champagne has grown inexorably through the new markets of Eastern Europe and right across Asia. But wiser heads in the Champagne community have been aware of an incipient danger. Dig below the surface, and the foundations of Champagne's boom seem rather less secure.

Cooperation, promotion, and renewal

During the grim 1930s, the first Champagne cooperatives were formed, to protect the existence of their member-growers. They were greatly helped by Comte Robert-Jean de Vogüé, a hero of the French Resistance who won the Croix de Guerre in both the world wars. As the head of Moët & Chandon, he made the highly imaginative and responsible proposal that the price of Champagne grapes be increased sixfold to ensure a decent living for the vignerons. He was dubbed the "red Marquis" for his pains by his reactionary fellow merchants.

Again largely on Vogüé's initiative, the Germans were persuaded to establish the Comité Interprofessionnel du Vin de Champagne (CIVC) in 1941. The success of the CIVC, based today in Epernay, is by far the most powerful and effective wine-promotional body in France, and owes much to the Germanic virtues of efficiency, realism, and attention to detail. In the 68 years since the CIVC's foundation, Champagne has become probably the greatest agro-industry in the country, with a track record that the Bordelais and Burgundians would surely give their eye teeth to match.

When America sneezes...

Volcanic activity in the financial world erupted in August 2007, triggered by the crisis in liquidity in the US subprime mortgage market. What started as a technical banking crisis, remote from people's everyday concerns, quickly became a widespread unease about the dodgy nature of much modern finance. Since then, as conditions for credit have become much stricter, consumer confidence in spending money on luxury goods has been weakened by the thought of imminent recession. Champagne is not immune to this change of mood, and the short-term prospects for expanding its new markets in the East are as likely to be as affected as those in traditional ones, since financial markets are now so interrelated.

The cold *douche* of market forces in a slowing world economic climate may yet, however, turn out to be a blessing in disguise for Champagne, dampening sales expectations and bringing a new mood of sober reflection to a bull market that risks losing control of prices. The growth of Champagne exports, at the giddy rate of 5–8 per cent annually since 2004, has created real problems in grape

Right: The statue in Epernay in memory of Comte Robert-Jean de Vogüé, recognized as a saviour of the region

ROBERT-JEAN DE VOGÜÉ
1896-1976
COMMANDEUR DE LA LÉGION D'HONNEUR
CROIX DE GUERRE 1914-1918
ET 1939-1945
MÉDAILLE DE LA RÉSISTANCE
RÉSISTANT DÉPORTÉ
CO-FONDATEUR DU COMITÉ
INTERPROFESSIONNEL
DU VIN DE CHAMPAGNE
PRÉSIDENT-DIRECTEUR GÉNÉRAL
DE MOËT & CHANDON

supply to meet world demand for the wine over the next decade. The situation has been exacerbated by the growers' habitual reaction in a boom market—hoarding their stocks, either in the speculative hope that their value will increase dramatically, or more likely because they do not want to pay too much tax at the end of each year. In the most recent round of price tariffs from growers (in 2008), there has been a hike of about 13 per cent. All of this fuels the current debate about revising the area of Champagne's vineyards, in an attempt to ease the pressure on grape supply without compromising quality.

Breaking point in demand and supply

In truth, any shortage of grapes will actually be felt most keenly after 2011, when the current AOC territory, totalling some 34,000ha (84,000 acres) will have been fully planted, with little prospect of any newly authorized vineyards producing extra volumes of Champagne for a further eight to ten years. Meanwhile, increasing world demand (even at a slower rate of growth), production near its extreme limit, and today's high level of growers' stocks at rising prices are a dangerous bend on the road to continuing prosperity—a hairpin that will need skilful negotiation if nobody is to be left on the highway. A thoughtful analysis of the grape-supply difficulty comes from Olivier Cossy, a Rémois *récoltant-coopérateur* and administrator of the Young Winegrowers of Champagne, a group whose past presidents include growers who have gone on to become some of Champagne's finest producers—men such as Alain Robert, Jean-Marie Tarlant, and Pierre Larmandier.

Cossy writes: "The breaking point between the theoretical maximum production of grapes and probable sales will happen around 2013. Put another way, if growth maintains its rhythm at about 2.5 per cent per annum—the average yearly increase of the past 20 years—Champagne will sell 384 million bottles in 2013." This projection is based on simple arithmetic. With the total surface area of 34,000ha fully planted by 2011, the maximum potential production, at available yields of 13,000kg (14.3 tons) of grapes per hectare, will be 383 million bottles. Assuming that sales continue to grow, there will be a deficit of production from 2013. This projection also depends, of course, on consumption and the continuing feel-good factor essential to increased global sales of Champagne.

An enlarged Champagne: limits and timescale

Meanwhile, the authorities have taken the first concrete steps in the long process of redefining the Champagne appellation and the limits of its notional expansion. In October 2007, the Institut National de l'Origine et de la Qualité (INAO), France's national wine authority, published a list of 40 new communes that might be included in such an enlarged appellation. Looking at the list, one is encouraged by the villages chosen as candidates. They are generally in good sites that are an extension of the classic Champagne zones, with the right soil and aspect. The valleys of the Vesle and Ardre to the northwest of Reims, prized for their mineral character, feature prominently. So do newly identified slopes to the southwest of Troyes, along the upper Seine Valley, where warmer summers would be ideal for the production of ripe, golden Chardonnays— very useful components in a well-balanced Champagne blend. More critically, the authorities have named two wine-growing villages in cold, wooded sites much farther north in the Marne for possible exclusion from the appellation. One of these—Germaine—has experimental vineyards owned by Moët & Chandon and the Vranken group. Germaine's possible ousting from the AOC should be seen as a political warning shot across the bows of the mighty that no one and nowhere will escape the scrutiny of the authorities' experts.

Above: The "no stock" sign has become a common sight at the premises of good producers as demand outstrips supply

In 2009, following exhaustive research and reports by its experts, INAO is issuing a decree in two parts redefining, first, where Champagne can be made and, second, where the grapes can be grown. The first part will freshly demarcate the total geographic area—some 9,030ha (22,313 acres), across 634 communes—where Champagne wine is vinified and transformed into the sparkling product. It includes, for instance, the Marne's departmental capital of Châlons-en-Champagne, which has no vineyards but is the headquarters of the famous house of Joseph Perrier. The second part of the decree will redefine the zone of grape production—those 313 communes, mainly across the Marne, Aube, and Aisne, whose wines can be used in any Champagne blend.

Then comes the tricky bit: a revision of those parcels of vineyards that are marginally situated, often quite far from the classic heartland of Champagne, and that may be included or rejected in an enlarged regional vineyard. This *révision parcellaire* will not start properly before 2010 and could take five years to complete—to say nothing of the appeals that will follow it! If the chosen parcels are eventually planted in 2015, it would not be until their third harvest that the grapes could be used and a further 15 months after bottling before the wine could be sold as Champagne. The first bottles coming from these new sites would arrive on the market towards 2020. Without wishing to second-guess INAO's final decisions, it would be surprising if Champagne's new vineyards amounted to more than 15 per cent of today's total surface area, and it may well be less. Champagne probably should remain what it has always been: a finite product.

The future for Champagne: a coherent vision

The prospect that Champagne will still be a tightly defined region making a high-quality product in reasonable quantities is unlikely to become a reality without a lively prior argument between the full-blown expansionists and the circumspect reformers who insist on a quality-first approach to any vineyard expansion. That the argument will be conducted the Champenois way—in whispered tones behind cupped hands—cannot hide the fact that there is a lot at stake. Essentially, the Champenois are sitting in front of a small cake, and there are plenty of aggressive players wanting a larger slice.

Fortunately, the moderate reformers—led by the all-powerful and responsible Moët-LVMH group (which includes Veuve Clicquot and Krug)—have the strongest cards, as well as a sympathetic listener in the new head of INAO, Yves Bénard, a highly intelligent and consensual negotiator and former president of the Union des Maisons de Champagne, which represented the négociants. Pitted against the reformers will be what we might politely call the young Establishment—the new merchants who have made great fortunes over the past 20 years and cannot resist the chance to grow further if a more root-and-branch extension of the vineyard is achieved, bringing them cheaper grapes and bigger profits. A cautionary tale of an ill-thought-out, very widespread expansion of a classic vineyard is Chablis in the 1980s. The ensuing fall in quality there has been checked only recently. Champagne, of course, is altogether a much bigger wine region, and the issues are more complicated. But the same vigilant principle of hanging on to top quality still applies.

Yielding not to temptation

The burning issue of the moment is the increasing yields of wine sanctioned by the authorities in order to give the Champenois breathing space before the new vineyards' wines come onstream around 2020. The current maximum amount of wine to qualify in extremis for the appellation is 15,500kg per hectare, which equates to 98.4hl/ha. If that sounds a lot, it is. As Tom Stevenson sharply observes, it "is 8.8hl above the limits at which producers of the lowliest *vins de table* can push their production before their wrists are smacked!" In fairness to the better houses and growers, it is

possible to make good, even excellent Champagne at quite high yields—big crops in great years like 1982, 1990, and 2004 make the point. But there is a limit, and that ceiling has now been reached. The Champenois have to get their house in order and reduce yields over the long term, before the European Commission does it for them.

In the same breath as Burgundy or Bordeaux

At the time of writing (early 2009), the challenging trading conditions in international markets for Champagne make it a good moment for all producers to do some hard thinking about the profile and strategy that they want for their product. Should Champagne really be sold in line with the hard-nosed practices of the commodity trader, where increasing market share is all? Or should it not be promoted instead as the great, unique wine that it can be, to be spoken of in the same breath as great Burgundy or Bordeaux? Since the prospects for expansion of the Champagne vineyards are necessarily limited, the second option is surely very much better for discerning consumers and producers alike.

Much of the euphoric talk about the potential of the Russian, Chinese, and Indian markets for Champagne ignores the fact that these markets are still in their infancy and will probably take ten years to come anywhere near the levels that classic markets like Britain and the United States currently reach. In the huge domestic market of France, Champagne sales in 2008 were 181.21 million bottles—more than double the exports to Russia, China, and India combined. It is also as well to remember that the buying power in the old communist giants and on the Indian subcontinent will remain concentrated in the hands of the very rich, making these promising future markets for Vintage and prestige cuvées that offer value rather than volume. Which is just as well, since volume, as we all know, is normally the enemy of quality.

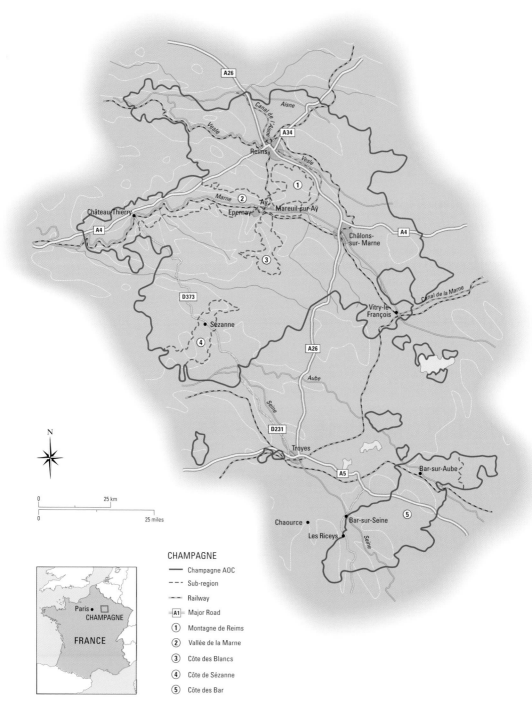

CHAMPAGNE

—— Champagne AOC
--- Sub-region
⊢•⊣ Railway
[A1] Major Road
① Montagne de Reims
② Vallée de la Marne
③ Côte des Blancs
④ Côte de Sézanne
⑤ Côte des Bar

Quality and Sustainability

Terroir—that mystical, French umbrella word covering the distinguishing climatic, geographic, and geological features of any piece of agricultural land—has particular force in Champagne. Vines in the Marne are planted at the northernmost limits of their cold tolerance, at latitudes of 49–49.5° north, the average temperature in Reims and Epernay rising no higher than 50°F (10°C).

About 180 miles (290km) southeast of the French Channel ports, this Marnais heartland of Champagne is subject to oceanic influences that ensure regular rainfall, with little variation in temperature from one season to another. But as you travel southwards for a further 100 miles (160km) to the Aube's Côte des Bar in southern Champagne, more continental influences prevail, historically bringing devastating winter frosts (as in 1957 and 1985) but also lots of summer sunshine. It is no accident that the Aubois vineyards produce the most succulent rosé Champagnes.

Rocks and soils

The most crucial feature of the Champagne terroir is its famous chalky subsoil, which keeps the vines naturally watered all year round—a real boon in the driest summers like 1989 and 2003. The rocky outcrops of *Champagne viticole* are categorized, in strict geological terms, as essentially "limestone" (75 per cent)—that is to say, chalk and marl as well as limestone proper. These naturally fissured soils generally provide good drainage that promotes the healthy vegetative cycle of the vine. The favourite home of both Pinot Noir and Chardonnay in Champagne is undoubtedly chalk. The finest, purest chalk type is belemnite (*see p.7*), which, being highly porous, acts as a reservoir, storing 300–400 litres of water per cubic metre. Limestones are comparatively less porous. The

Over: Sloping vineyards with varying exposures and gradients explain why some are more highly rated than others

marls, essentially calcareous clays, are rich in nutrients but can hold excessive moisture, promoting undesired vegetative vigour and fungal diseases.

Which grapes to plant where?

The nature of the Champagne subsoil historically determined the choice of plantings and led to the selection of one (or more) of the three main grape varieties best adapted to the particular district or vineyard in question.

Pinot Noir, accounting for 38.39 per cent of the Champagne vineyard, is planted mainly on the chalky grands crus of the Montagne de Reims, giving wines of majestic structure and balanced power. The great black grape, whose flesh yields clear, near-colourless juice when pressed gently and separated from the skins, is also grown on the Petite Montagne. There, elements of sandstone shape more supple wines of easy charm. Pinot Noir is also the principal grape of the Aube, covering four fifths of the marly soils that yield wines of bright, succulent fruitiness.

Pinot Meunier, covering 32.83 per cent of all vineyards, is better suited to the colder, more clay soils of the Marne Valley, because it is a hardier, late-cropping vine. Reference books have tended to denigrate Meunier as the least terroir-specific of Champagne grapes, a workhorse variety that gives palate-filling volume to a blend but does not age well on its own. In truth, the best vineyards of Meunier—around Epernay, on the Petite Montagne, along the Cubry Valley, and on the right bank of the Marne River above Damery—can produce fine and structured wines capable of long life, especially in the hands of such growers as Beaumont des Crayères, Collard, José Michel, and Jérôme Prévost.

It is worth noting that the proportion of Pinot Meunier in the Marne Valley has dropped by more than 7 per cent since the 1980s in favour of Pinot

Noir. This appears, at least in some cases, to have been driven by fashion and marketing, rather than by any serious concern to improve quality. It could certainly be argued that overall it is a retrograde trend, since the Marne Valley is ideal Meunier country.

Chardonnay, occupying only 28.51 per cent of the total vineyard, is the classic grape of the Côte des Blancs, grown on a deep stratum of belemnite chalk. Other outcrops of less porous, more friable chalk are located in the Sézannais (an extension of the Côte des Blancs), Vitry-le-François, and on the great hill of Montgueux above Troyes. In most typical Champagne blends, Chardonnay contributes crispness, precision, and verve to balance the expansive richness of Pinot Noir. When, by contrast, a Champagne is made from pure Chardonnay from the most privileged sites, it can age beautifully for ten, 15, sometimes 20 or more years, evolving a toasty opulence akin to great white Burgundy.

Other grape varieties, such as Petit Meslier and Arbanne, make up the remaining 0.27 per cent of *Champagne viticole*.

Slopes and *lieux-dits*
Sloping vineyards are the most striking feature of the Champagne viticultural landscape. This comes as no surprise in a marginal climate, when you realize that these hillsides provide an ideal terrain for vineyards that combine good drainage with excellent exposure to precious sunlight. The average gradient is around 12 per cent but can be much more spectacular. In the Clos des Goisses at Mareuil-sur-Aÿ, for example, Champagne's greatest walled vineyard, this south-facing slope drops down to the Marne canal at a maximum angle of 45 per cent, catching the full perpendicular strength of the sun and imbuing the grapes with high levels of sugar. The Goisses vineyard is just one dramatic example from the large mosaic of

Above: The crumbly texture of chalk, seen here in the hands of leading Avize grower Anselme Selosse, is vital to the vines

individually named vineyard sites, or *lieux-dits*. It is said that there are almost as many *lieux-dits* as there are acres in Champagne—some 84,000 at the last count. Many of these *lieux-dits* have evocative names such as Belles Voyes (beautiful vistas), Cendres (cinders), Les Froids Monts (chilly peaks), or (a personal favourite) Les Soupe-Tard (late suppers), which says a lot about the terroir and its history. Some years ago, CIVC technicians devised a zoning programme (*zonage*) to increase growers' understanding of their particular terroir(s). The completed research is now realized on a series of maps that detail (among other things) geographical formations, soil texture, frost zones, risk of erosion, and earth movements. This should allow growers to make the right decisions regarding grape variety or rootstock, grassing between the vines, minimal use of herbicides, and, most important of all, the timing of the harvest and making of the finished wine.

The *échelle des crus*

The *zonage* research should also deepen our understanding of the classification used for Champagne's vineyards, and may even make possible some refinements. The classification, known as the *échelle des crus* (ladder of growths), differs from those in Burgundy and Bordeaux. While Champagne's has a definite geographical anchor, it is essentially an index of price, based on the quality of grapes from classified vineyards. The *échelle* existed as early as 1911 but was formulated more thoroughly in 1919 as part of the restructuring of the Champagne industry after World War I. At that time, the finest grapes of the grands crus were rated at 100 per cent, the percentage dropping with declining quality to 50 per cent. Today the *échelle* rates the poorest grapes at 77 per cent; those of deuxième cru status at 80–89 per cent; the 43 premiers crus at 90–99 per cent; and the 17 grands crus at 100 per cent. Until 20 years ago, a legally binding annual agreement between the houses and the growers resulted in a fixed price for the grapes before the harvest. Thus grand cru grapes would sell for 100 per cent of the fixed price, and lesser ones sold according to their relative rating on the index.

Since 1990, a looser, quasi-free-market round of annual price negotiations between the houses and growers has operated, the only regulation being a reference price (or price ceiling) designed to place a limit on the buying of individual houses. This is supposed to prevent the most powerful firms from flexing their muscles and taking too large a share of the grapes. Until the economic maelstrom of 2008, that looked a forlorn hope in the previous boom times of the early 21st century, when it seemed impossible to buck the market. But now, with world markets in the severest depression since the 1930s, the reference price should be a more effective regulatory tool for the foreseeable future.

The quality of a Champagne is very closely linked to the quality of grapes from which it is made. Few serious houses will use grapes averaging below 90 per cent. And almost without exception, the prestige cuvées of the great houses are based on grand cru grapes. A few villages enjoy this highest ranking for only black or only white grapes. Although the rest qualify for grapes of either colour, those on the Montagne de Reims and in the Marne Valley are planted mostly to Pinot Noir, while those on the Côte des Blancs are given over to Chardonnay. The 17 crus or villages in this highest class are as follows:

Montagne de Reims: Ambonnay, Beaumont-sur-Vesle, Bouzy, Louvois, Mailly, Puisieulx, Sillery, Verzenay, Verzy

Vallée de la Marne: Aÿ, Tours-sur-Marne

Côte des Blancs: Avize, Chouilly, Cramant, Le Mesnil-sur-Oger, Oger, Oiry.

No classification is ever perfect, of course, and there are glaring flaws in the *échelle des crus*, which needs revision. It is patronizing, to say the least, to rate the best growths of the Côte des Bar at a derisory 80 per cent right across the board. Villages there like Celles-sur-Ource, Les Riceys, and Urville produce splendid Pinot Noir grapes. So while the inspectors at INAO ponder the expansion of *Champagne viticole*, they might also turn their minds to formulating a new ladder of growths.

Viticulture: the way forward

Cultivating vineyards on the cold 49th parallel north has never been easy for the Champenois. This challenging environment, and the folk memory of foreign occupation three times over the past 140 years, have bred an indomitable spirit and the will to succeed against all odds. No French wine region is better organized than Champagne, its coherent viticultural strategy now focused on such qualitative factors as planting density, selection of the most suitable grape variety and rootstock, and all-embracing research programmes.

The average planting density in Champagne is a model 8,000–10,000 vines per hectare. The greater the number of plants, the more the vines fight each other for nourishment, reducing the number of grape clusters per vine. All the vine's energy is channelled towards the clusters that remain, so boosting the concentration and quality of the juice. A well-nurtured vine should produce 12–15 clusters—enough to make one bottle of Champagne. Similarly, by reducing vegetative vigour and shading, high-density planting also favours optimal development of the vine leaves, which in turn promotes photosynthesis and better translocation of sugar from leaf to fruit.

Quality grapes

Finding the best strains of particular grape varieties is one of the crucial tasks of fine winemaking worldwide. The past century in Champagne saw a big shift away from a wide mix of vines to a trio of premium-quality varieties. In repeated trials, Chardonnay and the two Pinots were found to have the essential qualities to make fine Champagne: a good balance of sugar and acid; a rich, subtle taste; and a natural affinity with effervescence.

Two techniques were also developed to improve the quality within each variety. Massal selection involves taking cuttings from many vines and propagating them. Clonal selection involves taking cuttings from a single mother vine with certain desired characteristics—more or fewer fruity aromas, looser clusters for lower susceptibility to disease, or earlier ripening—and propagating them. In 1960, the Observatoire de Plants de Vignes was built in an area of Champagne with no record of wine growing, to reduce the risk of viruses. Researchers planted many hundreds of samples taken from vineyards throughout the appellation and observed their development. An official list of healthy, high-quality grapes has since been compiled, based on the continuous scientific analysis of these experimental plantings. There are now more than 50 authorized types of Pinot Noir, Chardonnay, and Pinot Meunier from which to choose.

Key vineyard work

For all wine growers everywhere, pruning is the most vital of vineyard tasks. Its timing depends entirely on the weather, which in Champagne is the joker in the pack that can quicken or stall vine growth and that regularly disrupts the best-laid plans of even the most meticulous vigneron. Pruning usually begins in the month following the harvest, which recently has been as late as early November; as the result of warmer autumns, the leaves stay green longer, giving the vine extra nourishment through photosynthesis. When the leaves stay green for a while after the grapes have been picked, instead of sending sugar to the fruit, the plant stores it in its wood, where it acts as a sort of antifreeze through the winter and provides food at budbreak in the spring, before the roots become fully functional.

After a break for Christmas, pruning of the vine resumes in mid-January and continues until late March. The main aim of pruning is to focus the plant's growth into a number of fruit-bearing buds, reducing the space it takes on the trellis, and

Above: Clonal selection can give looser bunches, while exposure to sunlight is secured through work in the vineyard

controlling excessive leaf production. Ideally, there should be a good balance of vegetative vigour and productivity—not easy to achieve, since these two requirements are often in conflict. The leaves make sugar to ripen the fruit, but a plant that is allowed to have too many leaves will set skimpy clusters that ripen poorly.

Typically methodical in honing this traditional skill for future generations, the Champenois Corporation des Vignerons runs a compulsory diploma course in pruning for young wine growers. There is, however, a gulf between good intentions and worldly realities. Since 2004, the increasing world demand for Champagne

seems to have tempted some wealthy growers, particularly on the Côte des Blancs, to allow their vines to produce more grapes than is reasonable. One hears stories of yields of 140hl/ha for Chardonnay from the best sites—but because this is 40 per cent above the official (recently increased) AOC maximum in extremis, much of the excess wine must legally be sold off for distillation. So what is the point?

Pruning techniques

Pruning has been such a fundamental tool of wine growing in Champagne for so long that it is no surprise to discover that the classic "Chablis" pruning technique is very similar to the method used in the 17th century, when the vines (then exclusively Pinot Noir) sprawled untrained, in a crowd (*en foule*), along the ground. The vines were pruned to long canes and were then buried at ploughing time to protect them from freezing. You can still see these burrowing vines in the two tiny plots of Vieilles Vignes Françaises behind Bollinger's old house in Aÿ. Dubbed "the Beast of Bollinger" by Tom Stevenson, because of its extraordinary ripe flavours, almost New World in their intensity, the Bollinger VVF cuvée is one of the rarest and most distinctive of Champagnes. This invites the question, "Why are more vines not planted in this way?" The simple answer is that grafted vines, resistant to phylloxera, such as are planted almost universally in Champagne, cannot be propagated by layering, as are vines *en foule*.

There are four approved pruning methods in Champagne:

Chablis pruning gives long canes with fruit buds along the length of the canes, which encourages a good balance of vigour and productivity. This makes it suitable for the finest Champagnes, as long as yields are kept at reasonable levels. A cane is wood that was new in the previous

growing season. It has smooth brown wood, and all of its buds are potentially productive. Grand and premier cru Chardonnays have to be pruned either by the Chablis method or by the Cordon de Royat method.

Cordon de Royat pruning is short pruning of spurs on one long "cordon"—that is, wood more than one year old, with rough bark. The cordon is unusually long, having short fruiting spurs cut from the prior year's canes. Spurs are used to temper the apical dominance of a variety like Chardonnay, especially when vigour is a problem. The sap flows more strongly to buds at the end of each cane, so if the canes are cut very short as

spurs, sap will be diverted to their buds rather than pushing a few unfruitful shoots of "bull wood" at the end of the plant.

Guyot pruning is basically cane pruning, similar to Chablis pruning, keeping one cane and one spur per vine, or two canes and two spurs per vine (Double Guyot). In this case, the spur is not for fruit but is to produce a well-located cane for the following year's crop. This method is particularly suitable for frost-prone regions, where some buds may be injured by the cold.

Marne Valley pruning closely resembles Guyot pruning. Used only for Meunier vines, it is

particularly suitable for these plants, giving them extra protection against frost.

Summer maintenance

Of the summer tasks necessary to control growth in the vineyard, the most important—mainly manual ones—are listed here.

Desuckering: This is the act of removing all non-productive water shoots that grow on old wood and drain sap away from the main buds.

Lifting: By the beginning of June, the shoots can be 20in (50cm) long, so it is necessary to lift them vertically by attaching them to wires

Above: Pruning has changed little over the centuries, and the winter months are still given over to this important task

running above the support wires. A few days later, trellising involves separating the shoots from each other and stapling them to yet more wires. This reduces the density of the canopy, allowing maximum exposure to light for photosynthesis and improving air circulation through the vines in order to prevent rot.

Topping: This is a sort of summer pruning that starts in mid-June/early July and can continue right through to the harvest. It is essential to prevent the vine from sprouting foliage at the expense of the grapes. All unwanted shoots and

31

leaves are removed to aid further light exposure, which promotes good ripening. Topping also stimulates the growth of new leaves that will be more effective in producing sugar than those that have been on the vines since springtime. (Middle-aged leaves photosynthesize most efficiently.)

Vendange verte: In July and early August some Champagne growers conduct a "green harvest", which involves cutting off a number of grape clusters in order to concentrate the sugar in those that remain. Others argue, reasonably, that this is a late-in-the-day expedient and no substitute for meticulous vineyard care, particularly a proper density of planting and skilful pruning earlier in the season. If it is done after the vines colour (veraison), the unripe clusters are easily seen, because they are still green, and can be quickly eliminated then.

Eco-friendly wine growing: ideal and reality

Since 2000, the avowed objective of the authorities in Champagne has been to convert the entire region to environmentally friendly viticulture over ten years. In simple terms, this is (to quote a CIVC document) "an undertaking to improve the protection of the land, the water, and the air that are all part of our heritage".

But far from being no more than an idealistic dream, "green" viticulture in Champagne aims to strike a realistic balance between economic, qualitative, and environmental requirements. It is a holistic approach that neither begins nor ends with production, yet its provisions relate to every stage in the cycle of the vine: vineyard design and planting in line with protection of the countryside; soil nourishment and preservation against erosion; protection against spring frosts by natural means; and ever-more-vigilant

Left: Although most vineyards belong to small growers, the large houses are keen to identify those in their ownership

waste handling and disposal. The days are long gone when town rubbish was used to make compost in the vineyards, including the blue plastic trashbags themselves, though these polluting *bleus de ville* really did disfigure the landscape up to the 1980s. Although eco-friendly methods are now almost universal, anecdotal evidence suggests that sales of both herbicides and pesticides are again on the rise, after a period when their use laudably declined in the early 2000s. As demand for grapes grows inexorably, one fears that some of the fine principles of vineyard care may be ignored.

Notwithstanding, the best young Champenois growers manage to strike a balance between, on the one hand, a sustained commitment to improve the environment and, on the other, a clear-eyed realism about the limitations that the marginal climate of Champagne places on their room for manoeuvre in the vines. A case in point is the admirable domaine of Veuve Fourny at Vertus, run by brothers Charles-Henry and Emmanuel Fourny. They made biodynamic trials, forsaking synthetic pesticides, in two of their parcels in 1995 and 1996. Mildew spread so widely that they had to spray the vines with copper sulphate every week, but they still lost much of the crop. Copper is allowed in biodynamic viticulture, because it is, to use the almost theological term of biodynamists, "elemental". It is also toxic and can degrade the soil, stalling growth of the vines. So the brothers preferred to use a non-toxic, synthetic product to reduce the use of copper sprays. At the same time, they employ organic fertilizer, grass over between rows, and use pheromones to cause "sexual confusion" among male butterflies, preventing them from mating and reducing the number of caterpillars that eat holes in the leaves, making them prone to rot. The brothers plan to be chemical-free by 2010, having steadily improved the health of their vines since the mid-1990s.

Art and Heart of the Cuvée

About a month before the harvest, the berries begin to ripen and change colour, depending on the grape variety: Chardonnay turns from green to greenish gold, Pinot Noir and Meunier to bluish black. As they approach maturity, the berries soften and become juicy and plump—they now look like real grapes. The exact moment of ripeness is when acidity begins to drop and sugar to rise. In Champagne, this is always a delicate calculation—the aim is to preserve enough acidity to ensure the essential "tension" of a great sparkling wine while, in the case of perfectionist producers, capturing the additional complexity that results from slightly later harvesting and full phenolic maturity. The old school of Champenois cellar masters may regard mention of the word "phenolic" as heresy, since the preservation of acidity has always been their main, almost obsessive priority. They would be entirely right, were it not for the current evidence of climate change, which is likely to alter the way Champagne is made over the course of the next decade. The likely challenge will be to protect the vitality of the wine coming from richer, potentially more complex grapes.

For the moment, though, in Champagne's northerly location, acidity in the grapes remains pretty high by comparison even with neighbouring Burgundy. Sugar content, particularly after poor summers like 2007, is much less dependable. Ideally, Champagne grapes should reach a potential alcoholic strength of about 10%. Of course, ripeness varies from year to year, depending on the weather. Grape maturity also depends heavily, however, on the cru and the grape variety, across the 318 communes of *Champagne viticole* that run from the Massif de St-Thierry above Reims down to Les Riceys close to the Côte d'Or border—a distance of about 120

miles (200km). In fact, sugar levels sometimes reach 13% potential natural alcohol in the finest old-vine sites of the Côte des Blancs. But as the great Mesnil grower Alain Robert once confided, "the *négoces* don't like these opulent, *gras* [fat] wines. In the main, with honourable exceptions, they much prefer blander, lower-alcohol wines that are easier to blend."

Every year, 100,000 pickers descend on the vineyards to do work that is as physically demanding as ever it was. For, unlike other wine regions in France, Champagne clings to the tradition of manual picking, because only the human hand has the dexterity to select whole, unbruised clusters of grapes. If the clusters were broken by the beating strokes of a mechanical harvester, the grapes would probably split and the hue of the seeping juice be tinted by the colour pigments, particularly in the black grapes—something to be avoided at all costs. The pickers are trained to pick the grapes carefully and to put them gently into plastic bins that are loaded on to trailers. These are then rapidly transported in a race against oxidation to the winery for immediate pressing.

Pressing: cuvée and *taille*

The grapes are pressed, as whole bunches, as quickly and softly as possible, according to the key Champenois principle of fractionated winemaking—that is, separating the brighter, clearer, free-run juice drawn off at the beginning of the pressing (the cuvée) from that extracted at the end (the *taille*, or "cut"), which becomes progressively darker due to the impurities found in the grape skins. The aim of this process is to coax all the natural freshness and dancing vitality from the grapes, though the separation of clearer and darker juices is of course more intricate than the simple principle might suggest. The cuvée, for example, is extracted by three successive pressings, or *serres*, which, in a standard-size press, produce a total of 20.5hl of juice. The best part—the *coeur de la cuvée* ("heart of the cuvée")—is the middle one of these pressings, giving an ideal balance of purity and structure.

To achieve this, it has normally been necessary for skilled workers to perform a manual *retrousse*—that is, to scoop the edges of the pressed grape "cake" and return them to the centre. Happily, there is now a brilliant new piece of technology that dramatically advances this crucial stage in the Champagne-making process: the *pressoir automatique à plateau incliné* (PAI), the Rolls-Royce of modern presses, from press manufacturer Coquard. This is designed to turn the pressed cake at an inclined angle that obviates the need for the manual *retrousse*. A full harvest-day's worth of *retrousse* is now reduced to an automated process lasting only three hours—with the added bonus of energy saving for the greater good of the planet. Some traditionalists suck their teeth at the punitive cost of the PAI, sticking stubbornly with their supposedly superior traditional Coquard vertical presses—but perhaps they have sentiment rather than reason on their side. At least for now, many producers use neither the traditional Coquard press nor the PAI but modern pneumatic presses.

After all the cuvée has been drawn off, the pressing is then repeated two or three times at progressively higher pressures for the *taille*. Since 1992, and the introduction of stricter quality controls, the total extraction of this *taille* has been restricted to 5hl (formerly 6.5hl). Although it has much the same concentrations of sugar as the cuvée, the *taille* has lower levels of malic and tartaric acids, which form the skeleton of all great white wines. It also contains more oxidants, minerals, pigments, and stalky, grassy elements. The first *taille*—the portion the houses want to have—does have some simple aromas

and attractive, if fast-maturing, fruitiness. Champagne's *chefs de cave* will use varying amounts of cuvée and *taille* depending on the desired style of their different blends.

Finally, in the pressing process, care is taken to avoid any risk of environmental pollution. The worst risk is in the water used for cleaning the presses after the reception of the grapes. This viticultural effluent, with its content of solid particles and organic substances, smells nasty and, more seriously, poses a threat to river and pond life. As a result of an in-depth study to prevent waterborne pollution, guidelines have now been put in place by the CIVC for all producers in Champagne, specifying methods for the proper management of water and other effluent.

Débourbage and fermentation

After pressing, impurities in the must (the pressed grape juice) are eliminated by *débourbage*, a process of settling that allows solid matter to sink to the bottom of the vat and clear juice to be drawn off from the top. An ultra-modern refinement of this method—ironically practised by Billecart-Salmon and Pol Roger, two of the traditional "greats" of Champagne—is *débourbage à froid*, which is a second settling of the must chilled down to about 41°F (5°C). The cold acts as a filtration and eliminates most of the natural yeasts and coarser lees. Oxidation of the must is also reduced, and these two houses certainly produce exquisite, fresh, long-lived Champagnes, partly as a result of this crucial procedure.

The clear juice then goes through alcoholic fermentation, which in most cases is conducted in stainless-steel tanks. In the mid-1990s, only a few top houses such as Krug, Bollinger, and Alfred Gratien, and the occasional great grower such as René Collard and Anselme Selosse, still fermented

Right: A growing number of producers use both stainless-steel and wooden vessels for fermentation and/or maturation

entirely in wood. Oak is once again in fashion, however, and is becoming the preferred vessel of fermentation for an increasing number of bijou houses and growers—particularly for their best, most structured wines.

The greater *matière*, or richness, of Champagne grapes today has not gone unnoticed by a growing number of Champenois producers who currently make their *vins clairs* wholly or partly in oak. Once it was just a handful of great *maisons* that stayed true to their oak *pièces* of 205 or 228 litres. Now some 100 houses and growers use wood in one form or another during the winemaking process —fermenting in different sizes of barrel and cask, maturing the wines in tonneaux, creating the *vin de dosage*—all for the added strength, suppleness, and complexity of flavour that microoxygenation in oak can bring to any fine wine with enough character and structure to cope with it.

Delving deeper, there are really three schools of oak in Champagne. First, the old school. These *anciens* have always used oak, usually older barrels, which may be anything from five to 30 years of age. For them, wood is not an end in itself, still less a fashion. It is an aid, a medium through which wine can best express itself, without being masked by an overtly woody flavour. Krug is the best-known example of this style, the family restricting the use of oak in small *pièces* to the first fermentation, after which the wine is stored in stainless-steel vats for optimal freshness.

Then there are the traditionalists who have returned to oak for its subtleties of aroma and flavour (when well managed), to emphasize a wine's personality or origin. Oak is a new field of play, often combined with the use of stainless-

Below: Small growers, such as Jérôme Prévost, have often been at the forefront of the return to small wooden barrels

steel or enamel vats to maintain an ideal balance when composing a blend or Vintage cuvée.

In the third school are the innovators. These *novateurs* are redefining oak as an essential component of their winemaking. Wood is perceived by them as incomparably the best method to make fine wine in Champagne, as distinct from an elegant expression of the world's best fizz. Innovators like Anselme Selosse, the distinguished grower in Avize, have brought modern techniques to Champagne—in Anselme's case, initially with the use of new oak, a "solera" system of reserve wines and *bâtonnage*, the stirring of the wine's lees in barrel. In the most marked cases, one can certainly speak critically of certain innovators' overtly woody Champagnes, which are anathema to many respected tasters. But equally, one should not labour the point, for addressing the issue of oak in Champagne is a learning curve even for some of the best producers, who, through observation and a flexible frame of mind, are adapting their methods and the proportion of oak to the different characters and structures of their wines as they change from vintage to vintage. Moreover, there is some cross-fertilization of ideas and methods between the schools—*anciens* employing some very modern aids to protect the wines from infection and spoilage, and traditionalists adopting *bâtonnage* as the wine matures in cask.

The art of blending

At this early point, after fermentation, the infant wine is much like any other still white wine, but it is transformed by what used to be known as the "Champagne method", now known as the "traditional method", and by the craft of blending. Traditional method is the EU-blessed name for the process of making a wine sparkle by allowing it to ferment for a second time in the bottle—a process now used for quality sparkling wine throughout the world. But intricate blending sets Champagne apart from lesser sparklers. The characteristics of as many as 300 crus must be memorized by the blender and their flavours married to produce a Champagne that mirrors the established style of the blender's house. It is often claimed that only the top merchant houses have the personnel and skills to master the art of blending, but this is not really true. In such a marginal climate, great growers can be as adept as the grandest *maison* at blending wines from different parts of their vineyards and from different years. It is merely a question of scale. The essential comparison is between the transregional blend of a big house, the character of many crus subsumed in a carefully honed house style; and the blend of a grower that may have up to seven components from contiguous villages and two or three vintages, reflecting more transparently their origin in place and time.

Great grapes: the raw material

As is their wont, the marketing departments of the big houses sometimes go into overdrive when describing the near-magical blending skills of their cellar master as the supreme art in Champagne. Vital and fascinating as the blending process can be, the crucial prerequisite for great Champagne, as for all great wine, lies in the vineyards. As the late Daniel Thibault of Charles Heidsieck, the finest Champagne blender of his generation, always scrupulously acknowledged, "*chefs de cave* are not sorcerers; it's the raw material, the grapes, that make the quality of Champagne".

The best cellar masters spend much of their time in the vineyards monitoring the growing cycle, many being the sons (or daughters) of growers: Jacques Péters, the Veuve Clicquot maestro, was born at the Pierre Péters estate in Le Mesnil; Richard Geoffroy, the supremo of Dom

Pérignon, is the son of a former president of the Union Champagne super-cooperative in Avize.

The greatest Champagnes are generally sourced from grand cru grapes in the finest sites, so the cellar masters have a fine palette of flavours to play with, for example, when composing the prestige or top Vintage cuvées of their houses. Among the 17 grand cru villages, a favourite hunting ground for Pinot Noir might be Aÿ, bringing harmony and texture; Verzenay, bringing acidity and structure; or Bouzy, bringing rich, exuberant fruit. For Chardonnay, it might be Le Mesnil, contributing minerality and staying power; Oger, contributing a rounder, more honeyed richness; Avize, for its "lead-pencil" elegance; Cramant, for its dynamism; Chouilly for its crisp, dry focus; and so on.

There could of course be interesting variations on this selection. Krug, for example, prizes Ambonnay as its favourite grand cru Pinot for its extraordinary finesse, based as it is on a deep stratum of chalk. For a lovely saline note, the subtlety of north-facing Verzy can be incomparable. Moving down to the top premiers crus, Mareuil-sur-Aÿ is a Pinot Noir grand cru in all but official rating, with an unsurpassed solidity and capacity for aging. For highly distinctive Chardonnay, Trépail above Ambonnay and Cuis at the top of the Côte des Blancs both have a fierce acidity that makes you want to grip the table for support but can be superb elements in a Vintage blend, as wines from fine growers such as Léclapart and Gimonnet will testify.

Nor should we ignore Meunier, as the majority of cautious houses are inclined to do when composing their Vintage cuvées, on the grounds that it does not age well. A soupçon of Meunier in the very greatest prestige cuvées, like William Deutz, adds palate-filling, spicy roundness; and one of the greatest Champagnes of the 20th century, the Krug 1981, had 19 per cent Meunier in the blend. No apologies, incidentally, for citing Krug once again, for this is the house, along with Pol Roger, Roederer, and Billecart-Salmon, by which all other Vintage cuvées are judged.

And so to the Non-Vintage blends. Here the palette of manifold flavours is like a tapestry of many threads. When I wrote my first book on Champagne, in 1994, Krug, as a bijou top producer of about 500,000 bottles of Champagne, was composing its Grande Cuvée from about 40 wines from 10–12 different vintages. Now, as production has increased, reflecting better access to the finest grapes as part of the Veuve Clicquot division, Krug has a larger palette of 70 or so wines from which to choose. And for the big beasts like Clicquot itself, making in excess of 11 million bottles, the number of crus that form part of the Yellow Label blend can exceed 200. Pinots of greater suppleness and bright primary fruit from the Petite Montagne and the Aube's Côte des Bar, Meunier from the best sites of the Valley of the Marne and Ardre, and golden ripe Chardonnay from the south-facing hill of Montgueux, above Troyes—these are some of the additional raw materials for a consistent, refined house style.

Sourcing red wine for rosé

Most rosé Champagne is made by adding red wine to a white Champagne blend (*rosé d'assemblage*), the aim being to preserve the sparkling wine's essential elegance and finesse. The winemakers of this style of rosé choose this fractional blending approach to avoid any overextraction of the colour pigments and tannins from the grapes. Because of intense demand by the great houses, the rarest thing on the Montagne de Reims and along the Marne Valley is fine red wine. The challenge is to find enough to tint the finest rosé to just the right hue, while imbuing the wine with succulent but refined flavours that never degrade into heaviness. So when Philippe Thieffry, the chief winemaker at

Veuve Clicquot, invited me to spend the day with him in their vineyards and tasting room, sourcing and blending fine red Pinot Noirs, I jumped at the chance. Since the days of the widow herself, Clicquot has been the role model for this serious style of vinous rosé.

On a typically cool April morning, we set off from Reims, skirting the southeastern Montagne and dropping down past Trépail towards Bouzy, the church spire peeping through the mist. Here, above the village, we were in supreme Pinot territory, where Clicquot has peerless sites. Walking through the vineyards, the topsoils threaded with white streaks of the famous belemnite chalk, the *lieu-dit* of Les Egarilles was the most striking, perfectly angled to face southeast and catch the morning and midday sun. No surprise to learn that this little vineyard is a major source of black grapes for the classic Grande Dame (white) cuvée. To its right, the equally privileged *lieux-dits* of Les Vaudayants and Clos Colin, with fractionally more southerly aspects, are prime sites for the Grande Dame Rosé. Farther south, the vineyard Au Moulin, at the limits of Bouzy

and Ambonnay, is usually a favourite source for the more vinous style of Clicquot Vintage Rosé.

The grapes are rapidly transported to Clicquot's village presshouse and cuverie, specifically designed to make red wine. A simple building, it is nonetheless very state of the art, with a box of the usual, magical, modern tricks. Gleaming stainless-steel fermenters, both small and large, fitted with computer-controlled *auto-pigeage* for punching down the *marc*, and the latest, gentlest *peri-statique* pumps all help capture the elusive, aromatic subtleties of exceptional Pinot Noir.

Adding the sparkle and removing the yeast

Once the blend is complete, the *liqueur de tirage* (a solution of wine, sugar, and yeasts) is added in carefully measured amounts. The wine is now ready for its second fermentation. The slow process known as the *prise de mousse* will produce the bubbles, and it is said that the slower the process is conducted in very cool cellars, the more refined the bubbles will be. The pressure created inside the bottle gradually rises to be five or six times that of the atmosphere.

As the second fermentation takes place, with the bottles binned on their sides (*sur lattes*), yeast cells die and decompose in the process known as autolysis, which adds complexity to the wine's aroma and flavour. The length of time that a Champagne is allowed to age at this stage is a key factor in its quality. Non-Vintage Champagne must be aged for at least 16 months in the bottle before sale, and Vintage Champagne at least three years. In practice, for the Champagnes that count, the best producers age their Non-Vintage for three or four years and their Vintage for seven or eight—though pressure of demand up to 2006 did often dilute this excellent principle for release.

Remuage is a process to remove the yeast deposits. The word in plain English is "riddling", which hardly has the same ring to it. Traditionally, the bottles are placed in holed racks called *pupitres* and are turned and tilted every day, eventually arriving at an almost vertical position, neck downwards. This allows the deposit to settle on the crown cap or cork. Much of this labour-intensive work is now carried out by a computer-controlled machine called a gyropalette, its prototype and patent the creation of the late Claude Cazals, a fine grower in Le Mesnil and Oger. In the case of some great houses, especially for cuvées such as Bollinger's Grande Année and Laurent-Perrier's Grand Siècle, hand-riddling is still preferred.

At this point, the bottles are taken from the gyropalette and stored vertically, upside down, to age gently in preparation for *dégorgement* (disgorgement), the technique for removing the cork or cap and expelling the sediment. The bottles are normally passed in an inverted, vertical position along a conveyor that freezes the liquid in the neck of the bottle, imprisoning the sediment in a tiny "sorbet" of near-frozen wine. The bottle is then up-ended by a *dégorgeur*, who removes the cap or cork, allowing the pressure generated by the gas to expel the little block of ice from the wine, which leaves the remainder clear and bright. This technique is known as *dégorgement à la glace*. The old method of *dégorgement à la volée*, which involves expelling the sediment without freezing it, is rarely used nowadays. On special occasions, it is wonderful to see how they do it, bringing the bottle upright in the split second after the cork has been drawn, thus preventing little more than the deposit from escaping.

Finishing touch: *dosage* and *mariage*

The addition of varying amounts of *liqueur de dosage* (Champenois wine and sugar, or occasionally rectified concentrated grape must), normally expressed as grams of sugar per litre of wine (g/l), results in the following official styles.

Extra Brut ("Extra Raw"): 0–6g/l *dosage*—very dry (Brut Nature, Brut Zéro, Pas Dosé: 0–3g/l)

Brut ("Raw"): 0–15g/l *dosage*—classic, dry

Extra Sec ("Extra Dry"): 12–20g/l *dosage*—dry to medium-dry

Sec ("Dry"): 17–35g/l *dosage*—medium-dry

Demi-Sec ("Medium Dry"): 35–50g/l *dosage*—medium-sweet

Doux ("Sweet"): 50–150g/l *dosage*—sweet.

After this finishing touch, the wine is ideally given at least 6–12 months for the *dosage* to "marry" with the wine before it is shipped.

Right: Bottles in their *pupitres*, at the end of their *remuage*, the yeast deposit ready for removal by *dégorgement*

Reims and the Montagne de Reims

The recorded origins of Reims are older than any other town in France, outside Provence and the Midi. During the first Roman occupation of what is now modern France (c.AD 57), when Paris was just a large village, Reims was the main city of Belgian Gaul, with a population approaching 100,000. Two millennia on, it is one of the great French provincial towns, with 248,000 inhabitants, a fine university, and one of the best children's hospitals in the land.

Reims is, of course, the headquarters of several of the greatest Champagne houses and quite a few smaller ones—about 40 firms in total. Veuve Clicquot, Charles Heidsieck and Piper-Heidsieck, Krug, Lanson, Pommery, Louis Roederer, and Taittinger read like a roll call of honour. Yet the venerable Ruinart, the first house to make sparkling Champagne in 1729, is the most atmospheric of all, its deep Roman chalk pits—les Crayères—classified as a national monument. Bruno Paillard and Alain Thiénot are excellent newer houses, both established in the 1980s, and two fine growers' cooperatives—Palmer and Jacquart—are also within the city limits.

Between them, Reims and Epernay account equally for nearly all the Champagne trade of the négociants. But while 90 per cent of Epernay's economy is bubbles, it is just 10 per cent for Reims, the city also having lively industries in textiles, clothing, and floor coverings. This is much more than a wine town. Chic shops, great restaurants and cafés, wide 1920s boulevards, and the superb churches of the Notre Dame Cathedral and the even lovelier St-Rémi Basilica all create a quasi-metropolitan feel. Paris never seems far away, and now it isn't. The latest TGV from Reims-Centre to the Gare de l'Est, a trip of nearly 100 miles (160km), is just a 45-minute ride. It takes only half an hour to speed on another TGV

Left: The great cathedral of Notre Dame still towers over Reims, where the kings of France were crowned until 1825

to Paris Charles de Gaulle from Reims-Bezannes at the foot of the Montagne de Reims.

Montagne de Reims

The Montagne is hardly a mountain, more a very large hill, some 12 miles (20km) long and 6 miles (10km) wide. Its highest point between Verzenay and Verzy lies 600ft (180m) above the Rémois plain and 900ft (275m) above sea level. The plateau at its top, bisected by the main Reims–Epernay road, is set in a 10,000ha (25,000-acre) national park of thick forests teeming with wild boar that are the favourite, perilous sport of Champenois *chasseurs*. For gentler nature-loving souls, one Montagne wood has some of the most remarkable trees in the world: les Faux de Verzy are ancient beeches, planted more than 1,500 years ago by the monks of the Abbey of St Bale. They have grotesquely deformed branches, like corkscrews that form parasols so weird that they would make a perfect film set for a horror movie.

The vineyards of the Montagne run continuously along its northern slopes from Villers-Allerand to Mailly and—for the very finest—along its northeastern slopes from Verzenay and Verzy through Trépail and down to Bouzy and Ambonnay. This is as ideal a district for exceptional Pinot Noir as the Côte des Blancs south of Epernay is for exquisite Chardonnay. These mostly grand cru sites, together with the great vineyards of Aÿ in the Marne Valley, have a common denominator: they are all on the *falaises* (cliffs) of Champagne, those rocky, east-facing outcrops of the purest belemnite chalk. It cannot be said too often that quite apart from the incomparable, crystalline, mineral flavours it seems to give to the wines, this type of chalk has a unique sponge-like texture that drains quickly after a downpour in a wet harvest, such as 2001, yet can store water deep down by the plants' roots to revive the wilting vines in a heatwave year like

Montbré

N44

Beaumont-
sur-Vesle

A4

Rilly-la-
Montagne

Villers-
Allerand

Chigny-
les-Roses

Verzenay

Mailly-
Champagne

Ludes

Verzy

Villers-
Marmery

Les Petites-
Loges

Forêt de la Montagne de Reims

Ville-
en-Selve

D9

D34

Billy-le-
Grand

Trépail

Louvois

Tauxières

Vaudemange

Fontaine-
sur-Aÿ

D34

D19

Bouzy

Ambonnay

D37

MONTAGNE DE REIMS

Grand Cru Vineyard

Premier Cru Vineyard

Village Border

A1 Major Road

0   3 km

0   3 miles

0   20 km

0   20 miles

Reims

Epernay

Marne

PARIS

Seine

Aube

Troyes

MONTAGNE DE REIMS

2003. Generalizations about wine are tricky, but one that does hold water is that it is impossible to make great wine where the texture of the soil cannot cope with the extremes of nature. The hillsides of the Montagne triumphantly can.

Sillery

The grand cru village closest to Reims is just 8 miles (13km) from the city along the Valley of the Vesle. Puisieulx, its neighbour, is a mile or two nearer the Montagne. Both villages have a fascinating history, associated with one of the great landowning families of Champagne—the Brularts of Sillery, who held high offices of state and ran immaculate wine domaines in the late 16th and early 17th centuries. The most famous member of the family was Nicholas Brulart, who served as chancellor of Navarre and of France itself under Henri IV. In 1621, he was ennobled, as Marquis of Sillery, and ten years later so was his son, as Marquis of Puisieulx. They poured money into these vineyards, acquired through marriage a couple of generations back. Soon the vineyards were lauded by the Brularts' contemporaries as being the equal of those of Aÿ. Their grand château at Sillery was looted and wrecked during the French Revolution, and in 1791 the head of the family lost his head to "Madame Guillotine".

The wily Jean-Remy Moët and the Ruinart family eventually acquired the twin vineyards on the restoration of the Bourbon monarchy after Waterloo. The fame of Sillery wine lasted for another century. The late Patrick Forbes relates that Thackeray's characters drank gallons of it, still and sparkling, and Forbes gives us one of the sweetest anecdotes associated with Champagne. The story goes that a Scottish landowner gave a dinner for his tenants, serving Sillery wine, made by Moët & Chandon. Doing his rounds of the table, he stopped beside an old lady, Mrs Macdoodle, apologizing that she could not take a glass because of her temperance principles. "Hoot, Laird," replied the good lady, "ye just pour it on ma bread and I'll eat it." Moët still owns a vineyard in Sillery, now planted with old-vine Meunier, which was the material for one of a trio of single-vineyard Champagnes released by the great house in the early 2000s. Ruinart retains holdings in Sillery and Puisieulx as key Chardonnay elements in its superb Dom Ruinart prestige cuvées. The only *récoltant-manipulant* to have vineyards entirely in Sillery is François Secondé.

Verzenay

Farther up the slopes from Puisieulx is the grand cru village of Verzenay, tucked between its famous windmill and lighthouse that has a contemporary eco-museum of Champagne-making. If ever the *chefs de cave* of the great houses had to make an invidious choice and nominate one key Pinot Noir element in the makeup of their long-lived prestige cuvées, it would probably be Verzenay. Because of its altitude, northeast aspect, and rude climate, as well as its superb subsoils, Verzenay so often expresses in its wines a vigour, precision, clarity, and vinosity, at once rich and austere, that together create one of the surest building blocks of the greatest Champagne blends. And no oenophile should miss the chance to taste a top grower's less blended version, particularly those of Michel Arnould, Jacques Busin, or Jean Lallement, who have plots in one or more of the village's best *lieux-dits*—les Correttes, les Pertois, les Bruyères, and les Hautes Coutures. Of Verzenay's 415ha (1,025 acres) of vines, 86 per cent is planted to Pinot Noir, which is particularly suited to these calcareous soils. Nevertheless, the little Chardonnay adds a gentle finesse, especially to the punch and power of the growers' Champagnes.

Verzy

Continuing south on the northeast flank of the

Montagne, the next village, Verzy, is now a grand cru, elevated in 1985 from premier cru status: the older *chefs de cave* used to say that the more modest status was the right one. Verzy is less voluminous, less powerful than Verzenay, which has an ideal balance of minerality and substance. Yet I have drunk some fine bottles of pure Verzy with a lovely saline character akin to Grand Cru Chablis. I know we are talking about the white juice of Pinot Noir rather than Chardonnay, but it's the terroir rather than the grape variety that speaks to the taster. Fresnet-Juillet is the village's best domaine, and it has been making its own Champagnes since the 1950s, when Gérard Fresnet started to dig his cellar out of the chalk; it took him nearly 40 years to get it right! His son Vincent is a fine winemaker, whose Champagnes are generous and well balanced, thanks to his Chardonnay vines at Bisseuil in the Marne Valley.

Villers-Marmery

Farther south are the premier cru vineyards of Villers-Marmery, which is preeminently the Montagne cru better known for Chardonnay than for Pinot Noir. Villers-Marmery wine tends to have a piercing acidity that works well in a blend but can make you grip the table if you taste it unblended; it's said that birds don't eat the grapes here because they are so astringent. The village does, however, have two excellent growers in Arnaud Margaine and Sadi Malot, who produce Chardonnay-led wines of finesse and poise. Heading down the Montagne's flanks, you come to the more attractive village of Trépail, also known for fine Chardonnay of brisk character. Domaine Claude Carré makes some good things; and in his 3ha (7.5-acre) vineyard David Léclapart—a disciple of Anselme Selosse and a committed biodynamist—creates exciting expressions of the great white grape.

Left: The famous windmill above the grand cru vineyards of Verzenay, whose wines are prized for their vigour and vinosity

Bouzy

The flanks of the Montagne finally drop down to their southeastern limit in the grands crus of Bouzy and Ambonnay. These vineyards vie for greatness with Verzenay but show a more opulent, *gras* character, usually shaped by the warmer conditions and therefore riper grapes. Quite apart from Champagnes from a string of first-rate growers, Bouzy is famous for its still red wine made from Pinot Noir. Standing in the vineyards as you arrive from the Trépail side, you can see why. The best sites such as Les Egarilles, Les Vaudayants, and Clos Colin face south or south-southeast basking in the midday sun, so precious in this northern climate. One of the best Bouzy reds is made by Paul Bara, and some of the most characterful rosés from this base come from Veuve Clicquot and top growers such as Edmond Barnaut, André Clouet, and Benoît Lahaye.

Ambonnay

Close by, Ambonnay was a prosperous *bourg* in the Middle Ages, built on the site of a Gallo-Roman villa. According to Eric Rodez, a leading Ambonnay grower, the discovery of an early Merovingian cemetery at La Fontaine de Crilly suggests that community life began on this spot. Later, at the beginning of the 11th century, the Templar monks of St John of Jerusalem built the village church, now a gem of Romanesque and Gothic styles. By this time, the vineyards were already part of villagers' livelihood, as revealed in carvings of grapes and vines on some of the church's pillars. And what vineyards they are today, spread across 370ha (914 acres) on ideal south-southeast-facing hillsides and a fabulous terroir. Look at the best Ambonnay *lieux-dits*, such as Les Crayères, and you notice streaks of chalk popping through the soil. These are just the tip of a deep stratum of chalk that goes down some 100ft (30m), imbuing the naturally voluptuous character

Above: An experienced hand in Ambonnay, where the standard of viticulture and winemaking is very high

of Pinot Noir grown here with an incisive minerality and racy dynamism that encourages comparisons with the most elegant Burgundies like Volnay. Little wonder that Krug jumped at the chance to buy a tiny Ambonnay plot in the 1990s; its first release, the 1995 Clos d'Ambonnay, is a very fine Champagne but no better than those of three or four village domaines that cost a tenth of the price. Ambonnay, with Verzenay, has one of the highest standards of winemaking on the Montagne, the work of artist-artisans such as Serge Billiot, Francis Egly, and Marie-Noëlle Ledru.

Louvois

Retracing one's tracks northwest from Ambonnay via Bouzy, one comes to Louvois, a village in fine, wooded, hill country that is between the best southeastern flanks of the Montagne and the westerly Valley of the Marne, where different conditions and soils prevail. Frankly, I have never quite grasped why Louvois is classified as a Montagne grand cru: it doesn't have the ideal aspect or, I suspect, the same great soils of, say, Verzenay, Verzy, or Ambonnay, and you don't find it that often in the composition of the greatest cuvées—except for those of Laurent-Perrier, which sources fruit from here. Certainly, the splendid approach, facade, and salons of the great château, once the seat of de Louvois, war minister of Louis XIV, make a fine setting in which the Nonancourt family and directors of the house can entertain important guests. In the village, I can vouch for the Champagnes of the domaine of the de Chassey sisters who make delicious wine at a very fair price.

Mailly-Champagne and the premiers crus

Taking the D26 road north, skirting Verzy, and then westwards, you will arrive at Mailly-Champagne, the last of the Montagne grands crus, this one facing north. Here the vineyards have some elements of clay as well as chalk, and they express themselves in wines that are certainly powerful but sometimes lack the crystalline focus of the "greats" of the east-facing slopes. Much of the production is in the hands of Mailly Grand Cru, a small group of growers farming 70ha (173 acres) of vineyards exclusively within the limits of the commune. The Champagnes are very well made and, for a cooperative, deftly marketed internationally. Shrewd fine-wine merchants such as Berry Bros & Rudd in London often use a cuvée of Mailly Grand Cru as their own-label Champagne—and very good value it is, too. For a further step up in quality, with a touch of classy minerality, the Mailly Grand Cru from Raymond Boulard is wholeheartedly recommended.

And so to the best premier cru villages on the north-facing slopes of the Montagne between Mailly and Villers-Allerand. The soils change progressively as you travel northwest—there is less pure chalk and more sandstone/clay, which suits the Meunier grape very well. In the hands of a top grower like Gilles Dumangin, in the pretty, flower-filled village of Chigny-les-Roses, Meunier can be transformed into the praised Grande Réserve Brut (50 per cent Meunier); it also accounts for all the red wine that is added to colour his succulent rosé. He successfully achieves finesse and fruit rather than substance and vinosity in these Champagnes, which is an intelligent recognition of the strength and limitations of his soils. And as something of an epicure, since 2001 Gilles has revived some forgotten Champenois specialities, such as a delicious Champagne confit that matches a delicate foie gras, or the grape chutney that is an ideal condiment for pâtés. Gilles also imaginatively uses cask aging and traditional solera systems to produce a range of alcohols such as *ratafia, marc*, and *fine de Champagne*. Chigny's best-known producer is Cattier—a négociant, but one with a real feeling for the land. Its 20ha (50 acres) of finely tended vineyards reaches its apogee in the 2ha (5-acre) Clos du Moulin, a true walled vineyard of Pinot Noir and Chardonnay. Made from a blend of three vintages, it matures very evenly into a fine, complex Champagne, in part due to the house's exceptionally deep cellars.

Going on to Rilly-la-Montagne, you come to one of the finest growers on the Montagne—Vilmart, whose eminence does not rely on particularly well-sited vineyards. But their 11ha (27 acres), with some old vines of more than 40 years, are tended with the greatest respect for the soils, and they are also brilliant winemakers, exhibiting a mastery of fermentation in oak, particularly for their top cuvées.

The Montagne reaches its limit in Villers-Allerand, a good premier cru close to a crossroads on the Reims–Epernay N51, where the Auberge du Grand Cerf serves some of the most refined cuisine, matched by one of the best cellars, in the Marne.

Here begins the Petite Montagne, which is really a northwestern extension of the Montagne proper, lying between the rivers Ardre and Vesle. The vineyards are among the most northerly in Champagne, but the wines are some of the friendliest, shaped by sandier soils mixed with clay that really makes this one of the best places for fine Meunier, on a par with some over the hill in Hautvillers and Dizy, overlooking the Marne Valley.

That is certainly not the whole picture, though. The village of Ecueil is famous for Pinot Noir, and there is no better exponent of it, skilfully blended with Chardonnay, than Alain Brochet of the Domaine Hervieux-Brochet. Alain and his wife Brigitte have farmed 15ha (37 acres) since 1980, and their greatest Champagne, the vintaged HBH, is a classic, long-aged cuvée, with a slight majority of black grapes (almost all Pinot Noir). The 1996, in particular, is well worth seeking out—an admirably evolved example of the vintage, fine, complex, and ample. Alain also produces an excellent Extra Brut, which marries the power of Pinot Noir with the friend-winning fruitiness of Pinot Meunier.

For the cellar masters of the *grandes maisons*, the Petite Montagne village of Villedemange, dominated by its fine medieval church, is a favourite source of the most refined Meunier, which belies its quite false reputation as a workhorse grape. Farther across towards the main Reims–Paris road, the great Ambonnay grower Francis Egly of Domaine Egly-Ouriet has some very old Meunier vines that make a lovely, complex Champagne for a gentle price. Farther on still, perhaps the most distinctive Meunier-maker of all, Jérôme Prévost in Gueux, says, "Meunier has interesting things to say, but you have to know how to make it speak."

Left: Altitude and exposure, as here at the high, northeast-facing Verzenay, help shape the style of the wines

Krug

As standard-bearers of the most prestigious name in Champagne, the Krug family have always made classic wines in an elegantly vinous style quite unlike any other. With such a daunting reputation for Champagnes that can age beautifully for 15, 20, even 30 or more years, you might think that Krug is a bastion of tradition run by old men with beards in three-piece tweed suits.

Not so. For although the family stays faithful to the winemaking precepts of founder Johann Joseph—particularly in fermenting the infant wines in small oak barrels—each successive generation since 1843 has been very open-minded in its approach to the composition of its cuvées. The Krugs are champions of Pinot Meunier, seen by some less imaginative houses as merely a workhorse grape. Not Henri Krug or his son Olivier. As supremely gifted blenders, they know it adds a palate-filling fruitiness and a whiff of the baker's shop to any cuvée, however grand. This free-spirited attitude to Meunier also applies to the making of Krug Vintages. The Krug 1981, one of the greatest Champagnes of the 20th century, has almost a fifth of Meunier in the blend, which says a lot about Krug's bold flair and the relative timidness of other great houses in shunning this, Champagne's third grape, in their best wines, for fear that it does not age well—rather a woolly generalization at the best of times. In the passionate words of Rémi Krug, Henri's brother: "We are mistrustful of tradition."

This shows clearly in the approach of the current generation. Now headed by Olivier, the winemaking team is young. Driven by a restless urge to find the best grapes without fear or favour, they sometimes scout vineyards that one would not immediately associate with Champagne's greatest house. The most radical of Krug's recent partnerships has been with the cooperative of Les

Right: Olivier Krug, the current generation of Champagne's most illustrious dynasty, with some of its hallmark barrels

As standard-bearers of the most prestigious name in Champagne, the Krug family have always made classic wines in an elegantly vinous style quite unlike any other

Riceys in the far south of Champagne, touching the border with Burgundy.

The three Riceys communes, just 40 minutes' drive east from Chablis, are well known to the cellar masters of the Marne as the fount of excellent Pinot Noirs of natural bright fruitiness and vinosity, expressed in its purest traditional form in the renowned, rare Rosé de Riceys. More important still, they are valued as a fine black-grape element in any well-balanced Champagne blend. The Riceys co-op apparently contacted Krug to say that it was embarking on a new project to enhance the quality of the wines from a 5ha (12-acre) plot of its finest vines. Would Krug like to be part of the project? The family did not hesitate to see the potential of such a collaboration, and the end result was a perfect deal, in which the family would accept only wine from that prime plot. So, every September, the Krug team travels the 120 miles (193km) to Les Riceys, there tasting exhaustively for the next 48 hours—"with no breaks for a proper lunch," says Olivier, a natural epicure, rather wistfully.

That the house takes as much trouble with these officially less highly rated but inherently fine growths from the Aube as with the grands and premiers crus of the Marne is just one aspect of this story of perfectionism. Blending at Krug, always a work of painstaking craftsmanship, now seems more rigorous than ever. In composing the crus from the difficult 2007 vintage that will make up the base wine for Grande Cuvée in 2014, the team made no fewer than 18 wines from Ambonnay (the family's favourite Pinot Noir grand cru) to give core strength to a blend of the broadest possible dimensions.

When I visited Krug to research my first book on Champagne in the early '90s, the blend might have comprised 40 to 50 different wines from 20 to

Above: A stone commemorating the building of Clos du Mesnil and the planting of the first vines there in 1698

25 different growths and six to ten different vintages: complex enough. But since 2007 and the installation of 36 stainless-steel double vats of small capacity, it is now possible to add, in Olivier's phrase, "72 extra colours to the already wonderful palette of wines we have for the blending exercise".

Those armchair critics who claim that Krug Grande Cuvée is not what it was have only a tiny grain of truth on their side. Great wine is not a monolith of fixed compositon and character. It changes and evolves, like all living things created by perfectionists. Krug today may lay more stress on freshness and finesse than when I first tasted it 40 years ago. But surely, with Champagne, that should be seen not as a fault but as a dynamic virtue, mirroring the changing taste preferences of the discerning modern consumer.

The Vintage wines at Krug are made with consummate skill but are less intricately composed, the thrust of the flavours deliberately illustrating the differing personality of successive vintages. The Krugs are careful to make them only in exceptional years. The 1996 is probably the greatest Champagne of an extraordinary vintage; the 1995, a lovely, low-key expression of harmony and refinement; the 1990, a sybaritic wine of opulent richness; the 1988 an aristocrat of reserve and grand austerity. Of the late-released Krug Collection wines, the 1985 retains an elegance and élan sometimes lacking in the rather foursquare Champagnes of this very intense year in their maturity. The Collection concept is that after about 20 years, Krug Vintages enter a "second life", during which the overall balance of their taste shifts as individual flavours become more intense. They are then judged ready to be re-released as collectors' Champagnes, representing the last bottles of an exceptional past vintage, which have been stored in the perfect conditions of Krug's cool, deep cellars in Reims.

Paul Krug II, Olivier's grandfather, used to say that the family's metier should be as perfectionist winemakers and blenders rather than owners of vineyards, let alone as high-profile exponents of single-vineyard Champagnes. That made sound sense, for the Krugs' greatest strength has always been, and is still, the intricate assembly of wines from many crus, and the touch of genius in the winemaking that is inimitably their own.

In 1971, the family began a project that proved to be a surprising and radically new expression of the Krug winemaking philosophy. As people who had always believed hitherto that their skills centred on the supreme art of blending, they bought a small, 2ha (5-acre) enclosed vineyard in the family's favourite Chardonnay grand cru, Le Mesnil-sur-Oger. The original aim, according to Henri Krug, was merely to secure an outstanding source of Chardonnay for Grande Cuvée, but this was quite quickly overtaken by the novel wish to make a single-site, varietal Champagne.

The vines at the eponymous Clos du Mesnil were in a poor state. Typically taking the long view, the Krugs decided on a thorough replanting

programme, so it was not until 1986 that the first Champagne from the *clos*—the 1979—was released. Athletic, taut, with a bracing acidity, the '79 reflected the relative youth of the vineyard and, of course, the strong minerality of Le Mesnil's soils. Some observers argue, with reason, that the aspect of the Clos vines—essentially due east—makes a good site, though not a perfect one, since there is little doubt that the more south-facing *lieux-dits* in Le Mesnil—above all, Chétillons and Moulin-à-Vent—yield riper grapes and arguably more complete wines. Clos du Mesnil can indeed have an austerity and reserve, a certain leanness in average years. But in 1981, the intensity of the year and the Krugs' fabled know-how resulted in a superb wine. And the 1996, from that warm summer, is particularly on song now and for the forseeable future. Other great warm vintages from

Le Mesnil include 1990, 1989 (rather underrated), and 1986.

The Clos d'Ambonnay, a tiny, walled, garden vineyard (0.685ha [1.7 acres]), was acquired by the family in the mid-1990s. For more than 100 years previously, the Krugs had prized the best wines of the village as perhaps the key Pinot Noir element in Grande Cuvée; and before the purchase they were already buying wine for the blend from this plot. The new aim, as at Clos du Mesnil, was to create the ultimate expression of a single-site Champagne in the Krug style, this time with the great black grape grown on an exceptionally deep stratum of chalk. Making its debut in 2008, the first released vintage was the 1995, based on vines with a decent maturity of about 20 years. The most striking aspect of the wine, reflecting of course the site but also the innate personality of this vintage, is its breed and finesse—a racehorse of a Champagne, very different from many heavy-limbed, fleshy "cart-horse" blancs de noirs. The 1996, when it is released, could be a more exotic animal of another stripe.

Krug Rosé, introduced by Henri Krug in 1983, stands apart from the rest of the house's cuvées. The Krugs are not looking here for the autolytic complexity that comes from long aging, but for very dry wines of exquisite fruitiness and purity of flavour—sensuous Champagnes that ally scents and flavours of woodland red fruits with the mushrooms and *sousbois* of the forest floor. The famous Paris chef Alain Senderens once created an entire lunch—from leek-wrapped lobster, to a mosaic of veal—around this exceptional rosé.

FINEST WINES

(Tasted in Reims, March 2008)

Krug Grande Cuvée
Bright gold; scents of quince, honey, and brioche, all wrapped in an exemplary freshness and a discreet minerality; the palate confirms, a burgeoning richness balanced by fine florality and great purity of orchard-fruit flavours. On top form.

Krug Rosé
Elegant, pale rose hue; purity of little red fruits—very Pinot Noir—and distinctive wild woodland aromas of moist earth, mushrooms, and forest floor. Exciting freshness, with an opulent note of hazelnuts. Long and fine. A gastronomic wine.

Krug Clos du Mesnil 1996
Green hints among the gold; typically discreet Clos nose at first, then lovely ripe Chardonnay scents of brioche and nougatine; pervasive minerality in a mouthfeel that becomes richer and more enveloping. Grand finale of sumptuous end flavours. One of the finest Clos du Mesnils so far.

Krug 1996★
Sustained yellow-gold; vigorous mousse; very fresh nose suffused with a strong, bouncy minerality. A quite splendid, majestic combination of flavours and textures—tight and crisp one moment, then a stunning array of every delicious taste one could imagine—from *glace à l'orange* and William pears, to lemons and prunes. Magnificent finale of great length and vigour. A Champagne that inspires a sense of wonder. Faultless. To 2030+.

Krug Clos d'Ambonnay 1995
A potentially very exciting Champagne, just emerging from its shell. Lovely Welsh gold, supremely elegant. In its aromas and flavours, it has a personality all its own—very sui generis. The aromas of star anise, crystalline fruits, brioche, and acacia honey are certainly emerging but will develop further complexities through to 2020. The palate as yet is very taut and precise.

Krug Collection 1985
Still shimmering, lustrous colour. Creamy mousse. Rich, sensuous aromas of roast figs, prunes, and *sousbois*—classic, aged Pinot Noir from a concentrated year. With its exceptional balance and texture, the wine has a claim to greatness, losing nothing in elegance or refinement.

Champagne Krug
5 Rue Coquebert, 51100 Reims
Tel: +33 3 26 84 44 20
www.krug.com

Charles Heidsieck

The third—and youngest—of the great 19th-century Champagne houses of Reims bearing the name Heidsieck, "Charles" has also generally been the best of the three for quality since its foundation in 1851 by Charles-Camille Heidsieck and his brother-in-law Ernest Henriot. Charles-Camille was, of course, the "Champagne Charlie" who was feted in music-hall and vaudeville songs for years after his eventful sales trips to the United States, and he was certainly the most colourful of the Champagne salesmen to take the US market by storm in the 1850s. By the start of the American Civil War he was selling 300,000 bottles a year, from New York to Louisiana.

Daniel Thibault's new brief was to make the finest Non-Vintage Champagne on the market. Since then there has been a fascinating series of Mis en Cave cuvées

But spending too long in the South was Charles's undoing. In 1861, he was arrested by the Unionists in New Orleans for being in possession of letters from French manufacturers offering to supply clothing to the Confederate armies. After four months in a swampy Mississippi jail, Charles returned to France a ruined man. But the firm survived and prospered, finding early new markets in South America and the Far East. In 1976, Joseph Henriot (a descendant of Ernest) bought the house and, under his nine-year rule, presided over the creation of some superb vintages of the Champagne Charlie prestige cuvée, old bottles of which still taste great today. In 1985, the firm was sold again to the Rémy Martin Cognac family, who already owned Krug.

The Rémy directors made a shrewd opening move in recruiting Daniel Thibault, Henriot's winemaker and reputedly the finest Champagne blender of his generation. Daniel's new brief was to

make the Charles Heidsieck Brut Réserve the finest Non-Vintage Champagne on the market. To do this, he was given carte blanche to buy the best grapes and, crucially, to increase his stock of reserve wines. The outstanding quality of Daniel's new cuvée was widely admired for its classic winemaking and the complexity of the blend. The first fermentation was in stainless steel, and technical treatments of the wine were kept to a minimum for optimal natural character. Certainly in Daniel's heyday, the NV was composed of up to 300 crus, 40 per cent of which were reserve wines. The sensuous yet elegant honey-and-vanilla flavours were stunning—and all achieved without the use of a single oak stave.

Daniel, a restless perfectionist, didn't stop there. In the mid-1990s, he conceived the revolutionary *mis en cave* notion for the Brut Réserve—that is to say, a Non-Vintage with a year specified on the label. "What's that?" said his less imaginative rivals and the lazier members of the press. Daniel calmly replied that he believed that Champagne connoisseurs should have full information about the age of the blend in order that they might gauge its stage of maturity. The phrase *mis en cave* effectively means "bottling date", and since the base wine is always bottled in the spring after the preceding harvest, "1997", for example, would indicate that the base wine would be the 1996 vintage. Since then there has been a fascinating series of Mis en Cave cuvées, the opulent yet lithe style of the wine a constant but also the various ages of the blend showing a wonderful repertoire of flavours from youth to distinguished middle age. Daniel died far too young—a chain-smoker, he did not look after himself properly—and I still keenly miss sitting at the feet of the master, with him reaching for an old bottle from his special fridge reserved for oenophiles wanting to learn more. Fortunately, Régis Camus, Daniel's friend and successor, is also a brilliant winemaker. A more

Right: Régis Camus, the quiet but determined and talented winemaker who has preserved the *mis en cave* concept

pliable character, Régis in his own quiet way has—thank goodness—successfully seen off attempts by his marketing department to kill off the *mis en cave* concept, which is too complicated for marketeers obsessed by a simple brand image. Although now consigned to the back label, the date of bottling is still clear for all to see, and the explanation of the idea is clearer and larger than it was. Bravo!

Daniel Thibault's other great legacy is the Blanc des Millénaires, a pure-Chardonnay Vintage Champagne of superb quality. Consistently blessed with a richness and creaminess vintage after vintage, it shows the kinder, often exotic-fruit character of great Chardonnay, yet it has a firm frame of acidity that is indubitably Champagne—certainly the kind of wine to convert drinkers who find most blanc de blancs too lean and austere. The grapes in the *assemblage* are a classic mix of the best sites of the Côte des Blancs: the minerality of Le Mesnil, the honeyed roundness of Oger, the raciness of Cramant, and the pure fruitiness of Vertus creating a complete wine of buttery, toasty loveliness. Yet it is always fresh and invigorating. Again, no wood is used in the making of this wine.

The Charles Heidsieck Vintage Champagnes, a classic mix of Pinot Noir and Chardonnay, are always very good examples of the year from which they come, and Régis is careful to make them only in harvests that really merit a vintage bottling. Personally, I am often just as happy with a Mis en Cave when the base wine is from a great vintage such as 1996 or 2002—and at a real cost saving, of course. The Charles Vintage Rosés are for those who like their pink Champagne subtle, pastel salmon in hue, well aged, with a Burgundian succulence that makes them ideal wines for food. The Millénaires has replaced Champagne Charlie as the prestige cuvée of the house, but if you ever see the 1982 Charlie in magnums at auction, inquire where and how they have been kept, and if all seems right, put in a bid—you could be in for a very rare treat.

FINEST WINES

(Tasted in April 2007)

Charles Heidsieck Brut Réserve Mis en Cave 2003★ [V]

Base wine 2002. A classic mix of all three Champagne grapes in equal amounts. 60% base wine, 40% reserve wines. *Dosage* 10g/l. Luminous, buttery yellow with green tints. Exotic, exciting aromas of mango, as well as citrus and orchard fruits. The toasty, buttery, rounded flavours are the beginning of the secondary stage of aging, with elegant autolysis likely to advance. Drink optimally from 2009. An exceptional Non-Vintage cuvée.

Charles Heidsieck Blanc des Millénaires 1995★

Lovely, even, ripe, butter-gold colour typical of great Chardonnay. The nose is still evolving, and one senses the minerality and depth of its grand cru origins; beautiful expression of fruit and burgeoning vinosity in a mouthfeel that is starting to be encompassed by a rich toastiness. Great length on the palate. Will live for years. 2008–20.

Charles Heidsieck Blanc des Millénaires 1985

Late-disgorged in 2007. Concentrated gold colour typical of this small-volume vintage, now at full maturity. Finely evolved, honeyed nose, with a fine, nutty note of pistachio. Intense, complex flavours—honey, brioche, buttered toast—with an intriguing end flavour of Oloroso Sherry and Asian spice. Pipped at the post by the potential of the 1995.

Charles Heidsieck Blanc des Millénaires 1983

Disgorged 2004. Sustained, burnished gold. My kind of great Chardonnay Champagne from a slightly underrated, actually beautifully ripe vintage. Remarkably fresh and vital, given its age—notes of honey and fig mingling with lemon peel and fresh cream. *Tout en finesse.*

Charles Heidsieck Champagne Charlie 1985

Although Chardonnay is marginally in the driving seat here (55%), it is Pinot Noir (45%) that dominates the flavours of this wine tasted at 22 years of age—not surprising, since Pinot often takes a long time to show in a blend. Moreover, '85 was a particularly intense year for the great black grape. Mid-gold; aromas of *sousbois*, mushrooms, very Burgundian; in the mouth, a warm, powerful Champagne, but one that has better balance and poise than several rather foursquare '85s now at full maturity.

Charles Heidsieck Champagne Charlie 1982
(In magnum) 50/50 Pinot Noir and Chardonnay. Splendid, deep gold; aromas of dried flowers (roses, peonies), apricots, and an intriguing note of white pepper. In the mouth, a Champagne of rare beauty—creamy, delicate, and sensual—Chardonnay seemingly in charge. A hedonist's delight, reflecting the sheer class of this very great year.

Charles Heidsieck Brut Rosé 1996
65% PN, 35% C. Salmon-brick, elegant hue; evolved Burgundian notes of mushrooms but not overdone. A charming, tender, balanced wine in the mouth, with a caressing softness. Exemplary harmony and balance, with evolving richness. An ideal Champagne for rack of veal, lobster, or even Bresse pigeon or Nantais duck.

(Tasted in Reims, June 2007)
Charles Heidsieck Brut Réserve Mis en Cave 1997
Base wine 1996. In a tasting of five Mis en Cave wines with Régis Camus, this was the greatest. Green-gold, hinting at its awesome structure; a vigorous and still wonderfully fresh bouquet. Massive, rock-like acidity, but a balanced, generous mouthfeel, round and fleshy, with flavours of peach and apricot. With its crunchy, chewy texture, this is a wine for roast chicken or guinea fowl. Outstanding.

(Tasted June 2008)
Charles Heidsieck Vintage Brut 2000
A lively, vibrant lemon-gold; signature, beguiling, Heidsieck nose, with white flowers and elegant autolysis; the perfect lead into a sensuous palate of buttered toast and torrefaction—real length, relief, variegated class.

Above: Grand cru Cramant, whose Chardonnays contribute elegance and race to Heidsieck's Blanc des Millénaires

Champagne Charles Heidsieck
12 Allée du Vignoble, 51055 Reims
Tel: +33 3 26 84 43 50
www.charlesheidsieck.com

Louis Roederer

The Roederers and Rouzauds, owner-managers of this outstanding Champagne house since 1827, are a classic example of an *haut-bourgeois* French family that has kept full control of its company through bad times and good. Intelligence, grit, and a wariness of banks were the qualities that another strong-minded Champagne widow, Camille Olry-Roederer, had in spades when she took over the reins in 1932. With 25 years of unsold stock, the firm was then nearly bankrupt. So Camille paid herself very little, and as the Great Depresssion eased, she ploughed the profits back into the business. With an entrepreneurial eye, she shrewdly saw the chance to buy at silly prices the great vineyards on the Montagne de Reims and Côte des Blancs that have been the house's rock ever since. She also knew when to splash out at the right moments. She would enter one of her champion trotters in a race and throw a victory party afterwards. Her Champagne would be on everyone's lips for months.

Camille Roederer's canniness has certainly been inherited by her grandson, Jean-Claude Rouzaud, the current president of Louis Roederer (now in alert semi-retirement) whose brilliant leadership of the firm, especially in the last quarter of the 20th century, earned him early on the unofficial nickname "King of Champagne". Certainly everything he touched seemed to turn to gold. Yet the recipe for his undoubted success has been a simple one: a combination of consolidated landownership; skilled financial management, involving slow, controlled growth; paying cash whenever possible for suitable acquisitions (such as Deutz Champagne and Ramos Pinto Port); and above all, perhaps, an unflagging commitment to top-flight winemaking.

Unlike several heads of great Champagne houses, Jean-Claude never went to business school but graduated in oenology and agronomy at the

Right: Jean-Baptiste Lécaillon, Roederer's *chef de cave*, in whose charge the wines have come ever closer to perfection

Jean-Claude Rouzaud's brilliant leadership of the firm, especially in the last quarter of the 20th century, earned him early on the unofficial nickname "King of Champagne"

famous wine faculty of Montpellier. Throughout his 40-year career, learning on the job about the severe challenges of keeping his firm viable and profitable, he has always had one foot in the vineyard and a warm, familiar, *tu/toi* relationship with growers.

It was indeed fortunate that after the debacle of the economic crash in Champagne in the early '90s, Jean-Claude was elected president of the Union des Grandes Maisons to hammer out a long-term programme of recovery and price control with the equally gifted and supple growers' leader Philippe Feneuil. Their rapport resulted in a decade of unparalleled prosperity for Champagne. Now that both men have left centre stage, it would be interesting to know what they think of the current risky scenario of grape shortages, high levels of growers' stocks, and rapidly rising prices at a time of impending recession. A sense of déjà vu, perhaps?

Roederer is better placed than most houses to weather any downturn. Its vineyards are enviably situated, mostly in grand cru sites, and carefully spread across three classic Champagne districts: at Verzenay, Verzy, and Beaumont-sur-Vesle on the northern slopes of the Montagne de Reims; in the sunny, south-facing hills of the Marne Valley at Mareuil, Aÿ, Dizy, Champillon, Cumières, and Damery; and deep in the best chalk of the Côte des Blancs at Chouilly, Oiry, Cramant, Avize, Oger, Le Mesnil, and Vertus. These vineyards represent more than two thirds of the firm's needs and have been slowly supplemented. In the early '90s, the Roederer holdings were 180ha (445 acres); in 2009, they were 218ha (539 acres), up by more than a fifth.

Just as well, because demand for the fabulous Cristal, probably the most sought-after prestige cuvée in the world, doesn't let up—and its peerless raw material comes exclusively from those equally fabulous vineyards. Across the compact Roederer range of its five cuvées, the attention to detail in winemaking has always been impressive. But with Jean-Baptiste Lécaillon, the present *chef de cave*,

the precision of the blends and traceability of the grapes that compose them are a further step up in the quest for perfection. The Brut Premier Non-Vintage is generally fermented in stainless-steel tanks of small capacity, the better to identify the individual character and flavour of each cru. Dominated by the two Pinots, its generous red-fruit flavours are enriched by the vanilla notes of about 20 per cent reserve wines aged in large oak tuns. Jean-Baptiste's style has been to introduce a controlled proportion of oak-fermented wines to the Vintage Champagnes for greater complexity, while avoiding the malolactic fermentation to preserve acidity—now a top priority at a time of climate change.

The striving for excellence in the most difficult circumstances was illustrated by Jean-Baptiste at a tasting of the 2007 *vins clairs* in January 2008. After one of the wettest summers on record, the Champenois in August '07 were facing catastrophe. Nature then looked kindly on the vineyards, a north wind drying the grapes and saving the harvest from drowning. The sun came out on the 26th, and those winemakers with enough nerve to wait saw the Chardonnay and, selectively, the Pinot crop achieve decent ripeness and good acidity. Jean-Baptiste and his team worked heroically to safeguard sanitary health in the vineyards, then picked selected top grapes at optimal maturity around 10 September. Against the odds, 2007 should be a vintage year at Roederer. The Chardonnays, particularly from Le Mesnil and Vertus, will make fine-drawn blanc de blancs in the house's distinctive style. And oak-fermented Pinot Noir from Roederer's best vineyards of Les Clos in Mareuil-sur-Aÿ and Les Montants in Verzy both scored highly in my notebook. 2007 is a year for the great terroirs, brilliantly expressed by the Roederer team. *Chapeau!*

Jean-Baptiste also has responsibility now for Roederer's latest glittering acquisition in

Bordeaux—the super-second Médoc growth Château Pichon-Longueville Comtesse de Lalande. To seal the deal, Jean-Claude and Frédéric Rouzaud had to take out a loan. True to form, Jean-Claude has insisted that it be paid back within two years. So father and son are not about to forgo growing orders for the very profitable Cristal. But there is little risk of its quality being compromised. As Jean-Claude quips, "There are no marketing people in the tasting room when we decide on the blend!"

FINEST WINES

(Tasted in Reims, January and April 2008)
Louis Roederer Brut Premier Non-Vintage★
Star-bright gold colour; poised, subtly opulent, Pinot-led scents of considerable distinction. Commentators talk of the full richness of Brut Premier; just as impressive is its freshness and finesse, a style Roederer jealously guards in our era of bigger and bigger Champagnes. Bravo.

Louis Roederer Blanc de Blancs 2002★
More sustained gold colour than usual, signalling the sublime maturity of the vintage. Composed of about half and half Le Mesnil and Avize, with just a touch of Cramant. "It spent a lot of time on lees to give added richness of fruit," says Jean-Baptiste. Poised yet opulent aromas, both citrus fruits and the broader *agrumes* taste of grapefruit; a rich, layered mouthfeel that has the best of all worlds: precise and racy, yet hedonistic and unctuous.

Louis Roederer Vintage 2004
Although not quite in the same class as the exceptionally successful 2002, this younger vintage is still a great success. More mineral-driven at the moment, and expressive of great Chardonnay, the most successful variety in '04.

Louis Roederer Vintage 2002
66% PN, 34% C. Just over a third of the wines in the blend were fermented in wood. Already this has a lovely creamy roundness and a brioche character from lots of lees stirring. Uncompromisingly sensuous Champagne.

Louis Roederer Cristal 2002
60% PN, from Mareuil, Aÿ, Verzenay, Verzy; 40% C, from Avize and Le Mesnil, touches of Chouilly and Cramant. Youthful colour with a tint of Pinot Noir; still very adolescent, yet with terrific finesse (note that minerally Chouilly) and the latent potential of all that richness and life-giving acidity.

Louis Roederer Cristal 1999
A good if quite showy example of Cristal, with expressive, golden fruit. But it does not really have the nth degree of class of a great vintage.

Louis Roederer Cristal 1995
I prefer this in terms of balance and harmony to the 1996, which is packed with acidity that it may never lose. Lovely, gently evolving colour of translucent gold, and a delicate filigreed cordon of bubbles; real ripeness and sustained power, but all very subtle and controlled. Some way from a distinguished maturity. Needs five years. Classic.

Louis Roederer Cristal 1988★
This bottle had a lower *dosage* than usual, to the enormous benefit of what is a very great Cristal. Exquisite, green-tinted Welsh gold, then that characteristic '88 promise of mouth-watering acidity given by the nose, but also a sensational smell of truffles. A faultless palate, with acids, green fruits, and a burgeoning richness all melding into one. Very long and fine to finish. Like the Krug '96, this is one of the finest Champagnes of my lifetime, creating a sense of awe.

Champagne Louis Roederer
21 Boulevard Lundy, BP66, 51053 Reims
Tel: +33 3 26 40 42 11
www.champagne-roederer.com

Taittinger

Taittinger is a fine tale of one family's entrepreneurial spirit and its aesthetic appreciation of the finer things in life. During World War I, Pierre Taittinger, an Alsatian and French officer, was billeted at the historic Château de la Marquetterie near Epernay, once the haunt of Voltaire and Beaumarchais. After the 1918 Armistice, Pierre bought the château and its vineyards in Pierry. A little later, in the 1930s, he acquired the defunct house of Fourneaux, which he eventually renamed Taittinger.

In the post-1945 period, the firm became one of the most powerful forces in the Champagne world, thanks to the energy and flair of Pierre's two sons— François, who died in an accident in 1960, and Claude, the chairman of the house in the latter part of the 20th century. He purchased fine vineyards, not only on the Montagne de Reims and Côte des Blancs, but also in the Aube, where he was quick to see its potential for producing excellent grapes. If that were not enough, in 1973, under Claude's aegis, Taittinger acquired sparkling-wine producer Bouvet-Ladubay; the Concorde hotel chain two years later; and in the 1990s, Domaine Carneros in Napa Valley, California. Claude also liked to surround himself with writers and painters, having especially good taste in modern art.

Yet the rapidly expanding business, which also included interests in construction and printing, would increasingly be prey to takeover bids. In 2006 the house was acquired by a Franco-American grouping led by Crédit Agricole. The good news is that in 2008 Claude's passionate nephew Pierre-Emanuel Taittinger climbed back into the driving seat to direct the firm, in that fast-vanishing sector of sizable family-owned houses that lies between the now-fashionable small growers and the huge conglomerates. A phoenix rising from the ashes, perhaps?

Right: Pierre-Emanuel Taittinger, the third generation to head the firm, which is now once again in family ownership

Taittinger is a fine tale of one family's entrepreneurial spirit and its aesthetic appreciation of the finer things in life. Its Comtes de Champagne is the benchmark of great apéritif Champagne

It is abundantly clear that there has been a reforming hand at work over the past few years. To quote Bettane and Desseauve, France's most thoughtful wine critics, "All the wines, and not uniquely the most prestigious, appear as brilliant representatives of a classic Champagne school, based on an apéritif-style elegance." Spot on.

The entry-level Brut Réserve, in particular, is so much better and fresher (with lower *dosage*) than I remember it in the mid-1990s, when I wrote rather crossly that it was maddeningly inconsistent. The Prélude cuvée is a frank expression of scented grand cru Chardonnay, bolstered by the deep flavours of Pinot Noir, while the Comtes de Champagne, always the jewel in the crown, shines more brightly than ever, especially in the supremely stylish 1998 vintage. And just to show that variety is the spice of life, the single-vineyard Les Folies de la Marquetterie, aged in oak *foudres* for ten months, is a splendid, exotic Champagne, in complete contrast to the rest of the line. It has as much character and sense of place as any grower's wine. *Vive la différence.*

FINEST WINES

(Tasted in Reims, January 2009)

Taittinger Brut Réserve NV
A blend of 35–40 crus, 40% C, 50% PN, 10% PM. The *dosage* has been reduced to 8g/l, and the wine (with a 2005 base) is vastly better for it. The Chardonnay content is higher than in a conventional NV, contributing to the excellent balance of incisive minerality and generous fruitiness.

Taittinger Prélude NV
This is actually a 2004 Champagne, even though the vintage is not mentioned on the label. 50% C, 50% PN. Made exclusively from grand cru grapes, this is a beautifully blended Champagne that shows the varied delicacy and depth of finer Chardonnay, here with a special iodic character. The Pinot adds a subtle, rich harmony to the blend. Impressive.

Left: Château de la Marquetterie, bought by the company's founder and now the source of its single-vineyard wine

Taittinger Les Folies de la Marquetterie NV
This single-vineyard wine is grown on the stony soils of Pierry in the Cubry Valley. 55% PN and 45% C, which spends ten months in large oak tuns. Ripe straw with gold hints. A real basket of all sorts of fruits—lychees, white and yellow peaches, even pineapple—that beguile the nose. The mouthfeel is also a celebration of the very ripe, vinous fruit so typical of 2003, with nice aerating effects of the large-format wood and just a hint of spiciness. Pure delight.

Taittinger Comtes de Champagne 1998 ★
This brilliant blanc de blancs prestige cuvée, made mostly from grand cru Chardonnay, first appeared in the 1952 vintage, while the rosé version made its debut in the 1966 vintage. Exquisite, crystalline green-gold. Wonderful, classy acids drive this exciting wine like the most streamlined TGV, its incisive scents perfectly foiled by a rich, leesy character, torrefaction, and minerality, all in complete harmony. A generous but always fine-drawn mouthfeel makes this the benchmark of great apéritif Champagne. The subtleties of the 1998 vintage and the elegant restraint of the Comtes style combine to make an outstanding bottle.

Champagne Taittinger
9 Place Saint-Nicaise,
51100 Reims
Tel: +33 3 26 85 45 35
www.taittinger.com

Veuve Clicquot

Among the big beasts of the jungle, Veuve Clicquot is probably the Champagne house most admired by rival merchants, cooperatives, and growers alike. Behind the glamour and the adroit marketing, it is certainly still the wine that counts. That achievement is largely due to the 30-year leadership of Jacques Péters, the remarkable *chef de cave* and roving ambassador whose professional competence, straight dealing, and simple humanity have both inspired his winemaking team and built a bond of trust with a network of hundreds of growers across the Marne and Aube. Champagne's farmers are happy to send their best grapes to Clicquot because they know that they will be transformed into the best possible wine. Jacques was due to retire at the end of 2008. It is hard to believe that such a vigorous man will really let go of the reins, for this house has always been a story of exceptional people driving themselves to the limits of their resourcefulness.

Veuve Clicquot herself was widowed at the age of 27 in 1806 and turned away from the price-conscious merchants of England and Holland to seek new customers in the East. In 1814, with iron determination, she penetrated an allied blockade and shipped her 1811 vintage to the imperial court at St Petersburg, opening the door to a Russian market that Clicquot was to dominate for the next 50 years. Mme Clicquot was also a great innovator and visionary in other ways. It was she who acquired the great vineyards of the house, now some 303ha (750 acres), comprising a large number of grands crus spread evenly from Cramant, Avize, Oger, and Le Mesnil on the Côte, to Verzy, Ambonnay, and Bouzy on the Montagne. Her cellar master Antoine Müller devised the technique of *remuage* (riddling), and together they shaped the style of vinous rosé Champagne that is still today

Right: Jacques Péters (left) with his successor Dominique Demarville, one of the brightest of the next generation

This house has always been a story of exceptional people driving themselves to the limits of their resourcefulness. Behind the glamour and the adroit marketing, it is certainly still the wine that counts

the best gastronomic match for veal as well as for game of all kinds.

Now part of the giant LVMH conglomerate, the house heads the group's Veuve Clicquot Division, which since 2004 has included Krug, a house with a similar wine ethos. Now producing 12 million bottles of Champagne a year, Veuve Clicquot is clearly an important buyer of grapes, particularly good Meunier from the Petite Montagne and along the northern Valley of the Ardre. The company is also a major purchaser of fine, golden Chardonnnay from the hill of Montgueux above Troyes, and bright, vibrant Pinot Noir from the Aube's Côte des Bar, from both the Riceys/Celles-sur-Ource sector and farther east around Bar-sur-Aube. For such a large operation, winemaking is naturally modern and state of the art. Yet among the gleaming stainless-steel vats, you'll notice smaller ones installed for the separate fermentation of parcels from better vineyards, so as to keep their own identities, which will later facilitate the blending. For vintages from 2009 onwards, there will be a return to the judicious use of oak for Vintage Champagnes. Quite a move, since no wood has been used here since 1961.

The renowned Yellow Label Brut Non-Vintage, made from at least two thirds black grapes balanced by up to a third Chardonnay, has maintained an admirably high level of quality over the years, especially given an annual production of 11 million bottles. Finer and with more finesse than it was before Jacques's time, it can nonetheless very occasionally slip below its usual excellence. Think for a moment why. Whatever the marketing people say, Non-Vintage Champagne does change from year to year—particularly when the base wine accounting for 60–70 per cent of the blend comes from a weak vintage like 2001 (too fragile) or 2003 (too low in the right acids). When the base fruit is below par, there is only so much a blender can do with corrective reserve wines. So it is encouraging to see that, unlike the much smaller Bollinger and Roederer, which will still be making a Vintage Champagne in 2007, Clicquot will not, preferring to keep the excellent wines from this challenging year to raise the quality of Yellow Label—a typically serious and far-sighted decision.

The Gold Label Vintage Réserve Champagnes have been the rock of the house's reputation for many years. They are honest expressions of the vintage in question, while always shaped in the rich, mouth-filling, invariably well-balanced, never overblown Clicquot style. Just how well they age was graphically illustrated by a rare tasting at the Manoir de Verzy in January 2008, when 12 great vintages between 1990 and 1955, were served in magnums without *dosage*. Exceptionally exciting was the "restrained exuberance" of the 1988 (to borrow a Rouzaud phrase); the gorgeous sensuality of the 1982; and the legendary power of the 1955, miraculously vital at 53 years of age, still rock solid and sustained at every level. Yet these occasions often spring a surprise, the greatest Champagne that day being the 1962, which outshone even the 1961, with every aroma and flavour you could wish for, and a texture that caressed yet energized the palate—supremely stylish. Younger vintages maintain a very high standard in the classic 1998★; the smoothly svelte 1999; and the potentially outstanding 2002, particularly for lovers of great Pinot. The Rosé Champagnes are equally impressive, and it has been fascinating to discover in some detail exactly how they are made (*see pp.40–41*).

La Grande Dame, first released in the 1985 vintage, is one of the top three prestige cuvées on the market. Compared with the Vintage Réserve range, where the emphasis in both colours is on vinosity, La Grande Dame stresses elegance, created by a higher proportion of Chardonnay in the blend. The 1998★ may be the greatest Champagne of the vintage, with the 1990 Rosé also at the head of the pack.

FINEST WINES

(Tasted in Reims, January and April 2008)
Veuve Clicquot Vintage Réserve Rosé
1996 Salmon brick; overwhelming chalky freshness; fine minerality, bounce, and length. Not yet ready.

1990 More evolved, with hints of orange; secondary scents of maturity, especially chocolate; complex, evolving flavours, greater generosity than the '96, but with exemplary minerality to balance the ripeness.

1989 Translucent, delicate salmon-trout hue; tiny bubbles; fine Pinot scents of little red fruits, with hints of *surmaturité* balanced by lovely, fresh flavours. Chardonnay, the supporting player, gives a cleansing vitality to the pure, *Pinoté* expression. Surprisingly subtle and silky for such a warm vintage.

1985★ More sustained colour than either the 1989 or 1990 (Pinot Noir was very concentrated in this small-volume year). Round and intense, but with lovely balance and vitality for a 23-year-old wine. Holding up better than the Vintage Réserve.

1978 Deepest, most dramatic colour, with hints of burnished leather. Supremely concentrated and intense on both nose and palate, but it doesn't taste overextracted. A masterpiece.

Veuve Clicquot Coteaux Champenois Rouge
2003 Deep, almost opaque, from the hottest vintage on record. You cannot miss the strong tannins and sheer heat of the vintage. An honourable effort in

Above: One of the precious Veuve Clicquot vineyards whose fruit is fine enough to make it into the prestige cuvée

atypical conditions. But not a wine to put away.

2002 Inviting, beautiful, sustained ruby, quite close to that of a fine Volnay. Seductive medley of orchard-fruit aromas, cherry, raspberry, and peach, even a touch of fig. Lovely, caressing mouthfeel, opulent yet lithe and very elegant. So 2002—ultra-stylish, the alcohol quite high but under control.

1989 All-new barriques, but the wine—pure Clos Colin—copes heroically. Compelling, lustrous ruby, with a hint of brick. Fine, evolving nose, gamey with hints of leather. The palate is *à point*, the fruit still alive at nearly 20 years of age, and wonderfully expressive of that glorious September. A fine, supple finale, with no hint of hard tannins. A classic case of an exceptional chalk terroir winning over the elements.

Champagne Veuve Clicquot Ponsardin
1 Place des Droits de l'Homme, 51100 Reims
Tel: +33 3 26 89 53 90
www.veuve-clicquot.com

Henriot

Henriot Champagnes are, at heart, Chardonnay-led wines of very high quality, reflecting Joseph Henriot's love of the great white grape. That passion is also expressed in two more recent acquisitions—the superb Chablis domaine of William Fèvre and the reborn Beaune house of Bouchard Père & Fils, which has a large slice of Le Montrachet.

Joseph himself has always been a complex character—an uncompromising guardian of quality and a wheeler-dealer of extreme agility. His family's attachment to the land and to the *négoce* is deep-rooted: vignerons in the Côte des Blancs since the 17th century, and lively Rémois Champagne merchants since 1808. But he is no sentimentalist. In 1985, he merged the family Henriot business with that of Veuve Clicquot and directed the two companies, each with its own identity, until 1994, when he went out on his own again—but not, one might add, before injecting more Chardonnay into the composition of Veuve Clicquot's flagship cuvée Yellow Label, which is the better for it.

Based in Rue Coquebert in Reims, the house is now run by Joseph's son Stanislas Henriot and still has the atmosphere of a family concern. The house likes to work with grapes from mature vines, on average 25 to 30 years old, and the vineyards have a high average rating of 97 per cent on the *échelle des crus*. Chardonnay, of course, represents a very large share of the stock, coming from the great villages of the Côte des Blancs: Chouilly, Cramant, Avize, Oger, and Le Mesnil. The supporting Pinot Noir villages are of equally grand status. No Pinot Meunier is currently used in any cuvée.

The whole vineyard is treated with the greatest respect; yield-boosting herbicides and fertilizers are entirely avoided. Yes, at Henriot, quality really

Right: Joseph Henriot has taken his family firm to new heights but is proud of his profound vigneron roots

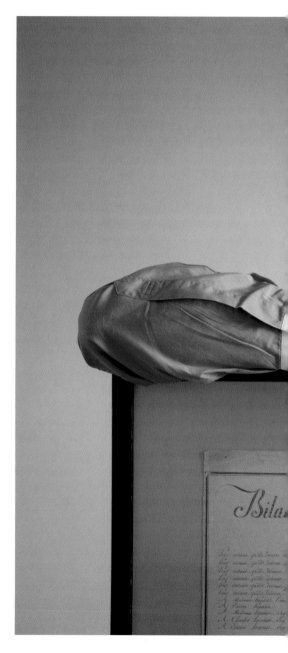

Henriot Champagnes are, at heart, Chardonnay-led wines of very high quality, reflecting Joseph Henriot's love of the great white grape

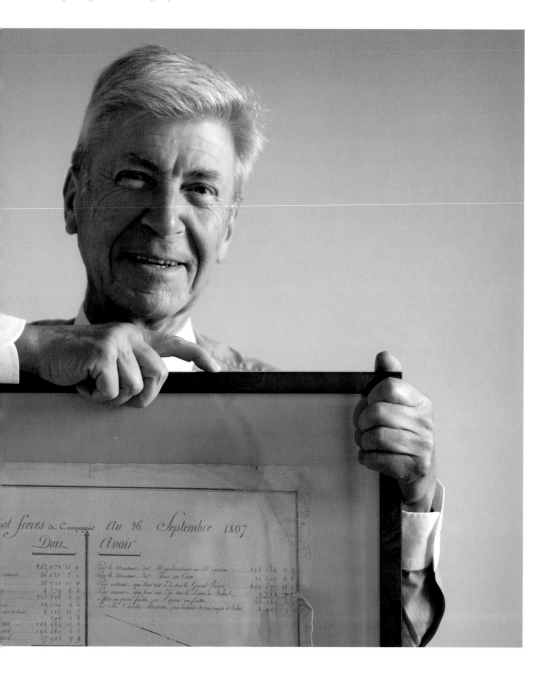

does count for far more than volume. The Chardonnay vines are pruned in the Chablis style, which means only two or three fruiting branches —not four. And during the winemaking, detailed classification is pushed to the limit. Wines of every origin and from every plot are vinified and stored separately, to respect the character of each cru. In this way, a broad palette of flavours is created that facilitates the blender's task.

Of the Non-Vintage cuvées, the Blanc Souverain Pur Chardonnay is an exemplary blanc de blancs aged for between three and five years. Its definition of subtle mineral flavours and perfect balance is a tribute to its first creator, Philippe Thieffry, now chief winemaker at Veuve Clicquot, who has one of the finest palates I know.

The Vintage Brut cuvées are a strong card, aged for a minimum of eight years but generally well worth keeping for at least a decade. The 1996 is one of the most successful Champagnes of that extraordinary year.

The prestige Cuvée des Enchanteleurs is the quintessence of the Henriot style. Driven by great Chardonnay with supportive Pinot Noir, it is a particularly long-lived Champagne that retains freshness, minerality, and endless complexity into distinguished old age. Made only in genuinely great vintages, it should not normally be touched until it is 13 years old, and it usually tastes better at 20. Excellent as the 1990 and 1995 are, they pale beside the 1988, which is one of the greatest Champagnes of the 20th century. The infant 2008 vintage, happily, looks to be in the same mould as its 20-year-old brother.

FINEST WINES

(Tasted December 2008)
Henriot Brut Souverain Pur Chardonnay NV [V]
100% C, from Mesnil, Oger, Vertus, Chouilly, and Trépail. Crystalline green-gold. Incisive lemon and mineral scents. Racy yet perfectly balanced; subtly vigorous yet with harmonious tastes of maturity. Good length, and the finish is as clean as a whistle. What a Non-Vintage blanc de blancs should be but all too often is not.

(Tasted August 2008)
Henriot Vintage Brut 1996★
52% PN, 48% C, from more than 15 crus—including Mareuil, as well as Verzenay and Verzy, and a touch of Montgueux (above Troyes) supporting Mesnil, Oger, and Chouilly. *Dosage* 10g/l. Intense golden colour; grand cru Chardonnay dominates on both the nose and the palate. Memorable interplay of ripe honey and vanilla flavours, with the purity of majestic acidity that contributes real vigour while being very delicate. One of the best 1996s. *Grand vin*.

(Tasted June 2007)
Henriot Cuvée des Enchanteleurs 1988
55% C, 45% PN, from 15 grands crus, with Le Mesnil and Oger, Mareuil, Aÿ, Verzy, and Verzenay key elements. *Dosage* 9g/l. The colour is star-bright yellow-gold, with more green highlights than in the 1990. The bouquet is compelling, mineral purity (so very Henriot) its hallmark, but also with slowly emerging notes of butter and hazelnut, all the time with a touch of classic austerity. The palate, like most very great wines, defies description, every component of fruit, vinosity, terroir, and lingering complexity in perfect harmony. Magnificent.

Champagne Henriot
81 Rue Coquebert, 51100 Reims
Tel: +33 3 26 89 53 00
www.champagne-henriot.com

Lanson

anson is one of the oldest Champagne houses. Founded in 1730, this proud family firm had a deserved reputation until the early 1990s for its distinctive, uncompromising, but unquestionably fine style of Champagne—full-bodied, bracingly dry, and with enough richness and vinosity in its Vintage wines to match fine cuisine. Happily, Victor Lanson, the outstanding head of the house in the mid-20th century, was a true wine man and noted gastronome. In the 1930s, he had been one of the first Rémois merchants to use the unsung but excellent Pinot Noirs of the Aube in his blends, and he always wanted his Champagne to be the sort you could drink right through a family meal.

As the First Gulf War and ensuing oil crisis of 1991 precipitated a crash in the Champagne market, Lanson became a pawn in the acquisitive battles of the big players. That year, Moët & Chandon bought the house and, in a cynical manoeuvre, owned it for just 175 days, before selling it on to a group headed by Marne & Champagne. As part of the deal, Lanson lost all 208ha (514 acres) of its magnificent vineyards (retained by Moët), while Marne & Champagne and partners were left with the Lanson name and business for which, amazingly, they paid the same price as Moët had done—including the vineyards!

When an important Champagne house loses its vital vineyard assets, any candid *chef de cave* will tell you that it takes a good 15 years to reestablish the best sort of contracted grape suppliers and build up reserve wines in the quest for top quality. That is more or less exactly what has happened at Lanson. Through all its travails, the house has been lucky to retain the Lanson family's *chef de cave*, Jean-Paul Gandon, who has been with them since the 1970s. A quiet, delightful man and very assured winemaker, Jean-Paul comes from Touraine, where he still keeps a vineyard between Amboise and Vouvray. At

Lanson, he has done a remarkable job since 1991, and there has been a real renaissance in the wines, coinciding with the arrival in 2006 of the enlightened new owners of the business—the Boizel Chanoine group. The CEO is Philippe Baijot, who must be the tallest man in Reims, a larger-than-life but very human character, who created the modern Chanoine Champagne brand. Certainly, his sunny personality has made everyone at Rue de Courlancy look a lot happier and much more confident about Lanson's future.

The entry-level Lanson Black Label's distinctive style owes most to the dominant Pinot Noir in the blend, which gives fullness and weight but is never heavy because freshness is kept intact,

Above: The gold caps and silver wires that adorn the Lanson range, which now includes a single-vineyard wine

the malo always being avoided at this house. There is no better Champagne with oysters. The Rosé Non-Vintage is aged longer and has more mature reserve wines in the blend; because it is a very dry wine, it needs that extra maturity, since this is very much a creation that respects the fruit in the wine rather than relying on the sugar content of a conventional *dosage*.

Lanson's best wine, I believe, is its vintaged Gold Label—not, as it happens, the most expensive Champagne in the range. A classic 50/50 blend of Pinot Noir and Chardonnay, in the excellent current 1998 vintage it has a pleasing austerity on the nose but superb depth, minerality, and presence on the palate. The top-of-the-line Noble Cuvée trio—pure Chardonnay, Rosé, and Vintage—stress balance and delicacy rather than full-on power. One sometimes feels that because of the non-malo winemaking, the desired delicacy turns out to be a lean, linear character that lacks the rich yet dry fruitiness that is Lanson's trump card. But that is a matter of personal taste.

From 2007, Lanson will make the house's first single-vineyard Champagne, the Clos Lanson, from the only (1ha [2.47-acre]) walled vineyard within the city limits of Reims. This vineyard is planted purely with Chardonnay of 20–50 years of age, and the wine will be made in oak barrels from the forest of Argonne, where the oak is gentle enough not to obscure the taste. The plot was formerly owned by Champagne Massé, which was bought by Lanson in 1976.

FINEST WINES

(Tasted in Reims, December 2008)
Lanson Black Label Non-Vintage
50% PN, 35% C, 15% PM. *Dosage* 11g/l. Bright yellow with green tints. The nose is all freshness, green apples and pears, while the palate is full

Left: CEO Philippe Baijot, who has led Lanson's renaissance since 2006, seen here with the company's royal warrants

but vigorous, with tastes of both citrus fruits, like lemons, and stone fruits, like cherries. The end flavours are so clean and brisk but without any harshness. A great Champagne for clams and sea urchins, as well as for oysters.

Lanson Rosé (Rose Label)
55% PN, 30% C, 15% PM. *Dosage* 9g/l. Lovely, subtle, wild-salmon hue. With slightly lower *dosage* and a higher proportion of reserve wines than the Black Label, this is a very superior pink, of elegant, creamy mousse and discreet tastes of little red fruits. There is no hint of heaviness, the natural taste of the grapes, artfully vinified, showing through strongly.

Lanson Vintage 1988 (Gold Label)
50% PN, 50% C. Fine, lustrous yellow-gold. Even with this amount of bottle age, the nose is slightly reductive on this tasting, but one almost expects that of non-malo Vintage Lanson. On the palate, it is splendidly powerful and rich, reined in by a discreet minerality. An exceptional wine from an exceptional vintage.

Lanson Noble Cuvée 1998
70% C, 30% PN. The best of the Noble Trio, due at least in part to the grand cru origin of the dominant Chardonnay. Luminous gold with green highlights. Real depth and marked acidity contribute to the powerful structure of this wine, though it still has fruitiness rather than minerality in the driving seat, making it less austere overall than the Noble Blanc de Blancs.

Lanson Vintage 1981
A magnificent wine from a small but highly concentrated vintage, recovered from the still-extensive Lanson wine library. At 37 years of age, it is still a vibrant gold, the fruit beautifully clear and dominant, with no hint of oxidation; vigour and elegance are here in perfect balance. A superbly long finish. Perfection, and as fine a non-malo Champagne as you will ever find.

Champagne Lanson
16 Rue de Courlancy,
51100 Reims
Tel: +33 3 26 78 50 50
www.lanson.com

GH Mumm

Like several famous families who founded Champagne houses in the 19th century, brothers Jules, Edouard, and Gottlieb de Mumm were German Protestants—in their case from Rüdesheim in the Rheingau, where they had vineyards and a sizable wine wholesale business. They opened their doors in Reims in 1827; 15 years later, Gottlieb's son, GH Mumm, joined the firm, and in 1853 it took his name, which has been the title of the company ever since.

In the heyday of Champagne prosperity in the 1880s, Mumm's flagship brand Cordon Rouge was better known than the house itself, particularly in the United States, its prime export market, where it was selling 850,000 bottles a year, aided by a vast advertising campaign. Certainly in the lavish brothels of New Orleans, "wine" meant Champagne, preferably Cordon Rouge.

For the Mumms, however, happy times were not to last. They remained German citizens, and so inevitably, on the outbreak of World War I in 1914, the house's assets, including all the vineyards, were confiscated by the French government. In 1920, this great house, the largest in Reims, was put up for sale and sold to the Société Vinicole de Champagne Successeurs. In 1955, the Canadian Seagram group acquired an interest in Mumm, later a majority one.

In the turmoil of the 1991 Champagne crisis, the house became vulnerable to takeovers, and after being bought by a Texan venture-capitalist group, it finally became part of the Pernod Ricard drinks empire in 2005.

Fortunately, Mumm does retain its important estate of 218ha (539 acres) in fine grand cru sites such as Verzenay, Bouzy, and Ambonnay on the Montagne de Reims, and in Cramant on the Côte des Blancs. Why, then, has the quality of the Cordon Rouge Non-Vintage been the subject of critical, sometimes downright hostile, comment over the years?

If you agree with the candid view of Champagne authority Tom Stevenson—and I do—that Mumm's reputation was destroyed by the poor quality of the wines made between 1982 and 1991, the prime responsibility must surely lie with André Carré, the *chef de cave* of the time. In December 1993, my tasting notes on Cordon Rouge NV (base wines 1990/91) read: "A fresh if clumsy wine in a green, immature style, artfully rounded out by a slightly higher than average *dosage* than is usually the case for a Brut [...]. A solid but unexciting product, fully priced and relatively poor value for money."

In fairness, the overall quality of the Mumm range did improve markedly under Carré's successors Pierre Harang and, in particular, Dominique Demarville (who has since moved on to Veuve Clicquot). Dominique's protégé, the talented Didier Mariotti, has also presided over the finishing touches of the current Cuvée R Lalou 1998—a superb wine. This recently reintroduced prestige cuvée, along with the now revitalized Cramant de Mumm, much improved by both Dominique and Didier, are encouraging signs. But more work still needs to be done on the Cordon Rouge NV, which seems to have slipped back into the clumsily balanced style of old—at least in my recent tastings. Moreover, some of the straight Vintage cuvées still seem to need an extra injection of tension and finesse to match their sturdiness.

FINEST WINES

(Tasted June 2007)

Mumm de Cramant NV
This is a rare sort of pure Chardonnay Champagne made in a different way from most blanc de blancs. It is a *demi-mousse* (bottled at low pressure) composed solely of grand cru grapes from the village of Cramant. To preserve its dynamism and

Right: The amiable and talented *chef de cave* at GH Mumm, Didier Mariotti, who helped reintroduce its prestige cuvée

freshness, the wine is aged for only two years and so, according to French law, cannot carry a vintage label; but it always comes from a single year. Pale yellow hue with silvery highlights; haunting, delicate aromas of white flowers and citrus fruits; a much-improved mouthfeel, at once mineral and softly kind, with lime and grapefruit flavours. The finale is longer than in the mid-1990s. Excellent.

Mumm Cuvée R Lalou 1998

In making this cuvée, 12 great vineyards of Pinot Noir and Chardonnay were first considered, then only seven were kept for the final blend. Lovely, luminous gold colour, suggesting both strength and elegance; Chardonnay, as usual, first drives the nose, citrus notes of La Croix de Cramant dominant, then Pinot Noir stirs itself distinctively in a subtle medley of orange blossom, nougat, and acacia scents. The palate is splendidly firm yet lithe, with beautiful cherry and red berry fruits, as well as spices; there is a lot of Verzenay-les-Rochelles and Bouzy-les-Houles in the Pinot makeup. Very long finish, with a classic note of austerity. The distinctive 1998 character of freshness, structure, acidity, and generosity is all there, making this one of the greatest wines of a fascinating year.

Right: The famous windmill now owned by GH Mumm at Verzenay, one of several grands crus in its extensive holdings

Champagne GH Mumm
29 Rue du Champs de Mars, 51100 Reims
Tel: +33 3 26 49 59 69
www.mumm.fr

Bruno Paillard

With his background, his exhaustive knowledge of Champagne, and his fine business brain, Bruno Paillard seemed destined from the start to become one of the most influential personalities and a force for good in the wine community. Born in Reims in 1953 to an old family of vignerons and brokers who had lived around Bouzy since the 17th century, Bruno started as a broker in 1975 (and he still keeps his hand in today). All the while, he dreamed of having his own Champagne house, and in 1981 he realized his ambition, establishing what is the youngest of the *grandes maisons* and still one of the smallest.

It is a measure of his achievement that, within 30 years of its launch, the Paillard brand now commands the same high prices as the market "greats" like Bollinger, Louis Roederer, and Veuve Clicquot. And with good reason, because the wines are impeccably made, aged longer than almost anyone else's, and beautifully presented. Every back label carries the date of disgorgement, so that the discerning drinker can gauge that bottle's stage of maturity.

With his exhaustive knowledge of Champagne and his fine business brain, Bruno Paillard always seemed destined to become a force for good

All this signals Bruno's credentials as a perfectionist wine man, but when you look at the gleaming steel-and-glass building that houses his office and cellars on the Epernay road out of Reims, you begin to realize that he is also a cool, analytical realist who always keeps a sharp eye on the bottom line of profit and loss. The ground-floor cellars are thermostatically set at an ideal temperature of 51°F (10.5°C) and streamlined so as to make optimal use of space, allowing the small working team to function most cost-effectively. Alice Paillard, Bruno's younger daughter, helps her father by managing the export business. For he is a busy man, who wears another hat as president of the Boizel Chanoine Champagne (BCC) group of seven houses, now the second largest in the region. In truth, the BCC's muscular clout is a thoroughly healthy check on the ambitions of the powerful LVMH group (headed by Moët & Chandon and Veuve Clicquot), whose policy under Bernard Arnaud does increasingly seem to monopolize the Champagne market, absorbing more and more vineyards from troubled houses in takeover battles.

But back to the bijou world of Champagne Bruno Paillard. Always vinified to rigorously uncompromising standards, these exceptionally fine Champagnes are very dry, of low *dosage*, always striving to be delicate and elegant, and, above all, natural. A clue to Bruno's tastes and preferences can be seen in the 24ha (59 acres) of vineyards he has acquired since 1981. His first purchase was in Oger, his favourite grand cru on the Côte des Blancs (mine, too), the wines, at their best, suffused with a magical mix of softness, generosity, and refinement. To this he has added fine sites in Le Mesnil—a crucial element in the longevity of the finest blanc de blancs—as well as equally good ones in Bouzy, which is in many ways the most sumptuously rich of the Montagne de Reims grand cru Pinot Noirs.

Of the three Non-Vintage wines, the entry-level Première Cuvée Brut is a classic *assemblage* of all three Champagne grapes. Of vivid gold colour, with a fine mousse, it is a model Champagne that manages the difficult balancing act of being fresh and incisively mineral, while showing lovely fruit and vinosity. This wine-like, gently oxidative complexity is achieved by fermentation of about 20 per cent of the blend in oak barrels, without imparting a woody flavour. The Rosé Première

Cuvée continues in the same elegant style: subtly coloured, freshly aromatic, with a purity of little red-fruit flavours—fine Pinot Noir, made more elegant by an undisclosed but significant amount of mineral, light-framed Chardonnay from the northern Côte des Blancs. The Blanc de Blancs Réserve Privée is an eclectic, typically uncompromising Bruno Paillard Champagne: 100 per cent Côte des Blancs Chardonnay, using a resuscitated traditional fermentation technique called *demi-mousse*. To activate the second fermentation in the bottle—which produces the bubbles—less sugar and yeast are added, producing a less fizzy, gently sparkling wine that is particularly suitable for Chardonnay wines: fine-drawn and ideal for drinking with *fruits de mers natures*.

The Vintage Brut always carries a beautiful illustration by a famous artist, each one changing with the successive vintage in a picture that seeks to reflect the essential characteristics of the year. The 1999, by Didier Paquignon, is titled *Flamboyant, Tumultuous*; the even greater 1995, depicted by Roland Roure, is rightly called *Balance and Completeness*.

And yet my favourite Paillard Vintage cuvée is the Brut Blanc de Blancs. It is made from a perfect blend of the greatest Chardonnay vineyards of the Côte, each contributing something all its own—in the case of the magnificent 1995, Chouilly giving cleansing briskness; Cramant, dynamism; Oger, that rounded softness; Le Mesnil, penetrating minerality; plus a touch of the friendly fruitiness of Vertus. The 1996 is not far behind, though it is not yet at its apogee.

The Paillard Prestige Cuvée NPU is made with the high-flown idea of making the greatest possible Champagne wine. Hence its tag: Nec Plus Ultra. Made only in outstanding years, the first vintage was 1990, then 1995, with the 1996 due to be released in 2010.

FINEST WINES

(Tasted in Reims between August 2008 and January 2009)

Vintage Brut Assemblage 1999
29% C, 42% PN, 29% PM, from 42 villages of the Marne. Low *dosage* of 6g/l. Gold rather than yellow-green. Svelte, ripe, elegant fruit on both nose and palate—enough to provide attractive drinking over the next five years. By no means exceptional, but well made.

Vintage Brut Blanc de Blancs 1996
100% Côte des Blancs Chardonnay, as described in main text, *left*. *Dosage* 5g/l. Vibrant, deep gold. A muted medley of candied lemon and gingerbread scents that soften an iodic character, slightly reductive for the moment. The 20% oak fermentation gives a nice touch of torrefaction to the palate, which has latent reserves of bouncy acids—so typically 1996. Still young-tasting but highly promising, too.

Vintage Brut Blanc de Blancs 1995
Composition as described in main text, *left*. *Dosage* 5g/l. For drinking 2009–2012, this is as near perfection as it gets. Very fine, sustained lemon-gold. Evolved, rich, classic style that retains the wonderful freshness of an outstanding Vintage Champagne, now approaching full maturity. An absolutely dazzling expression of great blended Chardonnays.

Prestige NPU 1995
A 50/50 blend of grand cru Pinot Noir and Chardonnay. An impressive colour: luminous gold, a real robe of depth and shimmering reflections. Lovely nose of exquisite, ethereal Chardonnay with the power of great Pinot bringing up the rear. The palate is very big and unctuous, and this is truly a luxury Champagne. But while one cannot deny the very high quality, I actually prefer the Blanc de Blancs 1995.

Left: The sharp-eyed Bruno Paillard, whose combination of passion and precision have brought remarkable success

Champagne Bruno Paillard
Avenue de Champagne, 51100 Reims
Tel: +33 3 26 36 20 22
www.champagnebrunopaillard.com

Piper-Heidsieck

It is not easy to rank Piper-Heidsieck in the pantheon of the great Champagne houses of Reims. Founded in 1834 by Christian Heidsieck, nephew of Florenz-Ludwig, the paterfamilias of the Heidsieck dynasty, Piper was always—is still—a famous *grande maison* with a loyal following in the United States, especially with movie stars. Yet before the house was bought by the Rémy Cointreau group in 1989, when it became a brother house to Charles Heidsieck, the Champagnes were generally lean, austere (no malo), and often rather charmless. In the course of the past 20 years, the late Daniel Thibault and his successor as cellar master, Régis Camus, have made the Piper style much richer, fruitier, and more appealing—essentially by selecting and carefully vinifying the best-quality Meunier, which has brought to the Non-Vintage blends a palate-filling roundness that makes the best sort of nightclub and party Champagne. It is also one that, because of its crowd-pleasing fruitiness, is good to drink at 30,000ft (9,000m). It is always a severe test for any Champagne to be served

In the course of the past 20 years, the late Daniel Thibault and his successor as cellar master, Régis Camus, have made the Piper style richer, fruitier, and more appealing

in a pressurized cabin, where the acidity in the wine is unpleasantly accentuated because of the effect of being airborne on the body's biorhythms. Yet Piper is also capable of springing a surprise to delight the pickiest wine connoisseur. Thanks to Régis's light winemaking touch, the vintage cuvées now have an elegance and élan that are a fascinating contrast with brother Charles. Régis's Cuvée Sublime is a little masterpiece: a demi-sec Champagne that is rich but not cloying and a great match with Asian cuisine. He has also revived, and continues to make,

what has been always the best wine of the house under the old regime and the new: Piper Rare.

The genesis of Rare is a heartening tale. In 1976, the summer skies over Champagne were more like Sicily's, white with heat; even in London that June, driving my then-girlfriend, a sister at St Mary's Hospital, to work every evening, we could have been on Rome's Via Veneto. Back in Champagne, from Reims to Bar-sur-Aube, from Epernay to Château-Thierry, rivers and springs were drying up, the earth was parched, the leaves on the wilting vines had turned deep yellow before their time. There was a real risk that the sugar in the grapes would negate any acidity. But Piper's cellar master and his team were determined to persevere. As the grapes came in—and a little later, as the *vins clairs* were first tasted—it became clear that Piper, against all the odds, had an extraordinary vintage of great purity—and one that could be enhanced in a special blend that contained a good proportion of wines from older vines, their roots having pushed deep into the porous chalk for life-giving water. Some of the wines came from Trépail on the southern Montagne, famous for the minerality and searing acidity of its special sort of Chardonnay, and Verzenay, on the northern side, renowned for its structure and power in Pinot Noir. This special '76 cuvée was given the name Rare as a reminder of the events that shaped it.

Ever since, special Vintages have been made in those years in which nature shows its mercurial character, always different but always fascinating. Since 1976, Rare has been produced another six times: in 1979, from a lateish harvest, but a wine of exceptional crispness; in 1985, an intense, small crop of Champagnes of firm intensity; in 1988, a record level of August sunshine and cooler September resulting in powerful wines; in 1990, another hot summer tempered by opportune rainfall, shaping a vintage of harmony and richness;

Above: *Chef de cave* Régis Camus, who has accentuated the differences between Charles and Piper-Heidsieck

in 1998, temperatures soaring to 102°F (39°C) in early August, before a rainy early September and returning sunshine, making it a winemaker's vintage, with some dramatic successes; and 1999, a triumph for Rare, supremely elegant, in a middling vintage that is less good overall than 1998.

Nothing stands still in wine, and Régis, making both Charles and Piper in the same modern winery on the outskirts of Reims, is evolving a distinctly different style for each house. His great achievement at Piper has been to enhance its exuberant fruitiness with a tempering finesse. The entry-level Brut now gets 24–36 months on lees, which retains a bright fruitiness yet ensures a rounded maturity of flavours. The Vintage is usually marked by a fine, citrussy character enhanced by a touch of toastiness. And the extraordinary Cuvée Sublime demi-sec is made up with a highish *dosage* of 40g/l, but you do not taste the sugar—masterly winemaking.

FINEST WINES

(Tasted April 2007)
Piper-Heidsieck Brut NV
55% PN, 25% C, 20% PM. Vital, green-tinted hue; a marked citrus character on both nose and palate; tight, dynamic, mid-weight, clean, pure, and frank, with decent maturity for an entry-level NV blend. An excellent Champagne for contemporary tastes.

Piper-Heidsieck Rosé Sauvage NV [V]
A high 20% of Pinot Noir vinified as red wine and then added to the blend helps shape this striking blood-orange rosé, though the colour is "wilder" than the nose or palate, with aromas and flavours of mandarins and exotic fruits. A good wine for meat and fish grilled on the barbecue. Crowd appeal.

Piper-Heidsieck Cuvée Sublime NV
Good aging on lees (a full 36 months) allays the significant dosing of this very fine demi-sec, which is, as a result, all balanced succulence and exotic spiciness. Try it with steamed lobster with ginger or duck with star anise *à la chinoise*. Exciting.

Piper-Heidsieck Brut 2000
Tasted twice, in April 2007 and August 2008. On the first occasion, still young and racy, with invigorating, lemony flavours on nose and palate; a coiled, still taut mouthfeel, dynamic, mid-weight, with admirably enlivening acidity that is sometimes lacking in 2000s. The second time, 16 months later—gosh, how the wine opened and blossomed. An expressive scent of lemon, then toast; lovely, smoky, mineral tones pervade the sprightly yet evolving mouthfeel, which has delicious fruit still framed by excellent acidity. A splendid result in a goodish but not great year.

(Tasted September 2008)
Piper-Heidsieck Rare 1999★
Pale gold with green lights and elegant bubbles. Fragrant aromas of white flowers (iris and jasmine) suggest grand Chardonnay, then the final whiff of liquorice hints at ripe Pinot Noir. Lovely, delicate flavours like emulsified lemon, lifted by a light spiciness. Very long finale and an enduring impression of silky finesse. An impressive '99, and greatly superior to most.

Piper-Heidsieck Rare 1998 (in magnum)
Deeper green-gold. Initial, finely subtle scent of sandalwood, then with air, gingerbread, orange blossom, and dried apricot presage dessert tones of meringue, cocoa, and liquorice. Now gentle, quite evolved, creamy flavours, dominated by mango and greengages. Very rich, complex, and mature. But even in magnum this wine is nearly *à point*, so do not wait much beyond 2010.

Piper-Heidsieck Rare 1988
Disgorged 1997. An intense, dark gold, typical of a mature, 20-year-old Champagne, with a gentle mousse. A very complex nose, initial whiffs of woodland plants—dried fern and humus—ceding to the scent of black truffles mingling with flowers like freesia, lily, and peony. Outstanding mouthfeel; flavours pervaded with the torrefaction of roasted mocha beans mixed with chestnuts, dried fruits, even a touch of grilled pineapple, completing a glorious, evolved mid-palate. Very fine fantail, almost Burgundian. Superb and absolutely ready.

An extraordinary tasting experience at every level. The colour is amber, the delicate mousse still lace-like and alive. The manifold aromas and flavours defy full description

(Tasted October 2007)
Piper-Heidsieck Rare 1979
An extraordinary tasting experience at every level. The colour is amber, the delicate mousse still lace-like and alive. The manifold aromas and flavours defy full description. There are pressed dried flowers, an enchanting touch of violets that melds into the monastic smells of wax and incense; unsurprisingly, given its age, vanilla, caramel, and coffee are also present. The palate is sui generis, the marine flavours of saline seaweed and iodine (much better than it sounds) merging with feisty, cumin-like spice and the peatiness one associates more with malt whisky. But that's more than enough imagery! This is a powerful Champagne that never degrades into heaviness.

Champagne Piper-Heidsieck
12 Allée du Vignoble, 51055 Reims
Tel: +33 3 26 84 43 50
www.piper-heidsieck.com

Ruinart

"In the name of God and the Holy Virgin shall this book be opened." So wrote Nicolas Ruinart on 1 September 1729, to record the founding of this, the first Champagne house. And thus did Nicolas fulfill the ambition of his uncle Dom Thierry Ruinart, the Benedictine monk and visionary who had already foreseen the social cachet and potential commercial success of sparkling Champagne on his tours of the royal courts of Europe. The breakthrough that turned this dream into a reality was Louis XV's royal decree in 1728 authorizing the transport of wine in bottles. Hitherto, wine could be transported only in cask, which of course was out of the question for Champagne. Nicolas Ruinart, as a natural entrepreneur, saw his chance and took it.

The firm gained many new customers in the slipstream of Napoleon's early victorious sweep across Eastern Europe, but after Waterloo the family also knew when to tack with the wind, as when Irénée Ruinart, as mayor of Reims and *deputé* for the Marne, welcomed the Bourbon Charles X to his coronation at Reims Cathedral in 1825. Like their forebears, succeeding generations were tireless travellers. Irénée's son, Edmond Ruinart, was received in 1832 by US President Andrew Jackson, to whom he presented a case of Champagne. Nearly 30 years later, Edgar, his heir, was travelling to St Petersburg, where he had an audience with the tsar. During World War I, the firm's premises were all but destroyed by German artillery, so with typical Champenois grit and sangfroid, André Ruinart, then head of the firm, quietly installed his working desk on a raft in the flooded cellar to ensure that the business could continue as usual. The house remained a family concern until it was bought in 1963 by Moët & Chandon, and it is now part of LVMH.

Since the early 1990s, production has steadily increased from 1.4 million to 2.5 million bottles. But wisely, Ruinart has been allowed to stay true to

Above: The suitably antique sign on the gates of Ruinart, the first sparkling Champagne house, founded in Reims in 1729

the founders' vision of a premier Chardonnay house of a very particular type. From the beginning, the firm has owned 15ha (37 acres) of Chardonnay at Sillery and Puisieulx on the eastern side of the Montagne de Reims. These Montagne crus give wines that are richer and rounder than those from the great growths of the Côte des Blancs, which, for all their mineral focus and elegance, are often leaner. When the Montagne and Côte Chardonnays are deftly blended, you have something very special, as best expressed in the prestige Dom Ruinart cuvées that are always among the greats of Champagne.

This unmistakable Ruinart taste—elegant, full, generous—also runs through the house's compact range of cuvées, a taste created in part by important stocks of reserve wines and in part by low *dosage*, to reveal the natural character of the wines. The entry-level "R" de Ruinart Brut Non-Vintage is the one Champagne that normally has a majority of Pinot Noir in the blend. It is in a style the French call *goût anglais*—that is to say, gently sparkling, supple, with a leesy, rich character that comes from extensive aging of the wine in broader contact with the lees for optimal autolytic flavours.

The 1999 "R" de Ruinart is really a more intense version of the Non-Vintage but better constituted than many Champagnes of this easy year. The Blanc de Blancs Non-Vintage blend, introduced in 1997, is an ideal apéritif—crisp and mineral yet smooth and rounded in the house style, with a fine freshness on the end palate. The Brut Rosé is more stylish and incisive than previously, with Meunier now eliminated from the cuvée, made with a majority of Chardonnay, a modicum of Pinot Noir, and good-quality red wine added.

In great vintages like 1998 and 1990, Dom Ruinart Blanc de Blancs has "the power and body of Pinot Noir in a Chardonnay", in the words of the late *chef de cave* Jean-François Barat, who made both of these highly successful wines. These two years do, however, display subtle differences. In 1998, an intensely hot August was followed by downpours in early September. The sun returned in time for the harvest, though the exact picking time was crucial to making great wines. Dom Ruinart '98 is certainly one of these, its precise, poised, racy flavours delivering a classic of the genre. The Dom Ruinart 1990, by contrast, saw a very warm summer with a record 2,100 hours of sunshine. Approaching maturity when tasted last in 2007, it had a lovely, golden colour, aromas at once sensuously ripe yet mineral, and a broad, luxurious mouthfeel—richer and silkier than the still adolescent 1996—with a

glorious, vanilla-like end note achieved without the help of a single oak stave.

The Dom Ruinart Rosé is made in the same way as the white—from top-flight Chardonnay, but with up to 20 per cent Bouzy rouge added. It is almost always an exceptional wine. The 1996 is predominantly pink-gold with some amber and copper lights; the aromas are fruity, delicate yet firm, suggesting great aging potential; and the palate is a fine amalgam of berries and orchard fruits, with a touch of liquorice, making it a gastronomic wine for lobster.

The 1988 is in the prime of a second life. Of exquisite and evolved salmon hue with copper highlights, the '88 has an extraordinary bouquet, that is freshly vegetal in the best sense and Burgundian in its sensual appeal. The palate is very elegant, of course, with its high Chardonnay content, but it also has the wonderful complexity that one associates more with Pinot Noir. Great Burgundy with bubbles?

FINEST WINES

(Tasted in Reims, June 2008)

Dom Ruinart 1998
Lustrous gold with green reflections. Complex nose, with lemon and grapefruit, apricot and plum, then a typically *gras* Montagne Chardonnay palate, rich, lithe, and long. Best from 2010.

Dom Ruinart 1988 Rosé★
Translucent salmon with copper highlights. Herbal, vegetal nose in the best sense, with hints of *sousbois*. Burgundian, very vinous mouthfeel, but elegant and very persistent, with a fantail finish. A Champagne for the table—especially Cantonese duck or milk-fed veal.

Right: Talented winemaker Frédéric Panaiotis, who moved from Veuve Clicquot to take over as *chef de cave* for Ruinart

Champagne Ruinart
4 Rue des Crayères, 51100 Reims
Tel: +33 3 26 77 51 51
www.ruinart.com

Pommery

The house of Pommery has an honoured place in the history of 19th-century Champagne. Founded in 1837 by Monsieur Pommery, scion of a wealthy Reims wool family, and the comically named Narcisse Greno, a consummate salesman. Surprisingly, in this dynamic period, they were not terribly ambitious, being content to specialize in still red wine. That all changed with the early death of Pommery in 1858, when his wife stepped up to the plate to run the business. Louise proved herself to be a strong-willed widow and brilliant entrepreneur. Over the course of the next three decades, until her death in 1890, she transformed the modest business into one of the most powerful and physically dramatic houses in Champagne. Her tangible legacy is the series of hideous but compelling edifices above Roman chalk pits that are still a landmark of the outskirts of Reims—the castellated facade whose towers and turrets are based, it is said, on the baronial mansions of her aristocratic British customers, such as the Dukes of Argyll.

Louise had her priorities right: qualité d'abord *(quality first). She also had a very clear idea of the style of wine she wanted to make: delicate, fine, and as dry as possible*

This *folie de grandeur* of the 1870s aside, Louise had her priorities right from the very beginning: *qualité d'abord* (quality first) was her motto, and she was quick to see the huge potential for sparkling Champagne in the English market. She also had a very clear idea of the style of wine she wanted to make: delicate, fine, and as dry as possible. Against all expectations, her legendary 1874 Vintage took Victorian London by storm. For sure, this was the first genuinely dry Champagne as we would know it, with a *dosage* of 6–9 grams

Above: The house's sculpted tribute to Louise Pommery, among whose achievements was the creation of its cellars

of sugar per litre of wine. Another of her achievements was the conversion of the Roman chalk pits into storage cellars, decorating them with sculpted bas-reliefs. The splendid carved blending vat in the reception hall, with a capacity of 100,000 bottles, was sent by the firm to St Louis, Missouri, for the Universal Fair of 1904; the carved figures on the cask depict Franco-American friendship. Yet Louise Pommery's supreme gift to her successors was the great vineyard estate that she acquired and increased during her tenure: 308ha (760 acres) of exceptional grand cru sites, the strongest concentration on the Montagne de Reims.

In contrast to this fascinating inheritance, Pommery in the latter years of the 20th century entered a long sleep and became a pawn of the big groups. In 1990, the Moët-Hennessy group (LVMH) woke everyone up when it acquired the firm and decided to go for volume sales, hoping to reach 8 million bottles by 1996. This goal of overly rapid growth had one deadly effect, causing a dip in overall quality, particularly of the Non-Vintage fighting cuvées, and some damage to Pommery's brand image as a whole.

LVMH then sold the brand in 1996 to the Belgian entrepreneur Jean-François Vranken but kept all the beautiful vineyard estate. You might well think that this would have triggered a further spiral downwards. But actually the corporate raider Vranken, now transformed into a major Champagne player, is an intelligent man, and he retained the services of Thierry Vasco, one of the most eminent of cellar masters. Certainly, if his 1998 Louise is anything to go by, all bodes well for the future of this justly famous prestige cuvée. It is one of the Champagnes that counts, and it is still made, as it always was in Louise Pommery's time, from Cramant and Avize for Chardonnay, and Aÿ for Pinot Noir—as a remarkable vertical tasting in 2007 showed. For quality and value, the Brut Royal entry-level Non-Vintage is also much improved under Thierry's stewardship.

FINEST WINES

(Tasted September 2007)

Pommery Cuvée Louise 1998
65% C, 35% PN. *Dosage* 6g/l. Lemon-straw; classic, mineral and grapefruit aromas; lovely freshness and exquisite balance, racy yet generous flavours, with a fine, pure, lemon-mineral finish. Chardonnay-dominant just now. Exceptional.

Pommery Cuvée Louise 1996 (magnum)
63% C, 37% PN. Similar *dosage* to the '98. Disgorged 1998. Still very youthful lemon-straw. Overriding sensation of high acidity on the nose; not yet much expression on the palate. A little reductive at this stage.

Pommery Cuvée Louise 1990 (magnum)
Disgorged 1999. Shimmering yellow-gold, indicating the ripeness of the harvest. Beautifully evolved yet controlled aromas of dried orchard fruits, apricots, even figs; gorgeous flavours of peach and cherry confit; sumptuous texture and long, long, long. No *dosage*: no need. Will live on till 2015 or beyond. *Très grand vin.*

Pommery Cuvée Louise 1989 (magnum)
Disgorged 1997. Yellow-gold, slightly less intense than the '90. Great richness apparent on the nose and magnified on the palate, but the mouthfeel is impressively not overblown—fine, fresh finish, though leaner than the 1990.

Pommery Cuvée Louise 1985 (magnum)
A pure Chardonnay cuvée from Cramant and Avize. The exclusion of Pinot Noir, very concentrated in '85, makes complete sense, since it would have been too burly for the delicate style of Louise. *Dosage* 4g/l. Disgorged 2005. Elegant, lustrous green-yellow; fine flow of little bubbles. Classy, sensuous nose of honey and crisp acidity. Perfect maturity on the palate, lovely minerality, mouth-watering purity of grand Chardonnay flavours, and a long, multitoned finish. A great wine, and a rare example of a blanc de blancs Louise. Who says low-*dosage* wines do not age?

Pommery Grand Cru 1982 (magnum)
In the absence of Louise 1982, this straight Vintage Pommery from one of the greatest postwar vintages was shown. And in fact this cuvée comes from similar sources as Louise. What a fabulous wine.

Champagne Pommery
5 Place du Général Gouraud, 51053 Reims
Tel: +33 3 26 61 62 63
www.pommery.com

Alain Thiénot

In his own quiet way, Alain Thiénot is one of the most impressive entrepreneurs of both Champagne and Bordeaux. Very discreetly, yet with formidable willpower, since the mid-1980s he has built a wine empire based on his ability to fillet a set of accounts with phenomenal speed when weighing the viability of any possible acquisition. In the 33 years since he set up his own Champagne house, he has taken control of Champagne Marie Stuart and Canard-Duchêne, and has a gentlemanly 50/50 share with his distant cousin, Jean-Claude Fourmon, in Joseph Perrier. He also owns several châteaux in the southern Bordelais that include the haunting, turreted Château Ricard, where he makes a Loupiac that is the finest nectar I know with foie gras.

Alain is no desiccated calculating machine; he is a true wine man with a very human face—direct and frank but also natural and warm. These qualities are reflected in his Champagnes, all made with skill and "feeling", based on his deep knowledge of Champagne acquired as a leading former broker. His handsome son Stanislas is a chip off the old block; he travelled the world, spending time in Washington, DC, and São Paulo in Brazil, then opened a wine bar in Paris with some friends, before returning to work with his father. Stan is now closely involved in the winemaking, and over lunch at Le Petit Comptoir in July 2008, he impressed me greatly with his intellectual honesty when dealing with searching questions on the ticklish issue of yields.

Putting aside my personal fondness for the family, I can report dispassionately that in the clinical atmosphere of a blind tasting, the entry-level Thiénot Brut NV always shows beautifully, being made with a very light touch and mild *dosage*. It is also great value for money. The Brut Rosé is made in the same mould, brimming with refined tastes of orchard fruits. The current 1999 Vintage is typical of this variable year: well and correctly made but not revealing huge character. More interesting is the single-vineyard all-Chardonnay La Vigne aux Gamins, which comes from old vines in grand cru Avize. Going against the modern trend, the Thiénots have given up making this wine in oak and returned to stainless steel, the better to express the true lead-pencil elegance of this privileged vineyard site. The Grande Cuvée is a prestige Champagne worthy of its rank. The 1985★ was one of the best wines of this tiny, super-concentrated year, the more impressive for being supple and not overblown —a virtue that shines through the line. The 1996 maintains this balance, while being a wine of real depth, with a lovely touch of grilled bread on the nose.

FINEST WINES

(Tasted in Reims, July 2008)
Alain Thiénot Brut NV★ [V]
A classic mix of all three Champagne grapes. A perfect house Champagne to keep chilled at home or in the restaurant: supple, fruity, friendly, and frank. It is also particularly good value.

Alain Thiénot Brut Rosé NV
Elegant, salmon hue. Like its white brother, fresh, frank, and supple, with pure, soaring flavours of raspberries and strawberries.

(Tasted August 2008)
Alain Thiénot Les Vignes aux Gamins 1999
A small production of 4,000 bottles. Shimmering, pure, pale colour with green highlights. A more reductive style, but one that will eventually better mirror the classy minerality, finesse, and potential length of flavour. Be patient. 2010–15.

Right: Alain Thiénot, here with his son Stanislas, is an astute businessman but also a real wine man with a human face

Champagne Alain Thiénot
4 Rue Joseph-Cugnot, 51500 Taissy
Tel: +33 3 26 77 50 10
www.thienot.com

Jacquart

A major player in Champagne, Jacquart is both a leading cooperative and a brand known internationally for the keen price of its often classy cuvées. Its beginnings were modest. It was founded in 1962 by 30 growers, mainly from the Côte des Blancs, who included René Robert, father of Alain Robert, the creator of the greatest of all Le Mesnil Champagnes up to 1999, which was his last released vintage. Jacquart's expansion over half a century has been dramatic: 700 member-growers now send their grapes from 1,000ha (2,500 acres) in 64 villages of the Marne to be made impeccably in an ultra-modern winery in Reims. Jacquart is a member of the powerful Alliance group of cooperatives, which includes the excellent Union Auboise (Veuve Devaux), the group led by the visionary Laurent Gillet.

The best wine is the Blanc de Blancs Prestige Cuvée Nominée. I remember the 1985, drunk in 1994, as a Champagne of rare refinement, and the 1990 may be even better

Their marketing is pretty effective, too. In 2001/02, a million bottles of their well-known Brut Mosaïque NV were shipped out to leading export markets such as Britain, the USA, and Japan. Made from a classic mix of white and black grapes (including 15 per cent Meunier), Mosaïque NV is a complex wine for little outlay, with scents of candied lemon, whiffs of the baker's oven, and a mouthfeel that is long and intense. If you are counting your dimes and pennies, the entry-level Brut Tradition is an easy, supple Champagne to keep in the fridge door for moments of consolation. The Vintage wines, now also labelled as Mosaïque for better brand recognition, are true standard-bearers of their years. The best wine in the cellar is the Blanc de Blancs Prestige Cuvée Nominée. I remember

the 1985, drunk in 1994, as a Champagne of rare refinement, and the 1990 may be even better. I look forward to tasting more recent as well as other more venerable vintages. Happily, there will now be greater opportunity to savour the older wines, as in March 2009 the company launched a new Oenothèque series.

FINEST WINES

(Tasted September 2008)
Jacquart Blanc de Blancs Mosaïque 1999
Mid-yellow; mature bottle aromas melding with incisive scents of lime. On the palate, mouth-watering acidity vies with an elegant leesy character. It benefits from airing and being served in wine glasses rather than flutes.

Jacquart Mosaïque Vintage 2002
Fine, luminous gold with green highlights. Rich scents of ripe fruit, with creamy, early toast aromas. Energizing mousse in a racy mouthfeel that encompasses sweet maturing fruit. Classic vintage, which should age very well.

Champagne Jacquart
6 Rue de Mars, 51100 Reims
Tel: +33 3 26 07 88 40
www.jacquart-champagne.fr

Palmer & Co

Palmer & Co is the brand name of the Société de Producteurs des Grands Terroirs de Champagne, which was founded after World War II by seven growers in the Côte des Blancs and the Montagne de Reims. This rather upmarket cooperative admits only members who have privileged vineyard sites. Today its holdings extend to 315ha (778 acres) of mainly grands and premiers crus on the Montagne de Reims, but there are also some choice plots on the finest Chardonnay hillsides between Chouilly and Vertus on the Côte des Blancs.

The winemaking is admirably classical and unhurried, taking place in a modern cuverie above deep, old cellars in the centre of Reims. Even today, processes like *remuage* are given plenty of time; there are good stocks of reserve wines; and the Champagnes are rested for three to six months after *dégorgement*. Almost unheard of for a working cooperative, Palmer has a library of old vintages back to 1947: I fondly remember drinking a bottle of the magnificent 1961 in 1994 with the director Jean-Claude Colson, whose company and sense of humor were as delightful and sparkling as his wines.

The entry-level Brut Non-Vintage is a 50/50 mix of highly rated Pinot Noir and Chardonnay and is well aged, with a fine, vinous complexity, deepening a Champagne of precise focus and enduring elegance. By comparison, the Rosé Brut is a very full expression of strongly constituted Pinot Noir, as you would expect from grapes grown in some of the best parcels of the Montagne. The Blanc de Blancs 2000 is a fine example of this forward and fruity vintage, with a medley of expressive grapefruit flavour, supple mouthfeel, and a nice touch of biscuity autolysis. The Cuvée Amazon comes in an original, somewhat bizarre, oval-shaped bottle that looks like a rugby ball. The wine inside is serious enough, though: a multivintage blend that is rounded but still fresh,

even if not normally for long keeping. By contrast, the Vintage Assemblage Brut 2002 is an exceptional Champagne from one of the greatest years since the Société was founded, and certainly worthy of long cellarage—to 2020 or beyond.

FINEST WINES

(Tasted August 2008)

Palmer & Co Brut Amazon de Palmer
A classic 50/50 *assemblage* of Pinot Noir and Chardonnay, usually a blend of three years—in this case, 2000, 1999, and 1998. Full, ripe, and rounded, this Champagne is now *à point*, and should be drunk by 2010 or shortly thereafter to appreciate fully the fine, toasty aromas and orchard fruit flavours of apricot and peach.

Palmer & Co Assemblage Vintage Brut 2002
Straw-gold. A golden, fruity nose; in a discreet way almost a hint of late-harvest wine. Lovely, velvety mouthfeel: toast, butter, torrefaction to come. Chardonnay-led, or so it seems at this stage. A real beauty in the making.

Champagne Palmer & Co
67 Rue Jacquart,
51100 Reims
Tel: +33 3 26 07 35 07

Henri Billiot

When I was researching my first book on Champagne in 1993, the Cuvée de Réserve of this small, 5ha (12-acre) Ambonnay domaine made a great impact, stopping me in my tracks with its depth of flavour and sinewy power. Serge Billiot, its creator, has always been happiest communing with his old vines, on which he lavishes the greatest care. The results in the glass are eventually spectacular, but Billiot Champagnes are not for the beginner, needing time to shake off an initial reductiveness.

The wines are made mainly in stainless steel, the malo avoided in the interests of fresh, precise, ethereal aromas in impressive balance with that profundity of flavours that still registers in my wine memory 15 years after I first encountered it. Serge, now approaching retirement, is slowly handing over the estate to his daughter Laetitia and her husband. The couple are keen to learn how Serge weaves his magic, since he tends to cultivate a certain playful mystery about his craft.

The Brut Tradition is made of 70 per cent Pinot Noir and 30 per cent Chardonnay (Serge is particularly proud of the strain of his great white grape). The quality of the fruit is such that he uses a proportion of the second pressings (the *taille*) to add a pretty fruitiness without detracting from the wine's finesse. The Cuvée de Réserve is virtually a blanc de noirs, with 90 per cent Pinot contributing its power. The Cuvée Laetitia, his best-known wine, named after his favourite little girl, is a perpetual blend of 20 vintages from 1983 onwards: a very complex Champagne made with a light touch. The Henri Billiot Vintage 2002 is one of the finest wines in a village of exceptional winemakers and one of the best years since 1945. In complete contrast, as a one-off, and very different from the rest of the line, the Cuvée Julie—named after Laetitia's daughter—is a full-on expression of

Right: The playfully mysterious Serge Billiot and his daughter Laetitia, for whom their impressive *cuvée perpétuelle* is named

When I first tasted the Cuvée de Réserve of this small Ambonnay
domaine, it made a great impact, stopping me in my tracks
with its depth of flavour and sinewy power

Above: Serge Billiot's stark winery and the basic tools of his trade. He is happiest when out communing with his vines

Champagne aged in oak barrels. But I think they need to reflect a little more about taming the wood impact on the aroma and flavour of this wine, because it is not yet in the distinguished, refined style that has made all of Serge Billiot's other Champagnes so sought after.

FINEST WINES

(Tasted in Ambonnay, January 2009)
Henri Billiot Cuvée Tradition NV
This 50/25/25 blend of the 2006, 2005, and 2004 vintages respectively was disgorged and *dosé* at 8g/l in December 2008, so the liqueur is not yet totally assimilated. Quite tight and young now, but lovely fruit, as in the past, so it should blossom after a few more months in bottle.

Henri Billiot Cuvée de Réserve NV
More intensity and depth than the Cuvée Tradition. Straw gold. The sinewy power of Pinot Noir is certainly there, but it is balanced and softened by a fat richness of texture. Mouth-filling, but with a really classy finish of minerality that is Ambonnay at its best.

Henri Billiot Vintage Brut 2002
Straw, with gold highlights. A really majestic Champagne, with acidity, fruit, vinosity, and a taste of the terroir harmonizing perfectly. As good a grower's Champagne as you will find in this classic and supremely well-balanced vintage.

Henri Billiot Cuvée Laetitia NV
A perpetual cuvée of 20 vintages (at the time of this tasting). Evolved golden colours and beautifully mature aromas and flavours—honeyed but with the brisk impact of the chalk. No hint of oxidation or of fading fruit. Long, multiflavoured finale.

Henri Billiot Cuvée Julie 2004
Vinified in tank and aged in oak *fûts*. A very big, golden Champagne, suffused with scents of acacia and vanilla, but the fine, honeyed fruit is seriously masked by the oak, which does give the wine far too woody a flavour. Perhaps they might consider fermenting in oak rather than just aging it there. That way, the wood and the wine might be better integrated, and it would protect the Champagne from oxidation through the inoculating effect of the infant wine's early contact with air.

Champagne Henri Billiot
1 Place de la Fontaine,
51190 Ambonnay
Tel: +33 3 26 57 00 14

Paul Déthune

The Déthunes are one of the oldest families in Ambonnay, having tended vines on the village's privileged slopes since the early 17th century. Records in the local registry actually date the official establishment of the domaine to 1847—a time of political turmoil and revolution in Europe that coincided with the great expansion of the Champagne trade internationally.

In the 1930s, Henri Déthune started to make and market his own Champagnes in order to provide a better life for his family. The business was then developed by his son Paul. Today, young Pierre Déthune and his wife Sophie have 7ha (17 acres) planted with Pinot Noir and Chardonnay in a 70:30 ratio, entirely within the Ambonnay grand cru

In the winery, handsome oak foudres *show the couple's respect for the best of tradition, though their Champagnes now have an extra dimension of quality*

Above: The welcoming sign at the Déthune domaine in Ambonnay, where the family has tended vines for centuries

vignoble and all farmed effectively on biodynamic principles. The house and outbuildings, in rough-cast stone, are beautifully covered with ivy that changes colour symbolically with the seasons. In the winery, handsome oak *foudres* show the couple's respect for the best of tradition, though their Champagnes now have an extra dimension of quality that comes from constant modern improvements, too. This is not an estate that is content to sit on its laurels.

The way they make their Brut Rosé is a case in point, a clever finessing of the *saignée* method. The pressed juice is given a short maceration (seeping) in contact with the Pinot Noir skins to achieve a pronounced colour that is neither really red nor rosé. Then, about 20 per cent Chardonnay is added to lighten and fix the colour, the latter being important for the consistency of the wine's appearance. The end result is a good balance of exuberant fruit, vinosity, and freshness. The Brut Non-Vintage is a bright, sleek wine that has the pedigree taste of the grapes' grand cru origins. The Blanc de Blancs shows the *gras* roundness of Montagne Chardonnay, which is particularly appreciated in Italy. The three best-known wines in the cellar are the elegant Blanc de Noirs, the Prestige Cuvée Princesse des Thunes, and the Cuvée à l'Ancienne. All of these are marked by *gourmand* flavours, aided by vinification in *foudres* and Champenois *pièces* of 205 litres.

FINEST WINES

Paul Déthune Blanc de Noirs NV
Burnished gold, deepened by what looks like a spell in wood. A round, rich wine, not as voluptuous as some but with a balance and elegance, an absence of heaviness, that gives it wide appeal. An adaptable wine for young game or hard or semi-hard cheeses such as Parmesan or Tomme de Savoie.

Paul Déthune Prestige Princesse des Thunes NV
A finely judged oxidative style, with a sumptuous bouquet of fine honey and acacia blossom, then a gentle, almost *demi-mousse* sensation on the tongue, allowing the wine to express its evolving complexity. Long and persistent finish.

Paul Déthune Cuvée à l'Ancienne NV
As its name implies, this is the most classic, old-fashioned Champagne in the range, and it's none the worse for that. Suffused with the leesy richness and evolved flavours of very mature grapes, it is a *Champagne di contemplazione*, as the Italians would say, to be drunk on its own after dinner.

Suffused with the leesy richness and evolved flavours of very mature grapes, the Cuvée à l'Ancienne is a Champagne di contemplazione

Right: Pierre Déthune, who intelligently adapts tradition to craft grand cru wines of exuberance and vinosity

Champagne Paul Déthune
2 Rue du Moulin, 51150 Ambonnay
Tel: +33 3 26 57 09 31
www.champagne-dethune.com

Egly-Ouriet

Francis Egly, who makes the wines at this exceptional Ambonnay estate, does not welcome journalists, but he was perfectly pleasant when I once managed to meet him. Although at a disadvantage in trying to write a vivid, contemporary profile of this painstaking vigneron and winemaker, I am a great admirer of these handcrafted Champagnes. Francis and his father Michel own 8.5ha (21 acres) of vineyards, largely in Ambonnay, but also in Verzenay, where they have another hectare, plus a few rows of vines in Bouzy. As well as these grand cru sites, Francis also cultivates a plot of very old Meunier vines at Vrigny, which make for a single-vineyard bottling of considerable charm, with a leafy, floral, and spicy character all its own. Francis is very eco-friendly. The Dijon soil consultant Claude Bourguignon advises him, and Francis has radically reduced the use of fertilizers and chemical pesticides.

The Eglys may make the finest blanc de noirs in Champagne, its only real rival (in a quite different style) being Billecart-Salmon's polished but pricier Clos Saint-Hilaire. The Egly wine is called Les Crayères, a plot of old Pinot vines planted in 1947. The deep soil is pervaded with chalk, giving a superb wine of power and finesse.

FINEST WINE

(Tasted June 2007)
Les Crayères Blanc de Noirs Vieilles Vignes NV
Based on the 2001 vintage, this is a voluptuously rich Champagne, yet with beautiful minerality and incisive focus. Subtly fermented in oak and not filtered, it needed a *dosage* of only 2g/l. An extraordinary result after a dreadful summer, when this special plot triumphed over the elements.

Right: Francis Egly, a passionate and perfectionist grower who crafts highly original wines from three grands crus

Egly-Ouriet
51150 Ambonnay
Tel: +33 3 26 57 00 70

The Eglys may make the finest blanc de noirs in Champagne,
its only real rival (in a quite different style) being Billecart-Salmon's
polished but pricier Clos Saint-Hilaire

Marie-Noëlle Ledru

Ambonnay is the favourite black grand cru of the Krug family, and with good reason. Pinot Noir on these chalky soils reaches great heights of voluptuous fullness, in tune with an incisive minerality. This dual character shapes wines of supreme breeding. Inevitably, pure Ambonnay Champagnes can be stiffly priced, as collectors discover their splendor. Imagine one's delight, then, on discovering an Ambonnay producer who quietly makes a range of immaculate Champagnes in a robust, *gourmand* style that faithfully reflects the terroir, ages beautifully, and is very reasonably priced. As you have guessed, this is no fashionable young Turk lionized by the press, but a kindly lady of unaffected charm and a certain age, who in another life and land might have been doing good works in Philadelphia or Cheltenham Spa.

Marie-Noëlle Ledru inherited her 6ha (15-acre) domaine from her parents. She works virtually alone, with no partner and just two employees. She does everything—from the tedium of the paperwork, to the love of tending her vines, on ideal south and southeast-facing slopes, then making the wines in stainless-steel or enamel-lined vats, with no desire to use oak, preferring to let her fabulous terroirs speak for themselves.

Roughly 85 per cent of her vineyards is planted with Pinot Noir in Ambonnay, and 15 per cent with Chardonnay in Bouzy. This ratio of black to white grapes in the vineyard is more or less followed in the *assemblage* of nearly all her Champagnes. The distinctive exception is the splendid, sturdy, vintage-dated blanc de noirs Cuvée du Goulté. The 2004 first intrigued me at a *World of Fine Wine* tasting in 2008, making me want to visit its creator. There's a serendipity of mature bottles in her deep cellars, with a classically vinous 1988, a lovely, rich, and harmonious 1990, and a bouncy and vigorous 1996. To taste such wines in Marie-Noëlle's parlour is an enchanting experience, with a nice touch of quirkiness. We were joined by her 17-year-old cat, Frémousse ("Funny Face"), who had hopped indoors to escape the glacial January day.

FINEST WINES

(Tasted in Ambonnay, January 2009)
Marie-Noëlle Ledru Brut NV
2005 plus reserve wines. *Dosage* 8g/l. Typifies the *gourmand* Ledru style. Vivid golden colour. Ample, generous, all aspects of scent and flavour showing a fine balance. Long and strong.

Marie-Noëlle Ledru 2003
Typical mix of 85% PN and 15% C. Same moderate *dosage*. Ripe hue. A Champagne that celebrates the golden fruit of this atypical, extremely hot year. But it is beautifully judged. The wine is still fresh and with absolutely no hint of oxidation.

Marie-Noëlle Ledru Cuvée du Goulté 2004
100% Ambonnay Pinot Noir. Paler gold. Powerful nose of aromatic complexity. A muscular palate, but fresh, poised, and vital. Still very young but with latent richness that will gradually unfold from 2010. A very natural Champagne from a great terroir.

Marie-Noëlle Ledru Brut Nature 2002
Non-dosé. A really intriguing Champagne in its natural state, without makeup. It could be made this way because of the richness of this great vintage. The first scents suggest fennel, menthol, then liquorice, reflecting the ripeness of the grapes. Powerful, nobly structured, and relieved by a fine, leesy touch. Keep until 2012 at least. Really fine.

Marie-Noëlle Ledru Brut 1999 [V]
A really successful vintage chez Ledru, in this case (against the trend) better than the 1998. Bright gold. Tiny bubbles. Energizing minerality, then lovely scents of honeysuckle, grilled almonds, and something more savoury, like sage. Beautifully pure flavours that speak directly of the privileged soils and the craftsmanship of this artisan. Great wine.

Right: Marie-Noëlle Ledru is the very image of the *vigneronne indépendante*, crafting authentically robust Ambonnay wines

Champagne Marie-Noëlle Ledru
5 Place de la Croix, 51150 Ambonnay
Tel: +33 3 26 57 09 26
info@champagne-mnledru.com

Edmond Barnaut

Leading Champagne growers in Bouzy since the 1930s, Edmond Barnaut is a family affair, with 12.5ha (31 acres) of enviable grand cru sites in 25 *lieux-dits* of Bouzy itself plus a little Ambonnay and Louvois—all blue bloods of the Pinot Noir family. Owner Philippe Secondé, grandson of the founder, is a frank, friendly man and natural communicator. He is the ideal sort of *récoltant-manipulant*, nurturing his own grapes to give reasonable yields, making the wines unhurriedly, and allowing them a respectable average of four years before release. Barnaut represents tradition at its best: enlightened winemaking without the flim-flam of fashion—and all at reasonable prices. On a recent visit, Philippe was away on business in Russia, but his wife Laurette and I tasted through the full range of Champagnes.

Traditional vertical presses are used here. The juice is separated into four or five parts, differentiating between young and old vines. The malo is encouraged, and the fine lees are kept in suspension—a classical sequence of Champagne-making and nothing particularly unusual. More remarkable is Philippe's method of solera-style "perpetual blending". In simple terms, the total blended quantity is double that bottled. The part that is not bottled is kept in vats and used as a base for the following year; to prepare the new blend, younger wine is added to refresh it. So this perpetual blend (or reserve cuvée) becomes more complex over time.

It shows in the Champagnes, which have multilayered nuances of flavour. The new Cuvée Edmond is a *Champagne de plaisir*, but serious, too. It is the one Barnaut Champagne with 20 per cent Pinot Meunier from the Marne Valley added, giving an exuberant, palate-filling roundness, balanced by the fine, racy flavours of grand cru Pinot Noir and Chardonnay that make up four fifths of this mature-tasting blend.

The vintage-dated Grand Cru cuvée is a classic Pinot/Chardonnay mix from low-yielding old vines. The Extra Brut (Zéro Dosage) is for aficionados of the bone-dry. The Blanc de Noirs is the youngest wine in the range, giving full fruit expression to its pure Pinot Noir content and the oomph of the Bouzy terroir—a bouncy, vinous Champagne.

And so to the Authentique Rosé, so named because it's a pink Champagne made the hard way. The skins of the Pinot Noir grapes are bled of enough pigment to colour the wine. This process is called *saignée* (a literal translation of "bled"). A recurring problem with this ancestral method is that the colour can be too dense and the flavours overextracted. At Barnaut, 5–10 per cent of Chardonnay added to the blend gives elegant balance and helps fix the colour.

Naturally, being *sur place*, Philippe makes a very good Bouzy rouge in sunny years like 2002. Yet his most original creation is his Clos Barnaut Bouzy Rosé, which is probably the only still pink wine in the Marne entitled to the Coteaux Champenois appellation. For the past three years, the little walled *clos* has been devoted to growing Pinot Noir for this unique wine. The grassy, organically complex soil of the *clos* is really too rich for Champagne but ideal for making a gastronomic still wine. Hand-picking of unbruised bunches, manual selection of the best grapes, and cold maceration to extract colour before a precisely timed fermentation result in a beautiful, clear, ruby wine, with expansive red-fruit aromas and flavours that are subtly rich but crisply mineral. With the freshness of a white and the structure of a red, Clos Barnaut drinks well with almost anything—sushi, smoked hams, air-dried meats, steak tartare, feathered game, fresh goat's cheese, or a *coupe* of fresh seasonal fruits. As a footnote, it is interesting that the complex tastes of the entire Barnaut range are achieved without the aid of a single oak barrel. "We want to illustrate the scents of nature, naturally harvested, in our wines," affirms Laurette.

FINEST WINES

Edmond Barnaut Extra Brut (Zéro Dosage)
This is made only in ripe years, which in the past had rendered its 90% Pinot content a bit weighty. Now a touch of young Chardonnay is added for freshness and zip, the sugarless style making it an ideal Champagne for the marine flavours of oysters. Exceptional wine.

Edmond Barnaut Blanc de Noirs
Deep yet bright copper-gold, classic blanc de noirs hue. Rich stone fruits (cherry, plum, and peach) pervade both aromas and flavours. Real Pinot punch and thrust on the palate, but as always with this winemaker, the mouthfeel remains perfectly poised and finely balanced.

Edmond Barnaut Authentique Rosé
A fine, not forced, ruby hue and lively bubbles,

Above: Philippe Secondé, his red paddle signalling his largely traditional approach and Pinot-based wines

reflecting all the matter in the grape skins. A complex range of Pinot's woodland-fruit flavours, such as redcurrant and wild raspberry, plus the citrus and grapefruit tastes of Chardonnay. This is a Champagne for strong creamy cheeses like Epoisses. Excellent.

Edmond Barnaut Grand Cru 1998 [V]
Bright gold, youthful colour. The Pinot-ish scents of morello cherries lead on to a full, ripe flavour with a touch of honey, all beautifully balanced by fine acidity—a characteristic of the 1998 vintage.

Champagne Edmond Barnaut
1 Place Carnot, 51150 Bouzy
Tel: +33 3 26 57 01 54
www.champagne-barnaut.com

André Clouet

Pierre and Françoise Santz-Clouet, and now their dashing winemaking son Jean-François, are the best sort of Champagne growers. Their 8ha (20 acres) of vineyards lie on the best middle slopes of Bouzy and Ambonnay, all grand cru sites in a domaine that is just the right size for perfectionist winemaking from great grapes, while providing a comfortable living for a family that still lives in the 17th-century village house built by their ancestor, a printer to Louis XV's royal court at Versailles.

An artistic sense of design obviously runs in the family, for in 1911 the great-grandfather of Jean-François created an ornate *ancien régime* label as a homage to their printer forebear. Finely evocative of the louche demimonde, the Clouets' Cuvée 1911 is still stocked at the bar of Paris's Folies Bergère, once famously painted by Edouard Manet.

The vineyards lie on the best middle slopes of Bouzy and Ambonnay, all grand cru sites in a domaine that is just the right size for perfectionist winemaking

FINEST WINES

André Clouet 1911
The Champagne is as richly interesting as its story. A pure Pinot Noir, this is an *assemblage* of the Clouets' ten best *lieux-dits* in Bouzy, and normally from three consecutive vintages, roughly half from the most recent year, and a quarter each from the preceding two. The wine has a sumptuous flavour and satiny texture typical of this great village but never tips over into ponderous heaviness, being made with a very light touch. The colour is vivid gold, the mousse swirling and creamy; the aromas are blossomy, with hints of acacia and honeysuckle that lead in to a peachy, svelte palate—very much a versatile *grand Champagne* that makes a special apéritif but also drinks beautifully with steamed lobster or salmon *en croûte*. Amusingly, each successive production of this special cuvée

is always precisely restricted to a symbolic total of 1,911 bottles.

André Clouet Silver Extra Brut NV
Another great Champagne here is the aptly named Extra Brut version of the Grande Réserve Brut, the latter wine being the mainstay of the range. Both wines are also 100% Pinot Noir, and normally a blend of three vintages. With minimal *dosage*, you can really taste the exceptional flavours of the Bouzy terroir in its natural state, and the proportion of the wine released this way has doubled in recent years. It is a fine wine for oysters or salmon tartare.

André Clouet Grand Cru Rosé NV
A typical grower's wine in the best sense. It is an intriguingly rich heather colour, and the primary Pinot aromas of raspberries leap out of the glass, yet the Champagne is admirably fresh, focused, and poised, thanks to the brisk acidity. This, like the Clouets' Bouzy rouge (8% of the blend), is made only in sunny years, and is the most adaptable of the wines with food. It would go well with *charcuterie*, dressed crab, roast Bresse chicken, veal *tonnato*, or a wide range of cheeses—from mild Coulomier or Caerphilly, to powerful Maroilles or Langres.

Right: Jean-François Clouet with some of the barrels he purchases secondhand from a famous Bordeaux château

Champagne André Clouet
8 Rue Gambetta, 51150 Bouzy
Tel: +33 3 26 57 00 82
jfclouet@yahoo.fr

Benoît Lahaye

A very serious young wine grower, Benoît Lahaye practises a thoughtful biodynamic viticulture of the very highest standard, adapted to the challenging conditions of growing grapes this far north. He is clearly a man with a genuine, deep respect for the environment, but one suspects that when faced with a horribly wet summer like 2007, he would protect his crop in extremis by necessary treatments rather than lose it because of too rigid an adherence to the teachings of Rudolf Steiner. His holdings are just over 4.5ha (11 acres): 1ha (2.47 acres) in Ambonnay; close to 3ha (7.4 acres) in Bouzy; 0.7ha (1.7 acres) in Tauxières; and 0.12ha (0.3 acres) of Chardonnay at Vertus. Yields are very carefully controlled, and he is progressively building up a stock of oak barrels (average age four years) from François Frères in St-Romain in which to ferment his wines. Production is limited to 40,000 bottles per year.

These are Champagnes with a real taste of their origins—a little dumb in youth but developing burgeoning complexities and a natural fine-wine character

My impression on a first visit in January 2009 is that these are Champagnes with a real taste of their origins—sometimes a little dumb in their youth but developing burgeoning complexities and, given enough age, a natural fine-wine character. Until then, and with hard times ahead, go for instant happiness with his least expensive wine—the aptly named Brut Essentiel, which is a lovely expression of Bouzy Pinot Noir lightened with a touch of Chardonnay. The Blanc de Noirs is a powerful, balanced, but young blend that needs a couple of years to show its undoubted pedigree. The Brut Rosé de Macération is really for those who like a pink Champagne that is really a red-wine substitute—deeply coloured and a good Champagne with *charcuterie* or spicy Asian cuisine. Even more serious is his 2004 Vintage Brut, which is aged under a cork rather than a crown cap in the belief that this will help ensure a long and distinguished life. It needs a lot of time. Top of the line is the splendid 2002 Vintage, now approaching maturity and with judicious *dosage*.

FINEST WINES

(Tasted in Bouzy, January 2009)

Benoît Lahaye Brut Essentiel NV ★
90% PN, 10% C. Largely based on the 2006 vintage. *Dosage* 6g/l. Inviting, bright Pinot colour, with tints of just-perceptible pink at the rim. Beautiful cordon of bubbles. Lovely nose of little red fruits: cherries, even raspberries. A beautiful expression of the exuberant Bouzy terroir on the palate but all controlled by an incisive mineral freshness. This is a Champagne to have at hand when friends drop by.

Benoît Lahaye Blanc de Noirs NV
A blend of wines from the 2006 and 2005 vintages. 60% Bouzy, 20% Ambonnay, 20% Tauxières. This shows the sustained power of mainly grand cru Pinot Noir. But at the same time, the middle palate is pleasurably *gourmand* and rounded, with a taste of quince. Good, fresh finish.

Benoît Lahaye Vintage 2002
The power and richness of great Pinots is very present, but as this Champagne approaches maturity, it has the finesse of six years on the cork and displays the balanced harmony of this exceptional vintage. A gastronomic Champagne, especially for feathered game and aged cheeses like Comté or farmhouse Gouda.

Left: Benoît Lahaye amid his carefully tended grand cru vines in Bouzy, where he crafts characterful, robust wines

Champagne Benoît Lahaye
33 Rue Jeanne d'Arc,
51150 Bouzy
Tel: +33 3 26 57 03 05
www.vitiplus.com/champagne-b-lahaye/

Mailly Grand Cru

Founded presciently in 1929, to protect the living of growers in this famous Montagne village against impending economic slump, Mailly has been a unique cooperative ever since. It continues to elaborate Champagne only from the wines of about 70 member-growers, who among them farm 71ha (175 acres) entirely within the grand cru limits of the commune.

The co-op has a thoroughly justified reputation for excellent cuvées, created by Hervé Dantan, one of Champagne's best *chefs de cave*, and astutely directed by Jean-François Preau, a great marketeer. Mailly Champagnes offer exceptional value for money, and around half of the 500,000 bottles produced each year are exported, to some 35 countries around the world.

The co-op has a thoroughly justified reputation. Les Echansons is consistently Mailly's finest Champagne, the peer of some of the best efforts of the grandes maisons

Of the half-dozen cuvées, the Brut Réserve is full of primary Pinot Noir fruit, palate-filling, and with a finish that reminds me of root vegetables—character it does not lack. If you like your Champagnes big and beefy, the Blanc de Noirs is a good Champagne for winter, made for rustic food like *pot au feu*, Thai chicken curry, or even a Maroilles cheese that is *à point* but not too overripe.

The Brut Rosé is strongly constituted but well balanced, with scents of the bakery, a nicely rounded mouthfeel, and a rightly judged *dosage* effectively married with the wine. The vintaged Les Echansons is consistently Mailly's finest Champagne, the peer of some of the best efforts of the *grandes maisons* but at a significant price saving. The 1997 and 1998 vintages show different faces of what is indubitably a top-flight wine.

FINEST WINES

(Tasted November 2008)

Mailly Grand Cru Les Echansons 1997
Normally a blend of 75% PN, 25% C, carefully selected from a few parcels of very old vines now more than 70 years old. Production is restricted to around 12,000 bottles in each vintage. Low *dosage* of around 6g/l. This is always a solid, powerful wine, and the 1997 vintage has this character in spades, but is tellingly relieved by the lovely ripe fruit that the Indian summer gave to the grapes. The *gras*, luxuriant mouthfeel balances the obvious power.

Mailly Grand Cru Les Echansons 1998
A very vinous, deep style, reflecting the extremely hot August this year. The aromas are tight and dumb even at ten years old, but one feels the tannins in the mouth—yes, white wines can taste tannic. Drink from 2010, by which time it should have emerged from its shell.

Right: The grand cru where member-growers have vines in 40 separate parcels, and from which all the wines are made

Champagne Mailly Grand Cru
28 Rue de la Libération,
51500 Mailly-Champagne
Tel: +33 3 26 49 41 10
www.champagne-mailly.com

Jean Lallement

Verzenay, the grand cru on the Montagne that faces northeast over the Reims plain, is a favourite element in the best Champagne blends, prized for the majestic acid structure and long life it brings, especially to the prestige cuvées of the great houses. Certainly, whenever I taste the older reserve wines in Veuve Clicquot's "library", Verzenay is invariably the Pinot star, rock stable and seemingly indestructible. As a result, even the numerous *récoltant-manipulants* in the village still send a good proportion of their precious grapes or still wines to the *maisons* of Reims and Aÿ, with which they have long-term contracts.

Jean Lallement, who owns 4ha (10 acres) in Verzenay, Verzy, and Ludes, is typical, having worked with Louis Roederer for some years. But this tiny estate, founded by his grandfather, has been discovered by alert wine scouts in the USA, UK, and Scandinavia, so when the current contract with the *négoce* expires in 2009, there are likely to

Small is very beautiful indeed, for these Champagnes show a muscular intensity in exquisite balance with richness and elegance

be another 2,500 cases supplementing the 1,700 cases now shipped abroad. Talking with Jean and his Lisbon-born wife, it is clear that they discreetly welcome these broader opportunities to deal direct. They also have three young children to provide for. When I happened to visit on a Wednesday, the kids were home from school, and at the right moment all trooped down the stairs, each presenting a cheek to be kissed by the unknown visitor. Ah, the heart-warming customs of French family life...

Jean makes three Champagnes for now. Small is very beautiful indeed, for the trio shows a muscular intensity in exquisite balance with

richness and elegance. Their magic owes much to the precision of the skilful winemaking. There is no oak here, and a longer time on lees, each year's new cuvée not normally being bottled until July, rather than earlier in the spring, which is the more common practice. The first Lallement Vintage Champagne will be released in 2009 or 2010 and should be well worth seeking out.

FINEST WINES

(Tasted in Verzenay, January 2009)
Jean Lallement Brut Tradition NV
80% PN, 20% C. Mainly 2005 with a little 2006. Moderate *dosage* of 6g/l. The least expensive of the current trio, but with all the hallmarks of Lallement's talents. Crystalline hue, creamy mousse, clarity of great Pinot-led expression on both nose and palate, a light hint of the lees, and very good length.

Jean Lallement Brut Réserve NV
From 30-year-old vines. Same *encépagement* and age composition as for the Tradition, but here everything has extra depth and intensity. Ripe straw colour. A brooding richness on the nose. Electrifying acidity on the palate, all in balance with the vinosity brought by the extended lees contact. A *ne plus ultra* of a Non-Vintage.

Jean Lallement Cuvée Réserve de Rosé NV ★
100% PN, 9% of which was vinified as red wine. Although marketed as a NV, this is in fact all from the 2005 vintage. Elegant, rose colour, with a hint of coral. The purest expression of Verzenay, a ripe strawberriness typical of this hot but not always easy harvest. Its brilliance as a gastronomic Champagne comes from the backbone of majestic acidity, providing a perfect partner to quick-seared tuna, maybe with a Pinot Noir sauce, though the wine is also strong enough to stand up to the spices of Szechuan cooking.

Right: Jean Lallement, who is expanding his range of excellent Verzenay wines with his first Vintage release

Champagne Jean Lallement
1 Rue de Moët & Chandon,
51360 Verzenay
Tel: +33 3 26 49 43 32

Michel Arnould & Fils

Patrick Arnould's Verzenay grapes are much in demand by the *grandes maisons*, and he still grows for Bollinger. But the best fruit from his immaculately tended 30ha (74 acres) of vineyards (80 per cent Pinot Noir, 20 per cent Chardonnay) is kept for his own Champagnes, which are now widely available internationally. If you are looking for a source of vigorous, vinous Champagnes that exhibit breed, balance, and creamy texture, then this is one of the two top addresses in Verzenay, along with Jean Lallement.

superb Mémoire de Vignes, from three parcels of old vines, some more than 40 years old, which is nearly always the best wine in the cellar.

The 2002 Mémoire de Vignes is destined to become a modern classic to vie with Egly-Ouriet or Billecart's Clos St-Hilaire as among the finest blancs de noirs

Respected authorities such as Michel Bettane and Thierry Desseauve note a welcome trend towards lower *dosage* in Patrick's wines. Indeed, this may be no bad thing, given climate change and the high level of ripeness in Pinot vintages like 2005 and 2006.

The Brut Non-Vintage is a true blanc de noirs (100 per cent Pinot Noir), blended from two vintages and aged for three years on lees. The winemaking is light-handed for an all-black-grapes cuvée, showing lithe fruit and full body, with the *dosage* well balanced and integrated. Never heavy or overextracted, it is the sort of Champagne that always seems to invite you to a second or third glass.

The Brut Réserve is definitely dry, made from two thirds Pinot Noir and one third Chardonnay, the latter giving a lift and precise definition to this superior cuvée. The 2002 harvest, great for most growers, was especially successful chez Arnould in both the straight Vintage and the

FINEST WINES

(Tasted December 2008)

Michel Arnould Carte d'Or Grand Cru 2000
A good standard-bearer for this forward, fruity vintage that will give pleasure for at least ten years from the harvest. *Gras*, palate-cloaking, and round, with no harsh edges. It has broad appeal, without ever being a contender of great class. A well-made wine.

Michel Arnould Grande Cuvée Brut 2002
70% PN, 30% C. An immaculate Champagne of great class—racy and athletic on both nose and palate, with a controlled opulence. Good length and perfect, moderate *dosage*.

Michel Arnould Mémoire de Vignes 2002
Pure 100% Pinot Noir, this is a superb wine destined to become a modern classic to vie with Egly-Ouriet or Billecart-Salmon's Clos St-Hilaire as among the finest blancs de noirs, given more cellarage (preferably until 2012). An ideal gastronomic Champagne, especially with fresh young game such as partridge or woodcock, or with a well-aged Tomme de Savoie cheese. Decant and serve in wine glasses rather than in flutes.

Champagne Michel Arnould & Fils
28 Rue de Mailly, 51360 Verzenay
Tel: +33 3 26 49 40 06
www.champagne-michel-arnould.com

Cattier

The Cattier family has lived in the pretty, flower-bedecked Montagne village of Chigny-les-Roses since the 18th century, becoming Champagne négociants in 1921. Thirty years later they bought Clos du Moulin, a 2.2ha (5.44-acre) walled vineyard in the commune.

The pride of the house, the Champagne from this plot is one of the few highly rated Non-Vintage prestige cuvées. Always a blend of three good vintages—the dominant, most recent vintage accounting for a minimum of 60 per cent—it is made from a classic 50/50 mix of premier cru Pinot Noir and Chardonnay. Of admirable consistency and ideal balance, Clos du Moulin has an intrinsic

The pride of the house, the Champagne from Clos du Moulin, is one of the few highly rated Non-Vintage prestige cuvées, of admirable consistency and ideal balance

quality that obviously has a lot to do with the scrupulous husbandry of the grapes, the smallness of scale allowing the vineyard workers to know each vine intimately.

The winemaking is equally meticulous, with only 80 per cent of the *cuvée* (16 of the 20.5hl from each pressing) being used. But another crucial factor is the aging of the wine: a minimum of seven years, in Cattier's cellars, which are some of the deepest in Champagne. Dug on three levels to a depth of 100ft (30m), they feature a series of magnificent vaults crafted in the Romanesque, Gothic, and Renaissance styles. With the TGV fast rail link from Paris's Charles de Gaulle Airport, the Reims train station on the edge of the Montagne is just half an hour away, and after a 15-minute taxi ride you can be sipping this splendid wine. On average, each release is limited to just 10,000 bottles.

The family also owns another 20ha (49 acres) of vines, predominantly in premier cru vineyards. The entry-level Brut Premier Cru is a blend of all three Champagne grapes, showing the palate-filling roundness of Pinot and Meunier, lifted by the citrus tones of Chardonnay. The Blanc de Blancs, pure Chardonnay, is delicate and discreet but still has plenty of body, due to the richer strain of Montagne Chardonnay in the blend; and the recently introduced Blanc de Noirs, pure Pinot Noir, has exuberant flavours of red fruits and a swaggering, joyful character.

FINEST WINE

(Tasted June 2007)
Cattier Clos du Moulin
50% PN, 50% C, in a blend of 1996, 1998, and 1999. Straw colour, green highlights; quite mature scents, with discreet, biscuity notes. On the palate, the wine is tight, a teenager, but after a little time in the glass, the Pinot Noir finally makes its presence felt, richly filling the palate. The most versatile of Champagnes, either as a grand apéritif or as a partner to feathered game or Comté cheese.

Cattier
6 Rue Dom Pérignon, 51500 Chigny-les-Roses
Tel: +33 3 26 03 42 11
www.cattier.com

Canard-Duchêne

Ludes is a pretty Montagne premier cru, with views over vines and meadows to Reims Cathedral. It is also home to Canard-Duchêne, the leading *maison* in a village with several fine growers. Founded in 1868 by the cooper Victor Canard and his *vigneronne* wife Léonie, the firm took off at the turn of the 20th century when their dynamic son Edmond became supplier of Champagne to Tsar Nicolas I and the Russian Court—a proud connection still recalled today with the double-eagle crest of the Romanoffs that adorns the firm's motif. Edmond's son, another Victor, was also a great and far-sighted wine man, who saw earlier than his rivals the potential for excellent Pinot Noir from the Aube in a good Champagne blend. As someone who represented the house in sales trips to the USA in the 1970s, I remember Victor fondly, as both a wonderful host and a purveyor of elegant wines, so typical of a good family business.

Veuve Clicquot acquired the house a decade later, and as much as I admire the Widow's Champagnes, those of its junior Canard partner went through a rough patch in the mid-1990s. In 1994, I was worried enough to write of the entry-level Brut: "[T]his wine had a suspiciously deep, tinted colour and a coarse flavour … (on two occasions)." Fortunately, things looked up with the arrival of a Péters protegé, Jean Dubarry, who cleaned up the Brut cuvée to match the Vintage wines, which have always been perfectly decent. Even better times arrived when the house was sold in 2003 to entrepreneur Alain Thiénot. Alain is always a force for good in Champagne, a former wine broker who knows the vineyards like the back of his hand—a reassuring talent allied to his famous ability to read a balance sheet of figures faster than anyone else!

With Canard's entry into the Alain Thiénot group, the thrust of its sales strategy in its target markets is a mixture of consolidation and change.

Traditionally, Canard is not an expensive Champagne. It is always meant to be an easy style of wine, stressing fruit, vitality, and cleansing acidity. Its customer base remains the French domestic market, that of the *coupe* served on the zinc bar. The management is, however, looking to tap the nascent markets of Eastern Europe and the fun-loving islands of the Caribbean. Apparently, Guadaloupe, which is still a *département* of France, has the highest per capita consumption of Champagne in the world—an isle of lotus eaters, where Canard has a strong presence.

The current range of Champagnes draws both Pinots and Chardonnays from 60 communes on a broad canvas: Ludes on the Grande Montagne; the Marne Valley; the Côte des Blancs; Sézanne, of course; but also quite a significant proportion from the Aube, which provides bright, early-maturing black grapes.

The entry-level Brut is a clean, fresh wine, round yet crisp, majoring on fruitiness rather than complexity. The Vintage cuvée shows good, leesy, mature flavour and is great value. But Canard's trump card is the Charles VII Grande Cuvée Blanc de Blancs, at once buttery, toasty, and floral. The Rosé version steers a confident middle path between voluptuousness and the fresh juiciness of orchard fruits such as cherry and peach.

FINEST WINE

(Tasted in Reims, July 2008)
Canard-Duchêne Grande Cuvée Charles VII
A multi-vintage, prestige, all-Chardonnay cuvée, and as such a comparative rarity. Evolving well: mature Chardonnay aromas and flavours of butter, toast and white flowers. Very good balance. This release will hold well to 2011/2012.

Champagne Canard-Duchêne
1 Rue Edmond-Canard, 51500 Ludes
Tel: +33 3 26 61 10 06
www.canard-duchene.fr

Vilmart & Cie

Vilmart was one of the estates setting the gold standard for grower Champagnes in the late 20th century. What struck me when I first met René Champs and his son Laurent in the early 1990s was their infinite painstaking capacity. On their 11ha (27 acres) of Pinot Noir and Chardonnay in Rilly-la-Montagne, they preferred a hand hoe for tilling the soils between the rows of vines, and no chemicals were used. "Respecting our natural environment develops exceptional flavours in our wines" were their watchwords then. They have since become the received wisdom of eco-friendly growers everywhere.

Now firmly at the helm, Laurent Champs directs everything with meticulous care. The wines are fermented in oak casks, most being large *foudres*. His perfectionist approach pays off best in his top-of-the-line Vintage Champagnes based on old vines of 40–50 years of age. The Non-Vintage cuvées are relatively simple wines by comparison. Essentially, Vilmart, like Rolly Gassmann in Alsace, are brilliant winemakers, but they do not have any grand cru vineyards, and this shows at the entry level.

Vilmart was one of the estates that set the gold standard for grower Champagnes in the late 20th century. What struck me was their infinite painstaking capacity

The Grande Réserve NV (70/30 Pinot Noir/Chardonnay) spends ten months in *foudres*, the straw-gold hue shaped by the time in oak. It shows simple green-apple fruit but is round in the mouth and of decent length. The Grand Cellier cuvée represents a clear step forward. Made from three vintages (currently 2004, '05, and '06), a third of the blend comes from Montagne Chardonnay, rounded and *gras*, shaping attractive scents of tangerine and lemon. Ample Pinot Noir fills the palate to

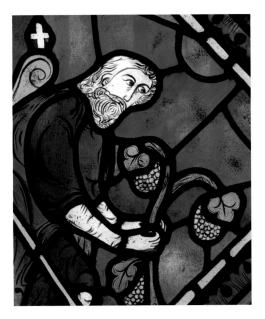

Above: Making stained glass is another craft René Champs practises with great skill, though the theme here is the same

finish a Champagne that is both a fine apéritif and good for the table.

Up again to the Vintage Grand Cellier d'Or, and we are now at the very fine level of Champagnes that made the house's reputation. They are as good as I always remember them. The Cellier d'Or 2002 is a beauty in the making. Dominated by Chardonnay (80 per cent) the nose is subtle, complex, and exceptionally well balanced. In the mouth, orchard fruits like apricot meld with luxurious buttery brioche flavours, finishing on a note of fine, life-giving acidity. It will give enormous pleasure from around 2012. The 2000 is in a different style—more delicate, with exemplary finesse and already *à point*.

The line reaches its apogee in the vintages of Coeur de Cuvée. As the name implies, the wines are made from the best part, the "heart" (or first pressings) of the *cuvée*. They are fermented in 225-litre barriques. The wood can dominate this

Laurent Champs directs everything with meticulous care. The wines are fermented in oak casks, most being large foudres. His perfectionist approach pays off best in his top-of-the-line Vintage Champagnes

great wine for several years until it approaches its maturity, but from about 9–13 years of age, it shows great class and new complexities every time you taste it. So give it plenty of air—or better still, decant and serve it in wine glasses rather than flutes.

A newly introduced blend, the Cuvée Creation, is another take on Chardonnay-dominated Champagne. More fine drawn, it is a summer wine, with restoring notes of lime and delicate touches of vanilla, made for great, subtly sauced sea fish like Turbot or John Dory.

FINEST WINES

(Tasted in Rilly-la-Montagne, January 2009)

Vilmart & Cie Coeur de Cuvée 2000
From the oldest (50-year-old) vineyards of the terroir; 80% C, 20% PN, all premier cru. Fermented and aged for ten months in barriques. Very fine, ripe, golden colour, shimmering; a real robe. Hazelnuts add a fine touch of soaring fresh fruit on the nose. Ample and luxuriant in the mouth, this Champagne has fine definition of vinous but balanced flavours. The wood is now quite integrated. Worth keeping, especially in magnums, until 2012.

Vilmart & Cie Coeur de Cuvée 1999
Expressive, up-front fruitiness, but there is a certain abruptness, a lean, linear character behind, that pales by comparison with the generous and complete 2000. Others may disagree, but this wine confirms my view that 1999 is not a great vintage.

Vilmart & Cie Coeur de Cuvée 1998
Chardonnay was particularly successful in 1998, especially when as well cared for and selected as it was here. A really subtle wine—still tightly coiled but slowly revealing all the mineral loveliness and exquisite acidity melded with generous fruit that is the signature of the vintage.

Left: Laurent Champs has now taken over from his father René and shares his perfectionist approach to winemaking

Champagne Vilmart & Cie
4 Rue de la République, 51500 Rilly-la-Montagne
Tel: +33 3 26 03 40 01
www.champagnevilmart.com

David Léclapart

David Léclapart is a biodynamist who farms and makes his own Champagnes from just 3ha (7.5 acres) in Trépail on the southeast-facing slopes of the Montagne de Reims, above Ambonnay. Although also planted with Pinot Noir, Trépail is particularly known for Chardonnay of feisty character and piercing acidity, traits much loved by Krug, among others. Since I last saw him, David has moved with his young family into his late grandfather's pretty house in the village. He was itching to drive us up into his vineyards to see what was a first for me in Champagne: ten Scottish black-faced sheep in a penned-off section, grazing the grass between the rows—the good life *à la française*? David is certainly a believer in the biodynamic creed, but more importantly he is an excellent winemaker with a "feeling" for fine wine that raises his craft to a higher level.

All his Champagnes are made from Chardonnay fermented in enamel-lined vats or used oak *pièces*, or a combination of both. The cuvées have poetic names—Amateur (connoisseur), Artiste (artist), Apôtre (apostle)—and are beautifully and elegantly labelled. The Amateur base wine made entirely in vat has real personality, a core of racy flavours, and the "tension" that classic Chardonnay Champagnes should have but often do not when overproduced. The Artiste (made half in vat, half in oak) usually shows a certain touch of wood initially, but the wine's greater strength and structure absorbs the oak flavour quite quickly.

David made some successful 2003s—a real achievement in a torrid year of weather extremes and the loss of three quarters of his Chardonnay crop through frost. The Amateur has a richness of fruit, concentration, and good acidity; because of David's meticulous work in the vineyard, he did not need to re-acidify. The Apôtre, wholly fermented in oak and now with 30 months on its lees in bottle, has a snowy-white mousse and intensity on the palate. David's Trépail Rouge, a 2003 still red wine from barrel-matured Pinot Noir, has a sustained ruby colour, a richness of fruit, extract, and ripe tannins that the heat of the summer brought to the grape. There's also a touch of minerally austerity on the aftertaste, which would ideally cut the richness of a marinated winter game dish like jugged hare. The biodynamic principles applied in the Léclapart vineyards certainly do seem to produce some interesting wines, particularly in difficult vintages.

FINEST WINES
(Tasted in Trépail, January 2009)

David Léclapart Amateur NV
Base wine from the 2004 vintage, tank-fermented. This is David's least expensive Champagne and a personal favourite of mine. An intense, vibrant, lemon-straw colour; exemplary purity of mineral, punchy scents typical of Trépail; real intensity of citrussy flavours signalling reasonable yields and generally admirable work in the vineyard. Long and racy on the finish.

David Léclapart Apôtre 2003
Oak-fermented. Snowy white mousse atop gently evolving lemon-gold. After extended time on lees, there are attractive, controlled notes of autolytic yeastiness on the nose. The palate is a miracle for such a hot vintage: very fresh and pure, with decent acidity (good vineyard work again and no playing around with re-acidifying). Beautiful quality of ripe, sturdy fruit, a characteristic of the small band of fine '03s. An excellent result for the year.

David Léclapart Trépail Rouge 2003 (Coteaux Champenois)
100% Pinot Noir fermented in 225-litre barriques. Intense, limpid, blue-tinted "Burgundian" ruby; properly ripe smell and taste of little red fruits and elegant tannins, but also an intriguing mineral end-note to remind you that this is still after all a punchy product of Trepail, and Champenois at heart. A very good wine for winter dishes like rabbit or wild boar.

Champagne David Léclapart
10 Rue de la Mairie, 51380 Trépail
Tel: +33 3 26 57 07 01

Raymond Boulard

The Boulard family's story is an object lesson in "what can be achieved from less exalted terroirs with experience, expertise, and vision". These apt words of my editor put me in the right frame of mind for my visit in cold January 2009 to this out-of-the-way domaine in the Massif de St-Thierry, north of Reims. A bluff, well-padded wine farmer in late middle age, Francis Boulard is a wonderful, playful character. Living up to his reputation, he creased his weathered features into an impish grin after his disarming greeting: "It's very good of you to visit us in our little Siberia!"

The story begins in 1952, when Raymond Boulard, Francis's father, created the domaine by purchasing a vineyard at La Neuville-aux-Larris on the right bank of the Marne, planted mainly with Meunier, some Pinot Noir, and a little Chardonnay. More than half a century on, the diverse estate is some 10.5ha (26 acres), including: a parcel of young vines in the Aisne part of the Marne Valley; a further prize plot of over 1.62ha (4 acres) of grand cru Mailly on the Montagne de Reims; and, perhaps the most surprisingly excellent parcel of all, the 3.03ha (7.5 acres) in the Massif de St-Thierry itself, which have been cultivated biodynamically since 2001.

The loving care with which Francis and his brother Dominic tend these scattered vineyards is exemplary. The vines are pruned short in the best traditions of the Royat and Chablis methods. Throughout the summer, a light deleafing is conducted to aerate the vines. A more radical green-harvest may be carried out in July, but only when conditions demand. The Boulards like to pick the rigorously selected grapes late, for optimal ripeness and key phenolic maturity, obviating the need for excessive chaptalization.

In the cellar, the same perfectionist approach is evident: delicate pressing in a membrane press; indigenous yeasts; and fermentations in a 50/50 mix of wooden barrels and stainless-steel vats, the brothers favouring Burgundy *pièces* for Pinot and Bordeaux barriques for Chardonnay. The stainless-steel fermenters are small in order to make wines from different terroirs separately. The malo is encouraged or blocked wholly or partially, depending on the style and quality of each cuvée. Remarkably, nearly every blend is available either as Brut Nature (no *dosage*) or as a Brut of 5–8g/l. No sugar is used in the *dosage*, the Boulards instead preferring the modern aid of rectified concentrated grape must.

The quality of the wines shows in the glass. The Cuvée Réserve, which accounts for 45 per cent of production, is a model of a friendly Meunier-led Champagne that is particularly good in the beautifully dry Brut Nature version. By contrast, Richard Juhlin, the widely respected Swedish Champagne expert, is surely right to prefer the Grand Cru Mailly in the Brut version, the moderate *dosage* better balancing the strong minerality and power that this great terroir habitually provides. The Cuvée Petraea is a complex perpetual blend of nine vintages from 1997 to 2005, fashioning a honeyed and finely evolving Champagne. But the greatest wine in the cellar—the more striking for its modest St-Thierry origins—is the scintillating, all-Chardonnay Les Rachais cuvée. First released in 2001 as a mini masterpiece in such a fragile year, the current 2002—a truly exceptional vintage—is a further step up thanks to its sumptuous fruit and complexity. Give it time (2010–12), and it should become one of the modern classics of Champagne.

FINEST WINES

(Tasted in Cauroy-lès-Hermonville, January 2009)
Raymond Boulard Cuvée Réserve NV ★ [V]
A 70/30 mix of Meunier and Pinot Noir from grapes grown on clay and limestone soils in the Marne Valley. Effectively a blanc de noirs, though not labelled as such. Base wine 2006, with older wines from 2004 and 2005 matured in oak barrels. In the

Brut bottling (with a moderate *dosage* of 5g/l), the wine is rounded, with a positive attack and good fruit definition. The Brut Nature is actually finer: straw-gold, very pure, mineral, and long, showing how classy Meunier can be at its best.

Raymond Boulard Grand Cru Mailly NV

A 90/10 mix of Pinot Noir and Chardonnay from the calcareous rock of this great Montagne cru. Base wine 2005, with 20% older wines of 2004, 2003, and 2002 made in oak barrels. The Brut version (5g/l *dosage*) is the better one, I suggest, showing all the round yet strong charm of its grand origin. A Champagne for pig's trotters or *tête de veau*.

Raymond Boulard Cuvée Petraea NV

60% PN, 20% C, and 20% PM. Essentially a perpetual blend of nine vintages (in this case, 1997–2005, the years being written on the label in Roman numerals), a new portion of the youngest vintage added every year to refresh the cuvée. Fermented in oak (*Quercus petraea*) barrels of an average age of five or six years, with a small proportion of new-oak Champenois *pièces* (205-litre capacity). Only natural yeasts are used, and there is no filtration. A lovely medley of evolving honeyed flavours, expressed in the roundness of Pinot Noir, the focus of Chardonnay, and the spice of Meunier. A truly original yet classically respectful Champagne.

Raymond Boulard Les Rachais 2002

Pure Chardonnay from silex limestone soils of the Massif de St-Thierry, the grapes having been cultivated biodynamically, without herbicides or other synthetic products. Fermented in eight-year-old oak barrels, with no fining or filtration, and given an Extra Brut *dosage* of only 2g/l. An exquisite Champagne with the purest, subtlest scents of Chardonnay, mineral and ethereal, and a haunting, fleeting spiciness. The palate is long and tight, since this is still very much a youngster, needing a couple of years to unfurl the full splendor of its nuanced complexities. Best from 2012.

Right: Playful Francis Boulard, who shows that great Champagnes can be produced from less exalted terroirs

Raymond Boulard
Route Nationale 44,
51220 Cauroy-lès-Hermonville
Tel: +33 3 26 61 50 54
www.champagne-boulard.fr

The greatest wine—the more striking for its modest St-Thierry origins—
is the scintillating Les Rachais cuvée, which should become
one of the modern classics of Champagne

Jérôme Prévost

A few miles northwest of Reims, at the foot of the Petite Montagne, the leafy village of Gueux is an easy commute to the city for its affluent residents, who include at least one eminent *chef de cave* of a great Champagne house. Nearly a century ago, during World War I, Gueux was a place of death and destruction: the village was right on the front line, and by the time of the Armistice, nearly every house had been razed to the ground by the Kaiser's artillery. One palatial mansion appears to have survived—or at least it was rebuilt after the war. This was, and is still, the property of the Louis Roederer family.

Jérôme Prévost produces just one wine, from old Pinot Meunier vines. The result is often the most intense and exotically spicy Meunier Champagne in the region

Right opposite the mansion is a charming little 1920s cottage that is home to one of Champagne's bravest small growers. Jérôme Prévost inherited his family's 2.2ha (5.4-acre) vineyard at the age of 21, in 1987. Being a smallholder, he was obliged at first to sell his grapes to the local cooperative. Eleven years later, Jérôme saw the chance to buy the cottage. It had good outhouses as well as an unusual but very practical "cellar", which was an old armaments store during World War I—durable enough to survive the bombardments of the enemy and a stable place to age fine wine.

He started to produce his own wine in 1998, thanks to the invaluable help given to him by the great Avize grower Anselme Selosse, who made space for Jérôme in his winery at harvest time. This arrangement continued for the next three vintages. Since then, the wine has been made back in Gueux. Note the singular noun—wine: Jérôme produces just the one, from old Pinot Meunier vines

planted in the 1960s. He aerates the soil by plough and applies biodynamic preparations to the plants. La Closerie is always the wine of a single year, fermented in oak, mainly barriques. Contrary to the received wisdom, the wine ages for a shorter time on indigenous yeasts in cask, rather than for a longer time on selected lees in bottle.

The result is often the most intense and exotically spicy Meunier Champagne in the region. Yet in each vintage, the venerable *cépage* says something different to the winemaker and the drinker. The 2006 is lithe and forward, with an attractive elegance; the 2005 is deeper, intense, and very vinous; the 2003 celebrates the wonderful fruit of the Meunier—indeed, in the extreme heat of that remarkable summer, it was actually the most successful variety. As it approaches maturity, the 2000 has a freshness and purity of fruit that gets better by the moment. *Dosage* is very moderate (4 g/l or less), well within the Extra Brut category.

Jérôme, a man of artistic sensibilities, is also something of a poet: read his back label, and you will see what I mean.

FINEST WINES

(Tasted in Gueux, January 2009)

Jérôme Prévost La Closerie Cuvée Les Béguines ★ Although officially a Non-Vintage Champagne, this is always a wine from a single year and barely *dosé*. Burnished gold from its extended spell in cask; toasty, spicy expression of very fine, pure Pinot Meunier aromas—like brioche fresh from the oven. Broad and rich, but impeccably balanced and intense. A masterly use of oak.

Right: The artistic Jérôme Prévost, who is one of the most courageous and creative of Champagne's many growers

Champagne Jérôme Prévost
2 Rue de la Petite Montagne,
51390 Gueux
Tel: +33 3 26 03 48 60
champagnelacloserie@orange.fr

Aÿ and the Vallée de la Marne

Crossing the Marne from Epernay, skirting the suburb of Magenta, a straight road takes you 2.5 miles (4km) northeast to Aÿ, one of the three great wine towns of Champagne. It may be the smallest of the three—more a large village, with only 800 inhabitants—but in terms of the Champagnes that are made here, it has the greatest reputation. To get an inkling of why it is such a special place for the vine, it is best to approach it from Dizy, on the western side. On your left, the majestic vineyards, the finest facing due south, slope down from the Montagne, the little town below, guarding the entrance to the Marne River valley.

During the Renaissance, Aÿ was known as the best *vin de la rivière*. Pope Leo the Magnificent, the patron of Michelangelo and Leonardo, was a Champenois who always ordered Aÿ wine for his own consumption; and several European monarchs in the 16th and 17th centuries drank the pale red of Aÿ in preference to Burgundy. Today very few red Champenois wines can be spoken of in the same breath as anything from the Côte d'Or or the Chalonnais, but one that makes a brave stab at it is the Aÿ rouge of Pierre Cheval of Gatinois.

The Champagne trade in Aÿ is dominated by some genuinely great houses—Deutz, Gosset, the recently much-revived Ayala, and, most famous of all, Bollinger. Yet in recent years some talented growers have come to challenge the *grandes maisons* as the standard-bearers of the finest wines of Aÿ. Great pure Pinot Noirs in different styles, depending on the exact location of their parcels and the winemaking style, include the aromatically complex, dense, but velvet-textured Cuvée Sire La Pelle of Roger Brun, the muscular yet super-fine, non-oaked, Les Noirs d'Aÿ of Gosset-Brabant, and the subtle silk and satin Vauzelle Terme of Jacquesson. Perhaps the most seductive of all is Claude Giraud's Cuvée Fût de Chêne, a rich, sumptuous, unapologetically oak-fermented Champagne, chiefly from the *lieu-dit* Les Valnons, artfully lightened with a little Chardonnay. These are some of the most striking wines in Aÿ.

Mareuil-sur-Aÿ

Just to its east, Mareuil-sur-Aÿ is officially not quite a grand cru—graded at 99 per cent on the *échelle des crus*—but its producers like to quote the old saying, "Aÿ has the reputation, but Mareuil has the wine." They are half-right. Certainly the best sites of Mareuil, especially the superb south-facing Clos des Goisses at the east end of the village, are vineyards second to none in Champagne, and sources of some of the most memorably special bottles. But on the other side from the Goisse hill, behind the statue of the Virgin, the soils are heavier and much less interesting—the rueful insight of Christian Gosset of Gosset-Brabant, who owns vineyards in Mareuil, so he should know.

But soil isn't quite everything. For several observers, currently the greatest wine in Mareuil is Billecart-Salmon's Clos St-Hilaire, from a small garden-like plot behind the family house, of correct but hardly exceptional aspect; and the subsoils are *tuffe*-like limestone and clay rather than classic chalk. Against the odds, the pure Pinot Noir made here can be magnificent (especially the 1996), but this has as much to do with the winemaking of François Domi, Billecart's gifted *chef de cave*, as with the terroir.

A fine 10ha (25-acre) Mareuil estate now gaining the recognition it deserves is Bénard-Pitois, for many years a regular supplier of great grapes to Pol Roger. The Bénard Réserve Brut shows a mastery of oak in a blend of 60 per cent Pinot Noir and 40 per cent Chardonnay; the finished Champagne is complex and deep yet florally fragrant with a touch of vanilla.

Right: Autumn sunrise over Aÿ, whose wines have been sought out by discriminating customers for centuries

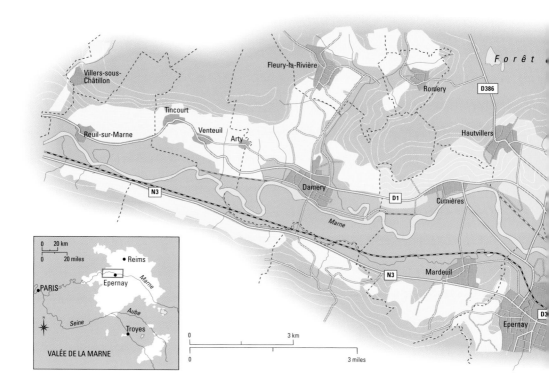

Up behind Mareuil, the premier cru village of Bisseuil is a good source of Chardonnay; nearby Tauxières also, for Pinot Noir. Down in the valley along the road to Châlons, lies Tours-sur-Marne, the last grand cru for Pinot Noir grapes only. The village is the HQ of Laurent-Perrier, in terms of turnover, the most successful, still family-owned business in Champagne. Across the street is A Charvet, a good small négociant with a 10ha (25-acre) vineyard. Their Carte Blanche is a well-aged blend of four years, with expressive flavours of Pinot Noir and Chardonnay. Their 1996 vintage is one of the best and deserves to be better known.

Dizy

Returning to Aÿ, retrace your tracks westwards over the hills and through the vineyards. On this second viewing, you begin to appreciate more fully what a big area the famous cru covers, with every aspect, north, south, east, and west—which, to be candid, results in a wide range of quality. After a couple of miles, you arrive in the premier cru village of Dizy, dropping down past the handsome church. On your left, is a handsome old house with a *clos* of vines *à la Bourguinonne* and a fine, traditional stone-built cuverie on the other side of the road full of large oak *foudres*. These are the premises of one of Champagne's most sought-after bijou houses, Jacquesson, which is owned and run by the passionate Chiquet brothers. They have an enviable inheritance of 30ha (75 acres) of vineyards in Dizy, Aÿ, Hautvillers, and Avize. Jean-Hervé Chiquet is the urbane face of the house—a charming, very humane man, warm and

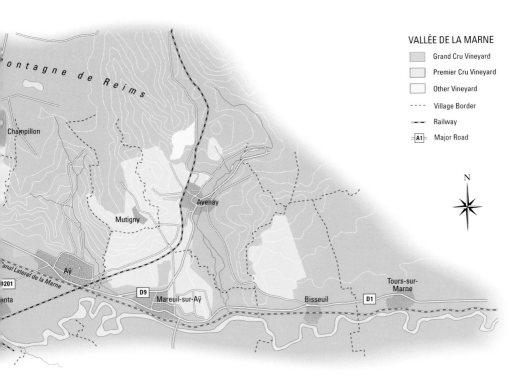

VALLÉE DE LA MARNE

- Grand Cru Vineyard
- Premier Cru Vineyard
- Other Vineyard
- ---- Village Border
- Railway
- A1 Major Road

N

Champillon

Avenay

Mutigny

Aÿ

D9

Mareuil-sur-Aÿ

Bisseuil

D1

Tours-sur-Marne

Montagne de Reims

Canal Latéral de la Marne

201

sophisticated, with a fine, mordant sense of humor and a love of his land. He is sometimes depicted as the businessman, but until the 1988 vintage he used to make the wines, too, with an admirably light and sensitive touch. His Jacquesson Prestige Signature 1988 is one of the very best Champagnes of that very great year. His brother, Laurent, a former architect, now makes the wines.

They are certainly extremely serious wines of real character and substance, nearly all the cuvées fermented in large oak tuns. I do, though, occasionally miss the simple delicious fruitiness of their old entry-level Champagne, called Perfection, which gave the purest pleasure without much, if any, help from a wooden stave. Its replacement, the numbered cuvées 728–735, is an interesting concept that tries to make the best

Non-Vintage wine that the most recent year and majority element in the blend can give, rather than trying to replicate the same style, year after year—character and individuality is the aim, rather than a consistent taste. These Champagnes strike me as wines for the table rather than apéritifs. I also have slightly divided feelings about the Jacquesson range of single-vineyard Champagnes. Since 2002, their prize Avize cuvée has been made from the one *lieu-dit* of Champ Gain, rather than three sites within the village, which gave the finished cuvée more complexity—certainly so in the case of the magnificent 1996. The Aÿ Vauzelle Terme, in fairness, is always classy and delicious, and so is their new baby, the Terres Rouges Saignée Rosé, from a vineyard on the border of Dizy and Hautvillers.

To experience a wholly different style of Champagne from another branch of the same family, walk five minutes down the road to the domaine of Gaston Chiquet in the Avenue du Général Leclerc. This estate is also managed by two brothers, Antoine and Nicolas, cousins of Jean-Hervé and Laurent. Here there is no wood in the cellar, the philosophy being one of more evolved tradition rather than the studied classical approach of Jacquesson. In the Gaston vineyards, meticulous tending of the plants and soils is obvious across the 23ha (57 acres) that the domaine owns in Aÿ and Hautvillers, as well as a new hectare of vines in the Valley of the Ardre close to Reims. They have particularly good vineyards on the mid-slopes of Dizy.

In the cellar, the best automated modern press works above deep cellars for long aging of the wines. Nicolas Chiquet is a quiet and thoughtful winemaker who always protects the natural pure fruit in his Champagnes while investing them with subtle complexities and perfect balance. Fine cuvées for the connoisseur these wines undoubtedly are, but they are also Champagnes of pleasure for everyone. Nicolas's Blanc d'Aÿ is a rare all-Chardonnay wine from the cru most famous for Pinot Noir—a rich, luxuriously textured Champagne that speaks more vividly of its origins than of the grape variety. The 2000 Vintage here is a great success, having far more charm, personality, and vinosity than the easy 1999, which some Champenois at the time of writing are trying to convince the outside world is an excellent one. There is no risk whatever that Nicolas would mistake a goose for a swan in that way. The Gaston Chiquet Special Club 1998 (a genuinely fine year) is a lovely wine: butter, brioche, and vanilla scents of Chardonnay, opulent in the mouth, with a hint of chocolate that is more Pinot in character. This is clearly a first-rate estate.

Hautvillers

For those with stout calf muscles, it is an invigorating walk from Dizy up to Hautvillers, which must be the most perfectly situated village in Champagne. In AD 650, St Nivard, the archbishop of Reims, was so inspired by the vision of a celestial dove alighting on one of its oak trees that he gave instructions for a monastery, St Pierre d'Hautvillers, to be built here. He could not have chosen a better place for a life of prayer and contemplation—on the southern edge of the Montagne de Reims, with heavenly views over the Marne Valley towards Epernay, the Côte des Blancs, and the plain of Châlons to the left beyond. Hautvillers was to become one of the most famous abbeys in Europe. A thousand years after its foundation, the Benedictine monk Dom Pierre Pérignon was probably making some of the first sparkling Champagne here. And it is always a memorable experience to be invited to taste great vintages of the famous cuvée that bears his name in an airy room off the old cloister, where it all began.

The village itself, with its honey-coloured stone houses, is delightful, and the wine from its south-facing slopes has always been good since at least the time of the Capetian kings of France. The Hautvillers Champagne I know best is Tribaut-Schloesser, founded in 1929 by a family of Champenois and Alsatian origin at nearby Romery. Their 20ha (50-acre) vineyard is planted mainly to Pinot Noir and Pinot Meunier, but there is also some Chardonnay. The straight Tradition Brut is a generous Champagne pervaded with the peach and apricot flavours of fine black grapes. Hautvillers also has a good cooperative producing good Champagnes, made, I remember, by a pretty, liberated young woman who did not like to be called "Madame".

Right: The Abbey of Hautvillers, founded in AD 650, at the top of the most perfectly situated village in Champagne

Cumières to Château-Thierry

Just below Hautvillers to the southwest, the premier cru village of Cumières probably has the sunniest slopes in the Marne Valley and certainly produces one of Champagne's most interesting red wines. René and Jean-Baptiste Geoffroy make the best Champagnes in the village. Duval-Leroy produces a very good pure Cumières Champagne in its Authentis range, and Pascal Leclerc-Briant makes another that would be better were it to be given more aging before release. Down into the valley, the bijou cooperative of Beaumont des Crayères at Mardeuil produces excellent wines from growers with small plots of vines, allowing for very tight control over the quality of grapes and meticulous parcel-by-parcel vinifications.

A little farther west, the village of Oeuilly is home to Jean-Mary Tarlant, one of the region's most distinguished growers, and a particularly fine exponent of the use of oak in Champagne-making. His majestic Cuvée Louis vies with Champagne's greatest wines and is the more impressive for coming from relatively modest terroirs on the south bank of the Marne.

Farther along, off the Dormans road, the cooperative of Leuvrigny has growers who own parcels in a superb amphitheatre of vines that catches the sun from every aspect at some time during the day. So it is not surprising that this co-op is a favourite source of Meunier for some of the greatest houses—Billecart-Salmon, Pol Roger, and Louis Roederer especially.

On the northern banks of the river at this point there are some exceptional producers. In Damery, the two best producers are Louis Casters and AR Lenoble; the latter estate was founded by a wine-loving Reims surgeon between the two world wars and now extends to 18ha (45 acres), including a prize slice of Chouilly at the top of the Côte des Blancs. Reuil, below Châtillons-sur-Marne, is the village where the legendary René Collard created

some of the longest-lived Champagnes entirely from Meunier. His son Daniel and grandson Olivier maintain the family's high standards, managing their own estates farther up the hill.

As you move westwards from Châtillons-sur-Marne, the soils become heavier, the chalk disappearing as the Marne flows towards Château-Thierry. According to American geologist James Wilson, author of *Terroir*, the geological strata here dip slowly into the Paris Basin, the Tertiary

Above: The broad sweep of vineyards in the Marne Valley means they are exposed to the north, south, east, and west

strata of marls and lignite clays in particular becoming more dominant as the chalk drops deeper underground. In Château-Thierry is the house of Pannier, founded in the 1970s as a cooperative of Champagne growers. Today the firm offers a range of very well-made Champagnes from grapes from the Montagne de Reims and Côte des Blancs, as well as the western Marne— all at attractive prices. Beyond the town, vineyards continue in little pockets as far as Charly and Nanteuil-sur-Marne, about 35 miles (55km) from Paris. This stretch of the Marne, as it broadens out and meanders towards the capital, is extremely pretty, the hilltops covered with woods of beech and oak, and golden wheatfields in summer surrounded by charming villages. Luckily, it has all been expressed for posterity in the paintings of Corot and the fables of La Fontaine.

Bollinger

Bollinger is the most uncompromising of the *grandes maisons*, having a certain classical idea of Champagne based on a very proud tradition. The house's attachment to the land goes back to the 15th century, when the de Villermont family, ancestors of current chairman Ghislain de Montgolfier, acquired vineyards in Cuis.

The house was founded at Aÿ in 1829 by Joseph Bollinger, a Swabian from Württemberg, and Paul Renaudin, a Champenois. Renaudin soon left the firm, though his name remained on the labels for 130 years. In the meantime, Bollinger had married a de Villermont and expanded the business rapidly. In 1865, he became one of the first merchants to ship a drier style of Champagne to England, and in 1870 to the United States. Later, the brand was ably represented in America by Julius Wile, the great New York wine merchant, until 1988.

During World War II, the widowed Madame Lily Bollinger took charge of the house. With no gasoline available to her under the German occupation, she toured the family vineyards on foot and bicycle. Remarkably, despite a totally depleted workforce, she continued to make and sell Champagne and, with a devoted companion, slept in the Bollinger cellars during Allied bombardments, including the American raid of 10 August 1944, which destroyed a third of Aÿ.

After the war, Tante Lily (as she was affectionately known to her family) bought prime vineyards in Aÿ, Grauves, Bisseuil, and Champvoisy, bringing Bollinger's wine estate up towards the level of the house's current holdings of 178ha (440 acres). These vineyards supply a little over two thirds of the company's needs, which gives Bollinger an edge over its competitors, particularly today when a major concern is the provision of grapes to meet the demand for Champagne in new markets such as Russia, China, and India.

Right: Ghislain de Montgolfier, ideally qualified by background and education to head this distinguished family firm

*Bollinger is the most uncompromising of the grandes maisons,
having a certain classical idea of Champagne based on a
very proud tradition*

Bollinger's rigorous approach to Champagne-making is based on its insistence on using only high-quality grapes from vineyards in the Marne. I remember once being given a firm but friendly talking-to by the late Christian Bizot, Lily Bollinger's nephew and successor, about how grapes from the Aube could never make great Champagne. Twenty years on, that looks like a questionable view. But Bollinger typically is standing its ground, which reinforces its image as a guardian of quality and exponent of the most classic style of Marnais Champagne—good, sound marketing, of course. In fairness, the house's use of highly rated grapes, and the juice from only the first pressings, results in generally excellent must, constituted strongly enough to allow for fermentation in wood for its Vintage Champagnes—Bollinger's glories.

Here the first fermentation is preferably conducted in small oak barrels, nowadays in Burgundy *pièces* from Bollinger's filial company Chanson, an old négociant house in Beaune. For Ghislain de Montgolfier, the barrel is "the life insurance for our grands vins". Bollinger is not looking for aromas of wood or for tannins in its Champagnes. New oak is avoided at all costs, the span of Burgundy *pièces* selected being normally between three and six years of age, though larger, often older casks are also used. Yet not all wines are suitable for oak fermentation, especially those that are lighter and more fragile, so they are vinified in modern vats. The marriage of wood and stainless steel is best seen in Bollinger's Special Cuvée Non-Vintage—the "Bolly" of its devotees' taste memory—where reserve wines stored at lower-than-usual pressure in magnum contribute to its special style. The house favours lodging reserve wines in magnums for more stable maturation, avoiding oxidation.

Interestingly, a little while back, when the time came to appoint a new *chef de cave*, Montgolfier wanted to have someone with an open mind, a candidate not steeped in the ways and preconceptions of Champagne. He chose a talented Alsacien, Mathieu Kauffmann. Together they have taken Bollinger to new heights, especially at the level of the vintage-dated Grande Année—the 1990, 1995, 1996, and remarkable 1997 are all exceptional. By contrast, it is a little difficult to understand their decision to pass over the 1998—generally one of the finest vintages of the decade—in favour of the 1999, which, for all its ripe, forward fruit, is not a great year for the long haul. (Nor is the unique "2003 by Bollinger", delicious though it is.)

No such qualms about Bollinger's RD (Recently Disgorged) Champagnes, which are released only in exceptional years. RD is a concept unique to Bollinger, of which there is no real equivalent in the Champagne community. There are other houses that very occasionally disgorge an exceptional wine quite late in its maturity, but none does it with the élan or regularity as this aristocratic firm has done since 1952. Before it eventually becomes an RD, this wine is originally a Grande Année, the prestigious Vintage Champagne of Bollinger, but in its reincarnation as RD it is one that has matured for a much longer period, from eight to 20 years, sometimes more. Throughout its long aging, RD develops subtle and multifaceted aromas, as well as creating a unique vinous style that is Bollinger's expression of great, expansive Pinot Noir, but it minds its manners in the company of elegant Chardonnay, which represents just under a third of the blend. RD vintages still generally available are the recently released 1997, less voluptuous than the Grande Année; the monumental 1996, still needing time; the lovely 1995, an ideal balance of body and finesse; and the magnificent 1988, now near full maturity, with that touch of austerity and tension of a real classic.

Bollinger's Vieilles Vignes Françaises (VVF) is the house's rarest Champagne. "To talk about this wine cultivated in the historic manner is to fling oneself into the past and boldly confront the archetypal taste of Champagne," says Montgolfier.

Above: Some of the small oak barrels, none of them new, used for the fermentation of Bollinger's Vintage cuvées

Pinot Noir was the only grape available in the 17th century, when the first sparkling Champagnes were made. Some 300 years later, the English journalist Cyril Ray was so astounded by the wines from Bollinger's ancient Pinot vines, these *vieilles vignes françaises*, that in 1969 he persuaded Madame Lily Bollinger to bottle them separately. Two tiny plots by the Bollinger house (a third in Bouzy succumbed to phylloxera in the late 1990s, causing the tiny stocks to dwindle further) still yield minuscule quantities of very intense wine from untrained vines that are allowed to sprawl close to the earth (*en foule*), absorbing the full heat of the soil for optimal ripeness. The 1998 is a classic, the power of the wine in balance with a finesse so characteristic of the year. The 1999 has more showy fruit but is softer and no marathon runner.

Bollinger's new cuvée—the first in 40 years—is its new Non-Vintage Rosé, which has lovely pure Pinot fruit, but as you would expect, there is a real wine behind the bubbles.

FINEST WINES

(Tasted June 2008 and January 2009)
Bollinger Special Cuvée Brut NV
Pale, brilliant gold, then the strong impression of ripe grapes from excellent base wine (2004), which results in vivid, red-fruit flavours and what tastes like a significant proportion of magnum-aged reserve wines. Mellow and fine. Immaculate balance.

Bollinger Grande Année 2000★
A welcome return to form in this fine 2000, better in every respect than the 1999: lovely, lustrous gold signalling an exuberant fruitiness and serious depth of flavour. Real charm, too: shades of the great '97.

Bollinger RD 1997
After tasting the Grande Année '97, this is a surprise at every level. Light, youthful gold; notably brisk acidity, crisp on the nose; athletic and racy, even a touch of leanness on the palate. The richness of the Grande Année is not there at the moment, making me wonder when this was disgorged.

Bollinger RD 1988
Gently evolved colour, green tints among the gold; the mousse more apparent and gently energizing on the palate; evolved, tertiary, oxygenated scents, green fruits, a touch of rancio—superb. Very complex flavours of maturity, ripe and vinous, yet still wonderfully fresh, with a classic end note of austerity. Outstanding.

Champagne Bollinger
Rue Jules Lobet, BP4, 51160 Aÿ
Tel: +33 3 26 53 33 66
www.champagne-bollinger.fr

Henri Giraud

Claude Giraud is one of the most engaging and interesting producers in Champagne. Bon vivant and most hospitable of men, he straddles the different worlds of grower and merchant with effortless ease. Claude always looks cheerful—hardly surprising, since he has had a head start in life. His family have been winemakers in Aÿ since the 17th century, and today he owns some of the finest vineyards, evenly spread across 30 parcels in 14 *lieux-dits*. With such fabulous grapes to call on, it is natural that Claude should be a committed exponent of oak, crafting some truly opulent wines. His approach to the whole subject is impressively honest and thorough. Logically, Claude concluded that his famous cru of Aÿ would best achieve a perfect affinity with oak from the Champenois forest of the Argonne, southeast of Aÿ near Sainte Ménehould. This little town was the birthplace of Madeleine Hémart, Claude's grandmother, who as a young girl had fallen in love with a cavalryman called Léon Giraud in need of shelter after the battle of the Marne. They soon got married.

Family history and sentiment were on Claude's side as the gentle, flattering Argonne oak had proved a natural nursery for the delicate wines of Champagne right up to the end of the 19th century. Until very recently, however, it had been virtually impossible to guarantee the origin of a particular type of oak. Undaunted by the challenge, Claude sought the advice of his old friend Camille Gauthier, a cutter of oak with an unrivalled knowledge of the Argonne forest and an experienced taster. Staves were cut and dried then sent to Vicard in Cognac, who made them into barrels and returned them to Aÿ. About a third of Henri Giraud Champagnes are now vinified in Argonne oak *pièces* of 228 litres.

Inevitably, since Claude Giraud has been the first man to reintroduce certified Argonne wood into winemaking in the Marne, decades after its

Right: Cheerful Claude Giraud, whose family has owned some of the finest Aÿ vineyards since the 17th century

*Claude always looks cheerful—hardly surprising, since he has had a
head start in life. His family have been winemakers in Aÿ since the
17th century, and today he owns some of the finest vineyards*

disappearance from Champagne, a fair amount of that oak is new. But as the result of continuing trials, comparing several types of oxidative and reductive winemaking, and different types of oak, it is quite clear that given proper aging in bottle (say eight to ten years) the wood in the house's Vintage Champagnes is easily assimilated. Much of this success is due to the ongoing research into oak that Claude continues each year with Château Latour.

The Henri Giraud Aÿ Grand Cru Fût de Chêne Cuvée may be the most complex Champagne in Aÿ. I venture to put my neck on the block because of the perfect and varied siting of those 30 parcels in 14 *lieux-dits*. Just two examples illustrate the point. The south-facing Les Valnons, lying close to the town in one of Aÿ's most prestigious valleys, is where Léon Giraud planted his best vines 75 years ago. He chose well, because the Pinot Noirs here have really broad shoulders, giving wines of calm force without loss of panache. In complete contrast, westwards, with the slopes facing east, Vauregnier (also known as La Cotelette) catches the early morning sun, its wines imbued with delicate minerality and tastes of mint and wild aniseed. As so often in Champagne, the surest path to greatness usually involves a little blending of sites, even at monocru level.

Inevitably, the Fût de Chêne range is among the most expensive in Champagne, though thankfully nothing like as dear as the fantasy prices now charged for certain single-vineyard Champagnes from houses powerful enough to employ marketing departments that dream up a figure and then double it. Happily, Claude has a new Champagne—Esprit de Giraud—that, with its pink brother, gives you a glimpse of the grand vin at a fraction of the price. The grape mix of all Giraud Champagnes is 70 per cent Pinot Noir, 30 per cent Chardonnay, save for the Esprit Rosé, in which the Chardonnay is reduced in favour of 8 per cent wood-fermented Aÿ rouge.

Left: One of the certified Argonne oak barrels that Claude Giraud has boldly reintroduced to the Marne Valley

FINEST WINES

(Tasted in Aÿ, January 2009)
Henri Giraud Esprit de Giraud NV ★
Thermo-regulated vinification, the wine then kept on lees in stainless steel for 12 months. Fine, golden colour. Attractive, stone-fruits nose (pear, peach) with touches of vanilla and white pepper. Fresh, vigorous mouthfeel, which assumes an elegant vinosity. Substance and minerality in fine balance.

Henri Giraud Esprit de Giraud Rosé NV
Same vinification and aging as for the Brut above. Rose-raspberry hue with orange nuances. Very fine bubbles. Intense but fine nose, crushed strawberries and biscuits on a spicy base, then scents of roses and peonies, with just a hint of oak from the Aÿ rouge. Fresh, full, round, and supple.

Henri Giraud Cuvée Fût de Chêne 1998 ★
Lovely, luminous gold. A very intense nose—confit of fruits, especially apricot, and grilled almonds—everything woven into a whole of awesome complexity. Great power on the palate, expansive, full, and very long. Fabulous *matière*, *gras*, opulent, and magnificent. More classic than the '96.

Henri Giraud Cuvée Fût de Chêne 1996
Among the best 1996s. Deep gold, light amber colour signalling the wine's power and partnership with oak. Evolving scents of vanilla and a touch of oxidative rancio character. Still pretty massive on the palate, the huge fruit and high acidity circling each other warily. A wine of exception.

Henri Giraud Cuvée Fût de Chêne 1995
Bright gold. Gently maturing nose, a real *corbeille de fruits*, yellow peaches with touches of candied lemon. A complete palate, moving upwards from primary fruits into a complex, subtly rich medley of flavours. Very classy. Oak now well integrated.

Henri Giraud Cuvée Fût de Chêne 1993
Golden robe. Confit of fruits and evolved aromas of mushrooms from great Pinot Noir; rich, honeyed palate, wood perfectly integrated, and sufficient acidity. An ace illustration of a virtual blanc de noirs from an underrated year.

Champagne Henri Giraud
71 Boulevard Charles de Gaulle, 51160 Aÿ
Tel: +33 3 26 55 18 55
www.champagne-giraud.com

Deutz

Several of Champagne's finest houses were founded in the early to mid-19th century by German immigrants from the Rhineland. William Deutz and Pierre Geldermann of Aachen were typical of these dynamic newcomers, establishing a Champagne business at Aÿ in 1838. Having first worked at Bollinger, Deutz was the accomplished winemaker, and Geldermann was (appropriately) the moneyman.

The house has always been one of the most discreet *grandes maisons*, eschewing publicity in order to focus on making classic Champagne from the best grapes in the finest villages. This concern to keep a low profile could have been embedded in the Deutz psyche by the scarring experience of the Champagne riots of 1911, when the firm's cellars were sacked by desperate growers. Not that the firm has ever lacked vigorous management—during the boom time of the 1980s, André Lallier-Deutz acquired the Rhône house Delas and sparkling-wine ventures in California and New Zealand.

However, in the aftermath of the First Gulf War (1990–91) and the ensuing crash of the Champagne market, the company looked overstretched. So, embroiled in the usual arguments with French family shareholders, Lallier finally sold 63 per cent of the company in 1993 to Louis Roederer, which has since become the owner of the business. Despite the changed ownership, the premises on Aÿ's Rue Jeanson still have the feel of the Deutz family's private residence, particularly in the fin de siècle salon and dining room. And Jean-Marc Lallier, André's son, is the company's export manager—a fine ambassador for the house, charming, articulate, and unpompous.

Since 1995 and the modernizing of the cuverie with a gleaming new extension, production has increased to 2 million bottles annually. The truly *sérieux* approach to Champagne-making that has made Deutz such a legend is alive and well. Tasting the *vins clairs* from the—how to put it?—"challenging" 2007 vintage, the Aÿ from the *lieu-dit* of La Côte was extremely impressive, with a fine attack and real depth of flavour, thanks to a properly restricted yield. Moreover, the entry-level Brut Classic—which I remember from the low period of the early '90s as table-grippingly acidic—is right back on song. Little surprise when one knows the age of the cuvée and provenance of the grapes, as at January 2008: base wine, the excellent 2004 vintage; Pinot Noir from Aÿ, Mareuil, and Bisseuil; Chardonnay from Le Mesnil and Avize; and fine Pinot Meunier from Moussy in the Cubry valley—a perfect recipe for a top Non-Vintage blend.

The vintage-dated Amour de Deutz has much more substance and vinosity than most blanc de blancs, but thanks to the light touch in the winemaking and the great grapes in the mix—largely Le Mesnil, with Avize—it retains an exceptional elegance and poise. The Brut 2002 is also a memorable expression of great Pinot Noir, which dominates the blend. This vintage is likely to be one of the top vintages for the noble black grape since World War II.

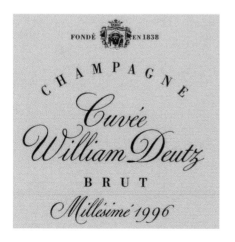

Right: Fabrice Rosset (seated), the company's CEO and chairman, and Jean-Marc Lallier of the original Deutz family

Yet it gets better. The prestige Cuvée William Deutz is, in my view, one of the three best luxury cuvées on the market—as much a very fine wine as a Champagne, and one that never needs to prove its greatness amid the big, burly flavours so prevalent today. Relying on subtle floral and herbal aromas, caressing texture, and long, multilayered flavours, it can be the ultimate apéritif for even the grandest occasion, or a natural for the table—as good with sushi and sashimi as with roast turbot or a simple tranche of Comté cheese. The 1998 vintage, as below, may turn out to be the best Cuvée William of the decade, the classic precision of the vintage perfectly suited to the subtle style of this great Champagne.

FINEST WINES

(Tasted in Aÿ, January 2008)
Deutz Classic Brut NV
Bright yellow with green reflection; fresh, frank expression of both citrus- and orchard-fruit aromas; splendid balance between a fine, vigorous attack, spirited but still gentle mousse, and a delightful fleshy roundness in the mouth. On top form.

Deutz Amour de Deutz 1999
60% Le Mesnil, 35% Avize, 5% Villers-Marmery. Youthful, pale yellow with green highlights. Classic, structured, grand Chardonnay aroma—mineral-rich; in the mouth, a real core of both citrus- and yellow-fruit flavours. The touch of Villers-Marmery adds good acidity to a Champagne that has much more about it than most '99s. 2009–18.

Deutz Cuvée William Deutz 1998★
Elegantly evolving gold with green flecks. Supreme, opulently voluptuous aromas, typical of Aÿ; lovely freshness on entry, then—with air—rich, meaty flavours return. Still very young, but with great latent complexity.

Champagne Deutz
16 Rue Jeanson, BP9, 51160 Aÿ
Tel: +33 3 26 56 94 00
www.champagne-deutz.com

Above: A statue reflecting the ethereal style of the wines, and the discreet sign of a house that has eschewed publicity

Gosset

Founded in 1584, Gosset is well known as the oldest wine house in Champagne. Wine is the operative word, for the style of this quirky family firm's creations has always been about the vinous flavours behind the mousse—as much when Albert Gosset's descendants first mastered the bubbles in the late 17th century as now, under the owning Cointreau family of Frapin Cognac.

The Cointreaus certainly insist on a continuity of old-style Champagne appropriate to its historic birthplace in Aÿ. There is little risk that this heritage will be lost under the present *chef de cave*, Jean-Pierre Mareigner, who was born in the town and lives and breathes the place in his professional and private life. Now in his 25th year with Gosset, Jean-Pierre has protected the inimitable vinous house style. But like all curious and dynamic winemakers wanting to raise their game, he has also presided over the introduction of novel cuvées that make the house more distinctive and better than ever.

In the mid-1990s, one could write a mildly sniffy note about the Gosset Brut Réserve, observing that it won more marks for flavour than for finesse. The surroundings have not changed much, but the Brut Réserve's successor, the Cuvée Excellence, is a big step up. It is a Champagne that combines delicacy, purity, depth, and abiding interest for a very reasonable price. The provenance of the 30 crus in the mix explains its high quality: good proportions of classic Chardonnay from Avize, Mesnil, Oger, and Chouilly, plus soupçons of the higher-acid examples from Trépail and Villers-Marmery that give race and dash; equally grand Pinot Noirs from Aÿ, Ambonnay, Verzenay, and Mareuil lend fine body and firmness; the supporting Meunier recruited from the best villages of Pierry, Châtillons-sur-Marne, and Reuil add volume and mouth-filling fruitiness.

The Gosset Grande Réserve has always been the fine ambassador of the house and is still so today. Made from three harvests, it is a longer matured multivintage Champagne that combines a delightful, perfumed floweriness with evolved flavours of roasted almonds and coffee, signalling the input of great Pinot and Chardonnay. A wine for food, it has enough presence to match duck or pheasant, as well as lobster or crab.

In the past, the Gosset Grand Millésime range was moulded in a highly distinctive, almost musky style that one either liked or did not: the sort of wine that takes no prisoners. So it was a very pleasant surprise to taste the excellent 1999, an exceptional success in a mercurial, mixed vintage. Made in a rigorously classic style, after eight years on lees, this Champagne remains fresh and vital, with a core of flavour missing in many '99s. It is certainly built to last (no malo) and already shows a mass of complex caramel and spice flavours that will unfurl further.

Jean-Pierre's undoubted masterpieces, first made with the enthusiastic support of the Cointreau family post-1994, are his prestige Celebris range. Be it the Celebris Blanc de Blancs (a blend of four vintages) or the Vintage 1998, both Extra Brut, these are collectors' wines whose magical melding of delicacy and strength has no need of the cosmetic help of standard *dosage* to show their beauty. The 2003 Celebris Rosé Extra Brut ★ is extraordinary. A magnificent success in a more than challenging year, it has an amazing delicacy of aromas that recalls a fine Volnay, leading on to voluptuous yet precise and lingering red-fruit flavours: *grand vin*.

FINEST WINES

(Tasted in Aÿ, November 2008)

Gosset Excellence Brut NV
42% C, 45% PN, 13% PM. *Dosage* 12g/l. Star bright, pale yellow. Even, fine, swirling bubbles, light and dancing on the tongue. Aromas show good balance of freshness and ripeness, whiffs of honeysuckle and jasmine ceding to fruity scents of pear and a touch of mango. The palate is lively and stimulating, Pinot flavours of peach and nectarine quickly establishing a grand presence. There is density and vinosity, the finish is long and fine. A model Non-Vintage.

Gosset Grand Millésime 1999 Brut

56% C, 44% PN. No malo. Fine, crystalline, pale gold, flashes of green. With seven years on lees, the nose is elegant and complex, an orchard-fruits character (apricots, peaches) enhanced by scents of lilac, honey, and a tart touch of pink grapefruit. The mouthfeel is very '99, lush and velvety, with a rush of Pinot flavours. But what gives it class is the incisive minerality of the Chardonnay, with cinnamon spice and vanilla adding further intricacies to the taste profile. Excellent. Drink to 2015.

Gosset Celebris 1998 Extra Brut

64% C, 36% PN. *Dosage* 3.5g/l. A classic, gently evolving hue for a ten-year-old wine—lovely, bright, clear gold with greenish tints and flashes of amber. Tiny bubbles form a creamy mousse, the cordon regular and persistent. Exquisite nose, at first scents of hawthorn and hedgerows, delicate yet assertive, then the finest smells of a fruit bowl—pear and peach, quince and dried apricot, with an end note of toast. The palate is a riveting, seesaw experience between the tastes of great Chardonnay and Pinot Noir—at one moment, lemon and citrus, the next, mocha and liquorice. Very complex. Superbly pure, dry finish.

Gosset Celebris Rosé 2003 Extra Brut

68% C, 32% PN, including 7% as red wine from grands crus Ambonnay and Bouzy. *Dosage* 5g/l. Given the huge challenge of intense heat during August 2003, this wine is a masterpiece, a stirring tale of the winemaker taming the elements. The colour is arresting and quite lovely—pale pink, salmon-trout hue, refined, luminous, crystal clear, but with a fleeting glint of copper signalling ripeness. Lively but lace-like flow of bubbles. Exciting scents, a mix of woodland violets and assorted herbs—all very Burgundian. To taste, this is a great wine that just happens to be sparkling: a wonderful potpourri of red berries, roses, even a touch of framboise eau de vie. Amazingly fresh finale, the low *dosage* just right for a pink Champagne, the ripeness of liquorice and the brisk spice of star anise in complete harmony.

Right: Jean-Pierre Mareigner, *chef de cave* of a house proud of its antiquity but producing its best wines now

Champagne Gosset
69 Rue Jules Blondeau, BP7, 51160 Aÿ
Tel: +33 3 26 56 99 56
www.champagne-gosset.com

Chef de cave *Jean-Pierre Mareigner was born in Aÿ and lives and breathes the place in his professional and private life. Now in his 25th year with Gosset, he has protected the inimitable vinous house style*

Ayala

The grand past of this Champagne house is symbolized by its august premises, the Château d'Aÿ, rebuilt in 1913 after it was burned to the ground during the growers' riots two years earlier. It was founded in 1860 by the Colombian diplomat Edmond de Ayala, and his bride Berthe Gabrielle d'Albrecht brought him the dowry of excellent vineyards in Aÿ and Mareuil that formed the base for the firm to become a distinguished *grande marque*, reaching its heyday in the 1920s and '30s. According to Elizabeth Bowes-Lyon, the late British Queen Mother, it was the favourite Champagne of her husband, George VI. Certainly in its very dry, unshowy, but excellent style, it matched the character of this shy but much-loved king of England, who steadied his people during the London Blitz of 1940–41.

By the end of the 20th century, weakened by stolid but unimaginative management and the Champagne crisis of 1991, the Ayala brand was in near terminal decline. In 2000, the owning Ducellier family gave up the struggle and sold out to the Jean-Jacques Frey group, which still has an impressive portfolio of wine investments in Bordeaux, Champagne, and the Rhône. Frey installed Thierry Budin, ex-director of Perrier-Jouët, who understood fine Champagne and did his best to restore the company's reputation. In 2005, Ayala was bought by the Bollinger group, the directors being clearly impressed by the potential of the wines. Ayala was reborn and has since prospered.

The recent success and more visible profile of the Ayala brand is due to the flair and judgment of Ghislain de Montgolfier, Bollinger's emeritus president and a distinguished agronomist. Montgolfier had the imagination to appoint his team's energetic marketing man Hervé Augustin to head Ayala. Always dressed with his trademark bow tie, Augustin had earlier restored the fortunes of De Castellane in the 1990s; even now, his colourful neckware always reminds me of that house's exceptional butterfly collection.

More tellingly, the two men quickly put in place the building blocks of recovery by taking a close look at Ayala's Non-Vintage range. The duo decided to make a real virtue of Ayala's famously dry style in a completely sugarless Champagne, launching a new fighting cuvée called Brut Zéro. This wine has succeeded because of the blend's excellent grapes, which have a high average rating of 93 per cent on the *échelle des crus*, and which, at least at the outset, came from ripe and sunny years such as 2002. Brut Zéro has been a tremendous success in the Champagne-by-the-glass market in London restaurants—perhaps a little too much so, since mature stocks had been exhausted by late 2008, and of necessity the base wine in the blend passed on to a younger vintage, to be released sooner than may be desirable for an Extra Brut Champagne.

A step up in qualitative terms, Ayala also makes a near-sugarless new rosé called Cuvée Rosé Nature, with a high proportion of premier cru Chardonnay and strong support from grand cru Pinot Noir, all from the outstanding 2002 vintage. This *assemblage* shows a particularly succulent ripeness that needs only minimal *dosage* to round it out into a lovely pink Champagne, great with sushi, salmon, and Asian treatments of spicy lamb.

The Ayala Vintage Champagnes are on song right now, as impressive in difficult years as in dream ones, and always fairly priced for their quality. The Cuvée Perle Brut Nature Blanc carries a vintage label and majors on Chardonnay, making four fifths of the blend, which, like the remaining Pinot Noir, comes from grand and premier cru sites. Although the wine receives no *dosage*, 2g of residual sugar per litre are artfully left in the wine to obviate any aggressively acidic edge. The 2002 has the sumptuous yet delicate elegance of a great year; the 2001 is leaner but with very pure fruit and great acidity.

Above: Hervé Augustin, sporting his trademark bow tie, outside Ayala's impressive premises at Château d'Aÿ

FINEST WINES

(Tasted in Epernay, October 2008)

Ayala Brut Nature Zéro Dosage [V]
48% PN, 34% C, 18% PM from great sites: Aÿ, Mareuil-sur-Aÿ, Bouzy, and Rilly (PN); Cramant, Mesnil, and Cuis (C); St-Martin d'Ablois and Venteuil (PM). Pale gold with green highlights. Punchy acidity on the nose. Potential depth and richness on the palate, but this blend, for now, tastes too young, the acids puckeringly brisk. Needs food and six to nine months. A 2004 or 2005 base?

Ayala Cuvée Rose Nature
53% C (Cuis, Vertus), 39% PN (Mareuil–sur-Aÿ, Verzy, Rilly), and 8% added red wine (Mareuil old-vines Pinot). Just a flick of residual sugar left in its Brut Nature state. Delicate pale salmon, with a flow of superfine bubbles. The intense aromas are led by Pinot Noir from a great vintage (2002), with the succulent fruitiness of the old-vine red wine. The high proportion of Chardonnay helps to give impeccably fresh, delicate, and poised flavours. Long and very fine.

Ayala Cuvée Perle d'Ayala 2002
80% C, 20% PN (all grands and premiers crus). *Dosage* 6.5g/l. Crystalline pale yellow with gold and amber hints. Lovely Chardonnay-led aromas of white flowers and lemon, and a note of white peaches. The palate is generous and open—peaches again and rich vanilla—nicely oxygenated, and multifaceted, thanks to being aged under a clamped, natural cork (not a crown cap). Class.

(Tasted August 2008)

Ayala Cuvée Perle d'Ayala 2001
Lemon green-gold, evolving colour, a certain leanness on the nose, but the quality of the fruit on the palate is irreproachable, signalling rigorous selection of the grapes. The acid structure is also admirable and will mellow gently with age (drink 2009–11). An excellent result and something of a miracle in this very difficult vintage.

Ayala 1999
Quickly evolving, medium-deep pastel yellow. Wispy, appley nose mingled with white flowers. Decent palate, if high-toned; fruity, easy rather than complex, but pleasant drinking. Very '99.

Champagne Ayala
2 Boulevard de Nord, BP36, 51160 Aÿ
Tel: +33 3 26 55 15 44
www.champagne-ayala.fr

Roger Brun

Vignerons since before the French Revolution, the Bruns are a well-known family in Aÿ, conceived with a visceral love for the town that was a cradle for the original 17th-century sparkling Champagnes made purely from Pinot Noir. Long before Dom Pérignon noticed the first bubbles in his early Champagnes around 1690, Aÿ was famous for its still wines, tinted a light red by the Pinot skins. Henry VIII, the Tudor king of England, would drink little else, and even as late as the 1850s, Pol Roger, in the early years of his Epernay house, regularly received orders specifically for the sparkling cuvées of Aÿ, where he too was born.

Roger Brun's great-grandfather, a cooper and red-wine maker, learned the art of Champagne-making while working for Moët & Chandon during the phylloxera crisis of the early 1900s. Philippe

Vignerons since before the French Revolution, the Bruns are well known in Aÿ, the town that was a cradle for the original 17th-century sparkling Champagnes

Brun, Roger's son, is now fully involved in the business and winemaking, and also has a fine bed-and-breakfast hotel, Le Logis des Pressureurs, right at the heart of Aÿ by the church. From their own vines, including a slice of the superb, early-ripening Aÿ *lieu-dit* of La Pelle, the Bruns make six cuvées, the entry-level Brut Réserve coming from grapes brought to the Brun presshouse from growers in 15 villages around Epernay. Intended as an apéritif wine, ideal for parties, this Champagne is Meunier-dominated (50 per cent vinified in stainless steel, with the malo induced, and then rested for six months). Traditionally dosed (11g/l), it is a charming, fruit-driven Champagne, but with the ameliorating presence of good Chardonnay and a touch of Pinot Noir. The Brut Grande Réserve is a step up for those

who like Pinot Noir. The great black grape makes up 60 per cent, the Meunier 10 per cent, Chardonnay accounting for the rest. In sum, this is probably the most typical of the wines from bought-in grapes, all from six premiers crus. Easy to drink, but with a capacity to age, all this is great value.

Now on to the exceptional Roger Brun Champagnes that really count. The Brut Rosé is very special: 100 per cent Pinot from the *lieux-dits* of Cumaine in Mareuil-sur-Aÿ and Grimbaud in Mutigny, it has a deep salmon, quasi-ruby hue because its colour is obtained not by the usual Champenois method of adding a little red wine, but by the much harder practice of *saigné*. The word means "bled", and the colour pigments in the Pinot skins are allowed to seep into the juice for a day or two to obtain the exact hue desired. In January 2007, after a long day's tasting, I felt pleasantly tired at the final appointment with Philippe. To cap the early evening, he opened a bottle of the 2005 Rosé. Wow! A shimmering, forceful hue reflecting the heat of that autumn, while the taste is akin to fine red Burgundy—a splendid Champagne for air-dried meats, sushi, and aged cheeses like Tome de Savoie.

Ever upwards, the Réserve Grand Cru is made only from Aÿ grapes, four fifths Pinot Noir, the rest Chardonnay, with 50 per cent reserve wine from the same blend. A wine for fine cuisine—young partridge, maybe, or roast chicken or guinea fowl, or again a *paillard de veau*.

Finally, two truly great wines fermented in oak. The Cuvée des Sires, a classic Aÿ 70/30 mix of Pinot and Chardonnay, has strength and finesse in equal measure, lemony aromas ceding to butter and toast with the years. At the summit, the single-vineyard version of the Cuvée des Sires from the La Pelle *lieu-dit* is a pure Pinot vinified in oak barrels—a forceful, muscular wine for dishes like grilled lobster or even Cantonese lamb with coriander.

Right: *Le style c'est l'homme même* (the style is the man): Philippe Brun crafts muscular, powerful Aÿ-based wines

FINEST WINES

(Tasted January 2008)

Roger Brun Réserve Grand Cru NV [V]
All Aÿ grapes. Typical aromas of apricot and apple.
Powerful, rounded mouthfeel, the Chardonnay
lending lift. A fine gastronomic Champagne.

Roger Brun Brut Rosé Premier Cru NV
This wine is from the very warm 2005 harvest, but
it does not carry a vintage label. Terrific, intense
but still elegant colour; soaring scents of Pinot Noir
and little red fruits; a gorgeous sensual palate of
raspberries, apricots, and yellow peaches, framed
with a real vinosity. Exceptional.

Roger Brun Cuvée des Sires Aÿ-La Pelle 2002★
A really powerful blanc de noirs, being pure Pinot
Noir from a top vineyard site. Deep, burnished
gold; profoundly scented, the aromatic fruitiness
tinged with the voluptuousness of the terroir. A
masculine wine of wondrous vinosity, which should
be reserved for the greatest dishes, especially
rich seafood or any sort of meat. Not a dance-hall
Champagne. Outstanding.

Champagne Roger Brun
1 Impasse St Vincent, 51210 Aÿ
Tel: +33 3 26 55 45 50
www.champagne-roger-brun.com

Gatinois

Pierre Cheval is one of the best small growers in Aÿ, but he looks more like a senior civil servant, which is perhaps explained by his unusual background. Pierre was born in the neighbouring Ardennes and, after studying in Paris, could easily have become a politician and a member of the ruling elite. But he came to Champagne as a young man, then fell in love with and married a Mademoiselle Gatinois, whose family had been growers in Aÿ since 1696.

Gatinois is actually best known for its excellent Aÿ rouge—a still red Pinot Noir that, in great years like 2002, comes closer than most others to the quality of decent Burgundy. The Champagnes from the family's 6.9ha (17-acre) estate of grand cru grapes are intense and long-lived, thanks to the high proportion of old vines, 90 per cent planted to Pinot Noir on the hillsides, and 10 per cent to Chardonnay on the chalkier soils at the bottom of the slopes.

The Champagnes from the 6.9ha (17-acre) Gatinois estate of grand cru grapes are intense and long-lived, thanks to the high proportion of old vines

As finished Champagnes, they are another example of being old-fashioned in the best sense. Deep-coloured and strongly constituted, they deserve storing for several years to show themselves at their best. The entry-level Grand Cru Tradition Brut, though officially a blanc, has a perceptible pinkish tinge and an assertive yet round fruitiness, the result of intricate blending from 29 *lieux-dits* on the estate and at least three years' aging on lees before release. There is a lot of wine here for your dollar. The Gatinois Réserve is made from a blend of two slightly older vintages and has a vinosity that comes from that extra time in bottle. The Vintage wines are quite special and, if you have a deep cellar,

are worth storing for your retirement or a very special wedding anniversary. A bottle of the 1988, drunk in 1994, was deceptively fine and delicate, for it had an iron-like strength behind the bubbles. The 2002 will be a classic—riper and more opulent than the 1988.

FINEST WINES

(Tasted in Aÿ, January 2007)
Gatinois Grand Cru Brut NV
If ever there was an entry-level Champagne that really tasted of its origins, this is it. Pure Aÿ, dominated by Pinot Noir, the colour is a restrained yellow with a faint hint of pink rose. Assertive, palate-filling, and round, this is a perfect winter Champagne for a fireside supper, though it will still taste pretty special on any other occasion.

Gatinois Brut Vintage 2002
90% PN, 10% C. Lustrous gold. Sensuous, perfectly textured grand cru Pinot Noir drives this great Champagne, its *gras* mouthfeel taming and harmonizing the inherent power and strength of the old vines. Also typically 2002, there is a lovely freshness coming from the Chardonnay. An exceptional wine, but try to keep it until 2015.

Right: Pierre Cheval may look more like a civil servant than a grower, but he produces fine, ageworthy Aÿ Champagnes

Champagne Gatinois
7 Rue Marcel Mailly,
51160 Aÿ
Tel: +33 3 26 55 14 26

Gosset-Brabant

Working in the Aÿ vineyards has been a tradition within the Gosset family since the late 16th century. In the 1930s, when Gabriel Gosset produced his first bottles of Champagne, he created the label Gosset-Brabant, adding the name of his wife Andrée Brabant to his own. Now, his descendants Michel and Christian Gosset manage this highly regarded estate, which comprises 9.6ha (24 acres) of vineyards, 5.6ha (14 acres) of which lie on the best hillsides of Aÿ in the *lieux-dits* of Asniers, Froide Terre, Croix Courcelle, and Loiselu. A further 3.5ha (8.5 acres) are spread across the premiers crus of Mareuil, Dizy, and Avenay, and there's a crafty 1.24ha (half-acre) of grand cru Chouilly (Chardonnay) to add élan to the blends. With such top material, one would expect the Champagnes to be good, but they are much more than that. Michel's and Christian's ethos is to produce Champagnes as different and distinctive as their land. Their winery is right opposite Bollinger's elegant *maison*, and the great house and the smaller estate clearly share mutual affection and respect.

The care given to the Gosset vines is based on knowledge, observation, and calculated protection. To ensure optimal concentration of aromas, the yields are controlled using natural manure, a short pruning, and the removal of unnecessary buds. As for winemaking, the grapes from each of the localities are kept separate and vinified parcel by parcel to facilitate selection at the blending stage. Other characteristics include a traditional vertical wine press; stainless-steel fermenters (no wood); malolactic fermentation for all wines; natural filtration; and the resting of disgorged Champagnes for at least three months prior to release.

Six cuvées make up the manageable range of Champagnes, all immaculately made with precision and focus. The brothers also make some 1,500 bottles of Aÿ Rouge, which is one of the best in the commune. The Tradition Brut is a classy staple for regular drinking and is the pouring Champagne in several Michelin-starred restaurants in London. The Grande Réserve is aged for longer and made only with grapes from Aÿ and Chouilly; the full-bodied, vinous Rosé is a wine for the table; and the supreme Gabriel Grand Cru 2002 is one of Champagne's jewels, in 2002 marrying power and finesse as never before, eclipsing even the exceptional 1999.

For me, Gosset-Brabant is now one of Aÿ's leading producers, right up there with Bollinger, Henri Giraud, and the brothers' namesake (Maison) Gosset, to whom they are related way back. The wines are excellent, and can be recommended without hesitation.

FINEST WINES

(Tasted in Aÿ, January 2009)

Gosset-Brabant Réserve Grand Cru NV
80% Aÿ Pinot Noir, 20% Chouilly Chardonnay. A 50/50 blend of 2003 and 2002. Green-flecked straw. Evolved scents of honey and vanilla dominate. The palate, though, is surprisingly fresh. A powerful wine, with good, mineral tension. Pretty superior Champagne.

Gosset-Brabant Noirs d'Aÿ Grand Cru Cuvée NV ★
Based on the 2004 vintage. Great, pure Pinot Noir from named sites (Asniers, Froide Terre, Croix Courcelle). Low *dosage* of 4g/l. A real cathedral of a black-grape Champagne: huge structure, extremely powerful, but also very fine, with a delicate aspect. Needs ten years to show at its best.

Gosset-Brabant Gabriel Grand Cru 2002
Predominantly Pinot Noir from the family's finest Aÿ *lieux-dits*, with 15% Chouilly from the named vineyard of Sorangeon. *Dosage* of 5g/l. Bronze straw. A truly great Champagne of real body and presence but also with real complexity and elegance. This really has everything.

Champagne Gosset-Brabant
23 Boulevard de Lattre de Tassigny, 51160 Aÿ
Tel: +33 3 26 55 17 42
gosset-brabant@wandoo.fr

Henri Goutorbe

The Goutorbes, one of the best-known families in Aÿ, really know their vines. This is because they were nurserymen before becoming wine growers. The nursery was founded after the Great War by Emile Goutorbe, then head vigneron at Perrier-Jouët. After a while, Emile devoted himself to his prospering nursery and gradually began to buy vines. His son Henri, who passed away in February 2009, integrated the two sides of the business after World War II. At the end of the 1940s, Henri and his wife Guilène still lived principally from the revenues of the nursery. But all the while, they were accumulating a considerable stock of wine that undoubtedly inspired their passion for finished Champagne, properly aged. René Goutorbe joined his father Henri on leaving school in 1970, putting all his energies and native shrewdness into the wine activities of the family. René expanded the vineyard on the strict criteria of selecting the best plants for their genetic character and their suitability for the increasing number of parcels. He was an early investor in stainless-steel vats but has stuck to a perfectionist classical approach to Champagne-making and aging. He is one of the rare producers who insist that all bottle formats—from the half, to the Methuselah—take the mousse in the bottle in which they are sold, rather than by the common practice of *transvasage*. And all Goutorbe Champagnes stay on their lees for at least three years.

The extent of the Goutorbe vineyards is currently an impressive 21.85ha (54 acres). The family has a thumping 10ha (25 acres) in Aÿ, a fine parcel in neighbouring Mareuil-sur-Aÿ, and good premier cru sites in Mutigny and Bisseuil, all ensuring an opulent style. In terms of texture, Goutorbe Champagnes, dominated by the Pinots of Aÿ, tend to be velvety rather than silky. The family's style is splendidly old-fashioned, generous, and full. All the wines go through malolactic fermentation, and in a modern touch, the *dosage* is based on concentrated wine must, not sugar. The real pull here is the range of mature, older vintages that the Goutorbes still sell. A recent tasting over dinner *en famille* was a delight, both for the wines and for the warm hospitality.

FINEST WINES

(Tasted in Aÿ, January 2009)

Henri Goutorbe Brut Prestige NV
Essentially 2003 plus reserve wine. Dominated by premier cru Pinot Noirs from Mareuil, Hautvillers, and Mutigny, with about 25% Chardonnay, mainly from Bisseuil. The richness of 2003 fruit and Goutorbe's traditional style combine to make a wine seductive enough to win over drinkers who find much Champagne too acid. Although soft and ready, this will drink well until 2010 at least.

Henri Goutorbe Special Club Brut 2002
Pure Aÿ wines, as always, in this Club cuvée. The magical *gras* texture of grand cru Pinot Noir pervades the mouthfeel in this great vintage wine so typical of 2002. It has perfect balance between a blueberry richness (thanks to Terry Theise for this analogy), a velvety opulence, and poised minerality. Long and fine. Exceptional.

Henri Goutorbe Special Club Brut 2000
Some critics found this vintage of Club structured and worth further aging. Maybe—but by early 2009 it had come on apace, revealing forward fruit and attractive roundness. *À point.*

Henri Goutorbe Special Club Brut 1998
A fine example of the fascinating and oddly still underrated 1998 vintage, with all its virtues of generous fruit and extract in balance with lovely, elegant acidity. Good life ahead. Drink 2010–15.

Henri Goutorbe Special Club Brut 1996
Lovely testament to the richness and vinosity of a great vintage that some savants said wouldn't last.

Henri Goutorbe Special Club Brut 1993
An illustration of how good Pinot Noir from Aÿ can be in this generally lean vintage.

Champagne Henri Goutorbe
9 bis Rue Jeanson, 51160 Aÿ
Tel: +33 3 26 55 21 70
www.champagne-henri-goutorbe.com

Laurent-Perrier

Bernard de Nonancourt, now in his late 80s, is one of the giants of Champagne, the last of the Mohicans who shaped the postwar Champagne trade before the corporate world took over. A natural leader who had fought with the French Resistance, in 1948 de Nonancourt took over the ailing family firm he had inherited from his mother, Marie-Louise (née Lanson). Learning from his wartime experiences as head of a *maquis* cell in the French Alps, he was extremely careful in his choice of colleagues to help him rebuild the firm. In the 60 years since then, Laurent-Perrier has grown from a tiny concern into the fourth-largest Champagne house, in which the majority of shares are still owned by the de Nonancourt family. Bernard's torch is now carried by his two daughters, Alexandra and Stéphanie, who actively

The highly individual style of these Champagnes owes everything to Bernard de Nonancourt's courage in thinking originally about what Champagne should be

work in the company. The sisters have been helped immeasurably since 1997 by CEO Yves Dumont, a great marketing expert and brand builder, and by winemaker Michel Fauconnet, who has worked at Laurent-Perrier all his life, succeeding his great mentor, Alain Terrier, as *chef de cave* in 2004.

The highly individual style of these Champagnes owes everything to Bernard de Nonancourt's courage in thinking originally about what Champagne should be, and to Alain Terrier's flair in turning those ideas into great wines. In a bold departure from conventional practice, the firm decided in 1957 to make a multivintage prestige cuvée called Grand Siècle. De Nonancourt believed that blending was what the Champenois did best, in this case ideally achieved by an *assemblage* of

three great years. Ever since, Grand Siècle has been one of the very best Champagnes. Intriguingly, like most sensible people, the de Nonancourt team does not always practise what it preaches, occasionally releasing a single-vintage version—Grand Siècle *exceptionellement millésimé*—in great years such as 1985 and 1990. The grapes at this level are from the greatest crus: Le Mesnil and Avize for Chardonnay; Ambonnay, Bouzy, and Mailly for Pinot.

Another of Laurent-Perrier's more innovative Champagnes, seemingly quite radical at the time of its first release in 1981, has been its Ultra Brut (zero *dosage*). Although bone-dry, it is never astringent, being made only in very ripe years, and it can be wonderfully refreshing on a summer's evening. Strictly speaking, Ultra Brut was less an innovation and more a return to the sugarless Champagnes that the house had sold in England in the 1890s. Laurent-Perrier is also the standard bearer of Rosé Champagne made by the *saignée* method—that is, by extracting colour from the skins of Pinot Noir rather than by adding red wine to a white blend. Laurent-Perrier Rosé Non-Vintage has been a huge success internationally and now commands higher prices than many mature single-vintage cuvées. Bizarre, but that is the power of good marketing.

The style of the entry-level L-P Brut Non-Vintage has aimed for a natural dryness, purity of fruit, and fine minerality, especially since 1974, when Alain Terrier became chief winemaker, with no love of Champagnes made in wood. Fermented in stainless steel, L-P Brut is always made with a far higher proportion of Chardonnay (55 per cent) than is usual for an NV. Its inimitable style has been faithfully guarded by Fauconnet. With its crisp, racy, subtly fruited character, the Brut reminds me of good Chablis with bubbles. The same shunning of oak applies to the Laurent-Perrier straight Vintages, which are more complex and concentrated expressions of the house style but with an increased use of Pinot Noir to give body and volume. The

Above: The sign outside Laurent-Perrier's corporate headquarters in Tours-sur-Marne and one of its vineyards

Cuvée Alexandra Vintage Rosé, first created for the wedding of Alexandra de Nonancourt, is an exquisite Champagne, a perfect expression of 80 per cent Pinot Noir blended with Chardonnay. It is certainly more elegantly Champenois than the all-conquering *saignée* cuvée.

FINEST WINES

(Tasted in Tours-sur-Marne, June 2007)

Laurent-Perrier Ultra Brut NV
This 55/45 mix of Chardonnay and Pinot Noir is made only in very ripe years with high natural sugar and low acidity in the grapes. These are selected from 15 special parcels that average 97% on the *échelle des crus*. Star-bright, crystalline yellow, with a fine stream of little bubbles. Exuberant, forward, lemony scents, then honeysuckle and a brilliant, saline, mineral whiff of the seashore. The palate is long and surprisingly powerful. Absolutely dry. A wine for oysters or sushi.

Laurent-Perrier Brut 1999
In the Vintage cuvées, the ratio is reversed to 55/45 of Pinot Noir and Chardonnay. Vibrant yet subtle lemon-gold. Equally vibrant scents of white flowers and an evolving medley of citrus and stone fruits. The palate has the L-P signature of richness, delicacy, and poise, wrapped in a gentle, creamy mousse. A nicely controlled touch of yeastiness adds enough complexity for ideal current drinking. An admirably light-handed take on this mercurial, often tumultuous vintage.

Laurent-Perrier Grand Siècle La Cuvée NV
An *assemblage* of three good vintages in a roughly 50/50 mix of grand cru Chardonnay and Pinot Noir, usually Chardonnay in a slight majority, largely from Avize and Le Mesnil. The current release is mainly 1997, with some 1996 and 1995. My tasting notes of June 2007 speak of lustrous straw-gold with green reflections. Chardonnay dominates on entry, with aromas of lily, brioche, and toasted almond. Elegant citrus flavours are the key notes, buttressed by the quiet power of Pinot Noir. The subtlety and substance of exceptional Champagne.

Laurent-Perrier Cuvée Alexandra Rosé NV
80% PN, 20% C, exclusively grand cru grapes, the Pinot notably from Bouzy, Louvois, Ambonnay, and Mailly. Beautiful, salmon-pink hue, fine bead of little bubbles. Exuberant, poised scents of wild raspberry and cherry, made more complex by candied lemon. The palate is round but racy, with a long, multitoned finish. *Grand vin*. Tiny quantities.

Champagne Laurent-Perrier
Domaine Laurent-Perrier, 51150 Tours-sur-Marne
Tel: +33 3 26 58 91 22
www.laurent-perrier.com

René Geoffroy

The vineyards of Cumières, high above the Marne and facing southeast towards Epernay, have one of the sunniest and best-exposed aspects over the valley. The village is famed for generous, exuberant, Pinot-led Champagne and one of the better red still wines of the region. The Geoffroy family are the village's preeminent growers and fine, ever-improving winemakers, whose roots stretch back to the 17th century, when Pierre Pérignon was making wine at Hautvillers, Cumière's neighbouring village farther up the hill.

The Geoffroys have 13ha (32 acres) of vines in Cumières, Hautvillers, and down the valley westwards in Damery and Fleury-la-Rivière. This is black-grapes country, so more than 80 per cent of their holdings are Pinot Noir and Meunier, the rest Chardonnay. Jean-Baptiste Geoffroy practises an eco-friendly viticulture that is close to organic but without the constraints that certification would impose. Jean-Baptiste and his father René insist on a rigorous selection of grapes at harvest, going to the expense of employing eight people to cut away any rotten berries. This is commonplace in Burgundy but quite rare in Champagne—a wine culture still alas atuned to high yields and volume.

Many of the wines have been fermented in oak for generations, and the malo is always avoided, no doubt to ensure the Champagnes retain precision and tension to balance the ripe fruit from these sunny vineyards. Jean-Baptiste now has a new house and cellar in Aÿ, with the winery and all his stocks under one roof, which will make his work much easier than in the dispersed cellars of old.

FINEST WINES

(Tasted March 2009)
René Geoffroy Brut Cuvée Expression NV
This entry-level Champagne, a 50/50 *assemblage* of 2005 and 2004, continues to evolve towards a more serious style, the level of Pinot Noir raised at the expense of Meunier. Fine, golden colour, with a hint of pinkish-grey coral at the rim. Finer and more elegant than the easy, fruit-laden style of old. Very well made, with a judicious touch of oak.

René Geoffroy Cuvée Volupté
Pure Chardonnay from the three *lieux-dits* of Les Chênes, La Montagne, and the vertiginously steep Tourn-Midi. It is all from the 2004 vintage, a year of minerality, tension, and (it has to be said) record yields, that suited Chardonnay better than the Pinots. Allied to the precision of flavours, there is indeed a sensation of voluptuous fruit, which is typical of the Grande Vallée de la Marne.

René Geoffroy 2000 Non-Dosé
A very distinctive Vintage Champagne driven by Chardonnay (70%) with just under one third Pinot Noir. The combination of no malolactic fermentation, no *dosage*, no filtration, and the super-ripe fruit of Cumières results in a wine that divides the critics. But while it may be an acquired taste, it is one that I could learn to like.

Right: Jean-Baptiste Geoffroy, whose family has vinified the fruit from the sunny slopes of Cumières for generations

Champagne René Geoffroy
150 Rue du Bois-des-Jots,
51480 Cumières
Tel: +33 3 26 55 32 31
www.champagne-geoffroy.com

Jacquesson

I t was a good time for Memmie Jacquesson to open a Champagne house in Châlons-sur-Marne in 1798, for it coincided with the rise of Napoleon as the greatest military commander of the age. On his way to a series of stunning victories across Eastern Europe, it is said that the emperor liked to stop in Châlons to stock up on Jacquesson's Champagnes—they might even have inspired him to greater heights of tactical brilliance before Austerlitz. Certainly, the imperial patronage propelled the house to prominence, and it soon became one of the most important Champagne brands. The firm was also a nursery of new ideas, fostered by Memmie's son, the brilliantly creative Adolphe Jacquesson, who helped transform the still primitive state of 19th-century Champagne-making. It was Adolphe who taught Johann Joseph Krug the art of blending and who encouraged the Châlons pharmacist Jean-Baptiste François to formulate the "réduction François", which lowered the incidence of exploding bottles from 25 to 4 per cent. Finally, in 1842, Adolphe patented the muselet, or wine muzzle, that holds the Champagne cork securely in place, now used for all sparkling wines worldwide.

Still one of the greats of Champagne, Jacquesson is nowadays a bijou house in Dizy, standing apart from the pack in its approach to the central task of blending a dry Non-Vintage cuvée. Jean-Hervé Chiquet, co-owner of the house with his brother Laurent, explains that "in the late 1990s we became aware that the fundamental principle of making a classic Brut Non-Vintage in a consistent style was limiting our possibilities of improving the wine". So in an attempt to escape these limitations, the Chiquets decided, with effect from the 2000 harvest, to prize excellence over consistency by crafting a wine that reflected the main vintage in the blend, rather than the replicated flavours of the traditional blends. Henceforth, the new aim was to give each

Right: Brothers Jean-Hervé (left) and Laurent Chiquet, who maintain their house's reputation for quality and originality

wine its own distinct personality, mirroring the character of the dominant vintage. It was therefore also essential to give each wine a clear identity.

First off, the Cuvée 728, being the 728th cuvée blended by the house since its foundation, was based on the forward, ripe, and fruity 2000 harvest that won immediate friends for its positive and solid character. Its successor, the 729, based on the fragile 2001 vintage, was a harder call but was still one of the best blends on release—fine-drawn and stylish, thanks to rigorous selection of the grapes and partial fermentation in large oak tuns. The Cuvée 730 is certainly the best so far. The base wine is 2002, probably one of the finest vintages in Champagne since World War II—as good as 1996, but of quite different character. After a lovely, warm, not-too-hot summer, and exactly the right number of refreshing showers before the harvest, the 2002's trump card is the gloriously ripe Pinot Noir, which, though making up only a third of this cuvée, pervades its deep, vinous flavour. The adroitness of the blending shows in the high level of Chardonnay, which contributes a racy bounce and crispness.

The Vintage Champagnes here are also highly individual, majoring on niche bottlings of monocrus, or single vineyards. The best known of these is the Grand Cru Avize, sourced from the family's three *lieux-dits* of La Fosse, Nemery, and Champ Gain. Personally, I believe that the Avize '96, undoubtedly a superb expression of Chardonnay, owes its greatness to the skilful blending of all three sites—with, may one guess, a parcel or two of more delicate wines from the higher slopes of the village? This great wine perfectly balances substance, racy minerality, and finesse, which leads me to mull over the Chiquets' decision to make a single bottling of Champ Gain alone in the 2002 vintage. This little vineyard is on the lower, deeper soils of Avize, where there are strong clay elements, as well as chalk, resulting in a super-intense, cruiserweight Champagne that

may not be everybody's idea of elegant Avize. The old wisdom, now a little out of fashion—that the blending of different sites makes for a more complete Champagne than one from a single source—is fundamentally sound, as in this case. But generalizations are always tricky, and I have no such reservations about other single-site Champagnes from this house.

Vauzelle Terme is the smallest of Jacquesson's great vineyards—just 0.3ha (0.75 acres), lying halfway up a south-facing vineyard in Aÿ, arguably home to the most complete Pinot Noir in Champagne. The soil is predominantly calcareous and has been formed by rich alluvial deposits over a bedrock of Campanian chalk that facilitates swift drainage of water. You do not have to be a geologist to appreciate that this is a privileged place for the great black grape. The 1996 crop was fermented in three 600-litre *demi-muid* casks, and early tastings revealed an exceptional Pinot of majestic structure. Laurent Chiquet used one of the casks to enhance the Jacquesson Grand Vin 1996; the other two were blended for a single bottling of Vauzelle Terme. My tasting note in 2004 read: "lustrous gold... ripe red fruits and gingerbread aromas... very 1996, rich, ample, vinous... but with cleansing acidity and a finale of magnificent purity".

Farther west from the home village of Dizy, Corne Bautray is the most surprising Jacquesson vineyard. The Chardonnay grown here should not be that exceptional; the vines lie high above the village, close to the woods and exposed to the southwesterlies. Nor is the soil the classic pure chalk; rather, it is heavier burrstone pebbles and clay, which yields a vigorous Champagne but one that finishes (do not ask me why) with a saline delicacy that raises it to the class of the truly fine. Corne Bautray is also remarkably consistent, shooting an ace in the fast-maturing, merely goodish 2000 vintage and something yet finer in the great 2002 harvest.

Above: The large oak tuns at Jacquesson contribute considerably to the full, rich, and round house style

And so to the Terres Rouge vineyard, so named after its rich soil, rising towards the boundary with Hautvillers. This is the most recent single-site bottling from Jacquesson, a full-blooded rosé made the hard way, by bleeding the Pinot Noir grapes of enough pigments to make the wine pink, rather than by adding red wine. This is a Champagne for the table, to accompany almost anything—tuna sushi, charcuterie, terrines, offal (especially sautéed kidneys), or even a stinky Maroilles cheese.

FINEST WINES

(Tasted in Dizy, April 2008)

Jacquesson Avize Champ Gain 2004
Lemon-gold. Racy minerality, a dashing élan characterizing both nose and palate. But this is still a wine played in one key, lacking a little of the complexity of the 1996, which was a blend from three sites. A very good Champagne nevertheless, more in the Avize mainstream than the fleshy 2002.

Jacquesson Dizy Corne Bautray 2004
Shimmering green-gold; fine, lace-like mousse. Incisive scents of Granny Smith apples. Rounded and full, but with fine, mineral tension. More elegant, if less explosive, than the 2002, veering towards a more classic and restrained style.

Jacquesson Dizy Terres Rouges Rosé de Saignée 2003★
Intense ruby colour, reflecting the heat of the harvest. Attractive, extrovert scents of strawberries. The mouthfeel is warm, and one senses the alcohol, but decent acidity keeps it all together. For food.

Jacquesson Avize Champ Gain 2002
Bright, clear gold; very ripe, *surmature* nose, like a late-harvest wine. Intense, supercharged flavours, again very ripe, to the point of being unctuous. You may either love this wine or be troubled by its size. The sort of showy Champagne that does well in blind tastings. But will it age?

Jacquesson Dizy Corne Bautray 2002 [V]
100% Chardonnay. Straw-gold; orchard-fruits aromas, so easy to confuse with Pinot Noir—the terroir speaking. Superb, explosive fruit on the entry and mid-palate, and that lovely saline aftertaste.

Jacquesson Aÿ Vauzelle Terme 2002★
A slight tint of Pinot pink to the hue. Classic Aÿ nose of peach, pear, and quince; also a touch of leather. Beautiful texture in the mouth, silk and satin, with perfect integration of fruit, wood, and vinosity typical of a great Pinot year. Really delicious. More generous than the 1996 and may, in time, be even better. Well-nigh perfect.

Champagne Jacquesson
68 Rue du Colonel Fabien, 51530 Dizy
Tel: +33 3 26 55 68 11
www.champagnejacquesson.com

Gaston Chiquet

Nicolas Chiquet is a quiet master of his craft, a fine exponent of what is best described as "evolved tradition" in Champagne-making. And a proud little story it is. Just after World War I, in 1919, Nicolas's grandfather and great-uncle, Gaston and Fernand, were among the first pioneering growers to turn from the *négoce*, keep their grapes, transform them into Champagne, and sell their finished wines under their own name.

Now 90 years on, Nicolas and his own brother's domaine is large for a *récoltant-manipulant*—some 23ha (57 acres) of excellent premiers and grands crus in Dizy and Hautvillers, Aÿ and Mareuil, with another hectare (2.47 acres) recently bought in the Ardre Valley northwest of Reims, a promising district for fruity, generous Meunier. Interestingly, Meunier and Chardonnay in equal proportions cover 80 per cent of the Chiquets' vineyards; but since they are planted mainly in privileged sites, these finished Champagnes preeminently give the drinker a real sense of place, of the special plots of earth from which they come—the antithesis of a big house's blend of many parts. The Chiquets' pure Chardonnay cuvée, for instance, comes exclusively and uniquely from Aÿ. In one sense, this is an alternative, hedonistic expression of the great white grape; but tellingly, it is the great terroir of the fabled commune (known better for great Pinot Noir) that speaks most clearly to the taster.

Yet Nicolas's talent has been to ensure that his Champagnes, naturally so opulent, also show a precision, freshness, and harmony that make them wines you actually want to drink and of which you always want to open a second bottle. In the poetic words of the distinguished Champagne and German Riesling specialist Terry Theise, Chiquet wines are "chiseled and articulate[....] the quiet heroes of Champagne"—rather like their maker. And here, bearing in mind the comparative richness

Right: Nicolas Chiquet, a brilliant winemaker who quietly continues a long family tradition of pure, terroir-driven wines

These Champagnes preeminently give the drinker a real sense of place, of the special plots of earth from which they come—the antithesis of a big house's blend of many parts

of the earth, that means no wood. For Nicolas, it is all a question of keeping the pure medley of fruit and terroir tastes in the glass—unmasked by oak—while guarding against the pervasive modern tendency towards overreductive, "clean" wines, which, alas, are all too often boring and soulless. Not always easy, with the unrelenting demand for top-drawer, bijou Champagnes like these.

Luckily, the fellow has his priorities right. Rather than buying a lot of expensive barrels, Nicolas has invested heavily in a tool for the most important part of the Champagne-making process—a PAI (*see p.36*). The result is the purest of juice, especially from the heart of the first pressings. One of the best modern advances in Champagne-making, this is the "evolved" bit of tradition for the Chiquets, keeping them abreast of the times. Yet the truly traditional asset of the house is its deep and extensive cellars—one of the reasons Gaston Chiquet bought the property on Dizy's Avenue du Général Leclerc in the 1930s. Here the Champagnes age beautifully—even the entry-level Brut Tradition, nearly half of which comes from Meunier, which is not supposed to last well but does so here.

In the fields, the vines are immaculately tended according to the tenets of sustainable viticulture. And although Nicolas prefers to blend the wines from a few sites for the greater benefit of the whole, there is no doubt that he has some fabulous *lieux-dits*, such as the perfectly located Le Haut de Souschienne, on the southerly mid-slopes above Dizy. Plainly, this is in every respect one of the best-managed estates in the Marne Valley.

FINEST WINES

(Tasted in Dizy, July 2008)

Gaston Chiquet Brut Tradition NV [V]
45% PM, 35% C, 20% PN. A 60/40 mix of 2005 and 2004. *Dosage* 8g/l. Pale yellow; smells of healthy, young fruit—not too concentrated, the tendency of '05 to dry extract being nicely mitigated by the

elegant acidity and crisp minerality typical of '04. The wine will gain in complexity, particularly on the palate, where the dominant Meunier already brings a charming roundness. Full of natural, unadulterated flavours. Worth cellaring.

Gaston Chiquet Blanc de Blancs d'Aÿ
This bottling of this famous Aÿ Blanc is actually all from the 2004 vintage—a lovely Chardonnay year—but is not labelled as such. It is sourced from several parcels, including one that faces west and is therefore dewy at dawn, gently warm by sundown. Elegant, green-flecked Welsh gold, with a gentle, soft mousse. Still a little shy on both nose and palate for the moment, but the rich, silky texture and uplifting acidity promise a *grand vin* from 2010.

Above: Gaston Chiquet owns several meticulously tended vineyards in Dizy, here within sight of its medieval church

Gaston Chiquet Cuvée de Réserve Club

A classic Champagne blend, being one third each of Chardonnay, Pinot Noir, and Meunier, from the 1998 and 2000 vintages. A gently evolved yellow-gold, with benign oxidation on the nose. Aeration releases spicy fruits and powerful, rich flavours that are elegant and controlled. It will develop further complexity over the next ten years.

Gaston Chiquet Brut Vintage 2000

60% PN, 40% C. *Dosage* 6g/l. Disgorged February 2008. Vibrant yellow with green lights. My sort of Champagne, with everything I look for: tension, punch, elegance, finesse. A peach of a wine, driven by great Pinot Noir. Nicolas says he prefers 2000 to 1999—so much more character rather than forward, flattering pleasantness. I could not agree more.

Gaston Chiquet Brut Tradition Rosé

Another classic blend of the three Champagne grapes, with 15% rouge from Dizy and Aÿ. An ideal mix of 2002 (a great Pinot year, rich and succulent) and 2004 (racy, mineral, excellent for Chardonnay). Star-bright, elegant English-rose hue. Pretty, *Pinoté* nose of little red fruits. Exuberantly fruity, but still taut and refreshing. Masterly winemaking.

Champagne Gaston Chiquet

912 Avenue du Général Leclerc, 51530 Dizy
Tel: +33 3 26 55 22 02
www.gastonchiquet.com

Billecart-Salmon

Among the half-dozen top family-run houses in Champagne, Billecart-Salmon is maybe the most distinctively Gallic— above the crowd, fastidious, knowing its strengths and sticking to them. The family came to Mareuil-sur-Aÿ in the 17th century and still lives in the village's most beautiful house and formal garden. Their ancestor, Pierre Billecart, a parliamentary counselor to Louis XIII, would probably smile on this discreet *vie du château*, still thriving in the 21st century. A greyhound at full pelt on Pierre's coat of arms, which long decorated the firm's labels, neatly symbolizes the exquisite Billecart-Salmon style and pedigree: elegant, fine-limbed, racy, and often first past the post in any Champagne stakes.

Nothing stands still in wine, of course, and brothers François and Antoine Roland-Billecart, who manage the house, are not in the least sentimental about the past. Though proud of their heritage and traditional wine values, they, like their father Jean before them, have always welcomed interesting modern techniques and moved with the times. As François once told me, tradition is an ailing body unless it receives regular transfusions of new blood and ideas. Even now, 50 years after it was first introduced, no Champagne-making technique is more radical than Billecart's treatment of the must. Borrowing an idea from the brothers' maternal grandfather, a brewer in Douai, they follow the first clarification process (*débourbage*) with a second, chilling the must down to about 41°F (5°C), which allows the coarser lees to be separated out. The temperature is then raised gently to a moderate 52–59°F (11–15°C) and fermentation proceeds slowly for about three weeks. Thus oxidation of the infant wine is entirely avoided. As proof that these wines do indeed live long and distinguished lives, the 1959 and 1961 Cuvée Nicolas-François Billecart,

Right: Antoine Roland-Billecart beside a stainless-steel tank used for the defining cold-settling of the must

Even now, 50 years after it was first introduced, no Champagne-making technique is more radical than Billecart's treatment of the must, borrowed from the brothers' maternal grandfather, a brewer in Douai

both fermented in oak, blew every other Champagne off the table at a famous blind tasting organized by Richard Juhlin in Stockholm in 1999.

If this proud firm ever had an Achilles heel, it was inflicted as far back as 1926, when Charles Roland-Billecart was forced to sell the family's vineyards in order to finance the increased Champagne sales he had achieved since the end of World War I. When François took charge of the house in the early 1990s, he could rely on solid contracts with an impressive network of excellent growers in the best sites—and he could call the tune, insisting on the most exigent standards regarding the quality of the musts delivered to the cellar. However, François knew that the balance of power was shifting in the vineyards, as more and more growers were holding on to their best grapes for their own Champagnes. So the firm steadily began to buy vineyards, some 30ha (75 acres) centred around Mareuil-sur-Aÿ, and also acquired 9ha (22 acres) rented in Damery, known for fine Pinot Meunier. Billecart—like Krug, Pol Roger, and Roederer—value Meunier highly as a pleasure-giving ingredient in a well-balanced Brut Non-Vintage.

As turnover increased in the run-up to the Millennium and beyond, the house hung on to top quality thanks to the exceptional skills of *chef de cave* and winemaker François Domi, one of Champagne's greats. Sticking to what they did best, however, caused the Billecarts a lot of financial headaches in the harsh 21st-century world of corporate raiding and changing ownerships. In 2004, the family knew they needed more financial muscle and sold a 45 per cent stake in the firm to the Reims-based Compagnie Financière Frey. Jean-Jacques Frey has a reputation as an efficient financial firefighter—

or as one great Aÿ grower cattily put it at the time, "You don't call in Frey on finding dry rot in the building, but when the roof has fallen in." This may be a classic example of Champenois gallows humor, but actually the wily Billecarts had the last laugh, because they secured a great deal, gaining access to 80ha (198 acres) of grand cru grapes owned by Frey, while retaining a majority share in the company and complete control of the winemaking. It all seems to work well.

With total production now touching 1.7 million bottles (more than three times what it was in the mid-1990s), the house draws grapes from more than 40 different crus—Pinot Noir mostly from the Montagne de Reims, but also some typically bright fruit from Merrey-sur-Arce in the Aube; Chardonnay from the Côte des Blancs, with a high proportion of grands crus; and Pinot Noir mainly from the sunnier right bank of the Marne in prime spots like Damery, but also from across the river in the amphitheatre of vines at Leuvrigny.

The buzz phrase of the moment in Champagne is *vinification parcellaire*. At Billecart, the wines are fermented, as much as possible, parcel by parcel of vines, rather than by grape variety, in order to identify the potential of each parcel. These are kept separate in serried ranks of polished stainless-steel vats so as to give the broadest possible repertoire of flavours at the critical blending stage. And since the triumph of the Billecart '59 and '61 in Stockholm in 1999, there has been a measured return to partial fermentation in wood for the grands crus that make up the vintage cuvées. Since 1995, Denis Blée, an expert in oak and the crus that suit it best, has supervised the project, having learned his craft from his years with Alfred Gratien,

Above: At Billecart there has been a gradual reintroduction of oak for some of the Vintage cuvées and for Clos Saint-Hilaire

the most rigorously old-fashioned Champagne house of the oak school. From a starting base of 50 barrels, the number has risen to 250, housed in a special building. Everything is done to avoid an overtly oaky flavour. The barrels are light- to medium-toasted, and still only a third of the wine in vintage cuvées sees wood.

The one cuvée that is totally oak fermented is Clos Saint-Hilaire. This pure Pinot Noir Champagne comes from a 1ha (2.4-acre) walled vineyard close to the house. The *clos* used to supply the 7 per cent of precious red wine that added the finishing touch to Billecart's renowned rosés, but it is now the source of arguably the greatest single-vineyard blanc de noirs on the market. The vineyard does not look that special. Its aspect—due east—is less favourable than that of the superb south-facing Clos des Goisses at the other end of the village. Saint-Hilaire's topsoils are also deeper and less chalky, composed of *tuffe* limestone. My own instinct is to throw away the viticultural manual and marvel at the wine, of density and controlled power, of old-vine fruitiness and vinosity, but one that never degenerates into heaviness, thanks to all the brilliant modern winemaking touches that are inimitably Billecart.

FINEST WINES

(Tasted in Mareuil-sur-Aÿ, April 2008)
Billecart-Salmon Clos Saint-Hilaire 1995
Evolving yellow-gold, very slow evolution on both nose and palate. A big, old-fashioned Pinot Noir Champagne, barely making its presence felt at every level. I'm not sure the zero *dosage* is quite right, since it is very, very dry. A very promising first effort. Will continue to improve until 2020.

Billecart-Salmon Clos Saint-Hilaire 1996 ★
A real step up by every test. Sublime daffodil colour, lace-like mousse, greater maturity than the '95 on the nose, yellow stone fruits—peaches, apricots— then a touch of fig. Rich yet lithe on the palate, its great power and structure reined in by a refinement that is superior than in the '95. Perfect *dosage* (3g/l). Is this the greatest blanc de noirs on the market? A masterpiece.

Billecart-Salmon Blanc de Blancs 1998
A roller-coaster year—record heat in August, rain in early September. By rigorous sifting of the best Chardonnay grapes (grand cru Oger leading the pack), this is a triumph of oak-sustained structure without woodiness. A lustrous green-gold hue and toasty creamy loveliness on both nose and palate. Perfect balance and length.

Champagne Billecart-Salmon
30 Rue Carnot, BP8, 51160 Mareuil-sur-Aÿ
Tel: +33 3 26 52 64 88
www.champagne-billecart.fr

Philipponnat

*A*ÿ *le nom, Mareuil le bon* is an old Marnais adage, implying that the wines of Mareuil are usually as good as, and sometimes surpass, those of its more famous neighbour. This applies supremely to the great walled vineyard of the village—Philipponnat's Clos des Goisses. Located on the dominant chalk hill of Gruguet, this 5.5ha (13.6-acre) vineyard slopes down at a dramatic angle of between 30 and 45° towards the Marne canal, the vicinity of water providing a natural defence against frost and cold nights. At the summit of the Gruguet, a statue of the Virgin smiles benignly down on Philipponnat's vineyard workers. Their grandfathers built this memorial as a token of thanks that their prayers had been answered and Mareuil saved from bombing during the American air raid of 11 August 1944. Aÿ had less luck; a third of the town lay flattened that night.

The old French word *goisse* signifies a painful task. And vignerons in the *clos* shiver at the thought of working on the hill in early March, when icy rain chills their bones and mires them in mud. That, of course, is the worst-case scenario. Otherwise, this is a dream walled vineyard, unique in Champagne for extent and size, its setting occupying the escarpment created by the river at a strategic point, where the Côte des Blancs, the Grande Vallée de la Marne, and the Montagne de Reims all meet.

The *coteau*, thus created, stretches eastwards for half a mile (800m) from the village of Mareuil along the road to Bisseuil. The subsoils are profound, dropping to a depth of at least 330ft (100m) and mostly composed of the purest belemnite chalk. Just as important, the topsoil is thin and poor, which allows the vines' roots to reach the mother-rock with ease, so pervading the wines with an incomparable minerality—always the sign of exceptional Champagne from a top terroir.

Right: Charles Philipponnat at home in Mareuil-sur-Aÿ, and happy to be back in charge of his prestigious family firm

Clos des Goisses is a dream walled vineyard, unique in Champagne for extent and size, where the Côte des Blancs, Vallée de la Marne, and Montagne de Reims all meet

It gets better still. The *clos* faces due south, the soils and vines catching the rays of sun in their full, perpendicular strength, maximizing their warmth and luminosity. What is more, the Gruguet hill provides a shield against the prevailing westerly winds. As a result, during the maturing cycle of the grape, temperatures in the *clos* are on average 2.7˚F (1.5˚C) higher than in the rest of Champagne, equaling those of Burgundy, 280 miles (450km) to the south. The main aim in the cellar is to give full expression to the power and richness of Pinot Noir, which is so suitable for this terroir, at the same time balancing that Pinot punch with a tempering incisiveness brought by Chardonnay. The great white grape covers some 2ha (5.1 acres) of the *clos*, the dominating Pinot Noir 3ha (7.5 acres).

In the vineyard, there are 14 parcels or *lieux-dits*, with evocative names like La Dure ("the hard one") and Grands or Petits Cintres—comically, *cintre*, in *argaud*, means coathanger. The grand sites in the warmest and steepest rows are reserved for Pinot, the little ones at the top or bottom of the *clos* for Chardonnay. The average age of the vines is a very respectable 30 years, the yields of grapes laudably restricted, their richness of sugar touching 11% ABV after the first fermentation and 12.5% ABV in the finished Champagne. The 14 parcels are vinified in pairs, so as to produce seven base wines.

Winemaking is very Champenois—rather conservative, and maybe even a shade too much so. Fermentations are conducted in stainless steel, the malolactic is invariably avoided to preserve freshness, and the use of wood is restricted to aging 20 per cent of the wines in oak rather than using it as a vessel for the first fermentation of the whole cuvée. The latter practice has always been followed at Krug, for instance, in order to give the baby wines an inoculation against oxidation, greater structure, and the prospect of a long and distinguished life. Where Krug has led, other star makers of single-vineyard Champagnes—such as Billecart-Salmon, Jacquesson, and Henri Giraud—have followed. It could also be argued that the proportion of Pinot Noir in the base wine of Clos des Goisses might be increased to 75 or even 80 per cent, for greater complexity and a fuller expression of this fabulous terroir. There need be no loss of balance if, in a flexible frame of mind, a few modern winemaking touches were to be carefully introduced.

None of this diminishes the track record of Clos des Goisses—indeed, vintages have been produced almost every year since 1956, which speaks volumes about this special piece of earth. Warmer years that release the full-on power and succulence of Pinot Noir are particularly impressive, like the honeyed 1976; the sensual, Mocha-like 1989; and the sumptuous 1990, which retains enough acidity to stay fresh into advanced old age. The 1985 Goisses, a small and very intense year for Pinot Noir, sticks in the mind as the centrepiece of a 1996 dinner in Paris, when this majestic Champagne was as perfect with roast woodcock as with a well-aged Tome de Savoie. Certainly, in full maturity (12+ years), the aftertaste of Clos des Goisses is imbued with very characteristic notes of crystallized stone fruits like cherry and mirabelle, even a touch of Kirsch making it a really original partner to roast Cantonese duck with ginger, star anise, and, at a push, plum sauce. The mature, rich Champagne seems to cope better with the spice and sweetness of the dish than a red wine would—even, say, a fine-drawn Burgundy.

On a happy note, after a miserable period under Marie-Brizard, in 1999 the new Boizel-Chanoine ownership asked Charles Philipponnat, then a vice president at Moët, to return and manage the family business. The Clos des Goisses of that year will be a fine, complex wine, decidedly superior to most Champagnes from this easy-drinking but slightly constituted vintage—a good omen.

Above: Philipponnat's steep-sloping Clos des Goisses is the source of the first great single-vineyard Champagne

FINEST WINES

(Tasted in Mareuil-sur-Aÿ, April 2008)
Philipponnat Cuvée "1522" 2000
The best of the blended cuvées, 60% PN, 40% C, all grands crus. Ripe, golden colour; subtle, iodine nose. A rich, round, Pinot-led palate, with a fleeting finale of dark chocolate, yet also crisp and mineral. A wine for lobster or scallops. Low *dosage* of 4g/l.

Philipponnat Clos des Goisses 1999
65% PN, 35% C. Elegant, yellow-gold. Although this is a big, powerful Champagne (13% ABV) with certain aspects more like a red wine than a white, there is still a filigree-like delicacy of Chardonnay aromas, with a whiff—would you believe?—of old furniture. Very good weight, balance, and length, with a caressing mouthfeel. Much better than most '99s. 2009–15.

Philipponnat Clos des Goisses 1991
After the big guns of 1989 and 1990, the 1991 shows a return to a more classic and incisive style of Champagne, stressing finesse and subtlety. Evolved scents of smoke and leather, ceding to black cherries and a lovely note of acacia honey. A lithe palate, Chardonnay making itself felt in flavours of lemon and cinnamon. Good finale without being overexpansive. Class—a Champagne connoisseur's Champagne. Ready now.

Champagne Philipponnat
13 Rue du Pont, BP2, 51160 Mareuil-sur-Aÿ
Tel: +33 3 26 56 93 00
www.philipponnat.com

Joseph Perrier

Joseph Perrier is one of the hidden jewels of Champagne—the only one of the old *grandes marques* to be based in Châlons-en-Champagne, the administrative capital of the Marne. Founded in 1825, the house was bought in the late 1880s by Paul Pithiot, great-grandfather of Jean-Claude Fourmon, the present head.

Jean-Claude is one of the last of that dying breed of grand Champenois still at the helm of a family business (in his case with the financial support of his cousin, the dynamic entrepreneur Alain Thiénot). An intriguing, playful character, Jean-Claude has the bearing of the Rémois establishment—his father Claude was Robert de Vogüé's right arm in rebuilding Moët after 1945. But he is also a free spirit, something of a rebel who likes to tweak the tail of the mighty by doing things differently in a highly individualistic Champagne style that is consistently excellent. At Joseph Perrier, these are real wines with a sense of terroir, as well as being deft examples of the blender's art. Another particularity is that its extensive cellars are all at ground-floor level at the base of beautiful chalk chambers with skylights, many feet beneath a mounded wooded hill, thereby achieving good humidity for the aging wines.

The house style is ripe and generous, shaped by the sunny location of the firm's 21ha (52 acres) of Pinot Noir and Meunier at Cumières, Daméry, and Hautvillers. Yet that richness is never overdone, thanks to brilliant blending with Chardonnay, a certain proportion of which comes from Cumières but also from one of Champagne's most interesting mini-zones close to Vitry-le-François. Here the Chardonnay vines lie on a deep bedrock of chalk, imparting a tension and focus to the wines that make Vitry an excellent (and less expensive) alternative source to the Côte des Blancs. Vitry Chardonnays are also arguably

Right: Joseph Perrier's directeur-général Jean-Claude Fourmon, whose great-grandfather bought the house in the late 1880s

purer and finer than the more rustic examples of the white grape from the Sézannais. The Vintage Brut cuvées are the rock of the house's reputation, released carefully in genuinely good years with plenty of age on the cork. I remember the 1985,

when I first tasted it some 15 years ago. At a recent vertical tasting of old vintages (*see below*), it still had all the power of this concentrated year quite intact. The real star of the Joseph Perrier range, however, is the prestige cuvée Josephine,

which can be a wonderful expression of ripe, mature Chardonnay, making up 60 per cent of the blend and pervading the wine's flavours. *Chapeau* to the company's talented cellar master Claude Defrain, who made it.

FINEST WINES

(Tasted in Châlons-en-Champagne, July 2008. The older vintages, from 1990 back to 1964, were disgorged by hand for this tasting.)

Joseph Perrier Brut Cuvée Royale Brut NV [V]
35% C, 35% PN, 30% PM. Bright, pale yellow. On the nose, there are abundant, ripe orchard fruits, particularly pear, with a hint of spices. Incisive Chardonnay on entry, then fine, mature Pinot Noir and Meunier fruit on the mid-palate, enhanced by a more moderate *dosage* (7g/l) than in previous cuvées. Decent length. Very good.

Joseph Perrier Blanc de Blancs Brut NV
An intricate Chardonnay blend from distinguished sources such as grands crus Chouilly and Le Mesnil-sur-Oger, and Bergères-lès-Vertus on the Côte des Blancs; from Cumières in the Marne Valley; and most distinctively of all, from Vitry-le-François. Vital, pale yellow-gold. Minerally, punchy, lemon-scented nose. Very original, tangy flavours on the palate, like the pith of a lemon (very Vitry), broadening out into a rich roundness and the sunny warmth that is presumably supplied by the Cumières. Lingering, fine finale. Excellent blending here.

Joseph Perrier Brut Rosé NV
Elegant hue, more pale rose than salmon. Pretty nose of little red Pinot fruits. Still very fresh, but ideally it needs another six months to show the wine's full natural character and structure, so it may be worth laying it down for a short while. This also benefits from a lower *dosage*.

Joseph Perrier Cuvée Royale Vintage 1999
Fine, flattering, fruit scents, Meunier leading the pack with the whiff of the baker's shop, which the palate confirms, with excellent fruit expression. Not a complex wine—an indicator of the vintage more than anything else—but better than many of the Vintage wines from this year.

Joseph Perrier Josephine 2002★
60% C, 40% PN. Still under wraps. A potentially great wine, words inadequate to describe its splendor from this fabulous vintage. Pale yellow-gold, with superb harmony and balance at every level—fruit, texture, vinosity. Perfectly, naturally ripe, so needs no *dosage*. This should improve with bottle age and develop into a great wine.

Joseph Perrier Josephine 1998
This excellent wine displays classic qualities of tension, minerality, and ripeness: a real core of flavour, with lovely complexity. Great class and poise. As good as it gets.

Joseph Perrier Josephine 1990
This bottle tastes prematurely evolved for such a highly regarded vintage. Lacks the vigour and vitality of a *grand vin*, at least today.

Joseph Perrier Josephine 1989
Always a very great wine in its youth and middle period; now into a tertiary life, it still holds up. Wonderfully evolved, roasted, toasted Chardonnay flavours, supported by the quiet power of Pinot Noir. The fruit is still vital—not drying out.

Joseph Perrier Cuvée Royale 1985
The initial concentration and power of this small, very Pinot year—hit by early winter frost—are still recognizable. Over 20 years it has undergone a lovely, balanced evolution, honeyed, gentle, and harmonious. Delicious.

Joseph Perrier Cuvée Royale 1975
Amber-gold, very evolved on the nose, now oxidizing quite rapidly. Hints of the former elegance and class of what has been a very fine vintage show in the vestigial scents of menthol and mint. But this is now past its best and on the slide.

Joseph Perrier Cuvée Royale 1971
The first great vintage of the '70s, rather forgotten, but maybe still the very best. This is still showing beautifully today: lovely, elegant, Welsh gold, not forced; caressing mousse; the old muscles have not atrophied, in a Champagne of awesome structure, vinosity, and finesse that just says, "Drink me." I did not spit this one out. Magical.

Joseph Perrier Cuvée Royale 1964
Another of the postwar greats—when in its prime. One still senses its backbone and stature, but the fruit is drying out now, leaving it all a bit dusty.

Champagne Joseph Perrier
69 Avenue de Paris, BP31,
51016 Châlons-en-Champagne
Tel: +33 3 26 68 29 51
www.joseph-perrier.com

Beaumont des Crayères

As demand for grapes exceeds supply and inflationary pressures rise, this highly respected bijou cooperative offers one of the best ratios of quality to price of any producer in Champagne. Created at Mardeuil in 1955, Beaumont now has 238 member-growers, farming 86ha (212 acres) of fine vineyards, most on the sunny premier cru slopes of Cumières and Hautvillers. These, together with its home village of Mardeuil, provide some of the very best Meunier, as well as bright, fruit-laden Pinot Noir. On these hillsides, close to Epernay, the soils are still chalky. The farther west you go towards Paris, the heavier the soils become.

The crucial key to quality, unusual in a cooperative, is that the size of an average Beaumont member's vineyard is only 0.5ha (1.25 acres). This smallness of scale allows for very strict control over the maturity of the grapes. For 20 years, until his departure in 2007, Jean-Paul Bertus, the exceptionally gifted *chef de cave*, vinified the wines with meticulous care and passion, winning excellent reviews for the finesse and richness of his cuvées.

I should declare an interest here: I was for 12 months a press consultant for Beaumont. The contract is now completed, however, and as an independent observer again, I can say in all conscience that the succession is assured under the new director, Olivier Piazza, another passionate wine man and *ingénieur agricole*, who is committed to the most natural methods of sustainable viticulture and winemaking. He is also something of a gastronome, attracted by the richness of Beaumont Champagnes and their affinity with fine cuisine.

The entry-level Grande Réserve Brut★ [V] is made largely from finer strains of Côte d'Epernay Meunier (50 per cent), which, with carefully selected Chardonnay and a touch of Pinot Noir, results in a poised Champagne, at once brightly fruity and of surprising finesse. This is the proverbial Champagne you can drink at any time of the day or night—which perhaps explains why it is often chosen as the pouring Champagne in Europe's better restaurants. The Rosé has bonbon, fruity, crowd appeal that comes from the high proportion of Meunier. Though well made, it is not a style I particularly warm to, but that is a matter of personal taste, not quality. In contrast, a personal favourite is the least expensive of Beaumont's Vintage Champagnes, the Fleur de Prestige, which costs less than the Non-Vintage cuvées of quite a few *grandes maisons* but is far superior—a distinguished, racy wine in its own right. Both the 1996 and the 1998 are exceptional. Of the other Vintage cuvées, Nostalgie is a substantial wine, made for the table, with increased amounts of both Chardonnay (65 per cent) and Pinot Noir (35 per cent), but no Meunier. The prestige Nuits d'Or has even more Chardonnay but is a Champagne that needs time. I find it lacks a little of the ready charm and open richness that is Beaumont's main virtue, without the mineral distinction of something from the Côte des Blancs. But then Mardeuil, of course, is black-grapes country. Newer releases include vintaged Blanc de Noirs and Blanc de Blancs, whose quality and potential should gradually become apparent over the next few years.

FINEST WINES

(Tasted in Mardeuil, July 2008)

Beaumont des Crayères Nostalgie 2000
Ripe yellow colour, tint of green; rounded, quite soft nose, the good, fruity expression heralding a generous, expansive palate, with no hint of asperity. The acidity seems a bit low, but the wine holds together well on the mid-palate; good extract, with decent length and a charming, spicy aftertaste. A very good 2000, for early drinking.

Beaumont des Crayères Nostalgie 1999
A paler, more classic colour than the 2000; taut and fresh on the nose. The palate is less easy to gauge, however—oddly, it does not confirm the nose. All a bit easy, *flatteur*. I could be wrong, but there seems to be a certain lack, at least for now, of the inner substance and vinosity of a good Nostalgie. Rather typically '99. To retaste.

Beaumont des Crayères Nostalgie 1998

Tasted twice: in July 2008 and again in August. The first time, an evolving gold colour and a quite advanced oxidative nose. The bubbles were faint and lacked persistence. Olivier thought there was a pressure problem. Yet the wine behind held up, with a sensual *confit de fruit* character and significant vinosity. The second bottle, at a *World of Fine Wine* tasting, was finer. My note read: "A better class altogether; luminous green-gold; that classy balance of maturity and minerality; a touch of austerity; as great on nose as on palate; fine lingering finish."

Beaumont des Crayères Nostalgie 1996

Typically '96, the aromas still brisk and partially formed, the bouncy acidity striking the nose. Equally characterstic of the year, the flavours are at a changing stage, with notes of mushroom and game. Will the aromas and flavours eventually be in balance? Today the '98 seems the better wine.

Beaumont des Crayères Nostalgie 1988

A lovely smell of toasty, fully mature, and evolved Chardonnay driving the blend. Great complexity in an exceptional mouthfeel of rare vinosity. A great wine from a great year. Ready.

Beaumont des Crayères Fleur de Prestige 1998

A special celebratory bottling. Still supremely fresh, with racy aromas of great purity, now touched with autolytic complexity; very full, ripe, and complete on the palate. A beautifully selected '98.

(Tasted April 2007)
Beaumont des Crayères Fleur de Prestige 1996

An extremely fine '96, successfully balancing exhilarating freshness and tender ripeness. Bright-green Chardonnay flashes among the gold; lace-like mousse; aromas of spring flowers mingle with hawthorn and honeysuckle. As the wine warms, a bouquet of pear, peach, and hazelnut emerges. The Champagne finishes with a mass of lemony freshness. Ace.

Champagne Beaumont des Crayères
64 Rue de la Liberté, BP1030, 51318 Epernay
Tel: +33 3 26 55 29 40
www.champagne-beaumont.com

Right: Director Olivier Piazza (left) and winemaker Pierre Lambert, in front of one of their traditional Coquard presses

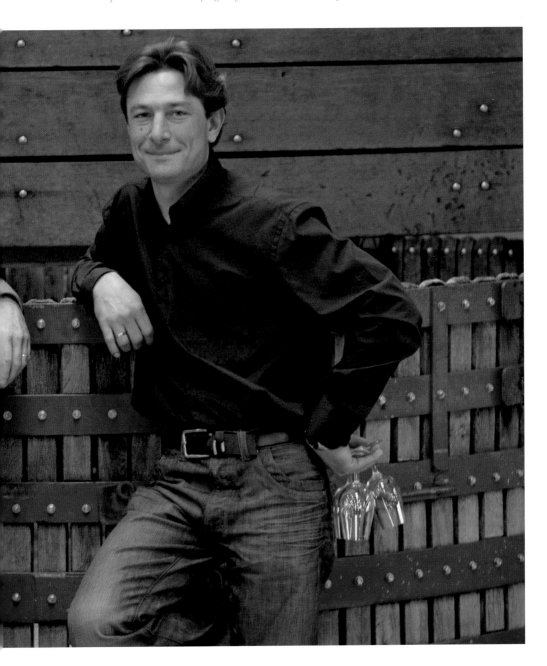

This highly respected bijou cooperative offers one of the best ratios of quality to price of any producer in Champagne. The Grande Réserve Brut is the proverbial Champagne you can drink at any time

Collard-Picard

For the Collard family of Reuil, in the Marne Valley, oak has always been the natural vessel in which to make their classic Pinot Meunier Champagnes. René Collard, the retired paterfamilias now in his 80s, is a legend in Champagne, if less well known outside France. He has always followed uncompromisingly traditional methods in order to make Champagnes that last for decades. The longevity of these remarkable Meuniers is created at the outset, with slow first fermentations in barrel, the gentle contact of air with the infant wine naturally inoculating it against later oxidation. The malo is avoided, and crucially, once the wines are bottled, they are perfectly stored in a very deep cellar some 100ft (30m) down in a chalk hillside.

That René has had complete faith in the durability of his wines is testified by the sight of amazing stocks of older vintages still in the cellar today. In 2007, there were 12,000 bottles of the 1990 and 8,000 of the 1976, with appreciable numbers of the 1975 and 1969. We tasted the splendid '75 (always a favourite vintage) with René's grandson, Olivier. Gold-bronze with green highlights, it had an extraordinary, multitoned nose of white flowers, caramelized apples (*tarte tatin?*), and spicy cinnamon. Naturally opulent in the mouth, with the touch of chocolate endemic to old Pinots, it was perfectly balanced by impeccable freshness on the end taste. Almost as good was the '85 Rosé, a salmon-brick colour, with well-preserved Pinot fruit and fine, tertiary, almost-Burgundian flavours of mushrooms and undergrowth. It has to be said that the '69 tasted a little maderized—a good excuse to go back!

Olivier and his wife Caroline, who owns grand cru Chardonnay vines in Le Mesnil, now have their own 10ha (25-acre) domaine—Collard-Picard—up the slope from Reuil at Villers-sous-Châtillon, where his father and mother also have their own estate under the name Collard-Chardelle. At Collard-Picard there is an impressive new winery complex, with an ultra-modern press that squeezes the grapes between two perforated stainless-steel plates, shortening the pressing time—a big advance. The recently installed 700-litre oak casks now play an integral role in the winemaking, following the tradition of *grandpère*, even if the oak is newer. In practice, the problem of woody flavours from new oak is not that great here, because of the much larger size of the casks and the partial use of stainless-steel vats, alongside the casks, to make the younger blends like the Cuvée Sélect Brut, a natural, fruity Champagne of beautiful freshness. The Cuvée Prestige, a blend of three vintages, is made from all three Champagne grapes and fermented in oak: ample and rich, with elegant acidity, wood and wine melding seamlessly. There is also a Vintage version of the Prestige, the 2000 and 2002 showing greater length and complexity after an extended period on lees. Collard-Picard is definitely a producer to watch.

FINEST WINES

(Tasted October 2008)

Collard-Picard Cuvée Prestige NV
A blend of 2003, 2002, and 2001 in a classic *assemblage* of Pinot Noir, Meunier, and Chardonnay, 50/50 black grapes and white. Suffused with fruit, this is full and *gras*, but retains some finesse.

Collard-Picard Rosé Brut NV
An *assemblage* of 2002 and 2001, this is a *saignée* Champagne from Pinot Noir and Meunier. The hue is so intense and deep, it is almost a red. A splendid wine for *charcuterie* or offal dishes like sautéed kidneys, or for Cantonese duck.

Right: Olivier Collard and his father Daniel, who have their own estates and together administer the wines of René

Champagne Collard-Picard
61 Rue du Château, 51700 Villers-sous-Châtillon
Tel: +33 3 26 52 36 93
www.champagnecollardpicard.fr

Tarlant

Pierre Tarlant was tending his vines in the Marne during the time of Dom Pérignon (c.1695), and the first bottles of the family's own Champagnes were made and sold in 1929. Today, Jean-Mary Tarlant and his son Benoît have 13ha (32 acres) of vineyards in the heart of the Marne Valley. Their 48 parcels in four different crus are located mainly on the southern side of the river in the villages of Oeuilly, Boursault, St-Agnan, and Celles-les-Condés. The soils here are diverse—on sand, small pebbles, limestone, and chalk—and also vary in composition from the top to the bottom of the slopes. Since the aspect of these vineyards is broadly north rather than south, the vicinity of the river is a vital influence in creating a benign microclimate. Meticulous, imaginative work in the cellar is necessary to realize the wines' full potential.

The family produce several single-vineyard Champagnes, but easily the finest is the superb, Krug-like Cuvée Louis, made from 60-year-old vines in their oldest vineyard

Fortunately, Jean-Mary is a consummate professional, a stalwart of the CIVC's technical committees and a past president of the Institut Technique Viticole. He insists on vinifying his different plots separately to reveal their true identity. That, Jean-Mary believes, is best achieved by fermentation mainly in barrel—in the Tarlant canon there is a kind of symbiosis between wine and wood through this small-scale vinification.

These are well-structured wines that also showcase the precision of their aromas and flavours. Always responsive, however, to the individual makeup of the wines, as well as to the weather, the Tarlants ferment certain cuvées in stainless steel to preserve their vitality. The model back labels helpfully supply the bottling and disgorging dates.

In line with their philosophy, the family produce several single-vineyard Champagnes, but easily the finest is the superb, Krug-like Cuvée Louis, made from 60-year-old vines in their oldest vineyard, Les Crayons, where the soil is chalkiest. It is always a blend of three vintages. The Tarlant Vintage wines are also worth seeking out, especially the excellent 1996, and there is a great rosé, available in both Brut and Extra Brut versions.

FINEST WINES

(Tasted March 2008)

Tarlant Cuvée Louis Extra Brut NV
50% C, 50% PN. *Dosage* 3g/l. Mainly 1998, with small amounts of 1997 and 1996. Fermented entirely in oak barrels (used four times before). No malo, the lees regularly stirred. The wine ages in barrel for seven months. Gold/yellow hue and a fine, crystalline cordon of bubbles. Powerful, expansive nose, the wood a judicious influence, with notes of dried apricots, vanilla, and toast. A majestic mouthfeel, strongly constituted, but round and *gras*, with a lovely, honeyed character. A wine for great occasions and high gastronomy.

Tarlant Brut Prestige 1996
Two thirds Chardonnay to one third Pinot Noir. No malo again—a daring step for a year suffused with acidity, but it all works beautifully. Fine, Chardonnay-led scents of buttered toast and brioche. Then, in the mouth, a sumptuous maturity of black fruit, a touch of liquorice, and very long finish.

Tarlant Rosé Zéro Dosage NV
A blend of 2003 and 2002. Dominated by Chardonnay with 15% Pinot Noir vinified as red wine. The ripeness of the grapes in these two years shows admirably, Pinot asserting itself with its little-red-fruits flavour and complementing the opulent, rich, and fleshy Chardonnay. An ideal alfresco Champagne for a barbecued veal chop.

Left: Benoît Tarlant, who, with his father Jean-Mary, allies respect for nature with technical brilliance in the cellar

Champagne Tarlant
51480 Oeuilly/Epernay
Tel: +33 3 26 58 30 60
www.tarlant.com

Louis Casters

Jean-Louis Casters and his son Johan are the fourth and fifth generations of a family of growers in Damery who were making their own Champagnes as early as the 1880s. Today, with négociant status, they own 7.5ha (20 acres) of vineyards in the Marne Valley at Damery, Vauciennes, Reuil, Binson, and Châtillon but also buy in grapes from a further 40ha (100 acres), especially in the Côte des Blancs. The house's main markets are fine restaurants across the EU, and some 70 per cent is exported.

I know their Champagnes the easiest way, for their lovely rosé in particular is often served by the glass from magnums in the Bistrot le 7 of Les Berceaux hotel in Epernay. After a sometimes stressful journey, there is nothing better to calm the mind and whet the appetite before a good dinner.

The approach of the Casters—like that of all enlightened producers—is one of evolved tradition. They treat their vines and soils with the respect that their grandparents did

In the vineyards and winery, the approach of the Casters—like that of all enlightened producers—is one of evolved tradition. They treat their vines and soils with the respect that their grandparents did, keeping yields reasonable in the practice of sustainable viticulture, which means avoiding use of chemicals and herbicides. In the cellar, they welcome modern technology insofar as it may enhance their careful work in the fields.

Their range of Champagnes is compact but full of interest and includes some unusual, rather recherché wines. The Cuvée Supérieure is made 100 per cent from the Meunier grape and is good as an apéritif but has the fruit to carry through a complete meal—as representative a Champagne

of this part of the Marne Valley as it is possible to be. The Brut Sélection is pure Pinot Noir, while the Grande Réserve is pure Chardonnay. The Cuvée Eugène comes largely from grand cru Chardonnay grapes. The finest Champagne in the cellar, however, is the Cuvée JL. Aged for a minimum of eight years, this a complex Extra Brut wine of real class. Casters also makes an old *marc de Champagne* and a *ratafia*, the local apéritif made from Champagne grapes and alcohol.

FINEST WINES

(Tasted in Epernay, October 2008)

Louis Casters Brut Sélection NV [V]
Although this is pure Pinot Noir, with a vivid peachy yellow colour and the full body one would expect, it is also a very precise Champagne of impressive finesse. A good Champagne for white meats, particularly chicken or milk-fed veal. Excellent value.

Louis Casters Rosé Brut NV
An interesting *assemblage* of roughly one third each of Pinot Noir, Pinot Meunier, and Chardonnay. The colour is a lovely lustrous salmon hue, and the bubbles are small and persistent. Creamy in the mouth, the Chardonnay particularly gives the wine a fineness and drive that is exceptional, yet there are also generous orchard-fruit flavours from the two Pinots vinified as Champagne and the little red wine that is added.

Louis Casters Cuvée JL Extra Brut
The top wine is a blend of 65% C, 20% PN, and 15% PM, and from the 1999, 1998, and 1997 vintages. Bright and still youthful in appearance: yellow with green reflections. Powerful, spicy, and long on the palate, in a hedonistic style, with exotic fruits and nuttiness to the fore.

Champagne Louis Casters
26 Rue Pasteur,
51480 Damery
Tel: +33 3 26 58 43 02
www.champagne-casters.com

Pannier

Pannier & Co is the brand name of the Covama Champagne cooperative of growers at Château-Thierry, the main town of the Western Aisne *département*, just 50 miles (80km) from Paris. They farm 624ha (1,540 acres) of vines, mainly of Meunier, in the Vallée de la Marne, but they also have access to grapes from the Montagne de Reims and the Côte des Blancs.

The wines are matured in deep medieval vaults and catacombs bought by the co-op when it moved to Château-Thierry in 1974. The winemaking is very competent and modern throughout the range, rising to genuinely fine at Vintage level, especially the prestige cuvée Egérie de Pannier—often a memorable bottle. The entry-level Brut Tradition is an utterly dependable staple Champagne driven by the predominant Meunier (more than 50 per cent)—pale yet vital colour, a fine persistent mousse, with clear fruit definition and a supple yet vinous flavour. The Blanc de Noirs, a more recent cuvée, is excellent—and impressive enough to be listed by Didier Elena at the Relais & Châteaux Les Crayères in Reims.

FINEST WINES

(Tasted in Château-Thierry, July 2006)

Pannier Blanc de Noirs NV
An *assemblage* of mainly Pinot Noir but with selections of fine Meunier, too. Vivid, bright yellow, with just a faint flick of pink at the rim. Ample orchard-fruit aromas—peach, cherry, apricot—soar from the glass. The palate is round, with real presence, but not overblown. A gastronomic wine.

Egérie de Pannier Rosé de Saignée NV
80% PN (the skins bled first to achieve the desired hue) and 20% C to add finesse. An unusual pink Champagne, with a distinctive flavour of orange zest, cooked fruits, and notes of caramel.

Egérie de Pannier Extra Brut 1999
50% PN (and a little Meunier), 50% C. One of the better 1999s: finesse, poise, and textbook balance, with admirable length. *Vin fin.*

Champagne Pannier
23 Rue Roger Catillon,
BP300, 02400 Château-Thierry
Tel: +33 3 23 69 51 30
www.champagnepannier.com

Epernay and the Côte des Blancs

Epernay, by way of its location and economic importance, is effectively the wine capital of Champagne. This pleasant little town of 24,000 inhabitants is plumb in the heart of the vineyards, situated between the top of the Côte des Blancs and the central part of the Marne Valley. And although just one tenth the size of Reims, Epernay makes as much Champagne. Providing nearly all the employment locally, 37 Champagne firms in the town are led by the giant of the industry, Moët & Chandon, which produces about 30 million bottles annually; it is said that a bottle of Moët is uncorked somewhere in the world every six seconds. For its vast size, Moët produces good Champagne that is getting better all the time, thanks to the excellence of its technical management and two great winemakers, Richard Geoffroy of Dom Pérignon and Benoît Gouez, the brilliant young *chef de cave* who has radically improved the quality of Moët's Brut Impérial.

Close to the Place de la République, Moët's huge yellow building dominates Epernay's Avenue de Champagne, a very grand street for a small provincial town, now partly converted into a pedestrian walkway to accommodate the many summer visitors. Opposite Moët's HQ are the two elegant 19th-century white buildings that were once the home of the Moët family, and behind their courtyard is a sunken garden and an exquisite orangery, designed by the French miniaturist Jean-Baptiste Isabey. Farther up the street is the grandiose Château Perrier, which now houses the town's library and fine museum. Farther still is a town house of the Pol-Roger family, No.44 Avenue de Champagne, which Winston Churchill once described as the most drinkable address in the world. He had good taste, for Pol Roger still makes the most consistently delicious Non-Vintage and the finest Vintage Champagnes of any house in Epernay. Right at the top of the avenue is the house of Mercier, whose

Champagnes are now sold mainly in the French market. Its cellar extends to 10 miles (16km) of cool subterranean galleries, which can be visited daily on the firm's miniature electric train.

For the curious connoisseur

Back in the centre of town, Champagne's governing body, the CIVC, has its offices, where it sits like Solomon in judgment on the competing claims of houses and growers. It is also a very effective promotional body for the whole industry. For the curious connoisseur who wants to dig beneath the surface, there are also bijou, family-owned Champagne firms off the Boulevard Maréchal Foch at the west end of the town, none better than a recent discovery for me, Vincent Testulat in the Rue Léger-Bertin, a source of excellent Champagnes at the right price and heard about the best way—by word of mouth. In his domaine of 18ha (44 acres) Vincent has some very good unsung vineyards on the surrounding hills, the Coteaux d'Epernay—a great location for the most refined expressions of the Meunier grape judiciously blended with Chardonnay and Pinot Noir. Both Vincent's vineyards and those of Thierry Laherte in the nearby village of Chavot, at the head of the Cubry Valley, lie on a fascinating transitional terroir. Here the chalk of the *falaises de Champagne* cedes to different soils of silt, sandstone, and not-too-heavy clay. Thierry insists on bottling wines from these soils separately, to show how diverse a domaine's Champagnes can be.

Epernay has my two favourite places to eat in Champagne. Les Berceaux hotel's Bistrot le 7 offers terrific-value brasserie dishes from the same great kitchen as chef-patron Patrick Michelon's main restaurant, which has one Michelin star but really ought to have two.

Right: Row upon row of vines run down the Côte des Blancs, the source of Champagne's greatest Chardonnays

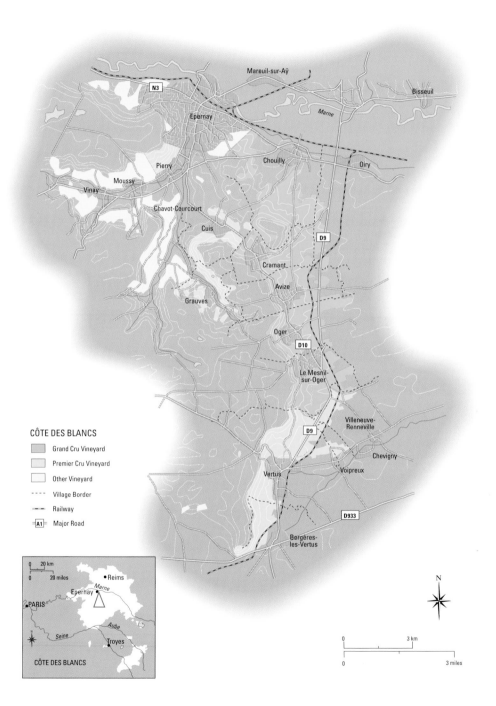

CÔTE DES BLANCS

Mareuil-sur-Aÿ

Bisseuil

N3

Epernay

Marne

Pierry

Chouilly

Oiry

Moussy

Vinay

Chavot-Courcourt

Cuis

D9

Cramant

Avize

Grauves

Oger

D10

Le Mesnil-
sur-Oger

Villeneuve-
Renneville

D9

Chevigny

Voipreux

Vertus

CÔTE DES BLANCS

Grand Cru Vineyard

Premier Cru Vineyard

Other Vineyard

Village Border

Railway

A1   Major Road

D933

Bergères-
les-Vertus

0   20 km

0   20 miles

•Reims

Epernay •

Marne

PARIS•

Seine

Aube

•Troyes

CÔTE DES BLANCS

N

0   3 km

0   3 miles

196

Côte des Blancs

The Côte des Blancs, as its name implies, is white-grapes country. A lozenge-shaped hill, about 600ft (180m) high, it stretches south of the N3 Epernay–Châlons road for 12 miles (20km) as far as Bergères-lès-Vertus, the village in the lee of Mont Aimé, where Tsar Nicholas reviewed the allied armies after Waterloo. Except in the commune of Vertus, which has sizable vineyards of Pinot Noir, the Côte is overwhelmingly planted to Chardonnay, which reaches heights of complexity and distinction as nowhere else in Champagne. Its dramatic slopes are steeper than those of the northeast face of the Montagne, and the Tertiary topsoils tend to be less thick. In the case of Le Mesnil, the topsoil is actually very shallow, the vine going almost directly into the Cretaceous chalk, making the wines of this grand cru the most searingly acidic when young but endowed with a splendid constitution—quite enough in great vintages to ensure a long, distinguished life of 20 years, and sometimes 30.

Cuis

The Côte is best approached by the prettier back road off the western roundabout of the Epernay ring road, rising steeply past Chavot to the first village of Cuis, home of Pierre Gimonnet & Fils, one of the most consistent producers of great Chardonnay Champagnes. The family, here since 1750 as grape growers, were making wine from the beginning, but it was the Great Depression of the 1930s that determined Pierre Gimonnet to begin making his own Champagne for direct sales to build a better life for his wife and children. His son Michel, who sadly died in 2008, greatly developed the range from 1955. And Michel's sons Olivier and Didier have taken the enviably large estate of 25ha (62 acres) to yet greater heights. Not for them the now-fashionable emphasis on monocru bottlings, for their ace card is the extent, size, and variety of their holdings in the best parcels of old-vine

Chouilly and Cramant, the northern grands crus of the Côte, allied to the cleansing vitality of their home vineyards of Cuis. They believe in blending this exceptional material across their range for the greater good and complexity of the whole. Food for thought for *maisons* and growers alike.

Cramant

The gradient gets steeper still as you climb to the hilltop village of Cramant. This was among the first communes on the Côte to be awarded grand cru status. As you stand on the ridge high above the amphitheatre of vines, with wonderful east, southeast, and even full south aspects, you realize how special a place this is for growing Chardonnay. The great white grape is clearly suited to this environment, naturally dynamized by the minerality of the subsoils in balance with a natural richness imparted by its ideal exposure to what warm rays of sunshine there are in this cold climate. In the sweep of history, Chardonnay was a relative newcomer, becoming dominant on the Côte only in the 18th century, when the price of land increased by 800 per cent. Each of the *lieux-dits* in Cramant has its own character. Talking to great growers here—such as Jacques Diebolt, Olivier Gimonnet, and Bertrand Lilbert—one learns that Pimonts on the western mid-slopes is known for its finesse, and La Croix for acidity and grip; whereas Gros Monts and Bouzons, on southeast-facing, steeper coteaux adjoining the Butte de Saran, contribute power and depth—especially from the 50- to 100-year-old vines that Diebolt and Gimonnet are lucky enough to have.

Chouilly

The large village of Chouilly to the east, just below Epernay, was formerly a premier cru but has been elevated to grand cru status. I have a great fondness

Following page: The commanding ridge above Cramant, one of the first villages on the Côte to become a grand cru

for the roundness and relative forwardness of Chouilly's Champagnes, which still retain a racy minerality. They are perfect wines, very versatile for food, especially fish. Since the early 1970s, R&L Legras has been the leading grower in Chouilly, making wines of great class at reasonable prices that are often the house Champagnes of some of France's greatest restaurants. Jacques Lameloise in Burgundy swears by it.

Avize

From the other side of Cramant you come down gradually to Avize. Along with Le Mesnil farther south, it is the grand cru of the Côte that arguably produces the most complete, ageworthy wines. Avize has a reputation for lead-pencil elegance, but this is a big commune with a diverse variety of subsoils, and there are plenty of parcels that yield powerful wines. The diversity of the terrain is due to a number of rills that penetrate the east-facing escarpment of the Côte at this point. Some of the big houses of Reims and Epernay own a lot of land here, but the Côte's growers are well represented by Avize's super-cooperative, Union Champagne, and there are also a half-dozen top-flight domaines in the village.

Lacking the great stocks of reserve wines that the great houses can call on, these small to medium-sized growers in Avize have developed a resourceful "perpetual" reserve based on the solera system, as used in Sherry-making. Each spring, the new cuvée is assembled, the total quantity of the blend being twice what is bottled. The other part is kept in tanks or barrels and used as a base for the following year. So, progressively, this perpetual blend, refreshed by new wine each spring, becomes more complex as the years go by. The celebrated Anselme Selosse's most renowned cuvée, Substance, is a perpetual

"solera" of 12 vintages. Anselme is sometimes depicted as the pioneer of the method; its "finest exponent" might be a more accurate description, since Claude Corbon, farther down the village, was doing much the same thing in the early 1970s, when Anselme was still a schoolboy.

In the Avize *vignoble*, such producers are very conscious of the subtle differences of soil, microclimate, and orientation of their various parcels, and growers such as Agrapart do separate bottlings in which to illustrate these differences. A more minerally wine might come from the *lieu-dit* of les Champs Boutins, a fleshier but fine one from Les Robards, where the house of Louis Roederer cultivates its vines biodynamically, the wine no doubt reserved for its sumptuous prestige cuvée Cristal. One of Avize's largest *lieux-dits* at the lower end of the village—Les Maladrieres du Nord—has a strong presence of clay that makes powerful wines for long aging. As in any great wine village, the various styles are an embarrassment of riches. Returning to the top of the village, it is worth the five-minute drive into the hills and the little village of Grauves. The two key growers here are Pierre Domi, respected for his generous, buttery Grande Réserve (50/50 Chardonnay and Meunier), and Driant-Valentin, who makes a very fine, mature Pinot-led cuvée usually composed of two vintages with an average age of seven years: aromatic, honeyed, and attractively unctuous, a wine for a *risotto aux cèpes*.

Oger

Moving south, you come to the grand cru of Oger, the prettiest flower-filled village on the Côte and source of some of its most beautiful wines. Oger has a gentle fragrance and roundness that comes from the consistent ripeness of Chardonnay grown in a sun-filled amphitheatre of vineyards that is the village's dramatic backcloth. There are very few growers making their own Champagnes here—

Left: Winter pruning on the slopes of the Côte des Blancs is the coldest vineyard task but also one of the most crucial

the *vins clairs* are snapped up by the *grandes maisons*—but two domaines deserve special mention. On the Avize road, opposite the village pharmacy, the small 6ha (15-acre) domaine of Jean Milan produces fine yet firm blanc de blancs. Henri-Pol Milan, the current head of the family, presses grapes very traditionally for Pol Roger, and his own Champagnes have been highly praised by Robert Parker, especially the single-vineyard La Terre de Noël that lies behind the house. Equally fine is his very complete Cuvée Symphorine, from his best hillside sites of Beaudure, Barbettes, Zailleux, and Chénets. The Clos Cazals, by the village church, is the location of Oger's other great Champagne, producing a brilliant 1996 and a sumptuous 1999 that is much better than many in that mercurial vintage.

Le Mesnil-sur-Oger

Continue south and you find Le Mesnil-sur-Oger, now probably the most prestigious Chardonnay grand cru of all, owing to the international prominence and quality of Krug's Clos du Mesnil, particularly in recent vintages such as 1996 and 1998, now that the vines replanted in the 1970s are approaching maturity. Le Mesnil is a large and diverse commune of some 420ha (1,040 acres), of which 320ha (790 acres) are owned by growers and about 100ha (250 acres) by the *grandes maisons*. More than 80 *récoltants-manipulants*, a highish figure, make their own Champagnes, and there is a fine cooperative, Le Mesnil, whose member-growers (included in the 320 figure above) own fine vineyards in the best sites. Where are they?

Well, by a process of elimination, the very high vineyards around the aptly named Mont Blanc and close to the woods should never have been included within the grand cru, according to Alain Robert, a great grower who produced magnificent Champagnes up to the end of the 20th century. And being such an exposed site between

two valleys, the upper side of the village has some good but not exceptional vineyards that include Krug's *clos*—the splendor of their Champagne has everything to do with the brilliance of the winemaking and those maturing vines. The Krugs say that the high walls of the *clos* are heat-retaining, accelerating the grapes' ripening. That's possible, but I always feel that Clos du Mesnil takes longer than most in the village to reach optimal maturity, which here means at least 15 years. I believe the best sites in Le Mesnil were graphically identified in 1985 by Charles Delhaye, a great Champagne man and president of Canard-Duchêne, a subsidiary house at the time of Veuve Clicquot, which still owns some of the best vineyards. Delhaye pointed out that if you look closely at the configuration of the terroir, the village is at the extreme north of the commune's vineyard area. Moreover, he argued that, to the south, in the direction of Vertus, there is a series of *lieux-dits*—Moulin-à-Vent, Musettes, Champs Alouette, Aillerands, and Rougemonts (he might also have mentioned Les Chétillons)—that have the most privileged exposure to the sun, a vital factor in achieving full balancing ripeness in grapes packed with that superb piercing acidity and minerality. Spot on. Le Mesnil needs the right sites in a hot year to show its full magnificence.

The village has had its fair share of inventive minds, not least the late Claude Cazals who, with his friend Jacques Ducoin of Mareuil-sur-Aÿ were co-inventors in 1969 of the gyropalette. Now, with Alain Robert's impending retirement, Pierre Péters, under François and Rodolphe Péters, is, with Krug, the leading Mesnil estate. Another fine producer is Christophe Constant at J-L Vergnon, who is revitalizing this old, respected domaine and realizing the potential class inherent in its fine vineyards. Lunching recently at Le Mesnil restaurant in the village, I was introduced to Philippe Gonet, a well-known local grower, who

Above: A commemorative plaque in Avize, recognizing the importance of Chardonnay to this leading grand cru village

offered me a glass of his excellent Brut; it is first-class and well worth investigating.

Vertus

And so to Vertus, the last and also the largest wine commune on the Côte—some 450ha (1,110 acres), all classified as premier cru. Geologically, there is a crucial distinction to be drawn between the vineyards on the east, Mesnil side of Vertus, particularly the calcareous, Chardonnay-compatible Monts Ferrés, and those richer soils on the west, adjoining Bergères, where much of the Pinot Noir is grown. Two great Vertus estates—Larmandier-Bernier and Veuve Fourny—make excellent minerally Chardonnay in the prize *lieu-dit* of Les Barillers on the Mont Ferrés. Vertus is the headquarters of Duval-Leroy, the most important house, with 200ha (500 acres) of vines. The redoubtable Carol Duval majors on Chardonnay, and any grapes she may have to buy in for her rapidly

expanding business are made with the same rigor and care as her own. Duval-Leroy is a rare example of a powerful merchant with its feet firmly in the vineyards, sharing the values of the vignerons: Carol always sends a birthday card to every one of the grape farmers who supply the house. Vertus is also the base for the fine cooperative of Paul Goerg, its cellars making the wines of the 117ha (290 acres) of members' vineyards. The Goerg Tradition is a fine Brut, much better and aged for longer (four to six years) than the entry cuvée of a middling *grande maison*. Among the independent growers, Yannick Doyard makes the supremely subtle Collection de l'An 1 oeil de perdrix (a great 2002), and Michel Maillard was until 2008 still selling his rightly named MM de Champagne Rare 1982, with the colour of golden leather and aromas of coffee, toast, and preserved fruit—a bottle for foie gras, especially if you find Sauternes too sweet.

Côte de Sézanne

After Bergères, the Côte des Blancs is separated from the Côte de Sézanne by the Marais (marshes) de St Gond. Sézanne is a typical, jolly French provincial town of 5,500 inhabitants. Its vineyard slopes share the same southeast orientation as those of the Côte des Blancs, but the soils are heavier and the wines broader and more rustic. Nonetheless, the cooperative of Le Brun de Neuville, south of the town at Béthon, close to the Marne border with the Aube, is an admirable source of fine Champagne at reasonable prices. It was founded in 1963, and 50 of its growers farm 150ha (370 acres), mainly of Chardonnay. Their finer selection of Chardonnay can upstage many more expensive bottles with its quality and value. There is also an excellent rosé, fruity and vital, yet with plenty of structure. And the Cuvée Lady de N Clovis is made with a light touch, belying its majority Pinot Noir element: all youth and charm with a lemony vivacity, it makes an ideal apéritif.

Moët & Chandon

Moët is a story of courage — the best sort that weighs all the risks and perils, then stiffens the resolve of the individual to seize the moment and go ahead with calm confidence.

Originally of Dutch origin, the family made its first recorded appearance in 1446, when the French king knighted the brothers Jean and Nicolas Moët after they routed a foreign army invading Reims. Almost 300 years later, in 1743, their descendant Claude Moët, a broker and wine grower in the Marne Valley, founded his Champagne firm in Epernay. With that strong family gene, Claude was very quick to see the potential for sparkling Champagne in the elegant cities of 18th-century France. But it was really his grandson, Jean-Rémy Moët, who made the brand famous through his friendship with Napoleon. Between 1805 and his death in 1841, Moët was the

Between 1805 and 1841, Moët was the most celebrated winemaker in Europe, and the company became the premier Champagne house—a position it has held ever since

most celebrated winemaker in Europe, and the company became the premier Champagne house— a position it has held ever since.

Like all good Champenois traders, Jean-Rémy was a brilliant salesman and natural marketeer. Playing the connection with the emperor for all it was worth, he built Epernay's Trianon—twin white Pavilions with a formal garden and exquisite orangery, still there and operational today, to accommodate Napoleon's court on its way to and from the battlefields of Eastern Europe. Jean-Rémy became the stuff of legend when he turned disaster into triumph after the defeat of Waterloo, inviting the marauding Russian cossacks to take his wine. He knew, of course, that they would get the taste for Champagne and be back as customers.

Less dramatic but just as important, Jean-Rémy was a true wine man, embracing modern ideas. He certainly studied the fermentation and aging process on a scientific basis, endlessly testing new techniques to bolster the quality of his wines and blends. This dual Moët trait of perfectionism and calculated risk-taking brought great riches to the company in the mid-19th century. By then, the name of the house had been changed to Moët & Chandon, to include the surname of Pierre Gabriel Chandon de Briailles, who had married Jean-Rémy's daughter. The family became the greatest vineyard owners in Champagne, the list of customers grew longer, and Richard Wagner consoled himself with a bottle of Moët when his opera *Tanhaüser* flopped at its 1861 premiere in Paris. By 1900, Moët & Chandon had about 16 per cent of the booming export market. In a downward dip in its fortunes, the firm then went through a period of stagnation until it was rescued by Comte Robert-Jean de Vogüé, the head of the house in the early 1930s.

De Vogüé, who actually preferred whisky to wine, was the best sort of aristocrat—visionary and bold, with a real sense of *noblesse oblige*. So in the dreadful years of the Great Depression, he proposed that the starving growers get a sixfold increase in the price of their grapes. And in 1935, he launched Champagne's first prestige cuvée—Dom Pérignon— in England and America, as a nectar to banish thoughts of the Fascist dictators, at least for an hour or two. With his loyal right-hand man Claude Fourmon, Comte Robert-Jean survived internment in a German deportation camp and, after the war, rapidly expanded the company's sales in new markets worldwide. In 1962, Moët became the first Champagne house to be quoted on the Paris Bourse. In the ensuing 40 years, the house expanded hugely. After acquiring Ruinart Champagne and the house of Christian Dior, the firm became the wine emperor in the Louis Vuitton-Moët Hennessy luxury-goods conglomerate, taking control of Veuve Clicquot.

Then Lanson and Pommery were bought and eventually sold on, but not before their beautiful vineyards had become part of the Moët wine estate. Of the company's many sparkling-wine ventures in Europe, the Americas, and Australasia, Green Point in Victoria is an Australian superstar, admired on five continents.

At home, the Epernay giant produces 30 million bottles of Champagne annually, a bottle being popped somewhere in the world every six seconds. For such a huge operation, the quality of winemaking at Moët is very high. That standard is built on the surest bases. First, the firm's immense financial muscle allows it to secure the best grapes, supplementing those of its own wine estate of 15,000ha (37,000 acres). Second, true to the Moët tradition of being willing to take risks, its winemakers are always innovative and meet any

challenge that Mother Nature can throw at them— never more so than in 2003. If you subscribe to the notion of "global warming", this was it: the hottest July and August ever, the earliest harvest for 181 years, wines of extraordinary fruit and extract but low acidity. If you prefer to call whatever is going on "climate change", again 2003 in Champagne perfectly illustrates the veering twists and turns of 21st-century weather sequences: the most severe winter frosts since 1957; a balmy March, causing perilously early budbreak; devastating spring frosts on 11 and 12 April that wrought terrible damage on the vines; then hail eight times in April and May, before the Saharan heat of the summer.

Moët's *chef de cave* Benoit Gouez and his team made a typically bold decision. They realized that it would have been futile to try to protect or radically "correct" the juice of grapes in which most of the acidity had been burned off. They preferred to let the grapes stay on the vine in the last week of August to settle down and take a drink from a few blessed showers. Then, when the grapes came in and the juice was tasted, they threw away the rule book and made a special and atypical wine that emphasized the glory of the fruit and its phenolic maturity. The blend majored on Meunier, which, of the three Champagne grape varieties, suffered least from heat stress and so brimmed with golden, palate-cloaking fruitiness. Then the team added rigorously selected Pinot, for the many wild flavours *le grand noir* produced that year, and of course Chardonnay that tasted more like white Burgundy, suffused with buttery, toasty succulence and a benign vegetative character.

The 2003 Moët Grand Vintage is part of a collection of sensual wines made in especially hot years—*les solaires*—distinguished by exceptional summer conditions. Even the greatly improved Moët Brut Imperial Non-Vintage seems to have a taste of the sun about it these days.

FINEST WINES

(Tasted in October 2008)

Moët & Chandon Grand Vintage 2003
A blend of 43% PM, 29% PN, and 28% C. Lowish *dosage* of 5g/l. The first delightful surprise here is the colour—not an overly ripe, deep gold, but rather an elegant, creamy blondness. Chardonnay, though marginally the smallest element in the blend, drives the aromas of vanilla, almonds, and hazelnut. The mouthfeel is framed by succulent summer fruits —apricots, yellow peaches, all very Pinot—and an opulence from the dominant Meunier, which also brings spiciness, notably gingerbread and the smells of the coffee shop. A powerful Champagne, but one with plenty of style. All in all, pretty impressive winemaking in challenging circumstances. For early drinking, 2009–10.

Moët & Chandon Grand Vintage Rosé 2003★ [V]
48% PN (of which 19% was vinified as red wine), 30% PM, and 22% C. *Dosage* 5g/l. The intention of the winemakers here was to make a rosé of real, no-holds-barred intensity, but one that finishes fresh and crisp. They have succeeded brilliantly. The blood-orange colour ceding to ruby tones speaks of the heat and richness of the scorching summer. The aromas are opulent yet poised—blood orange, yes, mingling with grapefruit, and a lovely floral hint of roses. In the mouth, hedgerow fruits like red currant meet more exotic, mocha-like flavours. But for all its size, the finale is amazingly brisk, racy, and herby, powerfully reminiscent of aniseed. Another great wine for Asian treatments of duck.

Moët & Chandon Grand Collection Vintage 1995
40% C, 50% PN, 10% PM. Low *dosage*. Disgorged November 2007. This vintage is a particular favourite. After a difficult spring and late flowering, the high summer months were very hot, with little rain. September, though, was cooler and, maybe because of that, saw perfect ripeness in the powerful Chardonnays and linear definition in the Pinot Noirs. A really classic year that will age beautifully, but the wines are always friendly and satisfying at any stage in their life. Pear and citrus-fruit aromas cede to apricot and other orchard fruits. The palate is a marvel of sumptuous richness and fresh vigour. One of Moët's very best vintages and, for some, superior and better balanced than the 1996.

Moët & Chandon Grand Collection Vintage 1990
Exactly the same grape mix and *dosage* as for the 1995. Disgorged August 2003. A cold snap of frost in April 1990 destroyed the crop over an area of some 7,000ha (17,300 acres) of vines. But summer brought the largest number of sun hours on record to this point. Then rain at just the right moment swelled the grapes. This is an excellent, even great, vintage, with that special touch of power and elegance. But although there is splendid harmony of rich, *surmature* flavours here, I actually slightly prefer the vigour of the 1995.

Right: Although Moët & Chandon needs to buy in most of its grapes, it also has its own vineyards, as here at Aÿ

Champagne Moët & Chandon
20 Avenue de Champagne, 51200 Epernay
Tel: +33 3 26 51 20 20
www.moet.com

Dom Pérignon

Benedictine cellar master at the Abbey of Hautvillers in the late 17th century, Dom Pérignon is (with a little poetic licence) dubbed the father of Champagne (*see p.12*). And Dom Pérignon—the wine—is certainly the daddy of all prestige Champagne cuvées, thanks to the imagination of another great Champenois, Robert-Jean de Vogüé. Undaunted by the effect of the Great Depression, de Vogüé persuaded his fellow Moët directors to relaunch an unused *marque* called Dom Pérignon, which had actually been bought from Mercier in 1930. He wanted it as a luxury Champagne for export markets.

It was a brilliant marketing coup, in view of Moët & Chandon's long-standing ownership of the ancient abbey and vineyards of Hautvillers. Remarkably, in the wake of the economic slump and the rise of the Fascist dictators, the first shipments arrived in London in 1935 and in New York the following year. It was an instant and resounding success, offering comfort and solace to wine lovers as storm clouds gathered over Europe.

So it was a real pleasure to return to Hautvillers in January 2008 to taste the most recent vintages with an old friend, Richard Geoffroy. Richard, Dom Pérignon's masterly *chef de cave*, is also a fully qualified medical doctor, drawn back to his roots in wine. His father was the president of Union Champagne, the greatest cooperative in the Marne Valley.

In terms of wine style, Dom Pérignon stays faithful to vinification of the still wines in stainless steel, resulting in Champagnes of precise, initially reductive flavours that can take a full decade, even 15 years, really to show themselves. Overly categorical verdicts on the wines when young are particularly risky. The essential DP style, however, is for floral aromas and a creamy middle palate that is never heavy—*finesse avant tout*.

Right: Richard Geoffroy, Dom Pérignon's inspirational *chef de cave*, in the suitably airy and light tasting room at Hautvillers

Dom Pérignon is (with a little poetic licence) dubbed the father of Champagne. Dom Pérignon—the wine—is certainly the daddy of all prestige Champagne cuvées

The Dom Pérignon Oenothèque series is a "library" of late-disgorged, late-released DP vintages, reflecting Richard's belief that the wines pass through three ages. The first release of the vintage (as Dom Pérignon *tout court*) still has the coiled reserve of youth (at 8–10 years of age). The first Oenothèque offering reveals the blossoming of proper personality in early adulthood (at around 18–20 years), while the second Oenothèque finally reveals the true character of full maturity, wrinkles and all (at around 35–40 years). Richard is convinced that the non-oxidative DP winemaking ensures a longer life. And it certainly works beautifully with the 1969, a real bouncer of a vintage that was packed with acidity for years and so is virtually indestructible. The 1975, however, a once superb but fine-drawn year, may be in decline. I think it might have been strengthened if it had been been fermented in oak, paradoxically gaining inoculation aganst oxidation by this early contact with air. But that is not the Dom Pérignon way.

FINEST WINES

(Tasted at the Abbey of Hautvillers, January 2008)

Dom Pérignon 2000
Vital, positive bright yellow, with gold and green highlights. Expansive, ripe scents of Pinot Noir and Chardonnay meshing together, already showing well. Round, *gras* palate; vigorous, with fine, mineral tones; still a touch foursquare but full of character. It will give real pleasure relatively young for DP. Reassuringly, it is not touching the reductive bottom of the range of maturity.

Dom Pérignon 1999
Lush, yellow gold; not inelegant. Soft citrus and stone fruits on the nose. Ripe, luxuriant palate; no hint of asperity, but lacking a little of the substance and complexity of classic DP. All up-front: a grandstanding wine.

Dom Pérignon 1998★
Brilliant, sustained gold. Classic, creamy citrus and red-fruit aromas in a magical balance of ripeness and mineral precision, typical of the best Champagnes of the vintage. The palate offers total confirmation of the nose: beautiful fruit expression, creamy yet chewy, with a fine, austere edge. The real McCoy—will age beautifully. This might be a snip. Tip-top but less talked about than the fashionable 1996.

Dom Pérignon 1996
Real, poised concentration here. It is a relief to report that the wine is much more balanced than many other 1996s. This one is so harmonious, so integrated. It is a big wine, quite vinous, and in that sense not a typical DP. Certainly excellent, but for me it is surpassed by the exquisite style and subtlety of the 1998.

Dom Pérignon Rosé 1996
Interesting to note that, in true DP style, Richard has not gone for the forward, oxidative style of other '96 rosés. This is more reserved and shy, but with great aging potential. Exquisite coral colour, and a vibrant but very controlled Pinot character on the nose. Captivating, fragrant-in-the-mouth, red-fruit flavours, so very Pinot. Perfect balance of ripe, elegant tannins and phenolic maturity. Lovely, crisp finish (Chardonnay making its presence felt).

Dom Pérignon Rosé 1990
Evolving shades of pink coral flecked with grey—a subtle, intriguing hue. The nose is at first reductive, but with air, sweet aromas of prunes, butter, and brioche rise up. That gorgeous, fragrant-in-the-mouth, red-fruit character is marked, as in the 1996, but here there is more vinous complexity coming from the secondary flavours of a wine approaching its 18th birthday. Outstanding.

Dom Pérignon 1969
Finally, a chance to taste a rarely shown vintage at nearly 40 years of age. Seamless, golden colour; clearly ripe and very mature nose but with that telltale punch of acidity typical of the vintage. Solid, robust, foursquare mouthful, relieved by a little creaminess. Not a typical DP vintage, but a vigorous wine in distinguished old age.

Right: Statue of Dom Pérignon at the Abbey of Hautvillers, his gesture seeming to reflect the wine's perfect proportions

Champagne Dom Pérignon
20 Avenue de Champagne, 51200 Epernay
Tel: +33 3 26 51 20 20
www.moet.com

Perrier-Jouët

Pierre Nicolas-Marie Perrier founded this Epernay house in 1811, adding the maiden name of his wife Adèle Jouët to the masthead of the new business. Its first shipments of Champagne reached England in 1815 and the United States in 1837. Charles Perrier, Pierre's son, was something of a commercial dynamo, a wily politician and the distinguished mayor of Epernay who built the Château Perrier on the Avenue de Champagne. As early as 1848, a Mr Burns, Perrier-Jouët's London agent, was writing to the house asking if the Champagnes might be made bone-dry, *sans dosage*, to satisfy the sophisticated tastes of his British customers. Burns was sent away with a flea in his ear, a man about 30 years ahead of his time. But from the early 1880s, following rival Louise Pommery's success with her Extra Brut 1874, the taste for genuinely dry Champagne was taken up in a big way by British society. By the time of his death in 1897, Charles had made Perrier-Jouët a leading brand in the kingdom, a favourite with both Queen Victoria and Sarah Bernhardt—the great actress reputedly liked to bathe in it.

Perrier-Jouët's excellent reputation had a secure base in the house's splendid vineyards, with particularly fine sites at Avize and Cramant on the Côte des Blancs

Charles Perrier had no children, and in 1934 the firm passed into the safe hands of Louis Budin, another fine mayor of Epernay who, with quiet dignity, looked after the welfare of the town's people throughout the ordeal of German occupation during World War II. Louis Budin and subsequently his son Michel were the builders of the firm's very high reputation for Vintage Champagnes through much of the 20th century.

This excellence had a secure base in the house's 65ha (153 acres) of splendid vineyards, with particularly fine sites at Avize and Cramant on the Côte des Blancs.

Mumm (later part of the Bronfman Seagrams empire) acquired a majority share in the business in 1959, but Michel was asked to stay on to land his greatest coup—the launch in 1970 of the firm's prestige Cuvée Belle Epoque in a Paris nightclub to celebrate the 70th birthday of the American jazzman Duke Ellington. The flower-adorned bottle was inspired by a fin de siècle decoration by glass designer René Lalique. It was an instant success and instrumental in making Perrier-Jouët the third largest Champagne brand in the USA by 1987. The first vintage of Belle Epoque, the outstanding 1964, was made from a classic mix of grand cru Pinot Noir and Chardonnay, with a smidgen of Pinot Meunier. On a personal note, the intense, rich, yet exquisitely elegant 1985 Belle Epoque is one of the greatest Champagnes I have ever tasted, the memory permanently etched with every nuance of flavour.

In the best of times, the '85 Belle Epoque would have been a hard act to follow. But the late 1990s and early years of the 21st century were a difficult period for the house, as it became the target of corporate raiders. With Seagram shedding its wine interests, it passed to a Texas group of venture capitalists, then to Allied Domecq, and finally to its present owners Pernod Ricard. In fairness, its latest home is a safe one. However, to be candid, I cannot say with any conviction that recent vintages of Belle Epoque, though more than respectable, are any longer in the same league of greatness as the half-dozen finest prestige cuvées on the market. Although still elegant and fine, P-J Vintage sometimes seems to lack the richness, vinosity, and complexity of old. In fairness, contrary to the usual

Right: Hervé Deschamps, the modest but talented *chef de cave* since 1995, one of his favourite vintages for Belle Epoque

asset-stripping habit of Champagne takeovers, P-J has been lucky enough to hang on to most of its precious vineyards. Any definite opinion of the ranking of Belle Epoque especially should wait until these younger vintages reach full maturity at about 13 years of age.

Meanwhile, let us enjoy those wines now in their prime and then look into one dramatic new release. The 1995 is a fine expression of Belle Epoque, since it is a Chardonnay year par excellence, and Chardonnay is Perrier-Jouët's forte—the white grapes for this vintage coming from the firm's superb vineyards in the grands crus of Cramant and Avize. These Chardonnays lead the blend (50 per cent). Great Pinot Noir from Mailly, Verzy, and Aÿ (45 per cent) is also important, creating a union of Montagne de Reims styles. And there is a touch, too, of superior Meunier from Dizy. The Champagne has been *à point* from 2008, the main impression one of freshness and purity, showing in the still green hints amid the gold and an evolving aroma of white peaches, with a note of toast. As air gets to the wine, this delicate, ethereal style is made more complex by buttery baker's shop flavours, particularly of brioche. The soupçon of Meunier adds a palate-filling richness that works well with the poised succulence of Pinot Noir. This was *chef de cave* Hervé Deschamps's first vintage, and it is still one of his favourites.

A new luxury version of Belle Epoque in the 2000 vintage was released in 2008. A pure Cramant Champagne from the *lieux-dits* of Bourrons-Leroy and Bourrons-du-Midi, it is intended to be Perrier-Jouët's ultimate expression of Chardonnay. Produced in tiny quantities for collectors of trophy wines, it was initially priced at an outlandish £35,000/$70,000 per case of 12. Apparently, Patrick Ricard had decided that this special bottling was going to be the most expensive of all Champagnes. But if you will excuse the bluntness, Monsieur, for Super Belle Epoque

Chardonnay to have any chance of being accepted by consumers long term, it is the market—not the producer—that decides the top price level of the greatest wines, based on a long track record of supreme quality over a run of vintages—as in the case of Romanée-Conti or Pétrus. Heigh-ho, undeterred, the P-J marketeers are tempting potential purchasers of Super Belle Epoque with some fantasy promotional devices—such as the option to "customize" their Champagne. That is marketing speak for choosing the exact amount of *dosage* to be added to the wine. Moreoover, P-J has chosen the 2000 vintage as the ambassador for this perfectionist concept of Champagne-making. This is surprising, since by any yardstick it is a low-acid vintage, good not great, and easy to drink on release—but will it age?

A far more revealing and worthwhile indulgence was an astonishing historic tasting at Maison Belle Epoque in Epernay in March 2009, spanning 20 of the house's best vintages from 2002 to 1825, the date of Perrier-Jouët's foundation. The tasting was chaired by Serena Sutciffe MW, and a dozen wine writers from Europe and Asia tasted four vintages of Belle Epoque back to 1964, followed by 14 vintages of PJ's Grand Brut, most served from magnum. My own favourite was the legendary 1985 Belle Epoque—as truly, opulently great as when I first tasted it 15 years previously. The 1982 Belle Epoque is another legend. Of the golden oldies, 1964, 1959, 1955, 1952, 1928, and 1911 were also awesome. The 1874 was the true "great" of its time, and the 1825 was probably the oldest bottle of Champagne in the world.

From the stratosphere to Planet Earth, Perrier-Jouët's best-value cuvée is the Grand Brut Non-Vintage. Tasted in 2007 with a sample based on the often tricky 2003 vintage, this Champagne was a surprise—floral, spicy, forward, and impeccably balanced. And on first tasting, the Grand Brut on a 2005 base also showed very well.

FINEST WINES

(Tasted in Epernay, October 2008 and March 2009)

Perrier-Jouët Grand Brut NV

20% C, 40% PN, 40% PM. *Dosage* 10g/l. The base wine for this NV release was 2005. Pale yellow/gold, shimmering. Fine, fresh aromas of apple, with notes of grapefruit and a stylish whiff of brioche. Good Pinot structure on the palate, a nuance of gingerbread and palate-filling fruitiness from finely sited Meunier (Dizy and Venteuil). Decent length.

Perrier-Jouët Grand Brut 1998

50% PN, 30% C, 20% PM. *Dosage* 8g/l. Straw/pale gold, with green highlights. A luxuriant nose, melding honey, peaches, and mirabelle plums, nicely exotic; the palate, however, is all elegance and restraint rather than volume or vinosity. A very good example of the lithe style in 1998.

Perrier-Jouët Belle Epoque Cuvée Spéciale 2000

A 100% grand cru Chardonnay from the Cramant *lieux-dits* cited above. *Dosage* 7g/l. Very pure, crystalline green-gold, with a refined cordon of tiny bubbles, persistent and evenly spread. Classic, dynamic, Cramant aromas, racy citrus fruits with ripe citrus notes, and a touch of vanilla as well. The palate is forward, the flavours round, charming, and ready to drink—typical of the 2000 vintage as a whole. This is certainly a very good, even excellent Champagne for drinking now—but one doubts whether it has the vinosity, complexity, and "legs" to carry it through to a distinguished old age.

Perrier-Jouët Belle Epoque 1999

50% C (Cramant, Avize), 45% PN (Mailly, Verzy, Aÿ), 5% PM (Dizy). *Dosage* 8g/l. Very elegant green-gold colour. Sensuous aromas of yellow peaches, papaya, and almond paste. Fine and taut on the palate, with relief, definition, and length—but like most Belle Epoques, this still needs more time to show its true worth (until 2012 or 2013 at the earliest). A better core of flavour than most '99s.

Perrier-Jouët Belle Epoque 1985 ★

A vital, evolving green-gold. Citrussy freshness cedes to toast, coffee, and pâtisserie scents, both elegant and concentrated. On the palate, the still-lively acidity is completely integrated into the vinosity of the mouthfeel. Creaminess and power in perfect balance.

Perrier-Jouët Belle Epoque 1982

Slightly deeper than the 1985, but still limpid gold. The nobility of the Chardonnay (49% of the blend) this year pervades the wine with it subtle nuances. Classy aromas of hazelnuts and almonds framed in a racy minerality. Less concentrated than the 1985—but what purity of flavours.

Champagne Perrier-Jouët
28 Avenue de Champagne, 51201 Epernay
Tel: +33 3 26 53 38 00
www.perrier-jouet.com

Pol Roger

If Champagne is all about pleasure, then Pol Roger is probably the preeminent brand to which astute connoisseurs turn first for the finest "bubbles". And we terroir zealots who champion the flavours of the *paysans*, the little guys, are always equally happy to bend the knee to Pol, the aristocrat of Epernay, because the Champagne is so damned good and so fairly priced. Quality has always been the watchword of this family house founded by Pol Roger in 1849, a turbulent time in European history. Pol himself made a great fortune in the heyday of Champagne prosperity that ran to the end of the 19th century. The family thereafter felt a sense of *noblesse oblige*, of the need to give something back to the community. Pol's son Maurice Pol-Roger was an outstandingly brave mayor of Epernay during World War I, protecting the townspeople against the worst excesses of the Kaiser's occupying forces; and he treated with contempt repeated threats of his own execution.

After the Armistice, it was Maurice who really made the Pol Roger brand famous, particularly in England, where, as a great shot and fisherman, he felt naturally at home. By 1935, Maurice had built the brand up to the number-one position in the British Isles, and even more remarkably, all his Champagnes were Vintage cuvées. In line with his robust tastes in field sports, Maurice was a Pinot Noir man, imbuing his wines with rich, mellow flavours in a style that also appealed to Winston Churchill, who first bought the 1911 vintage. Churchill's loyalty to the house was strengthened by his great friendship with Odette Pol-Roger, Maurice's daughter-in-law, whom he met in 1944 at a dinner party at the British Embassy in Paris. His memory lives on in Pol's Cuvée Sir Winston Churchill, one of Champagne's greatest prestige cuvées, driven by Pinot Noir and especially fine in such great black-grape years as 1985, 1996, 1998★, and, for the near future, the fabulous 2002.

Right: Christian de Billy (left) and Patrice Noyelle, with images of Pol Roger's most famous patron on the wall behind them

If Champagne is all about pleasure, then Pol Roger is probably the preeminent brand to which astute connoisseurs turn first for the finest "bubbles"

The straight Vintage Pol Roger is a particularly long-lived Champagne, and in really exceptional years like 1982, 1988, 1996, and soon-to-come 2002, it is often one of the best three wines of the vintage.

Yet, for many observers, including this writer, their favourite Pol Roger Champagne is the Blanc de Chardonnay, now prosaically renamed Blanc de Blancs on the questionable advice that it sounds more chic—quite the opposite, surely? This is the least expensive of Pol's Vintage cuvées, always delicious early on but holding well in good vintages for up to 20 years, as the vertical tasting below shows. Ironically, old Maurice had little love for Chardonnay, which he called *la flotte* (water). It was his grandson, the much-loved Christian de Billy, now semi-retired but happily still keeping a watchful eye, who began to buy Chardonnay vineyards in the 1950s. Their location around Epernay, in the Cubry Valley at Pierry, and in Cuis and Chouilly on the Côte des Blancs, makes for a fragrant, mineral style that matures quite quickly, to the impatient delight of its many devotees. There has been no wood in the cellars for many years, and there is none in the impressively refurbished cuverie, with its shining line of stainless-steel vats, their construction and shape masterminded by managing director Patrice Noyelle, a shrewd and effective Burgundian, who is holding the fort for the de Billy and Pol-Roger family. The cellar master, Dominique Petit, comes with impeccable credentials, having worked at Krug for 20 years. His first Pol vintage was 1999, a most promising debut, while his new baby, released in 2007, is the bone-dry Brut Nature Extra Cuvée de Réserve, one of the best genuinely sugarless Champagnes.

FINEST WINES

(Tasted in Epernay, July 2008)

Pol Roger Brut Nature Extra Brut de Réserve NV
An innovative departure for Pol: a truly bone-dry Champagne, *non-dosé*, with not a gram of sugar— rare, even in this category. A quite different blend from the excellent "White Foil" Brut—less reserve wine (about 10%), the base wine made from younger, riper fruit (33% PN, 33% PM, 34% C). Very fruity, primary scents; pure, super-clean yet rounded mouthfeel. Good length. Excellent winemaking.

Pol Roger Blanc de Blancs 1999
Elegant, light yellow, ripe-looking; the nose a little reductive today, more exuberant usually. The palate still needs time to unfurl, but this is already a sleek, sensuous Champagne. Very much better than most 1999s, but lacking the complexity and class of a great Chardonnay year like 1998, 1995, or 1988.

Pol Roger Blanc de Chardonnay 1998★ [V]
Evolving gold tints in the yellow-green hue; very fine, lace-like mousse; splendid smokiness overlaying classy lemon and honey aromas; rich, evolving mouthfeel, but with vital, mineral freshness and lovely, tart finale. A classic.

Pol Roger Blanc de Chardonnay 1995
A vintage that has stood a little in the shadow of 1996 but is actually a more classic year for Chardonnay—as here. A beautifully integrated wine: mousse, acids, fruits (including mango), and finesse all meshed together in an exquisite whole.

Pol Roger Blanc de Chardonnay 1990
Still very young-tasting, a monument of strength and vigour. Distinctive, pervasive quince fruitiness, with a still-developing smoky, buttery loveliness.

Pol Roger Blanc de Chardonnay 1988
Always a favourite vintage and still so today. The most complete Champagne of the flight, with every quality you could wish for: perfectly evolved aromas and flavours; ripeness and elegance; velvet mouthfeel, yet with an energizing tension and the austerity of the truly great.

Pol Roger Blanc de Chardonnay 1986
This '86 was always clearly superior to the vintage's average quality. Still all there, with no hint of degradation; masculine, but honeyed and opulent.

Champagne Pol Roger
1 Rue Henri le Large, BP199, 51206 Epernay
Tel: +33 3 26 59 58 00
www.polroger.com

Alfred Gratien

In 1867, Alfred Gratien, the founder of Gratien & Meyer in Saumur, diversified his interests by opening a Champagne house on Epernay's Rue Maurice Cerveaux. It is still there, in the original premises that are little more than working cellars. But do not be deceived, because for more than 140 years this modest operation has been the source of highly original and excellent Champagnes, made with the conviction that the old ways are best.

In 2004, the Gratien family firms in the Loire and Champagne were bought by Henkell, the market-leading Sekt producer. Big changes were expected, but the directors of the German giant knew they had a little gem in Epernay and wisely left young cellar master Nicolas Jaeger a fairly free rein to run the firm and make the wines—as

Above: Wicker baskets at Alfred Gratien's Epernay winery symbolize the company's conviction that old ways are best

The premium Alfred Gratien Champagnes are made in a rigorously classic style— fermented in oak, the malolactic always avoided to ensure a longer life

his father and grandfather had done so well for Gratien before him. Happily, Henkell's main input has been the new cuverie for the storage and blending of the infant wines. There is also a new range of second-label Champagnes made for earlier consumption.

Connoisseurs can rest easy. The premium Alfred Gratien Champagnes are made in a rigorously classic style—fermented in oak, the malolactic fermentation always avoided to ensure a longer life. The entry-level Gratien Brut NV has been the house Champagne of Britain's Wine Society ever since 1906. A big, full Champagne, with an autolytic, biscuity character, it was long based on a very high proportion of Pinot Meunier—Jaeger *père* was always chary about the exact figure, but it might once have been as much as 70 per cent. There's nothing

wrong with that, since it was good Meunier from the best, sunny sites of the Marne Valley, like Reuil and Châtillon, the home villages of the Jaeger family. More recently, there has been a higher proportion of Chardonnay and less use of the *taille*, mirroring today's preference for elegance and freshness. This adjustment makes for a finer Champagne *pour tous les jours* (every day).

The real glories are the Vintage wines. Well over half the grapes in a Gratien Vintage cuvée are Chardonnay from the greatest villages—typically, Le Mesnil, to give minerality; Cramant, to add dynamism and florality; and Chouilly, to lend a brisk, incisive purity of flavour. The Gratien non-malo style requires the drinker to be patient, often needing to wait ten years before popping the cork. The 1998, now approaching maturity, is a model of classic substance and linear precision, even surpassing the delicious 1997, one of the best Champagnes of that forward vintage. The prestige Cuvée Paradis does not carry a vintage label but is always from a single year. The 2002 is a sumptuous wine, again Chardonnay-driven. The use of Meunier in this top wine has already been reduced to 9 per cent and will be entirely phased out for future releases.

FINEST WINES

(Tasted in Epernay, January 2008)

Alfred Gratien Brut NV
42% C, 13% PN, 45% PM. As for the whole range, this is vinified in 228-litre oak barrels. Straw-gold; a fine, citrussy nose; well rounded and *gras* to taste, with a conventional *dosage* of 12g/l. More refined than usual, reflecting less *taille* in the blend.

Alfred Gratien Brut Rosé NV
A *rosé d'assemblage* with the same *encépagement* as for the Brut above, but with 9% Bouzy rouge added. Pretty, salmon pink, with an elegant cordon of bubbles; very fresh and incisive aromas. A full, vinous mouthfeel, yet no trace of heaviness.

Alfred Gratien Cuvée Paradis
Pure 2002. 70% C, 21% PN, 9% PM. A lovely buttercup yellow in appearance, signalling plenty of ripeness. Still a very lively mousse, with an athletic aromatic punch on the nose. Exceptional, already mature palate, fine yet mouth-filling and sumptuous. The high element of Chardonnay in the blend, especially from grand cru Avize, gives this wine real class. Already beautiful at the time of tasting, but this should rise even higher over the next ten or more years as the wine enters glorious maturity.

Alfred Gratien 1998
60% C, 20% PN, 20% PM. Brilliant gold; classic, Chardonnay-led nose, grilled bread, brioche; a very ample palate full of vinosity and complexity; fine, linear, precise finish. Exceptional. 2009–20.

Right: Nicolas Jaeger, who has succeeded his father and grandfather as *chef de cave*, stays loyal to the classical style

Champagne Alfred Gratien
30 Rue Maurice Cerveaux, BP3, 51201 Epernay
Tel: +33 3 26 54 38 20
www.alfredgratien.com

Boizel

Boizel is a fine tale of a family that—for all the stresses and strains of running a capital-intensive, modern Champagne business—has stayed remarkably faithful to the precepts and standards of the founders, Auguste Boizel and his wife Julie. This couple, both from old vigneron stock, took the plunge as merchants in 1834, opening their doors for business on Epernay's Rue St Rémy. Now, Evelyne Roques-Boizel, the fifth generation at the head of the firm, is one of those doughty Champagne women who meld Gallic charm and femininity with practical common sense and determination—inherited, in Evelyne's case, from her Dutch mother, Erica. The Hollander sense of a bargain is very strong at Boizel. What makes the house really worth following is the model teamwork of Evelyne and her husband, Christophe

A compact range of five excellent cuvées that, for quality and value, have few equals in Champagne—and all done without making a song and dance about it

Roques, the meticulous and cerebral son of a famous geologist. Christophe is a particularly acute buyer of grapes, and he oversees the winemaking, resulting in a compact range of five excellent cuvées that, for quality and value, have few equals in Champagne—and all done without making a song and dance about it. No spin here.

At a time when wines internationally get bigger and bigger, aiming for high scores on the 100-point scale, it is a tonic to hear Evelyne's calm explanation of their approach to Champagne-making. "We are lucky that our grape varieties, thanks to the soil and the climate, give very fine and delicate aromas. Our whole work is devoted to making sure that these aromas are never altered or deformed, so that they may express themselves completely." To this end,

Christophe patrols the vineyards all year round to choose the crus and hillsides where the three Champagne grapes show themselves best, in all their finesse. And with an injection of capital from the BCC group, arranged by the Boizels' powerful friends Bruno Paillard and Philippe Baijot, there is now more horsepower in the Boizel engine. This financing has eased the path to new sources of supply at a time of grape shortages, strengthening their existing base of excellent contracts, held for many years, with partner-growers.

The Boizel Brut Réserve is the calling card of the house and everything a well-blended Non-Vintage Champagne should be. A classic *assemblage* of a little more than two thirds black grapes and just under a third white, it shows those fine aromas and balanced, well-founded flavours one looks for, and all at a reasonable price, too—the sort of Champagne you keep in the fridge for any excuse and opportunity to drink it.

The Brut Chardonnay is an exemplary blanc de blancs and a genuine bargain. The grapes all come from privileged sites on the Côte des Blancs, chosen for their freshness, minerality, and generosity. Crucially, the wine is aged longer than normal and is usually a blend of two harvests of four to five years' age—rare indeed in a Non-Vintage Champagne.

The Brut Ultime is in the now-fashionable ultra-dry style. But this one is crafted with more care than most. Made only from sunny years of optimal maturity, Ultime has a higher percentage of fine Chardonnay but is still led by the supple richness of Pinot Noir, aided by the palate-filling fruitiness of a little Meunier. Of course, with no *dosage* to "round out" the wine, it is vital to have a pure and delicate balance in the wine, followed by a long, slow aging in the cellars to bring complete harmony. Ultime is an ideal Champagne to drink with sushi or sashimi, especially scallops or thin slices of raw tuna. The Vintage cuvées are of a similarly high standard. As usual, the couple make an individualistic choice of

the years they like. They opted for 1999—generally, I think, a less complex vintage than 1998—but in the Boizels' hands, the result is a resounding success of generosity and mineral finesse.

The greatest Champagne in the cellar is the Joyau de France prestige cuvée. First made by René Boizel in 1961, it is the apotheosis of the Boizel style, made only from grand and premier cru Chardonnay and Pinot Noir, a small percentage of which is vinified in oak. Joyau ages exceptionally well, particularly the blanc version, the marvellous 1995 being perfect to drink in 2009. The Joyau Rosé 2000, by contrast, captures all the orchard-fruits exuberance of Pinot Noir in a forward, fruit-laden year, tempered as always at Boizel by the incisive precision of great Chardonnay. *Chapeau!*

FINEST WINES

(Tasted in Epernay, November 2008)

Boizel Brut de Chardonnay NV★ [V]
Grapes exclusively from Chouilly, Cramant, Le Mesnil, and Vertus, from 2003 and 2004. *Dosage* 8g/l. Shimmering lemon-gold, indicating freshness and maturity, and a lovely, creamy, white mousse. Aromas of white flowers, minerals, and subtle ripeness. Of real quality and interest in the mouth, with a burgeoning, controlled, autolytic complexity and impressive length. Impeccable.

Boizel Vintage 1999
50/40/10 blend of grand and premier cru Pinot Noir and Chardonnay, plus Meunier from fine sites in the Marne Valley. *Dosage* 9g/l. Healthy, pale yellow-gold. Bewitching scents of yellow peaches and pears, with a hint of honeysuckle. Rich, warm mouthfeel of ripe, grandstanding Pinot reined in by brisk, mineral Chardonnay in fine balance. Consummate winemaking in a sensual Champagne, without quite the complexity of a '98 or a '95.

Boizel Joyau de France 1995
55% PN (Mailly, Verzy, Mareuil-sur-Aÿ), 45% C (Chouilly, Cramant, Avize, Oger, Le Mesnil). *Dosage* 8g/l. A really intense robe of yellow-gold, the touch of oak giving an extra dimension. As often in a maturing *grand vin*, the aromas of Chardonnay, still vigorous, are dominant: all white flowers and almonds. Then, with air and time in the glass, the greater weight of lazy Pinot Noir asserts itself superbly in the mouth: yellow peaches and William pears, with touches of vanilla and toast from the wood and the Chardonnay. A finale of great purity and length of flavour. Near faultless.

Boizel Joyau de France Rosé 2000★
65% PN, of which 8% is vinified as red wine, 35% C, all from great sites. A subtle pink hue with copper highlights. Luxuriant smells of cassis, orange zest, and quince—all very exuberant Pinot sensations. The mouthfeel is supple, silky, yet impressively crisp and refreshing. Very fine balance and length.

Above: One of the many proud reminders of the wine that has enriched the town of Epernay, home to Boizel since 1834

Champagne Boizel
46 Avenue de Champagne, 51200 Epernay
Tel: +33 3 26 55 21 51
www.champagne-boizel.fr

Charles Ellner

In October 2008, I was at the regular monthly Sunday *messe des vignerons* (vignerons' mass) in Epernay's Les Berceaux. And it was there that I tasted a very fine 1983, presented by a member of the Ellner family. I was intrigued to know more about this little house. As much a wine-growing domaine as a négociant, with 56ha (138 acres) of vineyards around Epernay and Sézanne, Charles Ellner was a thoroughly worthwhile visit, the consistently good Champagnes showing an admirable length of flavour that would put several *grandes maisons* to shame by comparison.

The founder of the house worked as a *remueur* at Moët around 1900, while he began to buy vineyards. His son Pierre developed the business between the two world wars. The firm is still independent, directed by the fourth-generation Jacques Ellner, who also makes the wines. Of the 1.3 million bottles produced each year, 75 per cent are exported across the EU and to North America, where the range has rightly won praise from *Wine Spectator*. The Brut Intégral is a fine, non-*dosage* Champagne, and the Séduction is indeed seductive. The subtle richness of the Ellner style owes a lot to reserve wines aged in oak.

FINEST WINES

(Tasted in Epernay, October 2008 and January 2009)

Charles Ellner Brut Intégral NV
35% C, 65% PN; a blend of 2002 and 2003. Pale yellow, abundant mousse. Though a minority of the blend, Chardonnay seems to dominate the bouquet. For such a bone-dry wine, the flavours are rich and lasting, reflecting the ripeness of the grapes and the admirable house style. Impressively long on the palate. A successful non-*dosage* cuvée.

Charles Ellner Cuvée de Réserve NV
60% C, 40% PN; a mix of 2002 and 2003. *Dosage* 10g/l. Ripe yet elegant yellow. A lot of freshness—the conventional *dosage* well integrated—and a certain complexity. Good balance and length. Very respectable.

Charles Ellner Cuvée Prestige 1999
60% C, 40% PN. *Dosage* 6g/l. An excellent standard for this mercurial year. Shimmering, ripe, golden colour. Lovely Chardonnay-led aromas of butter and vanilla. Tumultuous fruit that has a rich core, yet is fresh and long.

Charles Ellner Séduction 1999
55% C, 45% PN. This has the same moderate *dosage* as the Prestige but is more evolved, with a quiet richness and real refinement. Aptly named: a seductive Champagne.

Charles Ellner Brut 1983
This was the star wine at the *messe des vignerons* described above. A classic blend of 55% C and 45% PN. Aged, burnished gold but still vital hue. Honeycomb aromas, unctuous but not at all cloying. Superbly evolved on the palate, *gras* but perfectly balanced: complete. An exceptional wine, *à point* as it reached its 25th year.

Champagne Charles Ellner
1-6 Rue Côte Legris, 51200 Epernay
Tel: +33 3 26 55 60 25
www.champagne-ellner.com

V Testulat

In the heart of the Marne Valley, close to the Côte des Blancs, Epernay is the wine-trading capital of Champagne, home to more négocians than either Reims or Aÿ. It is certainly worth exploring this pleasant town beyond the *grandes maisons* of the Avenue de Champagne. The quiet side streets off the Boulevard Maréchal Foch have some splendid little houses that are off the radar of most Anglophone journalists and wine importers.

V Testulat is one such jewel, a bijou Champagne house founded by the Testulat family in 1862. In both spirit and reality, it is actually more a domaine than a *négoce*, with 17ha (42 acres) of choice vineyard sites in grand cru Chouilly and the best hillsides of the Côte d'Epernay above the town. Vincent Testulat, the son of the house, is a trained oenologist who, with his wife Agnès, is taking the firm to new heights of excellence. And the very reasonable prices charged make this little operation in the sedate Rue Léger-Bertin a real find. The solid 19th-century house and cuverie is a no-frills affair concentrating on essentials: stainless-steel fermenters of manageable size to ensure vinification of individual parcels of wine, and deep, dry cellars for optimal aging. No wood is used in the winemaking—as yet.

Agnès Testulat is from the Aubois village of Celles-sur-Ource, close to Les Riceys and equally prized for its bright Pinot Noir. Her cousins' Pinots are sent north to Testulat to add an extra touch of richness, especially to the remarkable blanc de noirs known as Carte d'Or. This is a powerful yet elegant Champagne and a steal at €10 a bottle cellar door. The Blanc de Blancs is also exceptional, driven by top-class Chardonnay from Chouilly—athletic, light, but with real persistence of flavour. The Cuvée Rosé Charlotte, named after the Testulats' two-year-old daughter, is an exuberant yet delicately fruity pink Champagne made from wines from the best hillsides. Red wine is added to give consistency of colour. Although composed entirely of black grapes, it is a wine that never degrades into heaviness.

The top-of-the-line, vintage-dated Cuvée Paul-Vincent, named after the couple's young son, is a classic mix of all three Champagne grapes from the very best family plots. The current vintage, 1999, has more substance than many Champagnes from this mixed year. The Testulats also make a velvety Ratafia from black grape juice, as well as a superior brandy. Quality and value are the name of the game at Testulat.

FINEST WINES

(Tasted in Epernay, October 2008)

Testulat Carte d'Or Brut NV ★ [V]
50% PN, 50% PM. *Dosage* 10g/l. An impressively powerful yet poised blanc de noirs—muscular but racy in a winning combination of Meunier fruitiness and Pinot strength. An excellent wine for white meat or game in a light Pinot Noir sauce. Great, too, with Beaufort or Tome de Savoie. Superb value.

Testulat Blanc de Blancs Brut NV
100% C. *Dosage* 8 g/l. Pale gold, green hints—classic hue; lace-like bubbles. Fine expression of green fruits, melding minerality with lemony freshness. A surprisingly depth of flavour and a silky texture. Average age of vines 25 years, from excellent plots in Chouilly and the Côte d'Epernay.

Testulat Rosé Cuvée Charlotte NV
50% PN, 50% PM. *Dosage* 10g/l. Lustrous ruby, positive yet delicate. Seductive strawberry fruitiness on nose and palate. Delicious—the more so for its cleansing acidity, which precludes any tendency to bonbon sweetness. Fine barbecue Champagne.

Testulat Cuvée Paul-Vincent 1999
A classic mix of Pinot Noir, Meunier, and Chardonnay in roughly equal proportions. A splendid success, with intensity, vinosity, and finesse in model balance. Everything Vintage Champagne should be, here from a year in which surging, foursquare fruitiness can overwhelm restraint and class.

Champagne V Testulat
23 Rue Léger-Bertin, 51201 Epernay
Tel: +33 3 26 54 10 75
www.champagne-testulat.com

Agrapart & Fils

O f all the winemaking growers in the Côte des Blancs, this 10ha (25-acre) domaine is gaining particular and quite deserved media recognition. For this is a model source of fine-drawn Champagnes, based on beautiful, scrupulously tended vineyards. The wines, too, are made with a clear intellectual grasp of the beneficial aerating effects that oak can bring to the estate's greater wines, balanced by a keen consciousness that they should remain as fresh and focused as the little cuvées. As Pascal Agrapart, the winemaker, puts it, "I am certainly Burgundian in the approach to my soils but very Champenois in the way I make my wines." There is nothing blowsy or overextracted in any of the Champagnes in this immaculate line.

Established by Pascal's great-grandfather, Arthur Agrapart, at the end of the 19th century, the estate has enviable holdings, mainly in the grand cru Chardonnay vineyards of Oger, Cramant, Oiry, and Avize, across which it has some 60 parcels. The Agraparts also have vineyards at Bergères-les-Vertus, Avenay Val d'Or, and Mardeuil. The average age of the vines is an ideal 35 years, but some plants are as old as 60 years. The soils are sensitively worked to maximize their microbiological life, so that the vines can push down the roots to the mother rock and feed on the full mineral elements that imbue the wines with the authentic tastes of the respective terroirs. The Agraparts are convinced of the differences at the heart of each site, related to the nature of the soil (in simple terms, strongest either in clay or chalk) and the vineyard's aspect. Treatments include homeopathic preparations for the vines and the use of organic compost and manure. There is little sermonizing talk of biodynamism, but the tending methods are very close to it. Manual, aerating *palissage* is practised in the vineyard, favouring the action of wind and sun—natural elements necessary for the defence

Right: Pascal Agrapart, a sensitive and skilled winemaker, with some of the *demi-muids* used for his top cuvées

Of all the winemaking growers in the Côte des Blancs, this 10ha (25-acre)
domaine is gaining particular and quite deserved media recognition.
For this is a model source of fine-drawn Champagnes

of the vine, preventing outbreaks of diseases such as botrytis, mildew, and oidium, reducing the need for further preventive treatment. At the harvest, picking is also manual and very selective, and the family likes to pick late for maximum maturity.

Winemaking is precise and intelligently varied according to the structure and weight of the wines. The *grands vins* are reared in larger oak barrels (*demi-muids*), the aim being not a woody taste but controlled oxidation (oxygen is not an enemy of wine—quite the reverse—since it has a protecting, strengthening effect on the infant wine). Thermoregulated stainless-steel vats are used to vinify the more supple wines. Malolactic conversion is encouraged for greater stability and complexity in the finished Champagnes. These are generally given low or moderate *dosage*, based on cane sugar,

The aim here is a pure expression of these privileged vineyard sites, Avize and Cramant having an exhilarating minerality and finesse

three months before release, the date of bottling and disgorgement clearly printed on the back label.

The entry-level blanc de blancs is an *assemblage* of all the communes where the family has vines—hence its name: Les Sept Crus. The vines in this blend are quite young, so the emphasis is on a driving fruitiness, aided by a conventional *dosage*. The vintaged Extra Brut Blanc de Blancs Minéral is a selection of the best parcels of Avize (les Champboutons) and Cramant (les Bionnes), which are vinified in both *demi-muid* casks and stainless steel. The aim here is a pure expression of these privileged vineyard sites, Avize and Cramant having an exhilarating minerality and finesse, in this case given wondrous complexity by the great 2002 vintage. The 2002 Cuvée Vénus, by contrast, is from

a 2∕4ha (60-acre) parcel of pure Avize in the *lieu-dit* of La Fosse. It is cultivated without mechanical tools, simply by man and a beautiful white mare called Vénus, who together plough the vines. Vinified wholly in cask, it needs no added sugar, thanks to the age of the plants and the richness of the vintage. The Avizeoise, also 2002, is the family's top cuvée, this time from the deeper clay and chalk soils of Avize's *lieux-dits* Les Robards and La Voie d'Epernay. It is the longest-lived of Agrapart's stable, with an intensity that makes it one of Avize's best. Because there are no large marketing budgets to factor in, these are also some of the best-value wines in Champagne.

FINEST WINES

(Tasted in Avize, January 2009)
Agrapart Minéral Extra Brut 2002
Dosage 4–5g/l. This is pervaded with an exciting minerality, mingling with the enticing scents and flavours of voluptuous yellow fruits and touches of liquorice that such a rich vintage can bring. The incisiveness of the terroir, though, is still in the driving seat, ensuring freshness and tension.

Agrapart Vénus Non-Dosé 2002★
From the soils of La Fosse, with more chalk than clay. Shimmering gold with green lights. Lovely scents of coffee-like torrefaction and grilled bread. No need for added sugar, because the palate is already so generous and palate-cloaking.

Agrapart L'Avizeoise 2002
From 50-year-old vines in the top Avize *lieux-dits*. *Dosage* 3g/l. Entirely cask-fermented and aged since 2003 in bottles sealed with clamped corks for longer life. It is mineral on the nose, but the palate is something else: large-scale and opulent, with great flavours of exotic fruits like mango and papaya (though not overdone), with aspects of toast and butter. A great Champagne for special dishes like lobster cooked with ginger *à la chinoise*.

Champagne Agrapart & Fils
57 Avenue Jean-Jaurès, 51190 Avize
Tel: +33 3 26 57 51 38
www.champagne-agrapart.com

Claude & Agnès Corbon

The history of the Corbon family is a very Champenois tale of survival, resource, and renewal. Agnès Corbon, who speaks perfect English, has recently returned from a marketing career with Unilever and the Mars Corporation to run this bijou Avize-based domaine for her father, Claude, who is easing into retirement.

The two earlier generations of the family had been grape growers and suppliers to the *négoce*—Agnès's grandfather finding the going so tough in the post-1945 austerity years that he became a coal merchant to feed his family. Claude, as his heir, began again to tend the family's small vineyards, but observing the troubles of 1968, when France almost tipped into revolution, he soon realized that to make a decent living he had to produce and market his own Champagne. The family now has 6ha (15 acres)—2ha (5 acres) in grand cru Avize and a further 4ha (10 acres) in the Marne Valley at Vandières, Verneuil, Vincelles,

and Trélou-sur-Marne, where Agnès's oenologist brother is the director of the local co-op.

Though taking a discreet backseat, Claude's presence and influence are still palpable. Behind the ruddy complexion and affability of a jovial vigneron, there's a sharp mind at work. Hearing that I was particularly interested in the terroir of Avize, instead of first proposing a standard trot through the current range, he casually asked if I might like to taste any of his pure Avize vintage cuvées made every year (though not always released) since 1971. That was remarkable enough, but nothing like as striking as his next words: "Of course, we could always taste the best vintages—the 1988, the 1982, the 1971 itself—but why not try two of the 'worst' years and one good one. I leave the choice to you." None of the Corbon Avize Vintages had been fined or filtered; none went through the

Below: A mural expressing the florality and fruitiness of Avize, where the Corbons are among the finest growers

malo; all were fermented in wood. So, on the trail of a little vinous history, I chose what I thought might be the promising 2000, the insanitary 1994, and a real "dog", the 1984, the most awful harvest of the late 20th century. Claude nodded gently.

Our preconceived idea of the relative ranking of the three Avize vintages needed adjustment after the tasting. Unsurprisingly, the 2000 was full of character and generous fruit; the 1994 had that very '94 *surmature* taste hinting at botrytis but was nonetheless pleasantly honeyed; the 1984 was hard and a bit ungenerous, but it was still alive and kicking and not as oxidized as many Champagnes would have been from this dreadful year. The experience was an object lesson in how no filtering or fining, allied to the magical touch of a master winemaker, can allow a Champagne from a great site to retain real richness and strength—despite all that the heavens can throw at it. As Agnès says, "It's all very different from selling Mars bars."

The Corbons still sell a good amount of their grapes to the *négoce*, but they also bottle and market about 15,000 bottles of their own Champagne, which go mainly to Italy—always a land of the most discerning Champagne consumers. Their Cuvée Prestige is a nicely complex, well-aged Non-Vintage wine composed of 50 per cent Chardonnay, the rest of the blend made up of Pinot Noir and Meunier in equal parts. It is made by a small-scale "solera" system, also favoured by other fine Champagne makers like Jacques Selosse and Edmond Barnaut. In this *cuvée perpétuelle*, half of the blend is drawn off and replaced with wine from the most recent year, so creating a blend of increasing complexity.

The top of the range is the Brut d'Autrefois, another solera-based blend but a much older one this time, composed of 95 per cent Chardonnay with 5 per cent Pinot Noir. The cork is secured with string, recalling the early days of sparkling

Left: Claude and Agnès Corbon, who produce excellent wines using both innovative and traditional techniques

Champagne during the reign of Louis XV, when the practice of *ficelage* was governed by a royal statute.

FINEST WINES

(Tasted in Avize, July 2008)
Corbon Cuvée Prestige NV
Aged for 12 months in a mix of large oak *foudres* and enamel-lined vats, then with six years on lees in bottle. The colour is an evolving green-gold, the mousse gentle yet swirling. The great thing about this wine is its scented aroma, on the nose but also in the mouth, giving the wine an elegant and refined texture. Grand cru Avize is in the driving seat, but Marne Valley Pinot Noir gives a supple touch of succulent orchard fruits, and Meunier contributes mouth-filling volume. Excellent.

Corbon Grand Cru Avize 2000
Evolved, brilliant gold in appearance. A big, rich wine that certainly has the forward, ripe fruit typical of the year, but the terroir shines through in its freshness, crispness, and minerality—all likely to allow this Champagne to age and grow more complex with ten years' further aging. An exceptional wine by any standard.

Corbon Grand Cru Avize 1994
A still vital yellow-gold sustained colour, lighter than bronze. Agreeable honeyed nose, not maderized. Telltale, *surmature* nose, with a hint of botrytis. Needs drinking, but very respectable.

Corbon Grand Cru Avize 1984
Deep bronze colour, still with a little mousse. A hard wine lacking generosity and fruitiness, but still alive, despite the difficulties of the vintage.

Brut d'Autrefois
Bottled in 1996 and with at least 11 years on lees, partly aged in oak barrels. Superb minerality and that svelte, *gras* texture of top-flight old vines. Avize melding brilliantly with a touch of Pinot Noir, which adds subtle hints of scented richness and restrained strength. Class.

Champagne Corbon
541 Avenue Jean Jaurès, 51190 Avize
Tel: +33 3 26 57 55 43
www.champagne-corbon.com

Franck Bonville

This Côte des Blancs estate is a princely inheritance for third-generation Olivier Bonville. His grandfather Franck, a grower in Avize, set up the house in 1946. Gilles, Olivier's father, developed the vineyards so successfully that the Bonvilles now have an unrivalled domaine in Avize, Oger, and Cramant, totalling more than 20ha (50 acres) and all grands crus.

With great material in such abundance to work with, it is hardly surprising that Bonville is an Avize estate that insiders often speak of in the same breath as Anselme Selosse. But everything in the Rue Pasteur is more discreet and low-key. The

The Bonvilles now have an unrivalled domaine in Avize, Oger, and Cramant, totalling more than 20ha (50 acres) and all grands crus

family like it that way, preferring to concentrate on making beautiful Champagnes in a subtle style to suit every occasion and most pockets. These distinguished expressions of great Chardonnay are reasonably priced compared with those of Anselme, their more famous neighbour.

A gentle, warm, and thoughtful fellow, Olivier is a trained oenologist, but he does not let his technological know-how get in the way of the family's vision of what great Champagne should be. With his inheritance of superb grapes, he takes a very measured, restrained approach towards oak—in fact, the only cuvée that sees any is Les Belles Voyes, a plot of 100-year-old vines in Oger that yields super-concentrated juice and needs the aerating effect of a barrel to bring it out and fully express its complexity, especially on the palate.

The rest of the range, fermented in stainless steel, has a natural richness in tune with precision and tension that makes it instantly recognizable as Champagne—there is no attempt here to attract Burgundian comparisons! Because of the scale and variety of the vineyard sites, Bonville Champagnes show considerably more complexity than those of many smaller mono-terroir growers. The *dosage* is conventional, at around 10 grams of sugar per litre. I might wish it were a gram or two lower, but that is just a personal preference.

FINEST WINES

(Tasted June 2007 and August 2008)

Franck Bonville Grand Cru Brut Blanc de Blancs NV [V]
A blend of all their vineyards and from several years. As the most popular and easy-to-drink Champagne in the Bonville range, the emphasis here is on floral aromas and pure fruitiness, yet in the mouth the peerless quality of the grapes and their origins shows through in a delicacy that fronts a subtle richness. Great class for a modest outlay.

Franck Bonville Grand Cru Brut 2002
The very powerful nose is dominated by liquorice (a sign of ripeness), with an oriental hint of star anise. The mouthfeel is ample and long, but there is admirable freshness supporting a honeyed unctuousness that is still very elegant. Winemaking of real class. Very 2002. A great vintage.

Franck Bonville Les Belles Voyes NV
From the family's plot of 100-year-old vines on a mid-slope of Oger facing east. Fermented in oak casks for two years. Strong, vivid yellow, the aromas quite developed, showing yellow fruits such as peach rather than lemon or lime. Still very tight and sinewy in the mouth. Needs another 2–3 years to start showing at its best. It is very interesting to taste Olivier's wine against the Clos Cazals, also an Oger wine, produced by his wife Delphine.

Right: Olivier Bonville, who crafts naturally rich but subtly stylish Chardonnay Champagnes exclusively from grands crus

Champagne Franck Bonville
9 Rue Pasteur,
51190 Avize
Tel: +33 3 26 57 52 30
www.champagne-franck-bonville.com

Jacques Selosse

Now in his mid-50s, Anselme Selosse is a visionary who has inspired a whole generation of younger growers by taking Champagne back to its roots in, to use his own phrase, "the essence of the earth". Certainly, his great achievement as a young 1980s graduate of the Lycée Viticole in Beaune was to introduce the handmade approach of classic white Burgundy-making to the corporate world of Champagne, which all too often has treated the product as a commodity to be spun as an emblem of the high life, remote from the land. Yet for all the highly distinctive style and often superb quality of his own wines, Selosse has always been more important for what he represents: leadership by example in staking a claim to a place at the top table of Champagne for the smaller grower-winemaker, tending his vines with respect, knowledge, and love, thus returning to the artisanal methods of *grand-père*.

At the family estate, Anselme has nearly 4ha (10 acres) in Avize, and parcels of 1ha (2.5 acres) each in Oger and Cramant—marvellous material for making some of the greatest wines of the Côte des Blancs. More recently, he has acquired similarly sized plots in Aÿ, Ambonnay, and Mareuil—*les grands noirs*—ideal sites for his exceptional pure-Pinot Champagne, Contraste. All the wines are fermented in used oak *pièces* from some of Burgundy's top estates. His vines are pruned hard to ensure a reasonable yield. Every week, he stirs the lees of the wines in barrels with a rod. So it is not surprising these are big, oxidative wines made in a broad, Burgundian style that has certainly expanded the taste spectrum of Champagne. His wines are aged for up to eight years, so occasionally a cuvée can show premature oxidation, like recent showings of his Version Originale, which can give off a whiff of overripe apples. But across the range these are some of the most exciting Champagnes, now available again in the USA—albeit at eye-watering prices, but worth it for the committed collector.

FINEST WINES

(Tasted in Avize, June 2008)

Jacques Selosse Initiale Grand Cru
Pure Chardonnay. In some ways, the most conventional and easy to understand of Anselme's Champagnes. Made from an artful *assemblage* of 2003, 2002, and 2001, each year bringing very different but complementary qualities. Dancing bubbles, creamy mousse, scents of hazelnuts, and a really together mouthfeel, everything in balance, the wood well integrated. Pleasure in the glass.

Jacques Selosse Contraste Grand Cru ★
Lustrous, burnished golden hue of *les grands noirs* of Aÿ and Ambonnay, the great Pinot sources of this superb wine. A huge structure, but with an impressively well-defined focus of balanced richness and precision. An endlessly complex finale, akin to great Burgundy from the Côte de Nuits. Yes, I know it's a white wine, but it has the power of a red.

Jacques Selosse Substance Grand Cru
A Champagne strictly for gastronomes and the greatest fish dishes. Made from a perpetual cuvée of 12 vintages of pure Avize. Boy, what substance in every department: deep bronze, almost amber colour, and an extraordinary intensity of aromas with that rancio touch of an old Amontillado Sherry; vibrant Mediterranean flavours all checked by the chalk and minerality of Avize's terroir. Sui generis. Magnificent. Decant and serve in wine glasses rather than flutes, as Anselme himself recommends.

Substance is a Champagne strictly for gastronomes and the greatest fish dishes. Sui generis. Magnificent. Decant and serve in wine glasses rather than flutes

Left: Anselme Selosse amid his carefully tended vines—an exceptional producer in the vanguard of grower Champagnes

Champagne Jacques Selosse
32 Rue Ernst-Vallé,
51190 Avize
Tel: +33 3 26 57 53 56
a.selosse@wanadoo.fr

De Sousa

From a family of Portuguese origin who came to Champagne between the two world wars, third-generation Erick de Sousa returned in 1986 to the domaine, now one of the three best in Avize. Over the past 20 years he has developed the vineyards while hanging on to top quality as a model practitioner of all that is best in Champenois viticulture and winemaking.

Erick has 9ha (22 acres) of grands crus, 2.5ha (6 acres) of which are enviably blessed with very old vines at Avize, Cramant, and Oger; these were his first to be biodynamically cultivated, now applied to the rest of the domaine. Like Anselme Selosse, Erick ferments in oak barriques, though his Champagnes can taste a little less oxidative and sometimes with

Erick de Sousa has developed the vineyards while hanging on to top quality as a model practitioner of all that is best in Champenois viticulture and winemaking

better wood integration than Anselme's. All the de Sousa wines go through the malo, and autolytic flavours are still induced through *poignettage*—a costly old method that involves using the wrists to shake the bottles and stir up the lees. Once common in Avize, the practice is now falling out of favour.

As a specialist in the *grands blancs*, Erick's Champagnes show classic Chardonnay flavours with a captivating savouriness akin to green olives, an analogy often cited in the tasting notes of authorities such as Bettane and Desseauve for the greatest wines of the Côte. The domaine's finest grapes from 50-year-old vines in Avize go into his prestige Cuvée des Caudalies: intriguingly, *caudalies* means seconds in reference to the length of time the flavours last on the palate! After fermentation in oak without chaptalization, the infant wine is added to a "solera" of reserve wines—a method used by some

of the greatest growers—in this case going back to 1986, so it is classed as a Non-Vintage. But now a Vintage version is released in exceptional years, with a string of conspicuous successes this century in 2000, 2002, and, a most delightful surprise, 2003.

FINEST WINES

(Tasted in Avize, July 2008)

De Sousa Grand Cru Cuvée des Caudalies NV
This multivintage "solera" wine is an object lesson in how to achieve that looked-for balance of freshness, minerality, and power. The mouthfeel is particularly captivating with a mousse that caresses yet energizes the palate, completely integrated oak, and perfect *dosage*. Long, multiflavoured finish. This certainly lives up to its title. Bravo!

De Sousa Grand Cru Cuvée des Caudalies 2003
A very intelligently composed Vintage Champagne, considering the challenge of the heat that summer. Everything is focused on the beauty of the ample Chardonnay fruit, so rich in natural sugars—the acids may be on the low side, but the capacity to age also depends on alcohol and extract, which are likely to make this wine live longer than doubters might think—until 2012 or 2015. A great effort.

De Sousa Grand Cru Cuvée des Caudalies 2002
Evolving into a classic beauty; gorgeous nose that allies the opulence, minerality, and freshness so typical of this vintage with the lead-pencil elegance of Avize. The palate closely mirrors the nose, with a seamless integration of oak and vinosity, and ends with a super-long finish. Drink 2010–25.

De Sousa Grand Cru Cuvée des Caudalies 2000
In a lighter, more forward style than the 2002, the 2000 is *à point* for current drinking (2009–11). *Tout en finesse*, the wood impact is rightly toned down, with an emphasis on purity of savoury fruits and elegant acidity—racy, fine, ethereal.

Right: Erick de Sousa, one of the three leading growers in Avize, who crafts concentrated grand cru Chardonnays

Champagne De Sousa
12 Place Léon-Bourgeois, 51190 Avize
Tel: +33 3 26 57 53 29
www.champagnedesousa.com

Union Champagne (De Saint Gall)

The Union Champagne is the outstanding cooperative group in Champagne, by reason of its location, size, and reputation for making wines of top quality. Based in Avize, the heart of great Chardonnay country, it takes in grapes from 11 smaller co-ops, whose member-growers own 1,200ha (2,965 acres) of vineyards, all classified as premier or grand cru. These holdings—the base for producing 12 million bottles of Champagne—are mainly in the Côte des Blancs but also include some great Pinot sites in the southern Montagne de Reims, particularly at Ambonnay.

The union's winemaking plant at Avize is a gleaming showcase of tall stainless-steel fermenters and one particularly vast blending vat, with everything done on the grand scale. The technology is very state of the art, the option of making non-malolactic wines to guard their acidity in warmer years effortlessly achieved. But this is no soulless wine factory. President Serge Lefèvre and his winemaking team are passionate about their *métier* and naturally curious about new trends that might improve their Champagnes. Monsieur Lefèvre himself has fine vineyards in Oger, a grand cru village that makes Chardonnays so beautiful that several growers there, Lefèvre included, were inclined to think that it would be a crime to mask their beauty with oak. But young Cédric Jacopin, the *oenologue* and deputy cellar master of the union, has recently persuaded his boss that a very limited use of oak would improve certain well-structured Champagnes, making them at once friendlier, more durable, and complex by the effects of gentle aeration through the staves of the casks. So, from 2011, a series of 50 larger *demi-muid* barrels will add their touch to the winemaking.

The union works well at two main levels within the industry. Its main activity is the production and supply of still wines (*vins clairs*) to the *grandes maisons*. Because of their superb origins, these wines are in great demand for prestige cuvées like Taittinger's Comtes de Champagne, Laurent-Perrier's Grand Siècle, and Moët's Dom Pérignon. But since 1984, the union has been marketing its own brand of Champagne—De Saint Gall. Year by year, production has quietly increased to the current 2.2 million bottles that are mostly exported across the EU and, more recently, with great success, to North America. The range is manageable, with just one blend of Pinot and Chardonnay, two rosés, and the rest all Chardonnays, rising to the prestige Cuvée Orpale, giving varied expression to the great white grape in Non-Vintage and Vintage bottlings. Because there is no need to factor in huge marketing budgets, as the *grandes maisons* do, these are some of the finest-value wines in Champagne.

FINEST WINES

(Tasted in Avize, January 2009)

De Saint Gall Extra Brut NV
Pure Chardonnay from grands crus Avize, Oger, and Le Mesnil; base vintage 2004. *Dosage* 4–5g/l. Yellow-gold. A very good expression of terroir. Beautifully dry but not austere. Very fresh and crisp, but also shows real volume and length.

De Saint Gall Blanc de Blancs Brut NV [V]
Base vintage 2005. *Dosage* 10g/l. A youthful character, white flowers; incisive, with a lively note of terroir balanced by a certain roundness.

De Saint Gall Blanc de Blancs 2002
The majority of grapes are from grands crus, and the malolactic has been partially blocked. Lemon-gold. Beautiful combination of roundness, volume, depth, and finesse. Splendid complexities to come.

Cuvée Orpale Blanc de Blancs Grand Cru 2002
Still a baby. *Matière*, but more finesse than richness.

Union Champagne (De Saint Gall)
7 Rue Pasteur, 51190 Avize
Tel: +33 3 26 57 94 22
www.de-saint-gall.com

Left: Cédric Jacopin, Union Champagne's winemaker, who oversees the production of 12 million bottles each year

Varnier-Fannière

A slim, neat man, Denis Varnier is a leading exponent of the non-oak school of winemaking in Avize, his fine-drawn, meticulous Champagnes a fascinating contrast to the wood-influenced, more oxidative examples of Anselme Selosse and Erick de Sousa, his more famous neighbours.

Created in 1950 by his grandfather Jean Fannière, Varnier's domaine is just 4ha (10 acres), composed of some 40 parcels of grand cru sites. Significantly, his largest parcels are located in Cramant and Oger, these two villages known for dynamic incisiveness and subtle roundness respectively. In Avize itself, the prize plot is the charmingly named Clos du Grand Père, close to the village pharmacy, where the vines are up to 70 years old.

When "bigness" is the order of the day for so many wines worldwide, it is a great pleasure to enjoy the subtle athleticism of these racy and refreshing creations

Highly competent in technical terms, Denis took a BTS diploma in Oenology at the Lycée Viticole in Avize. His aim is to improve the wine constantly, while respecting the best of tradition. The grapes are squeezed in a classic wooden Coquard press, the wines fermented in either stainless-steel or epoxy-resin-lined vats.

These are focused, precise Champagnes, made with a very light touch and relying, for their complexity and distinction, on the favourable exposures and privileged soils of the Côte des Blancs, where the grapes are grown. When "bigness" is now the order of the day for so many wines worldwide, it is a particular pleasure to enjoy the subtle athleticism of these racy and refreshing creations, which are well worth seeking out.

FINEST WINES

(Tasted in Avize, January 2009)

Varnier-Fannière Brut Zéro Grand Cru NV
Bright, clear yellow with green tints. A blend of 2006 and 2007. The purity of the great, dry Chardonnay flavours is the keynote here. The dynamism of this youthful cuvée is its strength, with its Cramant-like whiff of gunflint and model minerality.

Varnier-Fannière Brut Rosé Grand Cru NV
Again, a blend of 2006 and 2007. Made from grand cru Chardonnay with 8% red wine added. This is a white-wine maker's take on rosé, if you will: subtle, pastel pink; extremely refined, focused scents of lemon and grapefruit; a fine-grained texture and dancing acidity on the palate. Linear and focused, with a lovely, mineral-tinged fruitiness, the wine is at once incisive and gently expressive of cool-country cherries. Class.

Varnier-Fannière Clos du Grand Père NV
A blend of 2003 and 2004. A low, extra-brut *dosage* of 3g/l. A Champagne of weight and complexity, its quality due to the clay-rich soil of this little Avize plot and to the great age of the vines. Exotic fruit scents, particularly lychee, meld with aromas of vanilla. Excellent acidity lightens the dense and complex mouthfeel, and the finish is terrific—very long and elegant. A Champagne for the greatest fish, like whole seabass cooked in the tandoor, the great speciality of Le Foch, the admirable restaurant with the best quality:price ratio in Reims.

Varnier-Fannière Grand Vintage 2003
Bright, ripe, straw colour, and a fine, creamy mousse. More exuberant than the Clos du Grand Père. An intelligently made Champagne given this heat-wave vintage, and one that celebrates the ripe, golden Chardonnay harvested that year.

Left: Denis Varnier, who champions classic, focused, precise, unwooded wines from three grands crus

Champagne Varnier-Fannière
23 Rempart du Midi,
51190 Avize
Tel: +33 3 26 57 53 36
www.varnier-fanniere.com

Diebolt-Vallois

Jacques Diebolt looks like everyone's favourite uncle: a civilized, well-nourished vigneron and collector of antiques, whose comfortable frame belies a blazing talent for making supremely refined Champagnes. The Diebolt family estate of 10ha (25 acres) is of the right size to make a representative showing of Cramant's best. Much of the line is fermented in stainless-steel or enamel-lined tanks to preserve the verve and dash of the terroir, the finesse of the Diebolt style being highly prized by some of the world's great restaurateurs: the Prestige Brut is the pouring Champagne at the George V in Paris, and I have fond memories of his Vintage wines at Le Bec Fin in Philadelphia.

The Diebolt style is highly prized by some of the world's great restaurateurs: the Prestige Brut is the pouring Champagne at the George V in Paris

Yet Jacques's fabled lightness of touch and the quality of his Cramant sites have allowed him to make his most ambitious Champagne, the Fleur de Passion, in a different style, which, in the words of Richard Juhlin, "gives the [Cramant] cru another dimension". Fleur is vinified in old oak *pièces*, both the 205-litre Champenois size and Burgundian ones of 228-litre capacity. The malo is avoided, and the wines are neither fined nor filtered. In great years of good maturity, it is not chaptalized. The final result is an *assemblage* from several of Jacques's finest *lieux-dits*. But first, the wine of each privileged site is fermented separately. Pimonts, on gently rising slopes, to the west of the village, gives refinement, while Gros Monts and Bouzons, on steeper, southeast-facing *coteaux* abutting the Butte de Saran, contribute power and depth. I have only tasted the 1996 Fleur de Passion once, in 2007, but it was a very memorable experience.

FINEST WINES

(Tasted in Cramant, March 2007)

Diebolt-Vallois Fleur de Passion 1996
Jacques's light touch is well illustrated in this, his finest wine, in a great vintage. The 1996 is an *assemblage* of barrel-fermented wines from, among others, the top sites of Bouzons, Gros Monts, and Goutte d'Or. The oak is seamlessly integrated in this Champagne, which has lost none of its fresh purity after a decade in bottle. The vivid straw colour reflects the ripeness of '96, and the bubbles are fine and persistent. Scents of citrus fruit mingle with hints of the crystalline chalk. The mouthfeel is crisp and incisive, enhanced by full, orchard-fruit flavours: white peaches and nectarines. A masterpiece—complex, subtly powerful, yet ethereal.

Right: Jacques Diebolt, who crafts refined Cramant Champagnes served in some of the world's finest restaurants

Champagne Diebolt-Vallois
84 Rue Neuve,
51530 Cramant
Tel: +33 3 26 57 54 92
www.diebolt-vallois.com

Lilbert Fils

The dynamic, racy Champagnes of the hilltop village of Cramant have no finer exponent than the Lilbert family, who have lived here since the mid-18th century. Their estate is small—just 3.5ha (8.5 acres)—and the range compact, but their holdings are exceptionally well situated, chiefly in the finest *lieux-dits* of Cramant, where the average age of the vines is 40 years. In the perfectionist, uncompromising hands of the Lilberts, the wines have the purity and hardness of a diamond when young, but given enough time they are revealed as exquisite, crystalline expressions of great Chardonnay, at once electric in their mineral charge but with the gently burgeoning vinosity of fine wine as it ages.

The dynamic, racy Champagnes of the hilltop village of Cramant have no finer exponent than the Lilbert family, who have lived here since the mid-18th century

Finesse, grace, elegance are the watchwords, qualities that accurately describe the little Non-Vintage Brut that is made from a double *assemblage* of two to three different, generally consecutive years and from the family's three grands crus, which include Chouilly and Oiry, as well as Cramant. This is a textbook blanc de blancs, aged for at least three years on lees, showing floral aromas, a fine athletic attack that manages to be freshly incisive but also delicately expansive in its flavours, of yellow peaches and pears, as well as citrus fruits, with a delightful end note of fresh almonds that is long and persistent.

The Lilberts' Brut Perle is the modern name for what used to be the most distinctive category of wine in the village—the Crémant de Cramant. Originally, *crémant* signified a "creamy" Champagne—that is, one with lower than normal pressure. But the term was outlawed in Champagne by an EU directive and is now reserved for certain French sparkling wines from other regions of France. In its new guise, Lilbert Brut Perle is the most recherché and classic example of what is also called this *demi-mousse* or half-sparkling style of Champagne. It is made from a tough selection of grapes from old vines (the oldest being planted in 1930), and the wine is aged in the cellar for four or five years. It is an ideal gastronomic Champagne, best served with simple treatments of great fish like whole bass simply roasted—the better to show the purity of the wine's fabulous terroir.

The top of the range Vintage Brut is made only from the best *lieux-dits* of Cramant, the 2002 one of the finest and most perfectly balanced years in the past quarter of a century. None of these beauties has ever seen oak.

FINEST WINES

(Tasted in Epernay, October 2008)

Lilbert Cramant Grand Cru Brut Perle NV
A pale, very pure colour, suggesting a brisk, dynamic wine, all confirmed on the nose: incisive, mineral, and focused, with a definite sense of the deep chalky terroir; gentle mouthfeel, the mousse discreet on the tongue, then a silky vinosity dominates the middle and end palate without any loss of tension. The reference *demi-mousse* Cramant.

Lilbert Cramant Vintage 1982 Brut
An illustration of how exhilarating Cramant from the best sites can be. A benchmark of that crystalline, diamond-hard character that will allow this Champagne, already more than a quarter of a century old, to improve to 2020 or beyond.

Left: Bertrand Lilbert, who crafts exquisite, exclusively grand cru Chardonnay from Cramant, Chouilly, and Oiry vines

Champagne Lilbert Fils
223 Rue du Moutier,
51530 Cramant
Tel: +33 3 26 57 50 16
www.champagne-lilbert.com

Claude Cazals (Clos Cazals)

Clos Cazals is a genuine walled vineyard, one of only nine officially recognized *clos* in Champagne, covering 3.5ha (8.5 acres) in the heart of the grand cru village of Oger. It also encloses the family home of the Cazals family, which was once the country residence of Léon Bourgeois, founder of the League of Nations. The *clos* and the neighbouring well-known estate of Claude Cazals in Le Mesnil are now in the hands of the charming Delphine Cazals, whose father Claude invented and patented the gyropalette, an automated machine that effortlessly does the work of *remuage* in a few days—a task that used to take a skilled artisan a full month to complete manually.

Since 1995, the first vintage of Clos Cazals, Delphine has produced only 3,000 bottles from its oldest vines, planted in 1947. Such self-imposed restraint is probably wise, because this vineyard is not perfectly placed, being on the flat valley floor at the foot of the dramatic hillside amphitheatre of

Delphine Cazals and her winemakers have fashioned one of the prettiest, most beguiling Chardonnay Champagnes, which mirrors her own engaging personality

vines that make the most structured wines of the village. Remarkably, Delphine and her winemakers have fashioned one of the prettiest, most beguiling Chardonnay Champagnes, which mirrors her own engaging personality. But it is, one has to say, a wine that tends to be forward, fast-maturing, and needs to be drunk within a fairly short time frame—usually 10–12 years after the vintage. The 1998, for example, which was the loveliest expression of purity and toastiness in summer 2008, started to change early that autumn, and at the time of writing (January 2009) it showed the first signs of premature oxidation. Unprompted, Delphine admitted this quite openly,

which does full credit to her direct and spontaneous nature. There are no such anxieties, however, about the sturdy and magnificent 1996, the still youthful 1997, or the expansively fruity 1999, the most recently released vintage. It would be a fascinating comparison to taste Clos Cazals alongside Les Belles Voyes, the single-vineyard Oger Champagne of Delphine's husband Olivier Bonville, of the house of Franck Bonville.

Delphine's Claude Cazals Champagnes are typically those of a well-established *récoltant-manipulant,* with 9.3ha (23 acres) of finely sited vineyards around Le Mesnil. Her Cuvée Vive, with *dosage* of just 3g of sugar per litre, is a delicate, dry delight, clearly with a woman's touch in the way it is made. It is the favourite wine of her English agent Roy Richards, a taster of legendary ability. The straight Vintage, too, is always a pure and generously fruited Champagne, though I feel it would show more of its natural charms with a lower *dosage*, close to that of the refined Cuvée Vive.

FINEST WINES

(Tasted in Le Mesnil, January 2009)

Claude Cazals Grand Cru Cuvée Vive Extra Brut NV
Like all the Cazals wines, this is pure Chardonnay. Bright, lustrous gold. Lovely, delicate minerality on the nose. Rounder and more forward than usual on the palate, which is not surprising, considering the fragility of the base wine, 2001. Subsequent vintages are likely to revert to the tighter, better-constituted structure of old. But this is still a very good wine in the circumstances.

Claude Cazals Grand Cru Vintage 2001
Quite evolved yellow-gold. Evolved fruit on the nose, and on the palate, too, but the excellence of the origins still lends a fine mineral balance to the wine. The *dosage* of 12g/l seems to be slightly on the high side—a little less, and nothing of the wine's harmony would be lost.

Right: Delphine Cazals, whose sunny disposition is reflected in the wine from the vines around her family home, Clos Cazals

Claude Cazals Grand Cru Brut Nature 1999
The Vintage Brut here normally has a conventional *dosage* of around 11g/l. This Brut Nature cuvée version was something of an experiment, and a very successful one it was, too: quite delicious, with no hint of asperity.

Clos Cazals 1999
With its deep but elegant Welsh-gold hue, ripe but minerally driven nose, and lovely, silky but firm texture in the mouth, buttressing the expansive, rich fruitiness that is the mark of the small band of fine 1999s, this is a very successful vintage of Clos Cazals, with no hint of the advancing oxidation seen lately in the 1998. I suspect that the excellent health of this Champagne is due to the Chardonnay grapes being picked before the September 1999 rains, as well as to the above-average levels of natural alcohol.

Clos Cazals 1996
This is still the benchmark vintage of the *clos*. Somehow the ripeness of fruit endemic to classic Oger and the strong acidity of the 1996 vintage combine to make an iron fist in a velvet glove. A magnificent wine, with strength, suaveness, and finesse in equal measure.

With its deep but elegant Welsh-gold hue, ripe but minerally driven nose, and lovely, silky but firm texture in the mouth, 1999 is a very successful vintage of Clos Cazals

Right: Oger, the grand cru home of Clos Cazals, though the Claude Cazals estate also extends into neighbouring Le Mesnil

Champagne Claude Cazals
28 Rue du Grand Mont,
51190 Le Mesnil-sur-Oger
Tel: +33 3 26 57 52 26
www.champagne-claude-cazals.net

Jean Milan

Opposite the village pharmacy on the Avize road, this 6ha (15-acre) domaine has good claim to making the most focused and elegant wines in Oger, a Chardonnay grand cru that is certainly the equal of Le Mesnil, its better-known neighbour. From the 1860s, the family was growing grapes for the *négoce*. As Henry Milan, and later his son Jean, pressed the grapes for houses such as Krug and Veuve Clicquot, so they learned about making Champagne, thanks to the cellar masters of the houses with which they worked. Eventually the Milans became independent and, with their acquired savoir faire, began to produce and sell their own finished wines. It is no exaggeration to say that Milan is now a reference point among Champagne experts, and its traditional presses are still working for Pol Roger, the finest of Epernay houses, which remains very attached to this old process.

Henry-Pol, the current head of the Milan family, can appear a little gruff on first meeting—but this shy brusqueness masks a sensitive craftsman who has an exceptionally light winemaking touch. His beautiful daughter Caroline, who has inherited a brisk, businesslike approach, handles sales and marketing; behind the glamor is a woman of substance and discernment. Now registered with NM (*négociant-manipulant*) status, which in this case simply means that they can buy grapes from other growers, the Milans are increasing their production slightly, but they are very careful to buy only from vignerons they trust completely, most in Oger itself.

The purity of these Champagnes is remarkable, achieved by classic, generally rather conservative methods; there are wooden *foudres* but with one interesting modern tool: a little machine that disgorges the deposit from Champagne without freezing it—a facilitating refinement of manual disgorgement (*dégorgement à la volée*). The Milans believe, rightly, that this technique of non-freezing

Right: Henry-Pol Milan, current head of the family, and his son Jean-Charles, representing the fourth and fifth generations

This domaine has good claim to making the most focused and elegant wines in Oger, a Chardonnay grand cru that is certainly the equal of Le Mesnil, its better-known neighbour

Milan *Jules*	1841 - 1907
Milan *Henry*	1883 - 1972
Milan *Jean*	1920 - 1989
Milan *Henry-Pol*	1949 -
Milan *Caroline*	1971 -
Milan *Jean-Charles*	1983 -

CH
1864

protects the natural aromas in their Champagnes, all pure Chardonnay.

The family's compact range begins with the low-*dosage* Brut Spécial, a fairly young Champagne, tight and fine; then the Brut Millénaire, a more mature blend of two older years; rising to the very impressive Brut Réserve. Of the Vintage cuvées, Terre de Noël, from their oldest vines, is a highly original, distinctively mineral wine. The fuller, arguably finer Symphorine, is a blend of four of the family's finest *lieux-dits* in Oger. The new baby, a sort of prestige cuvée, is called Grande Réserve "1864", aged for eight years and partly fermented in wood, avoiding malolactic. Finally, there's Tendresse, a rich, lightly sweet Champagne, great with the spices of Asian cuisine or simple fruit flans. Altogether, this is a brilliant repertoire of wines.

FINEST WINES

(Tasted in Oger, July 2008)

Jean Milan Brut Millénaire NV [V]
This blend of 2003 and 2004 has a year's more age than the Brut Spécial NV. A sensual Champagne, creamy and splendidly ripe, with positive, unctuous flavours, reliving the dramatic heat of '03. Yet the chalky terroir, allied to '04's vitalizing acidity, freshens everything up beautifully. *Dosage* 8g/l.

Jean Milan Brut Réserve NV
A mature blend of 2002 and 2003, vinified in used Burgundy barrels, mainly of old wood. There is just a touch of oak in the finely oxygenated aromas and flavours. Intriguingly creamy and exotic, finishing with a lovely minerality, still fresh and firm. Class.

Jean Milan Terre de Noël 2002
With the current interest in single-vineyard Champagnes, this wine from "Christmas Earth" has been lavishly praised by Robert Parker and Milan's US agent Terry Theise. The plot lies just behind the Milan house on difficult, quite alluvial soil, planted with the family's oldest vines. Certainly, in this lovely vintage, this Champagne speaks of its origins—having, at least so it seems to me, an

Left: Above the cellar doors of the Milans' winery is a plaque recording family members back through five generations

extraordinary nose of freshly grated Parmesan, which is much better than it sounds. Today, this fine Champagne is a thoroughbred stallion still in the starting blocks, sinewy and athletic. Its very particular, smoky, intensely mineral character makes it an ideal wine for food—maybe roast turbot, then a little Beaufort cheese—rather than as an apéritif. Although certainly worthy, it maybe lacks that nth degree of restrained richness, *gras*, and harmony of a wine that creates a sense of wonder. Just now, anyway. Definitely one to retaste from 2010.

Jean Milan Symphorine 2002
Now we are really talking. Made from an *assemblage* of the Milans' four very best-located hillside *lieux-dits* in Oger, with the captivating names Beaudure, Barbettes, Chénets, and Zailleux. The greatness of these origins shines through in the glass, from the very first sniff to the last swallow: pebble-fresh, full yet lithe, opulent but racy, with great length and an aftertaste that lasts a good 90 seconds. The Symphorine is the real beauty here, and it is small wonder that this is the wine that Caroline wanted for her wedding. A perfect expression of balanced roundness and finesse that is quintessential Oger. To keep until 2010 and marvel at for a further decade.

Jean Milan Grande Réserve "1864"
This recently introduced prestige cuvée, whose name harks back to the year of the house's foundation, represents a *tirage* of only 1,000 bottles. A blend of 1998, 1999, and 2000, partly fermented in oak, it was aged on its lees for eight years. Towards the end of a hot afternoon's tasting, my palate may have been getting stale, since the wine was not saying much to me, save that there was substance here.

Jean Milan Tendresse Sec NV
In memory of Caroline's grandmother, this subtly soft Champagne, with a flick of sweetness, is the Brut Spécial with a judiciously raised *dosage* of 20g/l. An ideal match for wedding cake or a flan that has anything to do with apples —and most particularly, as an unusual partner for the finest tandoori lamb chops.

Champagne Jean Milan
6 Rue d'Avize, 51190 Oger
Tel: +33 3 26 57 50 09
www.champagne-milan.com

Salon

S alon is the story of an epicure, a perfectionist who created a unique style of Champagne that is now a legend. Eugène Aimé Salon, a cart driver's son, was born in the tiny village of Pocancy on the plains of Champagne Pouilleuse to the east of Le Mesnil-sur-Oger. As a boy, he loved to watch the growers making Champagne and dreamed of one day having his own vineyard. As a man who sought his fortune in Paris, Aimé became a successful furrier and later a politician. So with the means available, in 1905 he bought that dream vineyard of 1ha (2.5 acres) in Le Mesnil, his vision being to make the perfect Champagne entirely from Chardonnay in this, the grand cru that probably ages better than any other in the Côte des Blancs.

At first, Aimé's own Champagne was a hobby— he would offer it unlabelled to his house guests at Pocancy. But with increasing wealth he had become one of the greatest gourmets of his day and a member of that ultimate Parisian lunch club, Le Club des Cents, where contrary to malicious rumor you do not need to weigh 220lbs (100kg) to qualify for membership! More seriously, as an astute businessman, Aimé was quick to see the possibilities of so special a Champagne, and he decided to commercialize it. Conceived as always the wine of a single year, the first vintage was in 1911. Salon Champagne reached its zenith in the late 1920s and 1930s, when it was the house wine at Maxim's. Today the wine has a more discreet image, but it is certainly revered by connoisseurs, sommeliers, and wine critics, spoken of in hushed tones without a hint of criticism. Does reality bear out the legend?

Keeping it factual, only 35 vintages of Salon have been released in the century since it first appeared, which is striking evidence that it is made only in years worthy of the wine's mighty reputation. And unquestionably, by common consent, outstanding wines were made in 1928, 1949, 1964, 1971, and 1976,

Right: Didier Depond, managing director of Salon and Delamotte, is a child of 1964, one of Salon's greatest years

Salon is the story of an epicure, a perfectionist who created a unique style of Champagne that is now a legend, revered by connoisseurs, sommeliers, and wine critics

and excellent wines in 1955, 1966, 1975, and 1979. On my first visit to the house in 1994, I preferred the pure golden fruitiness of the 1983 to the super-ripe and gamey 1982. I was relieved to see that this was the late, great Harry Waugh's opinion, too, and when I had the bad luck to order two dud bottles of the '82 at Les Berceaux in 2000, I was not surprised that they had seen better days. This is a reminder that perfection, in even the most highly reputed wines, is an elusive reality.

More recently, the 1985 I have found a massive monster of a wine, tasting very reductive from being made in stainless steel, with no beneficial aeration that a short spell in a barrel of a certain age might bring. By contrast, the dense, intense 1988, the rich, opulent 1990, and the classic, likely-to-be-very-long-lived 1996 have been Champagnes that recall something of the great Salon vintages of the mid-20th century until 1976.

The dense, intense 1988, the rich, opulent 1990, and the classic, likely-to-be-very-long-lived 1996 have been Champagnes that recall something of the great Salon vintages of the mid-20th century

As an end note, it is perhaps a pity that just when top houses and growers are rediscovering the suppleness and complexity that judicious use of wood barrels can bring to Champagnes with enough substance to cope with oak, Salon has thrown out all those old *demi-muid* casks in which they used to age the wine, at least until the mid-1990s. Of course, many great Vintage Champagnes, like those of Pol Roger, Charles Heidsieck, and Dom Pérignon, see no wood, but they are blends of wines from different vineyards and villages. Salon is pure monocru Le Mesnil, whose mouth-puckering acidity and intense minerality surely deserve a helping hand from oak to bring it along and out of its shell, *non*?

FINEST WINES

(Tasted in Le Mesnil, June 2007)

Salon 1996
Very pale yellow colour, with hints of green, at once star-bright, crystalline, and lively. The nose is very complex, if masked by reduction, the first scents of green apple ceding to lemon and grapefruit. Then, after brief contact with air, richer tones of pear and kiwi emerge. This is a huge wine in the mouth, only partially formed just now, virile and muscular, yet with a latent richness and subtlety that will slowly unfold over the next 20–30 years. I still believe a carefully judged time in wood would bring on the wine, making it friendlier and even more complex.

Salon 1988
In this vintage, Salon shows a welcome return to form after, in my minority view, the massive and rather clumsy 1985. Lovely, still youthful lemon gold. Evolving nose of white flowers, mixed with walnuts, a hint of acacia, and spices, and a nice touch of austerity. In the mouth, it is dense and complex but beautifully balanced, long, and complete, with a multiflavoured finish. Classic stuff.

(Last tasted May 2006)

Salon 1983
A rather forgotten vintage but a good one, if the winemaker eliminated any rot in the later-picked Chardonnay. Lovely, lithe body and an exuberant expression of high-class Mesnil fruit, suffused with minerality and opulent, peachy ripeness. There is real charm here.

(Last tasted June 1995)

Salon 1966
I remember this opulent vintage for its extraordinary aromas, powerfully reminiscent of foie gras. The palate was equally unctuous, yet with perfect balancing acidity to cut the richness.

Left: The distinctive Salon logo, which also adorns the highly prized bottles, here at the company's HQ in Le Mesnil-sur-Oger

Champagne Salon
5–7 Rue de la Brèche d'Oger,
51190 Le Mesnil-sur-Oger
Tel: +33 3 26 57 51 65
www.salondelamotte.com

Delamotte

Right in the heart of the Côte des Blancs, this little house, founded in 1760, was long associated with Lanson. After World War II, the house passed into the hands of Bernard de Nonancourt of Laurent-Perrier, whose mother Marie-Louise was the sister of Victor Lanson. Delamotte has a big reputation among Champagne connoisseurs for a very good reason. The Chardonnay grapes used to produce its various wines come principally from the three "greats" of the Côte—Le Mesnil, Oger, and Avize. And for its entry-level Brut and Rosé Champagnes, the Pinot Noir is sourced from the top vineyards of the Southern Montagne, especially Bouzy, Ambonnay, and into the Valley at Tours-sur-Marne.

The Brut Non-Vintage is a classic mix of all three Champagne grapes. Nothing unusual about that, but in the glass this fine little Champagne has a real sense of place about it, with a Chardonnay-led scent of Mesnil-like apricots and a round vinosity that recalls Bouzy and Ambonnay in its Pinot makeup. The salmon-pink Rosé is composed of 80 per cent Pinot Noir—all Southern Montagne grands crus—and 20 per cent Le Mesnil. It is made by the traditional *saignée* method, extracting colour and complexity from the skins during fermentation. Allied to vibrant fruit, there is a touch of mineral flintiness that is Le Mesnil announcing its presence—ideal as a pre-dinner apéritif or with a roast Bresse chicken.

The pure Chardonnays are the strong suit of the house. The Non-Vintage Blancs de Blancs is way superior to the average, largely because of the high quality of the grapes—all from grands crus without exception. It is full-bodied, golden in colour, yet with a finesse and mineral drive that is invigorating. Flowery scents, especially roses, lead on to flavours that are lemony and clean, given added interest by hints of ginger and even angelica. The maturity of the blend shows in the autolytic, yeasty character on the middle palate.

The Delamotte Vintage Blanc de Blancs is a big step up and, in great vintages, can be among the finest Champagnes. The 1999 is a very good wine in this forward year, with a slightly decadent *surmature* ripeness and a smell of what is called *sousbois* (undergrowth) in Burgundy—great with steamed lobster or John Dory in vanilla sauce. The 1985 is fabulous, completely outclassing its sister house Salon's wine of the same vintage.

FINEST WINES

(Tasted at Le Mesnil, July 2007)

Delamotte Blanc de Blancs 1999 [V]
Slightly deeper in colour than its usual pale yellow. (August was hot before a rainy early September.) The fruit character on the nose is very striking, almost tumultuous. There is a real scent of orchard stone fruits, peaches mainly, and an intriguing Burgundian whiff of wild mushrooms. Richly fruity and opulent on the palate, it is a gastronomic wine that is certainly a real pleasure but not exceptional, lacking the concentration of 1996 or 1995.

Delamotte Blanc de Blancs 1985
From the frost-hit, tiny 1985 vintage, a Chardonnay Champagne that has a controlled intensity lifted by an extraordinary freshness, 22 years after it was made. The colour is remarkably youthful, vital green glints among the gold. The mousse is super-fine—so discreet as to be barely perceptible to the eye, but briskly dancing on the tongue. The nose first gives up minerals, then shows white flowers and a fruit basket of peach and apricot scents (very Mesnil-like in maturity). The palate is a superb amalgam of honey, vanilla, an arresting vinosity, and ageless structure. Some library stock is still available at the domaine—if you ever see it at auction, check that it has been well stored and make a bid. Very great.

Right: The discreet house of Delamotte is less well known than its sister house Salon but can be equally fine in its way

Champagne Delamotte
5–7 Rue de la Brèche d'Oger,
51190 Le Mesnil-sur-Oger
Tel: +33 3 26 57 51 65
www.salondelamotte.com

Champagne Le Mesnil

Certain critics disparage this cooperative as a wine factory that should not be spoken of in the same breath as the greats of Champagne. This is a big mistake. The scale of operation may be large, but the quality of the wines is excellent, based on the first-rate vineyards that its 553 member-growers own and tend in some of the best sites in Le Mesnil, the most ageworthy grand cru of the Côte des Blancs. The sheer competence and professionalism of the operation is illustrated by Champagne Le Mesnil's close relationship with the *grandes maisons* that are the co-op's main trading partners. It presses grapes for such great houses as Moët & Chandon, Veuve Clicquot, Piper-Heidsieck, and Taittinger, but also trades with smaller-scale perfectionists like Pol Roger and Bruno Paillard. It is even rumored that some of its wines find their way into the legendary Salon, just a few minutes' walk away across the village.

The quality of the wines is excellent, based on the first-rate vineyards that its 553 member-growers own and tend in some of the best sites in Le Mesnil

For the collector looking for great Champagne at kind prices, the good news is that Le Mesnil markets 8 per cent of production under its own label, now seen increasingly on export markets. The wines are first vinified in thermo-regulated stainless-steel vats at an ideal temperature of 64°F (18°C) and are then left on their lees for a little longer than usual before bottling in late spring. Gilles Marguet, the young and thoughtful director and wine supremo (who also has a pilot's licence), is worth listening to closely for his view of what makes great wine everywhere—from Pétrus and Margaux, to Montrachet and Le Mesnil: "With great terroirs, it's the texture of the soil rather than its chemical makeup that really counts. You can never make great wine when the vine is stressed

by too little or too much water." His implication, of course, is that Le Mesnil has the chalkiest soils on the Côte. They certainly drain superbly, as in the rain-hit harvest of 2001, but they also act as a sponge, creating a reservoir that can revive wilting vines, as in the heat-wave vintage of 2003. The remarkable quality of Le Mesnil's top cuvée, Sublime, especially in a fragile year like 2001, owes everything to the superb sites of the grapes, particularly the more southeast-facing *lieux-dits* of Chante Alouette and Moulin à Vent— plots where Moët and Veuve Clicquot also own vines.

FINEST WINES

(Tasted in Le Mesnil, January 2009)

Le Mesnil Grand Cru Brut NV [V]
Pure Chardonnay: 95% 2004, 5% 2002. *Dosage* 10g/l. Crystalline green-gold; abundant but gently textured mousse. Invigorating scents of white flowers, especially auberpines. Crisp, mineral, and long, with a fine mouthfeel. A model entry-level blanc de blancs.

Le Mesnil Grand Cru Millésime 2002
Evolving yellow-gold. The nose is rather animal for the moment, signalling the real *matière* of a great vintage, and there are also notes of grapefruit. The palate is excitingly dense and rich. A sleeping giant that will make a great bottle from around 2010.

Le Mesnil Cuvée Sublime 2001
A cuvée from member-growers' best plots in the village. Made without malolactic fermentation. Mature golden hue of some resonance. A fascinating potpourri of scents—from gunflint, to lemon confit. Athletic, elegant, and long on the palate. The succeeding 2002 will be very different: richer and more imposing.

Right: Gilles Marguet, director of Champagne Le Mesnil, which bottles its members' best wines under its own label

Champagne Le Mesnil
19–32 Rue Charpentier Laurian,
51190 Le Mesnil-sur-Oger
Tel: +33 3 26 57 53 23
www.champagnelemesnil.com

Pierre Péters

The Péters family is originally from Luxembourg, though as wine growers they have been around in the Côte des Blancs for quite a while. The domaine was formally registered by Pierre Péters in 1940 and now comprises 17.5ha (43 acres) in top sites of the Côte, mainly at Avize, Oger, and particularly Le Mesnil, where the family's slice of the *lieu-dit* Les Chétillons is one of the finest bits of earth in Champagne.

François Péters, the head of the family, is passing responsibility for the winemaking to his son Rodolphe, an oenologist who has returned to the domaine after working independently for several years. In February 2008, I had a humbling experience when I came here to taste the *vins clairs* of the 2007 vintage. Fearing the worst after a few days spent in Champagne the previous August, when it felt like November, I was amazed by the quality of the wines—a classic case of the greatness

The domaine has top sites in Avize, Oger, and Le Mesnil, where the family's slice of the lieu-dit Les Chétillons is one of the finest bits of earth in Champagne

of these terroirs winning over the pre-harvest weather. The Musettes vineyard in Le Mesnil was supple and round, with a ripeness shaped by the returning sunshine in the first weeks of September. By contrast, La Fosse, in the lower, clay-rich slopes of Avize, was altogether more powerful and burly, but with a lovely aroma of white flowers. Then the coup de grâce, Les Chétillons. At four months old, its mouth-puckering acidity, awesome punch, and mineral force were not for the novice, but—boy!— what terrific potential for the future. As Rodolphe dubbed it, *ce garçon difficile* ("this difficult boy") is likely to be a magnificent Chardonnay Champagne given 12–15 years in bottle. With great Le Mesnil

like this, you really do need to be that patient. And so it proved in our little vertical tasting of the Pierre Péters Cuvée Spéciale, which has always been pure Chétillons but never revealed as such—until now. In a clearer, simpler redesign, Rodolphe, in a bold stroke, has printed Les Chétillons for all to see as the originating vineyard of this remarkable wine. As Peter Liem has written on his excellent Champagne blog, let's hope that other producers follow suit.

FINEST WINES

(Tasted in Le Mesnil, February 2008)

Pierre Péters Cuvée Spéciale Les Chétillons 2001
From the most fragile vintage since 1984, this is a revelation. Clear gold. Classy, refined scents of nuts and white flowers; very fresh, healthy, and pure flavours; no hint of rot (thanks to vigilant vineyard care), and a real sense of this mineral terroir.

Pierre Péters Cuvée Spéciale Les Chétillons 2000
Greater depth of colour, signalling the ripeness of the year. More complex bouquet, melding citrus, lemony tones with dried fruits such as apricot. Broad and mouth-filling, with a hint of honey and notes of brioche. Although bigger than the 2001, this is a relatively forward Les Chétillons.

Pierre Péters Cuvée Spéciale Les Chétillons 1997
Beautifully preserved, fresh, chalky minerality, with interesting touches of coffee-like torrefaction on both nose and palate. An admirably slow and elegant evolution of flavours. *A point*, as one would expect from a relatively low-acid year.

Pierre Péters Cuvée Spéciale Les Chétillons 1989
An outstanding example of how Les Chétillons ages in a hot vintage. Superb minerality wrapped in beautifully preserved fruit and ample vinous fullness, touched with a lightly toasty end note.

Left: François Péters and his son Rodolphe, who produce scintillating wines from top sites on the Côte des Blancs

Champagne Pierre Péters
26 Rue des Lombards, 51190 Le Mesnil-sur-Oger
Tel: +33 3 26 57 50 32
www.champagne-peters.com

Guy Charlemagne

This property, based in an elegant village house, is one of the most respected names in Le Mesnil. Yet over the course of three visits to this firm, which was founded in 1896, I have learned to make a big distinction between their forward, entry-level Champagnes and the far superior Vintage cuvées—especially the cleverly named Mesnillésime—which are the basis for the affable Philippe Charlemagne's fine reputation.

A glimpse at the composition of his 13ha (32 acres) of vineyards gives a clue to the varied styles of the range. Philippe has, for example, 6ha (15 acres) in Sézanne, an extension of the Côte des Blancs that offers a different, more rustic and broadly fruity expression of Chardonnay. On the Côte des Blancs, there is the 1ha (2.47 acres) in Oger and 6ha (15 acres) in Le Mesnil, producing classically constituted blancs de blancs, the Mesnillésime cuvée being made from 60-year-old vines in the named vineyards of Vaucherot, Aillerande, and Masonière.

This is a domaine that likes to have plenty of approachable fruit and joie de vivre in its Champagnes. Mesnillésime can display the class and complexity of this fabled cru

Most of the line is fermented in stainless steel and the malo encouraged, for this is a domaine that likes to have plenty of approachable fruit and joie de vivre in its Champagnes. The Mesnillésime is the exception. Half the wine is fermented in tank, but the other half is vinified in oak barrels, with the malo blocked for extra vivacity. Mesnillésime, when on top form—as in vintages such as 2002, 1995, and 1990—displays the class and complexity of this fabled cru but, again, in a more forward and decidedly more opulent style than those of the two masters of old in the village, François Péters and Alain Robert, now both edging into retirement.

FINEST WINES

(Tasted in Le Mesnil, January 2009)

Guy Charlemagne Brut Extra NV
Made from 60% Sézannais Chardonnay and 40% Pinot Noir. Full *dosage* of 12g/l. Straw-gold. The first nose is quite mineral, ceding to sweet, ripe orchard fruits. The *dosage* is noticeable on the nose and confirmed in the mouth, which is broad and round, with street appeal but no claims to finesse. A party Champagne.

Guy Charlemagne Réserve Brut NV
Pure Chardonnay from Le Mesnil and Oger, a blend of 2005 and 2004. *Dosage* 10 g/l. Star-bright, pale yellow, fine bubbles. Exuberant grapefruit-like scents. A good, creamy mousse, with plenty of tension on the tongue. Fresh apples, then good tastes of the bakery—brioche and *viennoiserie*. Still at heart a *vin de plaisir*; good with cooked oysters or dressed crab.

Guy Charlemagne Cuvée Charlemagne NV
Grand cru Chardonnays, as for the Réserve, but from different vineyards. A little 2004, a bit more 2005. *Dosage* down to 8g/l. Pale yellow. Fine smells of grilled bread and orange confit. Silky mouthfeel. Nice balance, though finishes slightly short.

Guy Charlemagne Mesnillésime 2002
Pure Mesnil. 60% made in tank, with full malo; 40% in oak barrels, with the malo blocked. Shimmering pale yellow, with green highlights. Gorgeous nose that brings together acacia, honey, lime, and even smoked peppers. The palate is an exotic fruit salad, with peach and mango discernible. Perfect balance, though, and a long finale touched with vanilla. Intense yet very fine.

Guy Charlemagne Mesnillésime 1999
Although this wine may have been vinified as for the 2002 above, the difference in the vintages is very clear here. Exuberant fruitiness rather than great complexity. Lively but ready, good not great.

Champagne Guy Charlemagne
4 Rue de la Brèche d'Oger,
51190 Le Mesnil-sur-Oger
Tel: +33 3 26 57 52 98
www.champagne-guy-charlemagne.fr

André Jacquart

Champagne buffs old enough to have drunk the entry-level Brut of old André Jacquart of Le Mesnil in the early 1990s may agree with Michael Schuster, the distinguished British wine taster, that it was "the best Non-Vintage I came across then— at the right price". The good news is that the domaine is now reborn and has moved down the road to Vertus. The current business came together with the marriage of André Jacquart's daughter Chantal to Pascal Doyard, whose father Maurice had been a leading light in the CIVC, Champagne's governing body. The business is managed today by the next generation—Benoît Duval, Marie Duval-Doyard, and her husband Mathieu Duval.

Both sides of the family have brought great vineyards to the venture. No surprise, then, that the aim is to produce top-quality wines, which are beginning to show well— a real find

The interests of each side of the family were combined in 2004, both bringing great vineyards to the venture: Jacquart, 15ha (37 acres) of Mesnil and 1ha (2.47 acres) of Oger; Doyard, 5ha (12.35 acres) in Vertus and 1ha in Mesnil. The average age of the vines is 40 years. No surprise, then, that the aim is to produce top-quality wines. The experience of Marie and Mathieu—she having worked for French fine-wine organization Ficofi, he for several top restaurants—has further convinced them that the demand for luxury, niche products is there.

The better to reflect their privileged terroirs, they have further restricted yields and now vinify similar *lieux-dits* together. They have also invested in new presses and in more than 200 barriques, between two and six years old, where the wines are kept on their fine lees though there is no *bâtonnage*. Depending on the year, the malo may be blocked. The wines are beginning to show well—a real find.

FINEST WINES

(Tasted February 2009)

André Jacquart Expérience Premier Cru Vertus NV
A blend of three years, 60/40 Le Mesnil and Vertus grapes. Has the hallmark minerality of Le Mesnil and the forward fruitiness of Vertus—a fine combination for a superior Non-Vintage. Suffused with the fine, savoury green-fruit (olive-like) flavours of the southern Côte des Blancs.

André Jacquart Grand Cru Le Mesnil 2004
Pure Chardonnay from 50-year-old vines in some of the best southern *lieux-dits* of Le Mesnil, such as Mont Joli, Voizemieux, and Aillerons. Still very young tasting, but a deft, well-integrated use of oak is beginning to bring this Champagne out of its shell to reveal a palate of luxurious fruits—spiced pear and yellow peaches—framed with a racy but not aggressive acidity and elegant minerality. Very promising. Drink from 2010.

Champagne André Jacquart
63 Avenue de Bammental, 51130 Vertus
Tel: +33 3 26 57 52 29
www.a-jacquart-fils.com

Alain Robert

The worlds of wine and gastronomy have their fair share of special characters, of *garçons difficiles* who at first seem remote and guarded. But, like a fine wine, they grow on you, revealing warm, hidden depths every time you revisit them. One thinks of the Châteauneuf eccentric, the late Jacques Reynaud of Château Rayas, who would hide in a ditch and deny who he was when a so-called wine expert came to call. Or the manically obsessive Squadron Leader Pichel-Juan, owner of Sheriff House restaurant in Brockdish, Norfolk, England. As a restaurant inspector I remember once being slightly delayed for dinner chez Pichel-Juan because of fog, and there was the law-making Sheriff of Brockdish hopping up and down in the car park, mouthing the retort: "How can you expect to eat quenelles when you are four minutes late?"

My friend Alain Robert, the dean of Le Mesnil Champagne growers, is more reasonable and civilized, but he is also an acutely sensitive and fastidious man who has more than a few phobias—particularly of being photographed. As he enters his 60s and winds down his activities with no successor to the domaine, he is increasingly elusive, even with wine friends of long acquaintance. And yet it would be inconceivable to write a book on the finest wines of Champagne without paying tribute to this perfectionist producer who never releases any wine before it is seven years old, and in whose hospitable house I have drunk some of the greatest wines of the region—and indeed of *la belle France*.

The Robert de Robertsons, a noble family from the Nord *département*, moved south in the 17th century to become wine growers in Le Mesnil, planting Chardonnay, a grape variety much more suited to the deep Belemnite chalk of these hillsides than is Pinot Noir, which had previously been the sole grape used in Champagne-making. Alain's father, René Robert, was a prime mover in the Champagne cooperative movement, and he used to relate that as a child in the grim 1930s, to eat an orange on Christmas Day was a rare treat. By temperament, Alain prefers to work on a smaller scale. Until recently, he farmed 12ha (30 acres) of grand cru vineyards on the Côte, as well as holdings in the Sézannais and in the tiny Vitry-le-François sector southeast of Châlons-en-Champagne. All his wines are Chardonnay. The Blanc de Blancs Sélection, with at least seven years on lees, is made with the lightest touch (no oak) from his better vineyards and is a model of poised elegance in balance with deep, wine-like flavours. His greatest wine is unquestionably Réserve Le Mesnil Tête de Cuvée, the grapes coming from key sites in the village, near Krug's Clos du Mesnil and the famous slopes on the sunnier southern side of the village towards Vertus. The vines are up to 60 years old and are first vinified in 600-litre oak *foudres*. The wine is never fined or filtered.

As a perfectionist producer, Alain knows that this special wine, from such privileged soils, will taste searingly acidic when young so often needs, but seldom gets, a decade or two in bottle to show its mineral magnificence. Chez Robert, it always does—or rather, did. If you ever see the Tête de Cuvée at auction or on a fine-wine list, go for it.

FINEST WINES

(Tasted in Le Mesnil, June 2005)
Alain Robert Réserve Le Mesnil Tête de Cuvée 1986
Luminous Welsh gold. Aromas of succulent peaches and Asian spices. The palate confirms a seamless Champagne—long, richly complex, but in no way overextracted. Near perfection.

(Tasted in Le Mesnil, September 1999)
Alain Robert Réserve Le Mesnil Tête de Cuvée 1982
All the qualities of the 1986 but with even greater complexity and depth, and with superb expression of the greatest Chardonnay from what is probably the greatest terroir of the Côte des Blancs. 1982 was a beautiful vintage. Perfection.

Champagne Alain Robert
Rue de la République, 51990 Le Mesnil-sur-Oger
Tel: +33 3 26 57 52 94

Jean-Louis Vergnon

It was a stroke of luck finding this small grower in Le Mesnil, through the generous intervention of my friend Patrick Michelon, the great *chef-patron* of Epernay's Les Berceaux. Patrick suggested I have dinner in the restaurant with Christophe Constant, the *oenologue* and winemaker for Jean-Louis Vergnon, who is now in semi-retirement. Scuba diver and wine wizard, Christophe was not born with a silver tastevin in his mouth. His father is the owner of Epernay's best and least pretentious café, Le Khedive, a great place for a quick hot lunch. Christophe was a bright student at the oeno faculty in Reims and now manages the 5ha (12-acre) Vergnon domaine.

Although an intimate of both Anselme Selosse and Pascal Agrapart, Christophe adopts quite a different approach from these two Avize stars. He tends to emphasize the characteristics of the particular grapes in his cuvées, and there is nothing remotely shaming about their provenance. The largest parcel is in a top Avize site close to Agrapart's in the *lieu-dit* of La Fosse, and the rest of Vergnon's vines are in equally fine sites, notably in Oger and Le Mesnil itself.

These last two crus are the base of Christophe's most interesting wine—the Cuvée Confidence, a pure Chardonnay Brut Nature in both the great 2002 and the surprisingly successful 2003 vintage. If you think some Côte des Blancs Champagnes taste more dilute and loose-knit than they should these days, regain your faith with Confidence. The vital colour heralds freshness and zip; the aromas bounce off the nose with their minerality and zest; and the mouthfeel is all *croquant* yellow fruits, immensely refreshing, but with a rich, vinous character that says, "I'm a fine wine." Made for seafood, it is hard to think of a better partner for crayfish or carpaccio of scallops or veal, a dramatically delicious marriage.

The incisively dry style continues in the Cuvée Extra Brut Non-Vintage, based (at the time of my tasting) on the 2004 vintage, a bankable Chardonnay year. For those who like their Champagne a little less obviously dry, the Brut Classique, with a moderate *dosage* of 7g/l and full malolactic, is a winner, while the 2002 Brut Vintage is a true classic.

FINEST WINES

(Tasted in Le Mesnil, January 2009)

J-L Vergnon Cuvée Extra Brut

Pure Chardonnay from Mesnil, Oger, and Avize. Vinified in stainless steel. 2004 base with reserve wines. *Dosage* less than 4g/l. Crystalline, gold-green. Extraordinary freshness and finesse on the nose. The attack is clean, focused, and trenchant, with exemplary acidity that is the linchpin of quality holding everything together. Mineral, saline finish—perfect with oysters or a few slices of Parmesan. An original and successful Champagne.

J-L Vergnon Cuvée Confidence 2003

Pure Chardonnay grands crus, as above. *Non-dosé*. Very different to the 2002 tasted last year. Yellow colour with green reflections. The first nose confirms that promise—yellow flowers and fruits, quince, but also gingerbread, balanced by a fine minerality. The fresh attack cedes to the full body of the wine, the mouthfeel quickly assuming breadth and warmth. The wine is so *gras* that the absence of *dosage* is barely perceptible. Not typical of the Côte des Blancs in a normal year, but a fascinating wine whose voluptuous richness has just the right check of acidity to prevent it cloying.

J-L Vergnon Vintage Brut 2002

Dosage less than 8g/l. Typical yellow gold colour of a blanc de blancs approaching maturity. Intense *gourmand* nose, ripe pears at first, then perfumes of acacia and lemon zest waft up. The attack in the mouth is very fresh, and very classic Le Mesnil. Above all, the finale is powerful, long, and complex. A great wine from a superbly balanced vintage that was neither too firm nor too sunny.

Champagne Jean-Louis Vergnon
1 Grande Rue,
51190 Le Mesnil-sur-Oger
Tel: +33 3 26 57 53 86
www.champagne-jl-vergnon.com

Pierre Gimonnet & Fils

One of the great grower families of the Côte des Blancs, the Gimonnets produce what are probably the bluest of blue-chip Chardonnay Champagnes, famous for their finesse and rock-like consistency. The brothers Olivier and Didier Gimonnet start with distinct advantages. In Cuis since the 18th century, the family has amassed an important estate of 25ha (62 acres) in splendid sites, with old vines in the grands crus of Cramant and Chouilly. These are bolstered by their vineyards in Cuis, a premier cru notorious for its searing acidity, but one that brilliantly contributes a firm backbone to a style of wine that is supremely elegant, deserving the ultimate Champagne accolade: "restrained exuberance".

One of the great grower families of the Côte des Blancs, the Gimonnets produce what are probably the bluest of blue-chip Chardonnay Champagnes, famous for their finesse

It comes as no surprise, then, that winemaker Didier should reject the now-fashionable notion of monocru, or single-vineyard, bottlings for, say, his top Cramant and Chouilly sites. "To put all one's best wine into one cuvée would detract from the quality of the rest of the range, to the detriment of our customers' pleasure." Sound stuff. And when it comes to composing his best-selling Champagne, the entry-level Cuis Premier Cru Non-Vintage, his consummate blending skills in marshaling four different vintages of this punchy cru to craft a harmonious finished Champagne is an object lesson in how to do it.

Gimonnet's winemaking precepts expose in all its silliness the snide remark of a famous négociant who once said that growers can produce great Champagne but only by accident! Delving deeper into the composition of the Cuis cuvée, the successful aim is a vital, dancing wine, little dosed, technically perfect—the archetype of the Gimonnet style. This is a young, fresh Champagne, but to give it roundness and harmony, the house opts for the conserving of all its reserve wines on fine lees in bottle, rather than in vats, thus allowing these wines with more than two years of age to keep all their freshness.

Gimonnet's Cuvée Gastronome [V] is a concept of young Vintage Champagne that is seldom found among Champagne producers. Historically created by the family as a very superior pouring Champagne—*la coupe*—in fine restaurants, it is also a brilliant wine with the first courses of a fish lunch, especially oysters and crustaceans. Nearly half the Chardonnay blend usually comes from grand cru Chouilly, giving a signature elegance. Just under 40 per cent Cuis injects vivacious freshness; and the coup de grâce is the final addition of wines from 100-year-old Cramant vines, bringing a splendid roundness. Gastronome is always the friendliest, easiest Vintage cuvée in the range.

The Fleuron is Gimonnet's traditional Vintage cuvée, released uniquely in fine, often great years, and it is a judicious blend of the family's different terroirs representative of the vintage. Much in demand, it can account for 30–50 per cent of the harvest and probably has the best ratio of quality to price. I remember the 1999 Fleuron as a delicious bottle in 2007 at Les Berceaux's restaurant, priced at less than €60 a bottle. It is always aged on fine lees in bottle for at least four years, and then rested for three months before release.

The Special Club Vintage is the *ne plus ultra*, the summit of the range. Made from about three quarters grand cru grapes (notably with old-vine Cramant) and freshened with one quarter Cuis, it reveals real vinosity but still thrills with that wonderful freshness. There is also still a 1999 Vieilles Vignes bottling.

Right: Olivier (left) and Didier Gimonnet amid their Cuis vines, which contribute backbone and elegance to their blends

FINEST WINES

(Tasted October 2008)

Pierre Gimonnet Cuvée Gastronome 2004
An impressive, racy, vintaged blanc de blancs showing early the verve and dash of the potentially excellent 2004 Chardonnay fruit. The punch of Cuis and the elegance of Chouilly comprise nearly 90% of the blend, making this the ideal shellfish wine, while the roundness of old-vine Cramant makes it as good with turbot or Dover sole.

Pierre Gimonnet Cuvée Fleuron 2002
Green-flecked hue of some resonance; an athletic stream of visually elegant bubbles that give both a creamy and energizing mouthfeel. Still quite tight and adolescent, with a fine, green-fruit purity. Mouth-watering acidity.

Pierre Gimonnet Cuvée Vieilles Vignes 1999 ★
I have yet to taste this special bottling, but I leave it to Nick Adams MW, a great British taster, to describe it. "A truly magnificent wine—on the one hand, rich and multilayered, but counterbalanced by intense notes of minerals, flowers, and bread (autolysis). Beautifully dissolved mousse and creamy hazelnut flavours wrapped around a core of vital, racy acidity, with a long brioche finish."

Above: A pruner in one of the Gimonnet vineyards, which extend beyond their base in Cuis to Chouilly and Cramant

Champagne Pierre Gimonnet & Fils
1 Rue de la République, 51530 Cuis
Tel: +33 3 26 59 78 70
www.champagne-gimonnet.com

Laherte Frères

The small village of Chavot, in the Coteaux d'Epernay southwest of the town, is famous for its beautiful, part-Romanesque church set in the middle of the vineyards. It is also home to the Laherte family, whose 10ha (25-acre) estate is a model of what can be achieved in less well-known terroirs by a careful study of the soils, a viticulture of the highest order, and precepts of winemaking that are the best sort of evolved tradition.

This little corner of Champagne is geologically fascinating, a transitional district lying just above the Côte des Blancs at the entrance of the Cubry Valley, where chalk mixes and cedes to silt, clay, and marl. Apart from these Chavot and surrounding vineyards, the family have plots of Chardonnay in premier cru Voipreux (Vertus), and of Meunier in Boursault and Le Breuil (Marne Valley). For imaginative winemakers such as Thierry Laherte and his son Aurélien, the diversity of such terroirs across 72 dispersed parcels of vineyards is a gift that they have transformed into a fascinating series of Champagnes. In their rich variety, through the estate's policy of separate bottlings from specific parcels, Burgundy comes to Champagne, and the true identity of the vine is revealed. To the Lahertes, the terroir is more important than the oenologist's work of blending. Most of the cultivation is close to biodynamism, and certain parcels are actually tended that way.

The grapes pass into two traditional Coquard presses. Three quarters of the infant wines have been vinified judiciously in oak for the past 25 years, the aerating staves of the casks allowing these terroirs to breathe and fully blossom. Coopers are carefully chosen: François Frères in St-Romain and the local Jérome Viard, who specializes in lightly toasted casks, are the family's favourites. I do not detect any overt woodiness of flavour at the upper end of the range, as one critic has complained.

The Brut Tradition has a sense of place, freshness, fine orchard and hedgerow fruit flavours, and impressive depth. Thierry's wife's vineyard near Vertus shapes a blanc de blancs of delicate, fine, and racy character. Les Clos is a trial planting of all seven Champagne grapes extant in the Middle Ages (first release 2009). The 2002 Prestige shows subtle complexity, with a touch of smoke and vanilla that is not overblown. And the Rosé de Saignée is a Champagne for the table that benefits considerably from extra bottle age after release.

FINEST WINES

(Tasted in Chavot, January 2009)

Laherte Brut Tradition NV

This is a subtle amalgam of the estate's terroirs in the Coteaux d'Epernay, Marne Valley, and Côte des Blancs. 60% PM, 30% C, 10% PN. Mainly 2006 with reserve wines. Partially non-malo vinification. *Dosage* 6g/l. Vivid, fresh, bright yellow. Meunier drives the fruitiness of the blend, which is very pure tasting. Chardonnay gives it incisive length, and Pinot a touch of strength and real depth. Apricots and peaches shape the fruit profile. A really interesting entry-level Champagne of which you will never tire.

Laherte Blanc de Blancs La Pierre de la Justice NV ★

100% Chardonnay from the terroir of premier cru Voipreux. Vine stock chosen by *sélection massale*. *Dosage* 8g/l. Lemon-gold. Old vines contribute to the complexity on the nose, with a noticeable but discreet touch of menthol. Beautiful length and definition on the palate. A cracking Champagne.

Laherte Prestige Millesimé 2002

85% C from limestone and chalky subsoils in Charvot and Epernay; 15% PM from dominant clay with silt and chalky subsoils in Chavot, Mancy, and Vaudancourt. Low, extra-brut *dosage* of only 3–5g/l. Golden colour. Lively mousse. A complex medley of scents: honeysuckle, pear, and Asian spices, with just the right amount of smoky oak vanilla. Profound flavours, the pear fruit entwined with toast, brioche, and a fine, leesy character. Exceptional.

Champagne Laherte Frères
3 Rue des Jardins, 51530 Chavot Courcourt
Tel: +33 3 26 54 32 09
www.champagne-laherte.com

Duval-Leroy

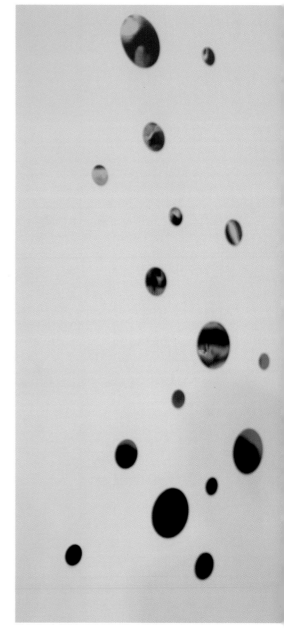

In the heart of the Côte des Blancs, Duval-Leroy is a family house that prospered during the heyday of Champagne expansion in the late 19th century. Based in Vertus since 1859, the family typically began to plough the trading profits into the purchase of land. Now, the firm's rock is nearly 200ha (494 acres) of beautiful vineyards, mainly Chardonnay, in all the grands crus of the Côte, as well as extensive holdings in Vertus, the fruitier character of their home village giving ideal balance to the blends.

In the 21st century, the higher profile of the house—now the ninth largest in Champagne—is very much to the credit of the dynamic Carol Duval, the current president. Belgian-born Carol is clearly made of the right stuff—another formidable, strong-minded widow in the Champenois tradition of such *grandes dames* as Lily Bollinger, Camille Olry-Roederer, Louise Pommery, and of course the Widow Clicquot herself. Since taking over on the death of her own husband in 1991, Carol has thoroughly yet thoughtfully modernized the production process, always with an eye for high, consistent quality. The incoming grapes are pressed gently in pneumatic presses, then drop by gravity towards the settling tank, retaining all their qualities; the fermentation proceeds slowly in stainless steel at a constant temperature of 61–68°F (16–20°C) for optimal character, delicacy, and bouquet. And in the best traditional practice, oak casks are used beneficially to aerate and age the main crus. On the commercial side, distribution channels have been developed, with branch offices in major EU cities; the product range has been increased; and export markets have been expanded. Yet what sets this house apart is the real sense of place in the Champagnes, which are at heart true expressions of great Chardonnay—the house's trump card. When I first wrote about the

Right: Carol Duval, Duval-Leroy's current president, who has grown the company to be the ninth largest in Champagne

Belgian-born Carol Duval is clearly made of the right stuff—another formidable, strong-minded widow in the Champenois tradition of such grandes dames as Lily Bollinger and the Widow Clicquot herself

Above: The basis of Duval-Leroy's success is its extensive vineyards, more than 40 per cent in grands or premiers crus

house in 1994, Duval-Leroy was in a sense one of Champagne's well-kept secrets, often providing excellent "buyer's own brand" Champagnes at keen prices to shrewd wine importers. Now, with the strategic building of the brand realized so successfully, the wines stand clear and undisguised.

The winemaking team knows well how important the quality of the grapes is in making good Champagne—an obvious enough priority, you might think, but one that is sometimes forgotten by rival négociants of similar size, who sometimes buy grapes of bland, nondescript character because they are easier to blend. Not at Duval. All the vineyards are cultivated by organic or biodynamic methods; more than 40 per cent of the holdings are in grands or premiers crus; and those grapes that are bought in, notably Pinot Noir from the Montagne de Reims, have to meet the same high standards as those coming from the house's own vineyards.

The sensibly manageable line of Champagnes shows a nice balance of classic winemaking and sharp, modern marketing. In keeping with today's trends, low-*dosage* cuvées and single-village/single-vineyard wines are now part of the line, in order to express in meticulous vinifications the diversity and range of Champagne styles.

The best-known blend is the Fleur de Champagne, the *cheval de bataille* of the house since its first release in 1914 and an *assemblage* of 75 per cent Chardonnay and 25 per cent black grapes. The name was coined by Raymond Duval, who thought its scents conjured up those of vine flowers in June. It is certainly finer and racier than the Non-Vintages of many *grandes maisons*, yet it also has a pleasing roundness. The Extra Brut also shows how it should be done—invigorating, fresh, naturally fruity. The Lady Rose is rare among négociants' Champagnes for being a pink made the hard way—by the *saignée* method of bleeding colour from the Pinot grape skins. The Femme de Champagne is a splendid

prestige cuvée made only in great years and built to last. Of the single-village/single-vineyard bottlings, I like best the Authentis Cumières, because this sunny site shapes an abundance of extract and fruitiness to make a highly individual Champagne.

FINEST WINES

(Tasted in August 2008)

Duval-Leroy Authentis Cumières 2003
In this atypical heat-wave vintage, the winemakers sensibly decided to emphasize the superripe fruit gathered on the sunny slopes of Cumières. Gold, with bronze hints—very 2003. Sensuous, rich, butter and toast scents. Opulent fruitiness caresses the palate. Spicy, confit-fruit flavours. Decent length. A lovely surprise.

Duval-Leroy Blanc de Chardonnay 1999
Medium-deep daffodil yellow. A fine-drawn, elegant wine with real class on the palate and better acidity than most 1999s.

Duval-Leroy Femme de Champagne 1996
Evolving lemon-gold colour, and mellowing, bready, ripe-fruit aromas (controlled autolysis). Mouthfeel still very young and vigorous, strong acidity boosting the finely shaped fruit. Still needs another two years. May yet be very great.

Champagne Duval-Leroy
Avenue de Bammenthal, 51130 Vertus
Tel: +33 3 26 52 10 75
www.duval-leroy.com

Larmandier-Bernier

Opinions differ about what makes a wine producer great, but everyone agrees that Pierre Larmandier's Champagnes are particularly natural and pure. When I first encountered the wines in 1993, it was those unadulterated flavours of great Chardonnay that struck me then, and they are with me still.

Although Pierre inherited 12ha (30 acres) of very fine vineyards in the Côte des Blancs, he did not study oenology, instead completing a course in business studies. Wags might say that this is the reason why the wines taste so good, made as they are with "feeling" and flair rather than secondhand technique. Pierre prefers to give a more rational and convincing explanation of his philosophy. "It

Opinions differ about what makes a wine producer great, but everyone agrees that Pierre Larmandier's Champagnes are particularly natural and pure

is not for reasons of tradition that our approach is natural," he insists. "It is just because it makes sense. The creation of any great wine begins in the grapes that contain the qualities and the authenticity that the winemaker seeks."

For him, the recipe for good-quality fruit is simple but demanding: respect for the soil, healthy vines, moderate yields, and mature grapes picked by hand. He is fortunate to work on superb terroirs, with a particularly old southeast-facing vineyard in Cramant, as well as other grand cru sites in Avize and Oger. He also has extensive holdings in Vertus, a terrain that he knows better than anyone, and which he expresses perfectly in his Terre de Vertus Champagne.

But for Pierre, the terroir is not enough in itself. What is the point of great land, he asks, if the grape variety and the vine plant—the instrument and the

performer—are not up to standard? His vines are biodynamically cultivated, partly so that their roots reach deep into the soil and reach the mother-rock, providing nutrients to the plant throughout the growing season. The grapes are picked late and by hand for optimal ripeness, both in natural sugar and for that phenolic maturity that gives the sought-after touch of complexity in the finished Champagne.

Pierre's three best wines are, of course, pure Chardonnay. The Brut Premier Cru Blanc de Blancs is made from a blend of all his Côte vineyards in Vertus, Cramant, Avize, and Oger. Both the alcoholic fermentation with natural yeast and the malo start spontaneously in stainless steel, and the infant wines spend the winter on their lees. Reserve wines from older vintages are stored in oak *foudres* and barrels. Disgorging is done by hand, and the *dosage* is a light 5 grams per litre.

With the Terre de Vertus, there is no blending for this single-cru Champagne, the Chardonnays coming from the *lieux-dits* of Les Barillers and Les Faucherets on the mid-slopes of the village. Fermentation starts in both big oak *foudres* and stainless-steel vats. No sugar is added—to respect the wine's purity from beginning to end. It is a Champagne of driving dynamism and tension.

The Vintage Cramant Vieille Vigne comes from the estate's oldest vines (aged between 48 and more than 70 years). Their deep root system, allied to the diversity of the venerable vine stock, adds to the complexity of the finished Champagne. Fermentation is in wood and steel. Chardonnay Champagne doesn't come any better than this.

Although there is almost certainly a commercial imperative that makes it unavoidable, the one slight regret I have about this outstanding domaine is that its top wine, the Cramant Vieille Vigne, tends to be released rather too young in its surely very long life. The 2004 vintage, for example, should ideally be left until around 2012, when it will finally start to show its full worth.

FINEST WINES

(Tasted in March and August 2008)

Larmandier-Bernier Blanc de Blancs Brut NV
Made mostly from the lithe, ripe 2006 vintage, with 40% reserve wines from 2005 and 2004, this is a Champagne that typifies Pierre's work in both vineyard and cellar. The nose has a smoky, gunflint character, mingling with pure, ripe, orchard fruits (particularly pears) and a hint of jasmine. It is, though, the mineral dynamism, vigorous yet refined, that pervades the long, fine flavours. Exemplary.

Larmandier-Bernier Né d'Une Terre de Vertus Non-Dosé Premier Cru NV
Although marketed as a Non-Vintage wine, this is from one year only: 2006. The nose really reflects the more chalky terroirs to the east of the village, combining with scents of linden (*tilleul*) and white flowers. This has even more drive and attack in the mouth than the Blanc de Blancs, but everything is perfectly balanced, with no hint of asperity.

Larmandier-Bernier Grand Cru Extra Brut Vieille Vigne de Cramant 2004
This is the purest statement of the terroir-based Larmandier style. The saline scents of the earth are unmistakable, but they are wrapped in exquisite aromas of green olives and a sage-like herbiness— no *maison* Champagne ever smelled like this! Latent, splendidly rich, deep flavours will unfurl, given more time (2011–12). Too young to drink at the time of writing.

Right: Pierre Larmandier, the highly principled and talented grower who crafts some of the greatest terroir-driven wines

Champagne Larmandier-Bernier
19 Avenue du Général de Gaulle, 51130 Vertus
Tel: +33 3 26 52 13 24
www.larmandier.fr

In the Vieille Vigne de Cramant, the saline scents of the earth are unmistakable, but they are wrapped in exquisite aromas of green olives and a sage-like herbiness—no maison *Champagne ever smelled like this!*

Veuve Fourny & Fils

The clue to the fine, mineral, and long-lived style of this rising Vertus star is found in its postal address: Rue du Mesnil. Most of its 12ha (30 acres) of premier cru Chardonnay vineyards lie on the Mesnil side of the town—more particularly, in the chalky terroir of Monts Ferrés, hillsides of ideal east and southeast aspect, which explains why you need to be patient and allow its Vintage Champagnes, especially, time to mature.

The widowed Monique Fourny, who was born in Flanders, has now passed the torch to her two extremely able sons, Charles-Henri and Emmanuel. The duo impress with their commitment to the environment, balanced by a thoroughly sensible awareness of the limits for manoeuvre that the weather can place on wine growers wanting to practise organic viticulture in the marginal climate of the Marne. Emmanuel, a trained oenologist but also an intuitive winemaker, honed his skills in Burgundy, where he learned the craft of fermenting wine in barriques with *bâtonnage*. He certainly talks more sense about the right way to make fine Champagne than anyone I know. It shows progressively as you taste up the range, the lightness of touch and the subtlest use of oak reaching its apogee in the family's single-vineyard Champagne, the Clos du Faubourg de Notre Dame, a scented beauty of poise, bearing, delicately expressive fruit, and great keeping qualities.

A particularity of the house is that its vineyards are more representative of Vertus than most other houses. This is best seen in the Grande Réserve, which is one Champagne in the range made with a touch of Pinot Noir from the Bergères, or western, side of the commune to balance the mineral saline character of the dominant Monts Ferrés Chardonnay. It is well distributed in America through Kermit Lynch.

The Fournys are also masters of low-*dosage* and zero-*dosage* cuvées, because they take great care to use wines from old vines, sometimes avoiding the malo when appropriate, to maintain the tension

and purity in the wines without any imbalance or flaw. The current Cuvée "R" Extra Brut—named in remembrance of Roger Fourny, Monique's late husband—is a splendidly incisive Champagne, and there is none better with a dozen oysters.

FINEST WINES

(Tasted in Vertus, January 2009)
Veuve Fourny Brut Nature NV
Zero *dosage*. Monts Ferrés Chardonnay from old vines, in a blend of 2006, 2005, and 2004. Pale

yellow hue with green highlights. Delicate perfume of green fruits; a hint of lime. Beautifully textured, crunchy fruits characterize a perfect, energizing mouthfeel. Very dry but finely balanced. An ideal apéritif before a serious dinner.

Veuve Fourny 2002

Non-malo. Pale yellow with green highlights. A fascinating bouquet that has the luxuriating richness of a great vintage, yet is rigorously precise and ethereal at the same time. Tasted blind, it could be confused with serious white Burgundy. Long and elegant in the mouth. Perfect balance and *dosage* (6g/l).

Veuve Fourny Grande Réserve NV

85% C, 15% PN. Much the same age as the 2002. Very pure and long, the little touch of Pinot Noir adding a friendly *gras* touch and weight to the flavours. *Dosage* just right at 5g/l. The best-selling Champagne here—and understandably so.

Above: Monique Fourny with her sons Charles-Henri (left) and Emmanuel, who craft perfectly poised Vertus wines

Champagne Veuve Fourny & Fils

5 Rue du Mesnil, BP 12, 51130 Vertus
Tel: +33 3 26 52 16 30
www.champagne-veuve-fourny.com

The Côte des Bar

Historically, the Aube has been part of the Province of Champagne since the Middle Ages, when Troyes was the provincial capital. The region has a long and honourable wine tradition based on seriously interesting soils and a semi-continental climate that brings warm summer and autumn days. Its vineyards lie on the Kimmeridgian strata of chalk, marl, and hard limestone that runs for 200 miles (320km) from the Haute-Marne and Aube through Chablis and on to Sancerre and Pouilly-sur-Loire. These remarkable chalky scarps thus support some of the best white wines of northern France—and on the same base it is no accident that the Aube produces arguably the most succulent rosé Champagnes.

Now known as the Côte des Bar, the main Aubois vineyards lie between 75 and 90 miles (120–145km) southeast of Epernay. They are divided into two subregions: the Barséquenais, centred on Bar-sur-Seine, and the Barsuraubois, on Bar-sur-Aube.

The Barséquenais

The western Barséquenais is the better known of the two—delightful undulating country with wooded hills and vineyards on sunny slopes above the river valleys of the Seine, the Ource, and the Laignes. Les Riceys in the extreme south, touching the border with Burgundy, is the largest commune in Champagne, actually composed of three villages: Riceys Haut, Haute-Rive, and Bas. The commune has three appellations—Champagne, Coteaux Champenois, and Rosé des Riceys—the last of which is one of the best and longest-lived (still) rosés. The wine is created by a short vinification of Pinot Noir, reaching a natural strength of at least 10% alcohol by volume. It is vital to stop the bleeding of the grape skins' colour at exactly the right moment, otherwise the sinewy, subtle taste of Riceys is lost. The better wines are given extra structure by being aged in oak and in a

great vintage can last well for 15 years. I remember the 1982 from Jacques Defrance (the finest producer) showing beautifully in 1998. The soils here are some of the richest in the Aube, producing Champagnes of very rich fruit and some vinosity. Just 5 miles (8km) north, towards Chaource, the twin hamlets of Avirey-Lingey are more open country, the wind whistling along the valley floor. On the protected slopes at opposite ends of the hamlets are two excellent Champagne growers: Serge Mathieu, who emphasizes purity of fruit in a range of Champagnes made in stainless steel, and Dosnon-Lepage, whose winemaker did his apprenticeship in Gevrey-Chambertin and now makes a sumptuous trio of cuvées vinified in oak.

Retrace your steps south to the village of Courteron, 1.2 miles (2km) from the Côte d'Or border, for the home of probably the most respected grower in the Aube, Jean-Pierre Fleury. His grandfather Robert started to make and sell his own Champagnes in the 1930s, and Jean-Pierre himself is the pioneer of biodynamic viticulture in the region, having converted the domaine strictly in line with the philosophy of Rudolf Steiner as early as 1989. His Champagnes are generous with a real naturalness of flavour, best expressed in the pure Pinot Noir Cuvée Europe and the Vintage Robert Fleury, which has 40 per cent white grapes in its makeup, including 20 per cent of the more rarely used Pinot Blanc. The 2000 is a great success, with a nice touch of oak in balance with floral and orchard-fruit flavours. Farther towards Bar-sur-Seine, the large village of Celles-sur-Ource has a thoroughly justified reputation for wines of great harmony and mellow richness. The hillsides have an ideal southeastern orientation, catching the full strength of the midday sun, while the nearness of the Ource mitigates against both heat stress and spring frosts. Richard Cheurlin's

Right: The sunny and tranquil village of Les Riceys, the largest commune in Champagne, right on the border with Burgundy

0   10 km

0   10 miles

N

Rizaucourt

D73

Arrentières

Colombey-les-
Deux-Eglises

D4

Bar-sur-Aube

D619

Argançon

Aube

Baroville

Meurville

D369

Bergères

Bligny

Urville

Clairvaux

A5

Eguilly-sous-Bois

D4

Noé-les-Mallets

D79

Bar-sur-Seine

Seine

Ource

Celles-sur-Ource

Essoyes

D70

Villemorien

Polisy

N71

Gyé-sur-Seine

Courteron

Seine

Avirey-Lingey

Les Riceys

CÔTE DES BAR

Vineyard

Rosé des Riceys Vineyard

A1   Major Road

0   20 km

0   20 miles

Reims

PARIS

Marne

Epernay

Aube

Seine

Troyes

N

CÔTE DES BAR

Cuvée Jeanne and Marcel Vézien's Double Eagle II are two of the finest Champagnes of Celles.

At the southern end of Bar-sur-Seine, the Union Auboise is a powerful cooperative of some 800 wine growers cultivating mainly Pinot Noir, transformed into still wines and Champagnes that are much in demand by the big houses of the Marne. But in recent years the Union has also developed its own upmarket brand, Devaux. The quality is very high, particularly that of the well-aged Grande Réserve, the prestige D Ultra Brut, and the D 1996, a finely evolved expression of that great vintage.

The Barsuraubois

The little town of Essoyes on the road east towards Bar-sur-Aube is well known as the place where Renoir had his country studio; the soft, gentle light must have greatly attracted him here. The Barsuraubois is more open country and noticeably colder than the Barséquenais. There are good sites for Chardonnay, because the soils are slightly more chalky and less richly Kimmeridgian. The villages of Meurville and Bligny are known to suit the great white grape well. There is also a small amount of Meunier grown in the Barsuraubois. But Pinot Noir, as always, is the star, particularly on the south-facing slopes of Bergères and Urville, about 8 miles (12km) east of Bar-sur-Aube.

Urville is the village of the Aube's greatest family Champagne merchant and grower—Drappier, who has a beautiful domaine of 41ha (100 acres) of Pinot Noir. The style of the Champagnes is unashamedly Aubois—joyful, brightly fruity expressions of the black grape—and it was obviously a style that appealed to Charles de Gaulle, a loyal customer, who lived in retirement nearby. Yet Drappier can make Champagnes as fine as anyone's, as shown by his wonderful Grande Sendrée Cuvée, which is consistently the Aube's best wine, the majority

Above: The welcoming sign at Avirey-Lingey, home to two of the Aube's best growers—Serge Mathieu and Dosnon-Lepage

Pinot Noir lightened with some grand cru Chardonnay from the Côte des Blancs.

The vineyards of the Aube actually spill over into the Haute-Marne east of Bar-sur-Aube. It is in this area towards Colombey-les-Deux-Eglises that new plantations of Pinot Noir are being considered for inclusion as part of the planned expansion of the Champagne appellation. So, too, are those villages to the south of the great hill of Montgueux above Troyes, whose golden Chardonnays have been a favourite element in the big Champagne houses' blends for years.

Drappier

The Drappiers are as Champenois as it gets. The family in the male line is probably Rémois in origin; the name means "draper" and suggests they were originally involved in the cloth trade, the main source of wealth in Reims in the days before sparkling Champagne was a commercial proposition.

Yet Troyes, the ancient medieval capital of the Aube, with its beautiful Gothic cathedral, has been the Drappiers' nearest city since the 18th century. From that time, they have been Champagne growers and merchants at Urville in the Barsuraubois, where they have a beautiful domaine of 41ha (101 acres) of Pinot Noir. Indeed, it was the father-in-law of André Drappier, the current head of the family, who in the 1930s was the first grower to rip out the inferior Gamay grape then used in Aubois Champagne-making and replace it with fine strains of Pinot Noir, earning him the nickname "Papa Pinot".

These Champagnes have real personality, in an opulent, hedonistic style that is a highly distinctive expression of Pinot Noir grown on rich, Kimmeridgian soils

This close-knit family business centres on a modern, pristine winery, which now includes some new oak *foudres* above deep 12th-century cellars built by winemaking Cistercian monks from the famous nearby abbey of Clairvaux. Michel Drappier, André's son, runs the whole business with immaculate care and quiet flair; he is certainly one of the most informative and open-minded of winemakers, having trained in both viticulture and winemaking at the Lycée Viticole in Beaune.

Right: Michel Drappier, who studied in Burgundy and is now one of Champagne's most reflective and talented winemakers

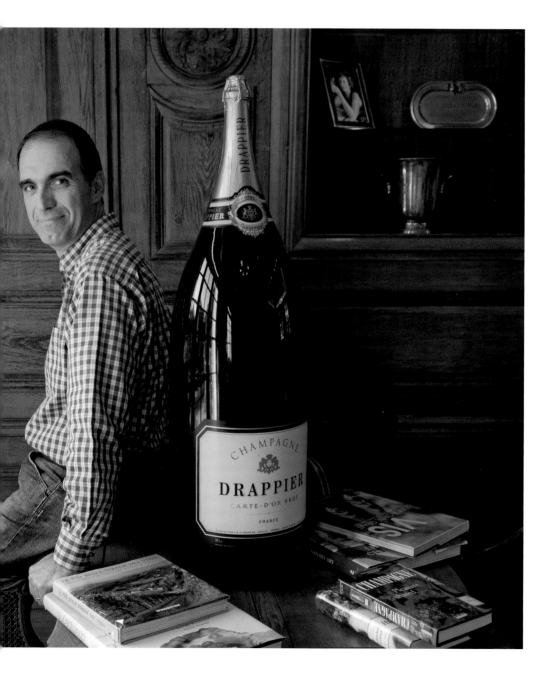

The Champagnes he makes are not just technically correct; they have real personality, in an opulent, hedonistic style that is a highly distinctive expression of Pinot Noir grown on the richer Kimmeridgian soils of the Côte des Bar. The Drappier style certainly appealed to Charles de Gaulle, when he was living in retirement at Colombey-les-Deux-Eglises, half an hour's drive from Urville. In our day, Sir Alex Ferguson, Manchester United FC's supremely successful manager, is also a fan. Michel, now in his 50s, has built important new markets across the EU and the Pacific Rim.

The entry-level Drappier Carte d'Or Brut Non-Vintage is composed of 90 per cent Pinot and a little Meunier. Of copper-gold colour, with a creamy, well-integrated mousse, it is round and supple, with flavours of little red fruits—a very consistent Champagne for those who like a less austere style. The straight Vintage cuvée is now renamed Millésime Exception and is a more intense expression of Carte d'Or, writ large.

The pink Val des Desmoiselles is one of the best Non-Vintage Champagnes I know. It is made by an adapted form of the *saignée* method, in which colour is bled from the skins and a smidgen of white wine is added to achieve a consistent colour year on year—always a challenge with this traditional method. The result is a succulent, seductive celebration of Aubois Pinot Noir.

The Signature Blanc de Blancs is richer than most, reflecting the better ripeness the Chardonnay achieves in the warmer summer climate of southern Champagne; but it is also tempered by the injection of minerally grand cru Chouilly from the northern Côte des Blancs, where Michel cleverly has a contracted, long-standing supplier.

No doubt, a little of this classy Chouilly finds its way into Drappier's Grande Sendrée, the house's prestige cuvée and one of the finest values in Champagne. It is, at heart, a wine from the finest south-facing slopes of Urville, and it has an interesting history. In the 1850s, there was a great fire in the village, reducing trees and bushes to cinders. Afterwards, on the razed slopes, the Drappiers planted a vineyard that became known as Les Cendrées ("The Cinders"). It was not until 1974, however, that the first vintage was made of Grande Sendrée, the "c" having been replaced by an "s" due to an error when the title of the vineyard was registered. The two best recent vintages of this great wine are the 1996 and the 2002—very different expressions of the same bit of earth.

FINEST WINES

(Tasted August 2008)

Drappier Grande Sendrée 2002★
Generally 55% PN, 45% C. Luminous, shimmering yellow-gold. A memorable array of aromas, rich-but-elegant Pinot dominant yet beautifully balanced by ripe, succulent, slightly exotic Chardonnay. In the mouth, the wine has an exceptional *gras* texture, rich but silkily gentle—so typical of this great, classic, but still adolescent vintage. Long, Burgundian-style finish, like the proverbial peacock's tail. Exceptional—and should be great—but wait to drink it at its peak, around 2011–12.

(Tasted June 2007)

Drappier Grande Sendrée 1996
Of deep, copper-gold colour, this vintage is atypical of the usual harmonious, silky style of Grande Sendrée. The nose is beginning to show notes of mushrooms and game, which suggests that the aromas are fast developing. Yet the palate fairly bounces with vigorous acidity. It will be interesting to observe its progress over next few years. Character it does not lack.

Left: Some precious, rare Methuselahs (each containing eight standard bottles) of the 1985 vintage still resting in the cellar

Champagne Drappier
Rue des Vignes, 10200 Urville
Tel: +33 3 25 27 40 15
www.champagne-drappier.com

Dosnon & Lepage

Wooded hills above windswept valleys are the Arcadian setting as you drive up from Les Riceys to the twin Aubois hamlets of Avirey-Lingey on the back road to Troyes. Catching the afternoon sun, the hamlets' best vineyards lie on slopes relatively protected from the wind corridor of the valley floor. Just 30 miles (48km) east of the Yonne *département*, the soils here are almost identical to those of nearby Chablis and Sancerre farther west down the long Kimmeridgian belt of hard limestone and clay that is the ideal cradle for some of northern France's best dry white wines.

Tiny though it is, Avirey-Lingey is home to two of the finest growers in the Aube region.

The duo of Simon-Charles Lepage and Davy Dosnon are young blades making exquisite expressions of golden Pinot Noir Champagne, mostly vinfied in oak

One, Serge Mathieu is rightly renowned for impeccable, non-wooded Champagne. By contrast, the duo of Simon-Charles Lepage and Davy Dosnon are young blades making exquisite expressions of golden Pinot Noir Champagne, mostly vinified in oak, to the evident delight of top Parisian restaurateurs and *cavistes*.

The boys cultivate 2ha (5 acres) of Pinot Noir with a little Chardonnay, also buying in grapes from a further 7ha (17 acres) of vineyards. They practise sustainable viticulture, grassing between the vine rows to encourage natural predators, tilling and ploughing to aerate the soil, and never using chemical treatments. The vines are pruned short à la Royau to control yields.

The duo believe that oak is the ideal vessel in which to express the best of these Aubois terroirs, though stainless steel is also used to make the more fragile wines. The result is a stunning trio of subtly rich, racy Champagnes that deserve to be much better known.

FINEST WINES

(Tasted October 2008)

Dosnon & Lepage Récolte Noire
A pure, *monocépage* Pinot Noir, this is an exceptional example of what the Aube does best. Pale yellow, with a lustrous hue; a luxurious, brioche nose; then a palate of crunchy green apples ceding to yellow peaches and pears. The oak is seamlessly integrated—there is real poise reining in the richness. Moderate *dosage* of 7g/l. Bravura winemaking.

Dosnon & Lepage Récolte Extra Brut
70% PN, 30% C. Under 5g/l *dosage*. Pale yellow, with fine bubbles; scents of pears and marshmallow, with lemon tones, the oak a little more obvious here. This still needs time to knit together, since it is less eloquent than the Noire at this stage.

Dosnon & Lepage Récolte Rosé
Pure Pinot Noir. Shimmering salmon pink, with a haunting bouquet of wild raspberries, apple, and even white chocolate—all of which are amply confirmed in a mouthfeel of supreme class.

Right: Davy Dosnon (left) and Simon-Charles Lepage, whose stunning trio of oak-fermented wines merits fuller recognition

Champagne Dosnon & Lepage
4 bis Rue du Bas de Lingey, 10340 Avirey-Lingey
Tel: +33 3 25 29 19 24
www.champagne-dosnon.com

Serge Mathieu

Along with Michel Drappier at Urville, Serge Mathieu's top-drawer domaine at Avirey-Lingey is one of the best two in the Aube, now managed by his daughter Isabelle and her husband, Michel Jacob, a fine, non-interventionist winemaker. Even more important, Michel is a scrupulous, eco-friendly guardian of the 11ha (27-acre) family estate: he's a pragmatist who stops just short of believing in the faith of biodynamism. The vineyard is mainly planted with the healthiest Pinot Noir but also with some excellent Chardonnay. There is no wood in the cellar here, the Mathieus preferring to let the purity of the grape and the character of the terroir show through, unoaked.

Tasting the Blanc de Noirs, one can see why. The colour is a striking burnished gold, almost bronze; the aromas of ripe, cherry-like Pinot melding with meat, spices, and leather lead on to a grand palate-filling mouthfeel uncannily like a mini Bollinger (Grande Année, not Special Cuvée!). Yet the most lasting impression is one of balance, finesse, and the lightest of touches in the winemaking—and all for under $30 a bottle retail. Michel also makes the refined Brut Sélect Tête de Cuvée, in which Chardonnay adds a delicate racy balance to the punch of Aubois Pinot Noir. This classy Champagne is now listed by Didier Elena at the two-Michelin-star Les Crayères hotel-restaurant in Reims.

When the family are not making wine or tending their vines, you are likely to find them on the golf course at Chaource, often playing a round or two with Michel Laroche, who drives over from Chablis, just 40 minutes away to the west.

Right: Serge Mathieu with his daughter Isabelle and her husband Michel Jacob, who is now making these stylish wines

Champagne Serge Mathieu
6 Rue des Vignes,
10340 Avirey-Lingey
Tel: +33 3 25 29 32 58
www.champagne-serge-mathieu.fr

*Serge Mathieu's top-drawer domaine at Avirey-Lingey is
one of the best two in the Aube. The lasting impression
is one of balance, finesse, and the lightest of touches*

Union Auboise (Veuve A Devaux)

Devaux is the prestige brand of the Union Auboise based in Bar-sur-Seine, 70 miles (113km) southeast of Epernay. This is a first-rate cooperative, aiming for high quality under the visionary leadership of Laurent Gillet. The Union is a powerful grouping of 800 growers farming 1,348ha (3,300 acres) of exclusively Aubois vineyards, which are now getting the recognition they deserve after nearly a century of anonymous provision of grapes for the blends of the *grandes maisons* in the Marne. Pinot Noir is the dominant grape variety of the Aube, but Devaux also has access to an increasing number of Chardonnay plantings. Contrary to inaccurate press reports, there is very little Aubois Meunier (a mere 6 per cent of plantings).

For such a large range of wines, the general standard is excellent, the Champagnes made with the best modern equipment but also a respect for tradition

For such a large range, the general standard is excellent, and *chef de cave* Michel Parisot is one of the brightest talents in the Aube. The Champagnes are made with the best modern equipment, but also a respect for tradition that includes large numbers of oak casks for aging the reserve wines. It shows in the Grande Réserve Brut, a blend of 50 crus, properly aged for three years. Bright green-gold, it has a nicely restrained note of autolytic complexity in balance with a pure fruitiness and incisive acidity. The traditional *oeil de perdrix* rosé is a gourmand's delight, brimming with the ripe, succulent fruit of Southern Champagne. The Union also vinifies the rare, still Rosé des Riceys. It is, however, the luxe D de Devaux range that should most interest the Champagne buff. Durably built and mouthfilling, the wines lack for nothing in breed and precision—though they are fully priced.

FINEST WINES

(Tasted in Bar-sur-Seine, June 2006)

D de Devaux Ultra Brut NV

A really good, sugarless Champagne that owes its success to deep wells of ripe fruit and vinosity in harmony with an impressive finesse and raciness. Versatile, too, great either as a winter apéritif or imposing enough to be served through a meal of fish and poultry—at least until dessert.

D de Devaux Rosé Brut NV

A subtle pink *oeil de perdrix* hue (with just 10 per cent vinified as red wine for addition to the blend, which has a high percentage of Chardonnay for the Aube). Very much an apéritif rosé. Refreshing, with notes of almonds and both hedgrow and orchard fruits. *Tout en finesse.*

D de Devaux Vintage 1996

An excellent '96, one that has already assimilated an elegant, not too raw acidity with the opulent fruit. Now entering a secondary stage, the flavours of apricot and orange confit are sensuous but not overblown. Precise winemaking. Ready at around 12 years old.

Right: Laurent Gillet, the inspiring leader of Union Auboise, which makes the most of its 800 grower-members' vines

Champagne Veuve A Devaux
Domaine de Villeneuve,
10110 Bar-sur-Seine
Tel: +33 3 25 38 30 65
www.champagne-devaux.fr

Richard Cheurlin

In the south of Champagne, the large wine village of Celles-sur-Ource is blessed with very warm summer days—200 sun-hours in a good year. Certainly since Gallo-Roman times, the finesse and generosity of its wines, tempered by the nearness of the River Ource, have enjoyed a great reputation. And even today they are often a step up in quality from those of other reputable communes of the Côte des Bar, having a better balance than the rich, sometimes extracted Champagnes of Les Riceys or the more aerian cuvées of the Barsuraubois. The great houses of Reims and Epernay are well aware of the virtues of Celles, but they keep quiet, preferring to add them as a extra little je ne sais quoi to their blends.

Richard Cheurlin is an outstanding Champagne-maker. Of his half-dozen nicely varied cuvées, there is one for every circumstance and mood

Richard Cheurlin is Veuve Clicquot's "man on the spot", supervising their observation post for the maturity of the grapes and monitoring the local presshouse. But Richard is also an outstanding Champagne-maker in his own right, from one of the oldest families of vignerons, here since the 16th century. By the sound of his postal address, were they refugees from religious persecution? There's nothing hunted about Richard now, who looks the very model of a contented wine grower, serene in his craft. With his ruddy complexion and Roman nose, he could have stepped down from a Renaissance tableau of villagers by a Flemish or Italian master.

Though Richard has the traditional inheritance of predominantly Pinot Noir vines, some as old as 40 years and grown only on the slopes, he is an intelligent modernist who embraces cold settling of the must in thermoregulated stainless-steel tanks, and all his wines go through the malo. Of his half-dozen nicely varied cuvées, there is one for every circumstance and mood. And he is a man close to my heart, a gourmand who loves good food, making some delicious suggestions of what to eat with each of his Champagnes. Richard's greatest wine is the vintaged Cuvée Jeanne, made in memory of his grandmother, the fermentation in oak handled in as masterly a way as the rest of the non-wooded range.

FINEST WINES

(Tasted in Celles-sur-Ource, June 2006)

Richard Cheurlin Carte Noire NV
Pale gold, the colour of ripe Pinot that drives the blend. Abundant, fine bubbles, discreet, emphasizing lovely fruit that leads on to a sensation of maturity in the wine. A nice touch of biscuity autolysis on the palate, which combines a grilled note with honeyed generosity and vivacity. A brilliant Non-Vintage at a bargain price. Great with *saucisson de Lyon* or grilled bass.

Richard Cheurlin Brut H NV
Clear yellow with green tints. A Chardonnay-led nose, white flowers, and fruits—white peaches especially. Very good maturity, with a vegetative finish in the best sense. Great fullness in the mouth, but the cleansing note of freshness and vivacity is still there. A long finish. Good with *fruits de mer* or as a drink with friends at any time of the day.

Richard Cheurlin Cuvée Jeanne 2002
Beautiful yellow robe flecked with intriguing aniseed-green lights. Persistent, very fine bubbles. A real palette of aromas, white flowers, orchard tones of peach and pear, then a lovely scent of the pastry shop, of *tarte aux pommes*, even a touch of caramel. Really fine in the mouth, powerful but poised and elegant, then a great finale, fresh and firm, with notes of vanilla. Exceptional. For foie gras or roast lobster with a vanilla sauce.

Champagne Richard Cheurlin
16 Rue des Huguenots, 10110 Celles-sur-Ource
Tel: +33 3 25 38 55 04
www.champagne-cheurlin.com

Fleury Père & Fils

Jean-Pierre Fleury was the pioneer of biodynamic viticulture in the Côte des Bar, having treated his vineyards according to the strict principles of Rudolf Steiner as early as 1989. The family had been grape farmers in Couteron, in the far south of the Barséquenais touching Burgundy's Côte d'Or, since the 1890s. But it was Robert Fleury who, in 1930, decided to make and sell his own Champagnes in bottle, as the way to escape from the deprivations and hardships that the Aubois vignerons in particular endured during the Great Depression.

Today Jean-Pierre has an estate approaching 20ha (50 acres), the health of his soils and vines being widely admired and emulated in the wine

The wines, which are fermented in oak, retain a floral expression and precision that naturally balance the rich, vinous flavours shaped by the local chalky marls of the terroir

community. Moreover, his wines, which are fermented in oak, retain a floral expression and precision that naturally balance the rich, vinous flavours shaped by the local, chalky marls.

Fleury's range of six cuvées has a shared weight and vinosity that make them very suitable for the table—from the subtly coloured rosé suffused with Pinot Noir flavours, through the evolved Brut Tradition, to the complex vintage-dated Cuvée Tradition, which has 20 per cent of the officially allowed but rarely used Pinot Blanc. The Fleury Champagne that consistently scores high marks is his Cuvée Fleur de l'Europe, which, for all the Pinot Noir in the blend, possesses remarkable finesse and poise. The sprightly character of Jean-Pierre's wines owes everything to the natural methods of work in the vineyard and explains the lightness of touch even in the very sweet Trilogie Doux 1995.

FINEST WINES

(Tasted in Courteron, April 2008)

Fleury Brut Tradition NV
The most traditional style of Aubois Champagne, driven by ripe, succulent Pinot Noir. Quite a deep, evolved, yellow, almost peachy hue, round and fruity on both nose and palate. Well-judged *dosage*.

Fleury Brut Rosé NV
Shimmering, subtle pink hue with salmon reflections. The wine looks very natural, and it smells and tastes that way, too. Particularly palate-filling mouthfeel, with a hedgerow-raspberry fruitiness melding into a burgeoning vinosity. A very good Champagne for spicy Asian cuisine, particularly crispy duck.

Fleury Fleur de l'Europe NV
The Champagne that best expresses Jean-Pierre's winemaking strength—supple, very pure, clean as a whistle, lovely roundness but with a dashing, energizing raciness that revives the palate. This is what all Champagne should be, with the extra bonus of an Aubois sense of place.

Fleury Cuvée Robert Fleury 2000
An *assemblage* of 60% PN, 20% C, and (a rarity) 20% Pinot Blanc, this is a finely evolving Vintage Champagne worthy of the genre. The nose is complex and multifaceted, with aromas of flowers and preserved fruits plus a touch of oak. Rather a Burgundian evolution on the palate, mushrooms especially, but not overdone. Fully mature.

Fleury Trilogie Doux 1995
A collector's item: a genuine and rare *cuvée doux*, a very sweet Champagne with a *dosage* of more than 50g/l. Sumptuous but not cloying, this is a dessert *mousseux* made with an admirably light touch. Subtly oaked, with a light touch of vanilla, toasted almonds, and confit of orchard fruits (especially peach) on both nose and palate. There's an intriguing hint of *eau de vie de mûre* (myrtle fruit brandy) on the finish. Great with *tarte tatin* or a host of Sicilian fruit pastries sweetened with *crème pâtissière*.

Fleury Père & Fils
43 Grande Rue, 10250 Courteron
Tel: +33 3 25 38 20 26
www.champagne-fleury.fr

Jean-Michel Gremillet

One of the great success stories of Aubois Champagne, this excellent domaine was created by Jean-Michel in the 1970s. It now extends to 27ha (67 acres), enviably situated on the steep, sunny Kimmeridgian slopes of Balnot-sur-Laignes, a hamlet that lies between Chaource, famed for its church and cheese, and the old stone villages of Les Riceys, renowned for Pinot Noir. The expansion of this dynamic enterprise has relied on the opportunity to buy in a certain proportion of good grapes from neighbouring growers, and Jean-Michel has been careful to deal with the best. Now officially a négociant, he is ably assisted by his daughter Anne and his son Jean-Bernard.

In a modern pristine winery full of gleaming, stainless-steel vats, the wines are made unhurriedly, with a classic attention to detail. The finished Champagnes receive their final *dosage* a good 15 months after the flowering of the previous year's vintage, then rest for three months before release.

The range of seven cuvées is a representative offering of the best of the Aube. None is more typical than the entry-level Brut Tradition, made from pure Pinot Noir: a Champagne of rich fruit and a taste of the sun, ideal for the table and very good value. The Brut Sélect—more than one third Chardonnay—is lighter-limbed and ideal as an apéritif or with smoked-fish canapés. The Cuvée des Dames is an exceptional blanc de blancs in a district known for black grapes. The Brut Prestige, a classic 50/50 Pinot/Chardonnay, is a *grand vin* with greater age on lees, perfect for the grandest fish or fowl. The Cuvée Evidence, with the Chardonnay aged in oak, shows exotic scents of vanilla and spice. The Rosé has all the succulence of this sunny corner of Champagne, and the Coteaux Champenois rouge gets better by the year. Last, and rarest of all, the still Rosé des Riceys has a lustrous, deep, salmon-pink hue. The flavours are haunting and fleeting, combining suave richness with fresh acidity and perfumes of violets and peonies. It is one of France's great pink wines.

FINEST WINES

(Tasted November 2008)

Gremillet Brut Tradition NV
100% PN of elegant, star-bright gold with ocher lights. The nose is very Pinot, surging upwards with red stone fruits—cherry and plum—but well balanced. On the palate, it is a generous, opulent wine, with enough presence to merit drinking with salmon *coulibiac*, young game, or offal.

Gremillet Cuvée des Dames NV
100% C. Although the blanc de noirs is more typical, this blanc de blancs is as remarkable, giving an individual expression of the great white grape on Kimmeridgian soils. Classic pale-gold colour, with green hints. Lovely benchmark Chardonnay smells of hedgerows—hawthorn and broom—and a touch of honeysuckle. Rich yet fine, palate-cloaking texture, and a long finish.

Gremillet Brut Prestige NV
50% PN, 50% C. Lustrous gold hue, with a hint of daffodil yellow. Subtle aromas mingle white flowers with a positive, Burgundian vegetative character. Lovely, swirling, creamy mouthfeel, the floral scents of the nose transformed into a toasty character, with superb length.

Gremillet Cuvée L'Evidence NV
50% PN, 50% C (oak aged). Pastel shade of Welsh gold, with silvery, green-flecked tints. The toastiness and spice of the nose make an impact that you either love or don't. That wood still dominates the mouthfeel, but interesting autolytic flavours of vanilla and wholemeal biscuits come through.

Gremillet Brut Rosé NV
This 100% PN Champagne plays to its Aubois strengths of warm summers. Vivid, intense, yet elegant salmon pink. Gorgeous, juicy, red-berry fruits make for a really seductive bouquet, confirmed in flavours and all nicely checked by good acidity. Great wine for food, especially sautéed kidneys, grilled *poussin*, or baked crab with ginger.

Champagne Jean-Michel Gremillet
Envers de Valeine, 10410 Balnot-sur-Laignes
Tel: +33 3 25 29 37 91
www.champagnegremillet.fr

Moutard

To call this producer individualistic and quirky, its range of Champagnes somewhat patchy, is an understatement—at least on past experience. But *vive la différence*, for Lucien Moutard, who sadly died in 2007, was one of the great, independent characters of the Aube. As Tom Stevenson pointed out, in the 1950s Lucien went to the trouble of reviving the Arbanne grape, a traditional Aubois variety, cheerfully defying officialdom, which wanted to suppress it. Arbanne is a very difficult grape to grow, and with its rather blowsy aromas—a poor man's Viognier?—not one that seems naturally suitable for making racy Champagne. But Lucien persevered and continued making his Cuvée Arbanne Vieille Vigne to mixed reviews. The real reputation of the house rested all the while on its range of digestifs and eaux de vie— their *marc de Champagne* is delicious.

Less well known than Cuvée 6 Cépages but of at least equal interest are Moutard's two terroir Champagnes, fine showcases for the Kimmeridgian soils of the Aube

Then, with the greater involvement of Lucien's son François in the vineyard and the winery, the wines improved markedly at the turn of the century, and particularly so with the launch of the Cuvée 6 Cépages in the 2000 vintage. This Champagne is indeed from all six varieties, including the tolerated Pinots Meslier and Blanc and the scented Arbanne. It has been given the "Bollinger treatment" of fermentation in Burgundian oak *pièces* and aging under a clamped cork in bottle for a longer life. This is now one of the more visible Champagnes on the market—due in part to its originality but also to its undoubted quality. Less well known but of at least equal interest are Moutard's two terroir Champagnes, which are fine showcases for the Kimmeridgian soils of the Aube's Côte des Bar: the Chardonnay Champ Persin and the Pinot Noir Vigne Beugneux. The advances that François has made in cellar management are typified by his readiness to have gone to the considerable expense of employing *débourbage à froid* (cold settling of the coarse lees) before fermentation. This ultra-modern technique dramatically clarifies the must and ensures purity of flavour, avoidance of oxidation, and long life in the finished Champagnes. Of the great houses, only Billecart-Salmon and Pol Roger use this technique. Being off the beaten track in *la France profonde*, Moutard's Champagnes are now great value, too.

FINEST WINES

(Tasted June 2007)

Moutard Cuvée 6 Cépages 2000
Moderately dosed at 6g/l, this Champagne has a fine, gentle texture in the mouth, the pure and direct expression of orchard fruits. The wood is well integrated and the different flavours of the six varieties add a touch of variety and character. Not a great Champagne, but one of undoubted quality.

Moutard Chardonnay Champ Persin NV
The Aube is better known for Pinot Noir than for Chardonnay, but this vineyard close to Buxeuil in the Barséquenais has matured well to deliver this excellent blanc de blancs. Long, elegant, and deep-flavoured, with none of the dilution that comes from overworked vines. Reasonable yields, of course. The best Champagne in the cellar.

Moutard Pinot Noir Vigne Beugneux NV
Packed with the orchard-fruit flavours of cool-climate cherries, even a touch of quince, this is a finely structured blanc de noirs—manly, palate-cloaking, but well balanced, with a long finish. It has enough clout to go the distance with a casserole of guinea fowl or breast of Bresse pigeon.

Champagne Moutard
Rue des Ponts BP1, 10110 Buxeuil
Tel: +33 3 25 38 50 73
www.champagne-moutard.fr

Year by Year 2008–1988

2008 ★★★★

The details of the vintage were not available at the time of writing. The weather patterns this year returned to a classic, slow sequence of a cool, gently warming spring and summer; a hot spell in late July; a cool but dry August; and a perfect September of sunny days and fresh nights. All this delivered a near-perfect vintage that could well be among the best of the past 20 years across all subregions.

2007 ★★

This was a year of wildly fluctuating weather patterns. January and February started windy and wet but also exceptionally mild. The only cold snap, with snow and hail, happened late: 19–25 March. April was hot enough to seem like late May. Although budbreak started on the usual dates (9–11 April), the very warm conditions in May led to early flowering at the end of the month.

A difficult July and a cold, wet August, which felt more like November, changed expectations of a very early harvest. By 20 August, disaster looked to be staring the Champenois in the face. Luckily, as often happens, a north wind then dried the grapes and saved them from drowning. The sun returned and continued through the harvest, giving adequate maturity, still with good acidity.

Yet nothing can disguise the fact that 2007 is a very variable vintage from district to district and even from village to village. Everything depends on the picking date, the standard of vineyard care, and the zone. It is a year for the *grands terroirs*, where the best growers looked after their vines and made rigorous selections. Bollinger, Roederer, and some growers may release Vintage cuvées.

2006 ★★★

The beginning of the year was marked by a serious lack of water during the first quarter, then by two

rainy, rather sunless months. The only positive feature was the absence of spring frosts. Warm, sunny weather returned in June, allowing for a fine flowering around 15–18 June. As the weather grew hotter in June and July, hailstorms struck right across the region: 600ha (1,480 acres) of vineyards were devastated. While the untouched regions benefited from the heat, it began to look like a rerun of torrid 2003, the vines wilting under the fierce sun. Then, in a dramatic twist, August was wet and cool, with the average monthly temperature 3.6–5.4°F (2–3°C) lower than normal. More important, accumulated rainfall was two or three times the monthly average.

Returning fine weather at the start of September accelerated ripening, and with the approach of the harvest the sanitary state of the grapes was, says the official line, "very satisfying, with the exception of a few foyers of botrytis". In fact, Champagne had never seen such widely different starting dates—as early as 6 September for Chardonnay in the Sézannais; as late as 25 September for Pinot and Meunier in the Montagne de Reims and the Marne Valley. The crop was of normal size (just under 13,000kg/ha), the richness in sugar excellent at 10.2% natural ABV, acidity a touch low. There is plenty of fruit and body, particularly in Pinot Noir; the Chardonnays are less interesting, perhaps lacking a little verve. I have no doubt that 2006 will give plenty of good drinking quite quickly, though its Champagnes are not true *vins de garde*. It may be a vintage year for some houses but not for guardians of tradition such as Bollinger or Jacquesson.

2005 ★★

An old Champenois saying has it that when the year starts mild and dry, at the Feast of St Vincent winter dies or comes alive again with a vengeance. Arctic conditions certainly returned on 23 January: snowfalls were frequent from the end of

January to mid-March. Grey skies and strong winds dominated the spring with alternate days of cold and warmth. This unsettled weather notwithstanding, the recorded rainfall since the autumn of 2004 was 40 per cent lower than average. The same weather pattern continued into late May, but flowering went well in mid-June, with ideally fine and dry conditions. July returned with extremes of heavy rainfall alternating with heat spikes, resulting in attacks of mildew in the middle of the month, which were repeated in August in parts of the Côte des Bar.

The violent twists and turns persisted into early September, causing real concern for the maturity and health of the grapes. Luckily, fresh weather resumed on 10 September and settled in for the duration, arresting, at least to some extent, the incipient grey botrytis that was forming on Pinot Noir and Meunier particularly. The harvest was fairly successful, with decent natural sugar levels (9.8% ABV) and a good-sized crop. Quality is variable, however, rot being a problem in the black grapes, so very strict selection was necessary. By contrast, there are some great Chardonnays, quite enough for some producers like Roederer and Jacquesson to make a Vintage Champagne. But overall, this is a tricky year, and nothing like as good as in Burgundy. Seek advice before buying.

2004 ★★★★

New Year began with snow and ice, but an unseasonably mild and dry period quickly followed and lasted until late March. A few cold days at the end of April did not hinder the advance of the vine, and although fresh, the dry sunny weather in May augured well for the growing season. Early June ushered in a chaotic period, with big swings of temperature, strong gusts of wind, and hail. But this did not affect the flowering a few days later, when it was already obvious that yields could be particularly high.

A wet, cool, and cloudy August engendered fears for the grapes' maturation, which was advancing very slowly. But the crucial first three weeks of September were dry and sunny, causing the grapes to swell spectacularly and ensure an excellent sanitary state in the vineyards when the moment of picking arrived—on average this was quite late, around 27 September. The harvest was conducted under calm, if grey, skies.

The record crop, exceeding even the huge harvests of 1990 and 1982, is a valuable corrective to the view that you cannot make good Champagne from high yields—you can, as long as the fruit is entirely healthy, properly ripe, and structured with the right acids. All these elements were in place this year. The wines show a consistent balance and fine aromatic profile and are true to their terroirs. The Chardonnays were most successful, with minerality, a lithe structure, and long, multitoned flavours—as successful here as in Burgundy. Pinot Noirs and Meuniers are elegant wines of admirable subtlety. It is a Vintage year for many houses.

2003 ★★

In this notorious, horribly difficult year, Nature dealt the Champenois three hammer blows: devastating spring frosts, violent hailstorms, and a high summer of such intense heat that the grapes burned on the vine. From the first days of January, glacial cold gripped the vineyards, sometimes accompanied by snow. In January and February, temperatures were between 10 and 21°F (−12 and −6°C). From 7 March, a very mild and sunny period followed until the end of the month. The vines woke up and budbreak occurred during the first eight days of April. Champagne then suffered the catastrophe of the most damaging spring frosts for 70 years: 43 per cent of the year's potential crop was destroyed, the Chardonnays of the Côtes des Blancs worst hit, though Pinot Noirs also took terrible punishment on the Montagne de Reims.

May brought a brief respite, but between 4 and 10 June, ferocious hailstorms hit the Montagne and the Marne Valley. Flowering went well in June, but this was certain to be a very small harvest.

It got worse. A very hot July was followed by a sweltering heat wave in August. Down in the Aube, the temperature at night did not drop below 86°F (30°C). The earliest harvest since 1822 started there around Bar-sur-Seine on 18 August. Even so, this was too late for many Aubois grapes, which had already shriveled, raisin-like, in the heat. Growers were luckier in the Marne, where late August showers revived the wilting vines. The harvest there started 5–7 September. These later-picked grapes were surprisingly fine, especially Pinot Noir and Meunier, which had high sugar levels, opulent fruit, and power, though because the acidity was low, they were hardly Champagnes as we know them. The best wines from this fiendishly challenging year came from producers who realized that it would be futile to try to preserve—or artificially boost—the meager acids in the wine. Instead, they threw away the rule book and respected what glorious fruit they had at their disposal. The Champagnes from such imaginative houses as Bollinger, Moët, and Duval-Leroy, who were prepared to respond in this way, can be hedonistic delights for early drinking. But do not expect too much of the vintage generally—the acids are too low. Approach with care, especially if you like your wine with age on it.

2002 ★ ★ ★ ★ ★

After several mild winters, a big freeze gripped Champagne from mid-December to mid-January. These hard conditions were very good for the revival of the soils, without any mishaps to the vines, because the cold arrived slowly.

The thaw started on 15 January, and pruning began in very mild weather, which remained rainy and windy until mid-March. So the vegetation was rather forward. Swelling of the buds began on 12 March, almost a month early, in the Côte des Blancs. April was mild in the main, dry and sunny. At the end of May and in the first days of June, a few hailstorms caused some damage. But a fine, warm, and sunny spell soon followed, and the flowering was rapid in mid-June. July and August were very variable. Storms on 27 August activated botrytis, which was quickly checked by fine, dry, sunny days that began on 10 September and lasted right through the harvest. This exceptional climatic sequence, blessed with good contrasts between day and night temperatures, was conducive to the concentration of sugars and the sanitary quality of the grapes. The vintage began on 12 September for the most forward vineyards and on 28 September for the later ones. Maturity achieved remarkable levels, with an average of 10.5% natural ABV. Acidity was very slightly below average, but that is often the case with exceptional vintages in Champagne (such as 1982). And 2002 is undoubtedly a great vintage in which yields were good but not excessive (just under 12,000kg/ha), and the quality of the Pinot Noirs in particular was magnificent. They are powerful yet perfectly balanced, expressive and silky, with distinctive flavours of spice, tobacco, and leather. The Chardonnays are rich and exotically scented, the best checked by an incisive minerality. Meuniers have a lovely, supple roundness. With fruit like this, 2002 is a vintage for nearly every producer.

2001 ★

The year started mild and wet, with very little sunshine. By the end of March, the accumulated rainfall was twice that of a normal month and the record of sun hours showed a drop of 20 per cent. It was a portent of miserable conditions to come, for although May and June were dry and warm and the flowering was successful, July saw the return of violent rainstorms, accompanied by hail, causing destruction of the potential crop across 55 communes and 800ha (1,980 acres) of vineyards.

In August, optimistic hopes of a decent harvest of good size were dashed in September by cold days, torrential rain (double the seasonal average), and the severest lack of sun for 45 years. The average of natural sugar in the grapes represented a measly 8.5% ABV. In short, this was the most difficult and fragile vintage since 1984. Very few houses or growers released a Vintage, but Ayala's Cuvée Perle is an honourable exception.

2000 ★ ★ ★

The year of the Millennium was rich in symbolism but a challenge for the Champenois as Mother Nature tested everyone. Unseasonal dry warmth marked midwinter and early spring. Interspersed with hailstorms, May continued particularly dry. A graver problem loomed on 2 July, when a freak storm of hailstones the size of pigeon eggs destroyed the crop across 1,900ha (4,700 acres) of vineyards. The vintage went on to be one of the most destructive years of hail ever. On the eve of the harvest, 13,000ha (32,120 acres) in 114 communes had been affected, and 2,900ha (7,160 acres) had suffered a total loss of the crop.

Fine weather returned during August, and it remained warm and dry to the end of the harvest, which started between 11 and 18 September. The abundant, fat grapes showed above-average levels of natural sugar (equivalent to 9.8% natural ABV) and were in an excellent sanitary state.

While purists may mutter about the slight lack of acidity, these Champagnes show rich fruit, giving plenty of pleasure for early drinking.

1999 ★ ★ ★

The growing season this year was unusual, marked by high temperatures and higher-than-normal rainfall. After a mild winter, budbreak in the first week of April was very early. From the beginning of May, violent hailstorms hit the vineyards and persisted until the end of September, causing damage to 2,800ha (6,920 acres), of which 500ha (1,230 acres) lost their crop entirely.

Flowering had gone very well, however, with grapes that were plump and plentiful. Everything looked set for a bountiful vintage of high quality when picking started on 15 September. But hopes of something special were dashed by heavy and persistent rain that, whatever the optimists may say, diluted the wines, particularly of the right sort of acids, and changed what might have been a great vintage into a goodish one, with plenty of fruit and easy charm but lacking the concentration of an exceptional year. In many '99s, there is something lacking on the mid-palate, which is why Krug, for example, will not release a Vintage cuvée. Other houses, however, such as Pol Roger and Bruno Paillard, made fine and elegant wines, as has the bijou house of Testulat. It may be a year that shows best in Chardonnays from top growers, like one really exceptional Champagne: Pierre Gimonnet's superb Vieilles Vignes Cuvée.

1998 ★ ★ ★ ★

A close look at the weather patterns this year scarcely gives much evidence of favourable conditions. There was a rapid succession of brief periods that contrasted dramatically and inspired little confidence in the even progress of the growing cycle.

Winter was generally mild, dry, and sunny, in spite of a few nights of snow and ice, as well as grey, humid skies on certain days. April was buffeted by wind and rain, and spring frost on 13–14 April hit 2 per cent of the vineyards. May and June alternated between heat (up to 90°F [32°C]) and cold (freak frost on 23 May). The flowering time was rainy but did not affect the outcome greatly, though the rain that followed in July encouraged outbreaks of oidium and botrytis. Then an August heat wave reduced the potential crop by between 5 and 10 per cent. But it also sowed the seeds of greatness in the best grapes, with latent extract and complexity. There were serious rainstorms at the beginning of September, but the sun put his hat on again from 14 September, and the harvest was gathered in dry and warm conditions. A good average level of ripeness was achieved in the grapes, which reached 9.8% natural ABV, with bracing levels of acidity (9.8g/l).

With such veering weather sequences, 1998 was a challenging year for winemakers who selected vigorously. In the finest wines, this is a real classic of a vintage—in my view, it outclasses 1996 for its balance and quiet complexities, allied to a generous and charming fruitiness. Examples from Krug, Pol Roger, Billecart-Salmon, and Mumm's René Lalou are quite exceptional, and it is also a top vintage for Dom Pérignon.

1997 ★★

Early on, this vintage looked like a catastrophe in the making, as frost, hail, *millerandage*, rot, and mildew afflicted the vineyards. But a hot July, a very warm August, and not a drop of rain throughout the harvest transformed the crop into a charming, succulent vintage of some concentration, with the lowest yields since 1985.

A forward year, with good levels of ripeness (10.2% natural ABV), it is for early drinking. Bollinger Grande Année and Alfred Gratien are exceptional. Excellent wines were also made by Louis Roederer (Blanc de Blancs), Billecart-Salmon (NF Billecart), Pommery (Cuvée Louise), and Jacquesson (Grand Cru Avize). It is also a good year for Coteaux Champenois, especially from Aÿ producers such as Gatinois.

1996 ★★★★

After a mild start to the year, on 20 February temperatures plummeted in certain sectors to −4°F (−20°C), but fortunately a rapid circulation of cold air prevented the ice from penetrating the cells of the vine. Frost returned in early May, along with rain and hail. After warm and sunny weather in early June, flowering started in the best conditions, but a sudden drop in temperature on the 19th retarded development of the little berries and caused *millerandage*, especially in the Chardonnay. Summer alternated between periods of rain and intense heat—not a great combination for the development of a classic Champagne. Luckily, after the anxiety of rain 12–20 September, clear sunny days, cool nights, and a strong north wind blessed the harvest to its end on 1 October, mopping up any rot and achieving both good maturity and high acidity in the grapes.

Initially, 1996 was hailed as one of the great vintages of the 20th century, on a par with 1928. But that judgment is being modified by more thoughtful observers. Although there are some truly great Champagnes of assertive character and vigour—Krug, Jacquesson Avize, Bollinger Grande Année, Beaumont des Crayères, and Billecart-Salmon stand out—there are others in which the bouquet is aging rapidly while the palate is still fiercely acidic. Will such Champagnes achieve a proper balance? It will be interesting to chart their progress over the next few years.

1995 ★★★★

There was nothing dramatic about the mild and rainy winter and spring weather until 20–21 April and 14–15 May, when falls in temperature to 25°F (−4°C) triggered devastating frosts. Nearly 600ha (1,480 acres) of vines were affected, principally in the Aube. For four weeks from mid-May it was cold and humid, but on 16 June, warm and sunny weather announced the arrival of the flowering, which went well. High summer was dry and hot, accelerating the maturity of the grapes. The harvest was picked under the same sunny skies.

Good alcoholic degrees (9.2% natural ABV) and normal levels of acidity promised powerful but refined wines—in other words, a classic vintage that has matured exactly to plan. Critics have allowed 1995 to stay in the shadow of the more dramatic, punchy 1996. But 1995 is certainly as good and arguably more consistent than the younger vintage. Close to being ready now, 1995 will hold well for another decade. It is a great Chardonnay year, especially for Charles Heidsieck Blanc des Millénaires and Bruno Paillard Blanc de Blancs, and also a very fine *assemblage* vintage for Jacquesson Signature and Veuve Clicquot La Grande Dame.

1994 ★

All you need remember about this vintage is that it was the year of rot. The sanitary state in the vineyards was generally poor, though Beaumont des Crayères and Claude Corbon still managed to make decent Vintage wines.

1993 ★★

A mild, sunny winter and quite a warm spring marked an uneventful start to the year. Then, apart from some devastating hailstorms in the region of Bar-sur-Aube and along the Marne Valley, the summer weather of a little rain alternating with plenty of sunshine appeared favourable for a harvest of excellent quality. But the harvest that started 8–20 September saw grey skies and frequent rain clouds, arresting maturity and causing dilution. The 1993s are healthy enough but tend to be lean and lack body. A few top houses such as Pol Roger, Henri Giraud, and Veuve Clicquot made surprisingly good Vintage wines based on Pinot Noir, the most successful variety.

1992 ★★

This year had a mild winter but a cool spring of unsettled weather—rather wet but without any fall in temperature at the critical time of budbreak. The flowering in June was satisfactory, though it was quite cool for the season and there was abundant rainfall. Thanks to a warm, dry summer, botrytis, very active at the beginning of July, disappeared, and veraison went well. Chardonnay was the most successful variety, picked first from 14 September, achieving above-average maturity (about 10% ABV) but with slightly low acidity—though Krug thought the vintage good enough to release a Clos du Mesnil. The Pinot Noirs and *assemblage* blends tended to be light, fruity wines, most already past their best.

1991 ★★★

This was the third year in a row that spring frosts wreaked havoc in the vineyards. The figures make bad reading: 47 per cent of all vines were affected, and 34 per cent of the crop was destroyed. A crumb of comfort was that, a month before the harvest, the grapes that remained swelled grandly, achieving high must weights. This was a small crop, but interesting cool-weather Vintages were made by Bollinger and by Philipponnat at Clos des Goisses, which still drink well today.

1990 ★★★★★

The growing season started precociously with early budbreak at the end of March, rendering the vines very vulnerable to spring frosts. They duly arrived on 4–5 and 18–19 April, hitting 7,000ha (17,300 acres) of vineyards across the region. After these cold snaps, the weather was a repeat performance of 1989: very warm, then emphatically hot right through the summer, registering, in the case of 1990, a record number of sun hours. Just at the right moment, there were blessed showers just before the harvest, which started quite early around 11 September. Beautiful maturity in the grapes (at about 11% natural ABV) and fine acidity make this one of the very best and most consistent vintages since World War II. Its evolution has been slow, but now the Champagnes are beginning to show their dazzling richness and sheer class, and the finest will continue to improve until 2020. The most successful cuvées are legion, but special mention should be made of Veuve Clicquot Grande Dame, Charles Heidsieck Blanc des Millénaires, and Roederer Cristal.

1989 ★★★★

Trumpeting the arrival of spring, the vine emerged quickly from winter. In March, temperatures as high as 81°F (27°C) were reached. The buds and leaves developed rapidly, making them more vulnerable to spring frosts, which hit the vineyards most seriously on 26–27 April. Some 6,000ha (14,830 acres), or a quarter of production, were affected. 1989 is the year of great heat, when Chardonnay vineyards on the Côte des Blancs bore grapes with up to 12% natural ABV. The conventional wisdom is that 1989s lack acidity. Although slightly below normal, the levels of total acidity were in fact satisfactory—and superior to those in other great warm vintages like 1964, 1953, 1949, and 1947. The greatest 1989s, such as Joseph Perrier Josephine and Billecart-Salmon Grande Cuvée, are magnificent and holding well.

1988 ★★★★★

The year began badly. After a mild winter and spring frost, the worst was feared in May when inspection revealed a reduced number of buds per vine, which was then made worse by *millerandage* and violent storms in late May. Hail hit the Barséquenais, and there was little prospect of an abundant vintage. The maturing cycle of the grapes a month before the harvest was slow, though the hardy Chardonnay was ripening best. For the first time, the date for the opening of the harvest was decided by each commune. Generally it was late, between 26 September and 2 October. None of this can make encouraging reading. Yet the final figures for maturity (9.6% natural ABV) and strong total acidity (9.4g/l) made this a classic vintage on paper.

In the end, 1988 turned out to be one of the all-time greats of the post-1945 era—Vintage Champagnes for connoisseurs who like a certain austerity and a wonderful minerality in their wine. Among the most magnificent successes were Jacquesson Signature, Krug, Veuve Clicquot, Pol Roger Cuvée Spéciale PR, Roederer Cristal, and Henriot Cuvée des Enchanteleurs.

Below: It need not be kept under a key as impressive as this one at Moët & Chandon, but Champagne should be well stored

Champagne Gastronomy

Champagne is not a land of plenty in the way that Alsace, Burgundy, and the Lyonnais obviously are. A glimpse at the map reveals Champagne's troubled history and helps explain why the region lacks a rich gastronomic tradition of its own. First settled by the Gauls as the Roman Empire fell, the emerging Duchy of Champagne under the Merovingian kings of France (5th–8th centuries AD) stretched for 200 miles (320km), from lower Belgium through the Marne and Aube to the gateway of Burgundy—a vast province that corresponds today to the French administrative region of Champagne-Ardennes. Strategically placed at the crossroads of western Europe, this land has been fought over for centuries—in more recent times, during the Franco-Prussian conflict of 1870; during World War I, when old Reims was all but destroyed; and at the end of World War II, when so many towns and villages of the Ardennes were devastated while the Battle of the Bulge raged. Remember, too, that Greater Champagne has one of the coldest and mistiest climates in France, so conditions have hardly been conducive for the development of a vibrant food culture based on exceptional products.

What Champagne does have is excellent game, particularly wild boar, venison, rabbit, and hare from the Ardennes; those strange pork chitterling sausages from Troyes called *andouillettes* (an acquired taste); and fine white asparagus grown along the banks of the Marne. Best of all are four of France's great cheeses made at the limits of the province. Maroilles is a semi-hard cow's-milk cheese from the Thiérache district famous for its fortified churches, about 55 miles (90km) north of Reims. Named after the Abbey of Maroilles, it is redolent of harvest time, being given to grape pickers after a backbreaking day in the vines.

Nicely *à point*, it is a great cheese for blanc de noirs Champagne or fine Belgian beer. But beware: Maroilles becomes stronger as it ripens, so eat it while it is still semi-hard and before its pungency clears a carriage on the Métro or subway.

Brie is probably France's best-known soft cow's cheese, now eclipsing Camembert on the shelves of supermarkets around the world and produced in industrial quantities. It is worth buying the superior Brie de Meaux, named after the town 40 miles (65km) east of Paris, close to the Aisne district of Champagne. This farmhouse version has a more flaxen colour and much more flavour than the impenetrable prepacked Brie sold on Main Street.

Langres is a soft cow's-milk cheese that takes its name from the medieval walled town between Chaumont and Dijon, said to be the second-chilliest place in France. The best Langres cheese from the nearby Haut-Marne village of Bassigny can be as punchy as Maroilles but with a lovely saline character that matches Brut Champagne or Chablis perfectly. Talking of Chablis, if you are driving from there towards Troyes, you come to the Aube village of Chaource, famous for its snowy, soft, creamy cheese of whitened crust and mild, fruity flavour. Its odd name is believed to be a corruption of *chat* (cat) and *ourse* (bear).

Actually, there is nothing at all bearish about Chaource, which is often used by imaginative chefs in the preparation of the gutsy *andouillettes* to soften their pungent character. The fine medieval city of Troyes is the place par excellence to try these sausages. Being made from pig's intestines, or *chaudons*, they are certainly not for the squeamish. But in the hands of a master butcher such as Gilbert Le Meille, these chitterlings are washed very thoroughly, then cut and dressed by hand to produce a highly distinctive speciality that adventurous epicures will not want to miss, despite their popular reputation.

Left: Champagne is a very versatile wine but especially suited to fish, such as this John Dory at Restaurant Patrick Michelon

Such robust fare and other peasant dishes like pig's trotters and *potée champenoise* (a soup-hotpot of pork, chicken, ham, and vegetables) are hardly rarefied gastronomy. Yet the wine of Champagne has been a natural partner for food and a favourite ingredient of haute cuisine preparations since at least the 18th century. In Menon's account of suppers at the court of Versailles in 1755, Champagne was chosen in preference to other wines for 90 per cent of recipes with the word *vin* in their title. Plainly, the great blond wine of the Marne was playing a pivotal role in the early development of haute cuisine, bringing to heavy, cream-rich dishes a touch of the panache that has been Champagne's trump card ever since.

In the 19th century, Carême was cooking salmon à la Rothschild with a *mirepoix* that was moistened with four bottles of Champagne. In our more health-conscious times, at the home stove or the restaurant range, modern cooks know how useful just a splash of Champagne can be in lightening dishes, particularly fish and chicken. Its acidity prevents sauces from browning and also deglazes a pan of butter and oil. Moreover, a great still Champenois blanc such as Moët's Château de Sarran can bring a magical touch to a lightly sauced roast turbot.

In the 21st century, Champagne has developed a cuisine by adoption, drawing on the finest meat and poultry from Paris's Rungis market, fruit and vegetables from the Ile de France, and the freshest fish from the Brittany coast, delivered the next morning through France's superb overnight distribution system. Champagne's chefs are constantly creating new refined dishes to match the supreme subtlety of the wine, as well as revisiting old staples for the highly sophisticated clientele that is the modern Champagne trade. Here is a selection of favourite tables to suit every taste and budget—from a grey-slated Ardennais inn serving the finest wild boar, to Rémois temples of gastronomy, alongside marketplace bistros, and even a fusion restaurant, for times when you tire of *grande cuisine*.

The other gastro-rich towns of Epernay, Châlons, and Troyes are selectively covered, and in the far south of Champagne, two great places are reviewed in Bar-sur-Aube and Colombey-les-Deux-Eglises to show that the regional gastronomic tradition is alive and well in *la France profonde*. Gently priced menus and reasonable wine mark-ups are also noted. *Bon appétit!*

Favourite tables in Champagne

In rating these restaurants—a very personal selection—I have used a five-star system, the sole criterion being the quality of the cooking. As restaurant critics know all too well, such ratings will never adequately replace the written word in fully valuing the taste of a dish or a wine. But we have to live with rankings, since many modern consumers seem adrift without them. So, if the following reviews do not seem to marry with the ratings, follow the words. All of the recommended restaurants merit three, four, or five stars, as defined here:

★★★

Good to excellent cooking; prime ingredients prepared with skill; sympathetic service.

★★★★

Exceptional cooking achieved with a mix of imaginative originality and a sense of classical balance but free of modish culinary tricks.

★★★★★

Outstanding cooking, worth a long journey to enjoy; impeccable but human service; a great wine list; likely to be very expensive but always worth it.

Above: Michelin-starred Patrick Michelon raising a welcoming glass of Champagne at his eponymous restaurant in Epernay

Restaurant Patrick Michelon, Les Berceaux, Epernay ★★★★★

Patrick Michelon comes from Mulhouse, the smoky industrial city of southern Alsace, but he has made his reputation as an outstanding chef in Champagne. Having gained two Michelin stars for his cooking at Aux Armes de Champagne at L'Epine, in 1996 he and his wife Lydie bought the venerable, creaking Les Berceaux hotel in the heart of Epernay. Patrick's cuisine has a special contemporary tempo—very open to new ideas, often from the Mediterranean, but always rooted in the Champagne tradition. Local wines and Champenois ingredients are used in recipes wherever possible and suitable for such highly original cooking.

An innovative summer starter on the €69 menu is the *vitello tonnato à ma façon*. Patrick's way with this classic is carpaccio of rare white tuna with fillets of fresh anchovies and capers, as well as the traditional veal. A choice for autumn is the warm foie gras with vine peaches and their confit in Cumières wine. The wild turbot cooked at low temperature with cèpes and leaf spinach is as good as it gets; the roast milk-fed piglet is unsurpassed; and the lovely *clafoutis* of local Cerfeuil cherries is sinfully rich, as is Patrick's Royal Suisse tiramisu, so the *poêlée* of strawberries with cardamom comes as a perfect reviver.

Along with those at Château les Crayères and Le Grand Cerf (for both of which, see below), the Berceaux wine list, effortlessly explained by sommelier David Mangeard, is one of the best three in Champagne. Fairly priced throughout, it shows a nice balance between the finest cuvées of the great houses, often fully mature, and the best of top growers' Champagnes, such as Gimonnet's Fleuron 2002 for under €60. The young staff are swiftly professional yet very natural, as they are in Les Berceaux's Bistrot le 7, where you can eat from the same great kitchen. In this less formal setting you can enjoy, for example, a terrine of rabbit, one of the best steak tartares in France, and *oeufs à la neige*, with a couple of glasses of fine wine, water, and coffee, all for under €40. The pouring Champagne of the month—usually a discovery from a promising vigneron or bijou house—is served stylishly from magnums. If you have just one dinner in Champagne, you should eat here in either room.

13 Rue Berceaux,
51200 Epernay
Tel: +33 3 26 55 38 84
les.berceaux@wanadoo.fr
Restaurant closed Monday and Tuesday;
Bistrot le 7 closed Wednesday

Les Crayères, Reims ★★★★★

One of the grandest Relais & Châteaux in France, Les Crayères was built in the confident first years of the 20th century (1904) as an imposing town house by the aristocratic de Polignac family of Champagne Pommery. It still has a club-like atmosphere and is the natural place of celebration and hospitality for the top men and women who run the great Champagne houses. The most impressive thing about Les Crayères, however, is that, despite its grandeur, there is a delightful, unforced atmosphere of welcome and goodwill to all, the staff taking their lead from the owners, Xavier Gardinier and his son, whose properties run from orange groves in Florida to Château Phélan-Segur in St-Estèphe. No absentee landlords, they are often here, and anybody who knows them will vouch for the fact that theirs is one of the most unaffected and least pompous of the great wine families of France.

Since 2005, the new chef Didier Elena, a Monaguesque and protegé of Alain Ducasse, has offered a cuisine that is an innovative mix of high sophistication and confident simplicity, creating a contrast of polarities on the plate that really work. His *lapereau de ferme* is an intriguing starter—stuffed rabbit, Genoa-style, is served cold with a warm *estoufade* (casserole) of the shoulder. Another is simply roasted langoustines with green mango and avocado. Fine entrées run from fillet of seabass with September tomato, slow-cooked as a confit, to a prime piece of beef with shallots cooked in Pinot Noir. The simplicity of Roussillon apricots with almonds and gooseberry is beautifully matched with a classic Melba sauce.

The Crayères wine list is outstanding and very fairly priced for such a grand place. Alongside a fine selection of Non-Vintage Champagnes from blue-chip *maisons* (such as the excellent Alain Thiénot at about €50), as well as the right vintages of prestige cuvées (back to Dom Pérignon 1959), there is a good balance of the best growers' Champagnes, especially strong in blancs de noirs from Egly-Ouriet and Serge Mathieu. There are magnificent mature vintages of Médoc classed growths and the finest Côte d'Or grands crus; the showing of Domaine Leflaive and of Domaine Colin-Deléger's Bâtard-Montrachet is particularly enticing. But again impressively, it is not all internationally famous names. For quality and value, there are the super Mâcon-Lamartine 2004 and 2006 from Lafon for €49 and fine-drinking Mercurey for much the same price. Service is everything it should be: attentive, highly professional, yet warm. There were plans to open a bistro in 2009.

64 Boulevard Vasnier,
51100 Reims
Tel: +33 3 26 82 80 80
crayeres@relaischateaux.com
Closed mid-January to mid-February

Le Foch, Reims ★★★★

Jacky Louazé has first claim to being the best fish chef in Reims, and his landlocked restaurant is superior to several famous ones on the Brittany coast, and indeed in Paris itself, all at fair prices for the supreme quality of freshest seafood. Jacky's great dish is whole seabass (the coldwater type the French call "bar") cooked in a tandoor-style clay pot—magical. Preface this with his modern take on cannelloni of Mont St-Michel mussels with shallots in a light curry sauce, or, if you are in the mood for offal, mignons of sweetbreads and Sherry with pig's trotters. Another fine fish option is roast sea bream with "Marco Polo" spices and sauté of artichokes. For dessert, there is none finer than the *moelleux* of chocolate with crème St-Dominique and apricot sorbet. Close to the central pedestrianized Place d'Erlon, the dining room itself is not as sophisticated as the cooking—it's cozy, solid, and bourgeois, rather like *la patronne*, Mme Louazé, who keeps a kindly but firm eye on proceeedings at front of house. There is a good list of Vintage Champagnes and the classics of France.

36 Boulevard Maréchal Foch,
51100 Reims
Tel: +33 3 26 47 48 22
mjackylouaze@aol.com
Closed 24 July–22 August, part of February, Saturday lunch, Sunday dinner, all Monday

Jacky Michel at Hotel d'Angleterre, Châlons-en-Champagne ★★★★

As its name implies, this site was the headquarters and mess for British officers during World War I. After the Armistice it became a bank, and since the 1980s it has been the best place in town for haute cuisine and an ideal hostelry in which to rest your head and eat a fine continental breakfast the morning after. Chef-patron Jacky Michel carries the torch for gastronomy in Châlons, his cooking being right up there with the greats of Epernay and Reims.

His style is a nice blend of tradition and modernity. Start, maybe, with a classic warm foie gras with peaches, or be adventurous and choose the tartare of tuna and cod accompanied by cream of cucumber and mint. Exceptional main courses run from fillet of turbot with confit of carrots in cumin, to sweetbreads sautéed with gingerbread and fennel, and *meunière* of farm chicken *au lard* with vegetable-stuffed tomato and basil. Jacky's chocolate soufflé is the best in Champagne. Like Les Berceaux, the Angleterre now has a good bistro, Les Temps Changent, in the same building. Here the pouring Champagne is the excellent Claude Corbon, from this fine grower in Avize. The

restaurant's *cave* is as good as its cuisine, with fine vintages in particular from Joseph Perrier, the one old *grande marque* Champagne to be based in Châlons itself.

19 Place Monseigneur Tissier,
51100 Châlons-en-Champagne
Tel: +33 3 26 68 21 51
Closed August, Christmas, Saturday lunch, Sunday, and Monday lunch

Le Grand Cerf, Montchenot ★★★★

At the foot of the Montagne de Reims, on the N51 road to Epernay, this handsome inn has elegant dining rooms for classic cuisine, which the kitchen

Above: One of the sumptuous lobster dishes at Le Grand Cerf, whose chefs have a particular talent for fish

has perfected over the years, with a particular talent for fish such as *poêlée* of fresh cod with algae and red berries, and a series of its speciality, lobster, done differently depending on the season—with melon in spring and summer, and *poire confit* come October. Also in autumn, *ris de veau* (sweetbreads) with chestnuts and truffles is a sumptous treat. The *gratin de fruits rouges* makes a fine dessert.

The Cerf's great strength is the superb selection of great Champagnes to match every flavour imaginable, deftly suggested by an outstanding sommelier, the well-padded Hervé. This is the place to discover the best growers' Champagnes, like the magnificent Gaston Chiquet 1982, a magnum of which was keenly priced at €192 in 2006. The inn has a lovely garden for pre- or postdinner drinks, and solicitous service by staff, several of whom used to work at Les Crayères.

59 Route Nationale Montchenot,
51500 Villers Allerand
Tel +33 3 26 97 60 07
Closed Sunday night, Tuesday lunch, and
Wednesday

Version Originale, Reims ★★★

In the Boulingrin district of the city, its social hub, Christophe Mertes's smart contemporary restaurant has been a big hit with discerning Rémois. For his cooking is certainly different, inspired by ideas from all over the world—a touch of Thai, a hint of creole, some North African spices, a bit of French. Dim sum of squid with lemongrass and chili, coriander lamb with spiced couscous, Louisiana blackened red fish and paprika, magret of duck with star anise—all extend the spectrum of taste in this city reared on haute cuisine and regional Champenois staples. A full-bodied pink like Philippe Brun's saignée rosé Champagne suits this food well. The service is swift and simpatico.

25 bis Rue du Temple,
51100 Reims
Tel: +33 3 26 02 69 32
Evo@vo-reims.fr
Closed Sunday and Monday

Le Boulingrin, Reims ★★★

Built in the 1920s after the destruction wrought by World War I, Le Boulingrin has preserved the delightful Art Deco style with some very pretty frescoes of the period. It is also the meeting place of the Rémois bourgeoisie—you may see the Krugs talking to the Billecarts, or either of these families greeting their doctor!

The cooking is sound, its strong card the exemplary freshness of the oysters and the fish of the day, such as roast brill in a light béchamel-and-parsley sauce. The steak tartare and *frites* is as it should be. A fine *tarte tatin* for dessert, and young, fruity wines *en carafe* complete a pleasing experience. The old stained-concrete market opposite the brasserie is to be restored shortly, an initiative of the dynamic lady mayor of Reims.

48 Rue de Mars, 51100 Reims
Tel: +33 3 26 40 96 22
boulingrin@boulingrin.wanadoo.fr
Closed Sunday

Au Sanglier de l'Ardennes, Oignies-en-Thiérache ★★★

Exactly 1 mile (1.6km) over the border from Champagne-Ardennes, into the Belgian village of Oignies-en-Ardennes, is a granite-and-slate inn typical of the Ardennais forests teeming with wild boar. Chef-patron Buchet's speciality is, of course, *sanglier*, the tastiest and tenderest fillet of boar you will ever encounter. But there is also much else to delight fastidious palates, thoroughly deserving of the restaurant's Michelin star. Foie gras de canard and panaché of brill and turbot were other first-rate dishes enjoyed in 2006 as part of a five-course, €50 dinner with wine—terrific value for money, as was the chintzy bedroom for another €50, which included great coffee and Ardennes ham for breakfast. As often in Belgium, the cellar is more interesting and varied than a comparable inn in France: a Niersteiner Auslese was a rich yet incisive match with the foie gras.

Oignies-en-Thiérache,
5670 Namur (Belgium)
Tel: +32 60 39 90 89
Closed Sunday night, Monday, and Tuesday

Bistrot du Pont, Pont Ste-Marie ★★★

Barely 2 miles (3km) east of the exquisitely restored medieval heart of Troyes, this pristine Parisian-style bijou in Pont Ste-Marie is frankly a better bet and sounder value than most of the big restaurants in the city. Kick off with the best *andouillettes de Troyes* (from Gilbert LeMeille) or superb deboned pig's trotters, pan-fried by the sure hand of chef-patron Yves Brousset. Another excellent choice might be the salad of warm red mullet, followed by the entrecôte steak with trompette mushrooms and creamed courgettes, then a little cheese from the well-kept board, and the strawberry gâteau with crème anglaise, plus say a little *pichet* of delicious Aligoté and maybe another of fresh Beaujolais—bistro food at its best. There are also excellent budget-saving menus at €25–35 that fully deserve the Michelin bib for good value.

5 Place Charles de Gaulle,
10151 Pont Ste-Marie, Troyes
Tel/fax:+33 25 80 90 99
Closed Sunday night and Monday

La Toque Baralbine, Bar-sur-Aube ★★★

This excellent restaurant in the pretty market town of Bar-sur-Aube offers the superb-value cooking of chef-patron Daniel Phélizot. Already awarded a Michelin bib, a full rosette must be coming soon. From the menus at €25–40, you can dine exceptionally well on tuna tartare with spices, thin Chaource tart with basil oil, finely layered rabbit terrine, fish of the day in the lightest of sauces, and slices of duck magret with sweet-and-sour flavours, finishing with nougat glacé with candied fruits. The wine list is exceptional value, too.

18 Rue Nationale,
10200 Bar-sur-Aube
Tel: +33 2 25 27 20 34
toquebaralbine@wanadoo.fr
Closed Monday

Restaurant Natali, Hostellerie de la Montagne, Colombey-les-Deux-Eglises ★★★★

Chef-patron Jean-Baptiste Natali, who earned his culinary spurs at the Palme d'Or in Cannes, has returned to the renowned restaurant his father established in this Haute-Marne village, best known as the home of Charles de Gaulle. Jean-Baptiste's cooking shows a love of Mediterranean flavours, beautifully wrought. The carpaccio of cèpes in roasted pistachio oil, and fillet of John Dory with *poivrade* of artichokes and *rillettes* of turtle are quite exceptional. In the autumn, pigeon and partridge are also transformed into exquisite creations of modern cuisine. The wine list is excellent, while staff are deft, swift, and gracious.

Rue Pisseloup,
52330 Colombey-les-Deux-Eglises
Tel: +33 3 25 01 51 69
Closed Monday

The Finest 100

Producers or wines appear in alphabetical order within their category.
A star (★) indicates what is, in my opinion, the finest of the fine or the most important in its category.

Ten Best Non-Vintages
Bollinger Special Cuvée Brut
Henri Giraud Esprit de Giraud★
Charles Heidsieck Brut Réserve Mis en Cave 2003
Jacquesson Cuvée 730
Benoît Lahaye Brut Essentiel
Moët & Chandon Brut Impérial (since 2006)
Pol Roger Brut Réserve
Louis Roederer Brut Premier
Jacques Selosse Initiale Grand Cru
Alain Thiénot Brut

Ten Best Vintages
Bollinger Grande Année 2000
Pierre Gimonnet Cuvée Vieilles Vignes 1999★
Henri Giraud Fût de Chêne 1998
Charles Heidsieck Blanc des Millénaires 1995
Piper-Heidsieck Rare 1999
Henriot 1996
Krug 1996
Pol Roger Blanc de Chardonnay 1998
Louis Roederer 2002
Veuve Clicquot 1998

Ten Best Rosés
Boizel Joyau de France 2000
Louis Casters
Henri Giraud Esprit de Giraud
Gosset Celebris 2003 Extra Brut
Jacquesson Dizy Terres Rouges 2003
Krug
Jean Lallement Cuvée Réserve de Rosé
Moët & Chandon Grand Vintage 2003
Ruinart Dom Ruinart 1988★
Veuve Clicquot 1985

Ten Best Blanc de Noirs
Billecart-Salmon Clos Saint-Hilaire 1996★
Roger Brun Cuvée des Sires Aÿ-La Pelle
Paul Déthune Blanc de Noirs
Dosnon & Lepage Récolte Noire
Egly-Ouriet Les Crayères Vieilles Vignes
Gosset-Brabant Noirs d'Aÿ 2004
Jacquesson Aÿ Vauzelle Terme 2002
Krug Clos d'Ambonnay 1995
Serge Mathieu Cuvée Tradition Brut
Jacques Selosse Contraste

Ten Best Prestige Cuvées
Deutz Cuvée William Deutz 1998
Dom Pérignon 1998
Drappier Grande Sendrée 2002
Gosset Celebris 1998 Extra Brut
Joseph Perrier Josephine 2002
Louis Roederer Cristal 1988★
Pol Roger Cuvée Sir Winston Churchill 1998
Taittinger Comtes de Champagne 1998
Alain Thiénot Grande Cuvée 1985
Veuve Clicquot La Grande Dame 1998

Ten Top Houses (and Their Winemakers)
Billecart-Salmon (F Domi)
Bollinger (M Kaufmann)
Gosset (J-P Mareigner)
Charles Heidsieck and Piper-Heidsieck (R Camus)★
Jacquesson (L Chiquet)
Krug (E Lebel)
Bruno Paillard (A Paillard)
Pol Roger (D Petit)
Louis Roederer (J-B Lécaillon)
Veuve Clicquot (D Demarville and P Thieffry)

Ten Top Domaines
Franck Bonville, Avize
Clos Cazals, Oger
Gaston Chiquet, Dizy
Diebolt-Vallois, Cramant
Egly-Ouriet, Ambonnay
Pierre Gimonnet, Cuis
Larmandier-Bernier, Vertus
Pierre Péters, Le Mesnil
Jacques Selosse, Avize ★
Vilmart, Rilly-la-Montagne

Ten Rising Stars/Domaines to Watch
Raymond Boulard, Cauroy-lès-Hermonville
Richard Cheurlin, Celles-sur-Ource
Collard-Picard, Villers-sous-Châtillon
Dosnon & Lepage, Avirey-Lingey
Charles-Henri and Emmanuel Fourny, Vertus ★
Gosset-Brabant, Aÿ
Benoît Lahaye, Bouzy
Thierry and Aurélien Laherte, Chavot
Jean Lallement, Verzenay
David Léclapart, Trépail

Ten Top-Value Champagnes
Beaumont des Crayères Grande Réserve
Boizel Brut de Chardonnay
Raymond Boulard Cuvée Réserve
Canard-Duchêne Brut
Louis Casters Brut Sélection
Henriot Brut Souverain Pur Chardonnay
Laherte Frères Blanc de Blancs La Pierre de la Justice
Le Mesnil Grand Cru
Vincent Testulat Carte d'Or Brut
Alain Thiénot Brut ★

Ten Market Leaders
Duval-Leroy
Lanson/Boizel Chanoine Group
Laurent-Perrier
Moët & Chandon ★
GH Mumm
Perrier-Jouët
Taittinger
Union Champagne
Veuve Clicquot
Vranken

Glossary

assemblage blending of wines and/or different years

agrumes citrus fruit; often used to describe the aroma/flavour of grapefruit

autolysis biochemical process in which yeast cells are broken down. In Champagne production it occurs during the *prise de mousse* and is increased by long aging of the Champagne laid sideways in the bottle on fine lees, adding a desired complexity to the finished taste.

barrique small oak barrel of 225 litres (59 US gallons), the term and size most used in Bordeaux

cave cellar—in Champagne, almost invariably underground

chef de cave(s)/cellar master technical director responsible for the production of Champagne in the cellar; usually an oenologist in charge of blending

CM Champagne that has been made by a cooperative. See also *cooperative-manipulante*

cooperative-manipulante (CM) a cooperative making and marketing Champagne

Coteaux Champenois appellation (controlled name of origin) for still white, rosé, and red wines produced in Champagne

crayère Gallo-Roman chalk pit used as a Champagne cellar

crémant in Champagne, a now-obsolete term for a gently sparkling wine with around 3.5 atmospheres of pressure. In 1994, its use on a Champagne label was forbidden; the term now only applies to certain sparkling wines in other regions of France.

cru a specific commune or village producing wine, usually of good reputation and quality

cuvée (1) the first and best pressings of the grape (= 2,050 litres [541 US gallons] of juice) in Champagne; (2) a Champagne blend

débourbage the separation of pressed grape juice from solid matter prior to fermentation

débourbage à froid a very modern technique, still not widely accepted in Champagne, of clarifying the must and eliminating the coarser lees by chilling it down to 41°F (5°C). The aim is to maximize the finesse of the wine and avoid oxidation.

dégorgement disgorging—that is, removal—of the deposit that forms in a bottle of Champagne as a result of the second fermentation

dégorgement à la glace disgorging of the deposit from a bottle of Champagne that has passed neck down on a conveyor through freezing brine. The deposit is thus captured in a near-frozen pellet or sorbet, then expelled from the bottle.

dégorgement à la volée disgorging by hand, without freezing

demi-mousse literally half-mousse, or gently sparkling. Now the accepted term for making the formerly named *crémant* Champagne. *Perle* or *perlé* is another term for the same thing.

demi-muid wooden cask, usually oak, with a capacity of 600 litres (158 US gallons)

dosage liqueur of mature wine and sugar added to a bottle of Champagne to round out the wine. In the wrong hands, it can be used to mask the immaturity of the blend. Expressed in percentages or in grams of sugar per litre. A more modern *dosage* is made from rectified concentrated grape must.

échelle des crus classification of the Champagne crus or communes expressed on a percentage scale. It is geographically based but is essentially an index of price,

based on the quality of grapes from individual vineyards. Deuxièmes crus rate 80–89 per cent; premiers crus 90–99 per cent; grands crus 100 per cent.

foudre large wooden cask

grand cru one of 17 Champagne villages rated 100 per cent on the *échelle des crus*

grande marque now-defunct term for a leading Champagne house belonging to the Syndicat des Grandes Marques ("great brands") founded in 1882. The association no longer exists. Its old member houses are now known informally as Grandes Maisons.

gras literally "fat"—complimentary tasting term used for a wine with a fleshy texture

gyropalette computerized *remuage* (riddling) system in a metal container holding up to 500 bottles

lees sediment; the by-products of fermentation, particularly dead yeasts, that fall to the bottom of the tank or barrel in the winemaking process

lieu(x)-dit(s) named vineyard site(s), usually on privileged terrain

liqueur de tirage a liqueur containing sugar and yeasts added to the still wine as it is bottled to create the bubbles

malolactic fermentation conversion of piercing malic acid into milder lactic acid to make wines softer and rounder—but also more complex; known informally as "the malo"

marc Champagne term for a pressing of 4,000kg (8,818lb) of grapes; informally sometimes refers to the "cake" of pressed grapes

méthode traditionelle EU-sanctioned name for what used to be called the *méthode champenoise*: the classic way of making sparkling wines by inducing a second alcoholic fermentation in the bottle that creates the bubbles

millésime vintage

millésimé vintaged

monocru Champagne from a single cru (village or vineyard)

mousse stream of bubbles in a sparkling wine

mousseux fully sparkling wine of five to six atmospheres of pressure

négociant-manipulant (NM) Champagne merchant (négociant) who is permitted to buy grapes or wines from other sources for his blends. Some or all of the wines may come from the NM's own vineyards. All the famous houses are NMs.

NV Non-Vintage

pièce small oak barrel—in Champagne of 205 litres (54 US gallons); in Burgundy of 228 litres (60 US gallons) capacity

premier cru in Champagne, a wine commune rated at 90–99 per cent on the *échelle des crus*

prise de mousse literally the "taking of the mousse", or the creation of bubbles in a Champagne, by the second alcoholic fermentation in bottle

pupitres inverted wooden desks with holes in them, used for *remuage* (riddling) of the deposit in a bottle of Champagne

récemment dégorgé (RD) recently disgorged. Applied to very high-quality Vintage Champagnes that have been aged in bottle for a longer time than a straight Vintage would have been. They are disgorged a few weeks before release. The term RD has been patented by Bollinger, the leading producer of this style.

récoltant-coopérateur (RC) small grower without the means to vinify his own Champagne, who has it

made for him from his own grapes by one or more cooperatives. The grower then sells the Champagne under his own label. However, an RC Champagne is not a true grower's wine, since grapes from the *coopérateur* may have been blended with others.

récoltant-manipulant (RM) grower making Champagne from his or her grapes but allowed to buy in 5 per cent from other sources

remuage riddling. The turning and tilting of Champagne bottles so that the deposit may settle on the cork or crown cap. See also gyropalette; *pupitres*

reserve wines older wines than those from the current vintage kept in reserve to add a harmonious, mature balance to a Champagne blend

Société de Récoltant (SR) company formed by wine growers belonging to the same family who pool resources

sur lattes (1) applied to Champagnes that have been laid on their sides; (2) near-finished Champagnes awaiting disgorgement, which are sold on by the producer and labelled as the buyer's own product—a rather murky practice that enlightened voices say should be banned

taille second and third pressings of Champagne grapes. The third pressing is now effectively discontinued for use in Champagne-making and is sent for distillation.

tête de cuvée finest juice from the first pressings, sometimes known as the *coeur de cuvée*

vendange vintage or harvest (in the sense of picking the grapes)

vigneron wine grower

vins clairs Champagne term for still wines after their first fermentation and before they are transformed into sparkling wines

François Bonal,
Le Livre d'Or de Champagne
(Editions du Grand Pont, Lausanne; 1984)

Nicholas Faith,
The Story of Champagne
(Hamish Hamilton; 1988)

Patrick Forbes,
Champagne: The Wine, the Land, and the People
(Gollancz; 1967)

Richard Juhlin,
4000 Champagnes
(Flammarion, Paris; 2004)

Don & Petie Kladstrup,
Champagne
(Wiley; 2006)

Tilar J Mazzeo,
The Widow Clicquot
(HarperCollins; 2008)

Maggie McNie,
Champagne
(Faber & Faber; 1999)

Cynthia Parzych & John Turner with Michael Edwards,
Pol Roger & Co
(Cynthia Parzych Publishing; 1999)

Tom Stevenson,
Christie's Encyclopedia of Champagne & Sparkling Wine
(Absolute Press, London; 2009)

Tom Stevenson,
The Sotheby's Wine Encyclopedia
(Dorling Kindersley, London; 2007)

Serena Sutcliffe,
A Celebration of Champagne
(Mitchell Beazley, London; 1988)

James E Wilson,
Terroir
(Mitchell Beazley, London; 1998)

Index

Author's Acknowledgments

It would not have been possible to write this book without the unstinting help of many houses and growers in Champagne, who opened their greatest bottles for me—often at unsociable times of the day or night. I hope they will forgive me if I say a *grand merci* to them all generally. I must, though, mention several friends who gave sterling backup when I most needed it: Louisa Thomas Hargrave, pioneering *vigneronne* in Long Island, New York, for constant encouragement and for suggesting many invaluable corrections to the chapter on viticulture; Philippe Thieffry of Veuve Clicquot for his insights into making pink Champagne; Patrick Michelon of Les Berceaux on all matters gastronomic and for board and lodging on more than one occasion; the always hospitable Jean-Hervé Chiquet of Jacquesson, who provided detailed maps of the Montagne de Reims, Vallée de la Marne, and Côte des Blancs; Philippe Wibrotte of the CIVC in Epernay, Françoise Peretti of the Champagne Bureau in London, and their staff who arranged many trips and appointments.

I owe a particular debt to Piers Spence, director of co-edition publishing at Quarto, and to all those at Fine Wine Editions, especially Sara Morley, Stuart George, and Vicky Jordan, for support given without question. My greatest debt of all is to Dr Neil Beckett, scholar, dream editor, and Champagne specialist, for his gentle but clear guidance in improving the text at every stage. I am a lucky man.

Photographic Credits

All photography by Jon Wyand, with the following exceptions:
Page 6: Manuscript, Musée Condé, Chantilly; The Art Archive / Alfredo Dagli Orti
Page 12: Anonymous, *Louis XV of France*, Château de Chambord; Wikimedia Commons
Page 14: Leon Bakst, *The Luncheon*, State Russian Museum, St Petersburg; The Gallery Collection / Corbis
Page 29: Valérie Dubois, Chardonnay grapes; CIVC
Page 34: Alain Cornu, Pinot Noir grape; CIVC
Page 315: Gardin Berengo, The "smiling angel" on Reims Cathedral; CIVC